Silicon Valley Python Engineer Interview Guide

Jianfeng Ren • Andric Li

Silicon Valley Python Engineer Interview Guide

Data Structure, Algorithm, and System Design

 Springer

Jianfeng Ren
Google
San Diego, CA, USA

Andric Li
University of California at San Diego
La Jolla, CA, USA

ISBN 978-981-96-3200-8   ISBN 978-981-96-3201-5   (eBook)
https://doi.org/10.1007/978-981-96-3201-5

Translation from the Chinese Simplified language edition: "硅谷Python工程师面试指南：数据结构、算法与系统设计" by Jianfeng Ren and Andric Li, © China Machine Press Co., Ltd. 2024. Published by China Machine Press Co., Ltd.. All Rights Reserved.

© China Machine Press Co., Ltd. 2025

Jointly published with China Machine Press Co., Ltd.

The print edition is not for sale in Mainland China. Customers from Mainland China please order the print book from: China Machine Press Co., Ltd.

This work is subject to copyright. All rights are solely and exclusively licensed by the Publisher, whether the whole or part of the material is concerned, specifically the rights of reprinting, reuse of illustrations, recitation, broadcasting, reproduction on microfilms or in any other physical way, and transmission or information storage and retrieval, electronic adaptation, computer software, or by similar or dissimilar methodology now known or hereafter developed.

The use of general descriptive names, registered names, trademarks, service marks, etc. in this publication does not imply, even in the absence of a specific statement, that such names are exempt from the relevant protective laws and regulations and therefore free for general use.

The publishers, the authors, and the editors are safe to assume that the advice and information in this book are believed to be true and accurate at the date of publication. Neither the publishers nor the authors or the editors give a warranty, express or implied, with respect to the material contained herein or for any errors or omissions that may have been made. The publishers remain neutral with regard to jurisdictional claims in published maps and institutional affiliations.

This Springer imprint is published by the registered company Springer Nature Singapore Pte Ltd.
The registered company address is: 152 Beach Road, #21-01/04 Gateway East, Singapore 189721, Singapore

If disposing of this product, please recycle the paper.

Preface

I am currently employed at Google as a software engineer. Like many developers, I thoroughly prepared for interviews, and practice on leetcode was particularly painful and exhausting. However, I found that despite the challenging process, there were many benefits:

- First, my code has become more concise, and my programming is now more efficient.
- Second, my system design skills have improved, allowing me to approach real-world problems with clearer ideas.
- Lastly, due to my thorough preparation and stable performance, I secured a compensation package higher than the average software engineer.

During my interview preparation, I summarized some valuable experiences, which I now share with readers in this book.

One point to clarify: why does this book use Python? Compared to C++, Python is more concise and allows easy access to many built-in functions. Using Python for "leetcode grinding" avoids the hassle of dealing with intricate details.

This book is divided into three parts:

- **Data Structures**: Covers basic applications of lists, stacks, queues, priority queues, dictionaries, sets, linked lists, trees, and graphs.
- **Algorithms**: Explains algorithms such as binary search, two-pointer techniques, dynamic programming, depth-first search, backtracking, breadth-first search, and includes practical exercises with real interview problems.
- **System Design**: Includes both theory and practical examples, covering topics like multi-threaded programming and case studies on machine learning system design, including search ranking systems and Netflix's movie recommendation system.

Key Features of This Book

- Fresh Content: Most cases are practical problems frequently used in interviews at major companies.
- Free Code: Includes a large amount of tested code.
- Experience Sharing: A comprehensive summary of my accumulated interview experiences.
- Practical Insights: Detailed explanations paired with numerous examples.

The completion of this book would not have been possible without the encouragement of my late mentor, Professor Jiang Liyuan. Though he has passed away, his inspiration was the reason I decided to write this book. I dedicate this book to my beloved teacher!

Special thanks to Dr. Du Yaqin, my junior colleague, who took the time out of her busy schedule to review and edit the entire manuscript. And I also thank my daughter, Jasmine Ren, who is currently high school student in Bishop School in San Diego, provides the proof reading in the book.

San Diego, CA, USA   Jianfeng Ren

Competing Interests The authors have no competing interests to declare that are relevant to the content of this manuscript.

Contents

1	**Technical Interview Process**		1
	1.1	Non-technical Phone Interview	1
	1.2	Technical Phone Interviews	2
		1.2.1 Introduction (5 Min)	2
		1.2.2 Technical Challenge (30–50 Min)	3
		1.2.3 Asking Questions (5–10 Min)	3
	1.3	On-Site Interviews	3
		1.3.1 Present Yourself Confidently and Professionally	4
		1.3.2 Emphasize Clear Communication	5

Part I Data Structures

2	**List**		9
	2.1	The Basics of Lists	9
		2.1.1 Create a List	9
		2.1.2 Add Elements to the List	10
		2.1.3 Delete an Element from the List	13
	2.2	Example 1: The Maximum Number of Consecutive 1	15
		2.2.1 Problem	15
		2.2.2 Approach and Explanation	15
		2.2.3 Code Explanation	15
		2.2.4 Complexity Analysis	16
		2.2.5 Explanation of Steps in the Code	16
		2.2.6 Testing the Code	17
		2.2.7 Expected Output	18
		2.2.8 Explanation of Test Cases	18
	2.3	Example 2: Binary Addition	19
		2.3.1 Problem	19
		2.3.2 Approach and Explanation	19
		2.3.3 Code Implementation	20
		2.3.4 Complexity Analysis	20

		2.3.5	Explanation of Test Cases	21
		2.3.6	Expected Output	22
		2.3.7	Explanation of Test Cases	22
	2.4	Example 3: Random Indexing		22
		2.4.1	Problem	22
		2.4.2	Problem Analysis	23
		2.4.3	Explanation of the Code	23
		2.4.4	Reservoir Sampling Algorithm	23
		2.4.5	Code Implementation	23
		2.4.6	Expected Output	25
		2.4.7	Explanation of the Output	26
		2.4.8	Complexity Analysis	26
	2.5	Example 4: The Next Maximum		26
		2.5.1	Problem	26
		2.5.2	Problem Analysis	27
		2.5.3	Code Implementation	27
		2.5.4	Explanation of the Code	29
		2.5.5	Expected Output	30
		2.5.6	Explanation of the Output	30
		2.5.7	Complexity Analysis	30
	2.6	Example 5: Valid Decimal Number		31
		2.6.1	Problem	31
		2.6.2	Problem Analysis	31
		2.6.3	Rules for Valid Numbers	31
		2.6.4	Code Implementation	32
		2.6.5	Explanation of Code	33
		2.6.6	Test Cases	34
		2.6.7	Expected Output	34
		2.6.8	Complexity Analysis	35
3	Stack			37
	3.1	Stack Basics		37
		3.1.1	The Time Complexity of Stack Operations	37
		3.1.2	How to Implement the Stack Operations in Python	37
		3.1.3	Applications	41
	3.2	Example 1: Minimal Removal to Get Valid Parentheses		42
		3.2.1	Problem	42
		3.2.2	Key Idea	42
		3.2.3	Solution Explanation	43
		3.2.4	Test Function	44
		3.2.5	Expected Output	45
		3.2.6	Complexity Analysis	45
	3.3	Example 2: The Dedicated Time of the Function		45
		3.3.1	Problem	45
		3.3.2	Problem Analysis	46

		3.3.3	Key Concepts	47
		3.3.4	Example Walkthrough	47
		3.3.5	Approach	47
		3.3.6	Code Implementation	48
		3.3.7	Explanation of Code	49
		3.3.8	Testing the Code	49
		3.3.9	Expected Output	51
		3.3.10	Complexity Analysis	51
4	**Queue**			**53**
	4.1	Basic Knowledge of Queues		53
		4.1.1	How Queues are Implemented	53
		4.1.2	Implement Queues with Lists	53
	4.2	Example 1: Design a Circular Queue		58
		4.2.1	Problem	58
		4.2.2	Problem Analysis	58
		4.2.3	Key Concepts	59
		4.2.4	Example Walkthrough	59
		4.2.5	Code Implementation	60
		4.2.6	Explanation of Code	61
		4.2.7	Testing the Code	62
		4.2.8	Expected Output	63
		4.2.9	Complexity Analysis	63
	4.3	Example 2: The Shortest Subarray That is Summed is Greater Than K		63
		4.3.1	Problem	63
		4.3.2	Solution Approach: Sliding Window with Deque	64
		4.3.3	Code Implementation	65
		4.3.4	Explanation of Code	66
		4.3.5	Complexity Analysis	66
		4.3.6	Test Cases and Main Function	66
		4.3.7	Expected Output	68
5	**Priority Queues**			**69**
	5.1	Implementation of Priority Queues		69
		5.1.1	Implement Priority Queues with Lists	69
		5.1.2	Implement Priority Queues Using HEAPQ	70
		5.1.3	Use queue.PriorityQueue Implements Priority Queues	71
	5.2	Example 1: Minimum Cost of Employing K Workers		72
		5.2.1	Problem	72
		5.2.2	Approach and Explanation	73
		5.2.3	Code Explanation	74
		5.2.4	Complexity Analysis	75
		5.2.5	Explanation of Steps in the Code	75
		5.2.6	Testing the Code	75

		5.2.7	Expected Output.	76
		5.2.8	Explanation of Test Cases	77
	5.3	Example 2: Split an Array into Consecutive Subsequences		77
		5.3.1	Problem	77
		5.3.2	Approach and Explanation.	78
		5.3.3	Code Explanation.	78
		5.3.4	Complexity Analysis	79
		5.3.5	Explanation of Steps in the Code.	80
		5.3.6	Testing the Code	80
		5.3.7	Expected Output.	81
		5.3.8	Explanation of Test Cases	81
	5.4	Example 3: Traffic Light		81
		5.4.1	Problem	81
		5.4.2	Solution	82
		5.4.3	Explanation	84
		5.4.4	Complexity Analysis	84
6	**Dictionary**			85
	6.1	Basic Knowledge of Dictionaries		85
		6.1.1	Create a Dictionary	85
		6.1.2	Dictionary	87
		6.1.3	Access Elements from the Dictionary	88
		6.1.4	Remove an Element from the Dictionary	89
	6.2	Example 1: The Sum of the Subarrays is Equal to K.		91
		6.2.1	Problem	91
		6.2.2	Solution Approach: Prefix Sum with Hash Table	91
		6.2.3	Code Explanation.	92
		6.2.4	Complexity Analysis	93
		6.2.5	Extension: Two-Pointer Method for Positive Numbers.	93
		6.2.6	Test Cases.	93
		6.2.7	Expected Output.	94
		6.2.8	Explanation of Each Test Case.	95
		6.2.9	Conclusion.	95
	6.3	Example 2: The Maximum Value from the Labels		95
		6.3.1	Problem	95
		6.3.2	Solution Approach.	95
		6.3.3	Code Implementation.	96
		6.3.4	Complexity Analysis	97
		6.3.5	Testing the Code	97
		6.3.6	Expected Output.	99
		6.3.7	Explanation of Test Cases	99
	6.4	Example 3: Insert/Delete/Get Random Value O(1)		99
		6.4.1	Problem	99
		6.4.2	Approach	100
		6.4.3	Code.	100

		6.4.4	Complexity Analysis	102
		6.4.5	Testing the Code	102
		6.4.6	Explanation of Test Cases	103
		6.4.7	Expected Output	104
	6.5	Example 4: Least Recently Used (LRU) Cache		104
		6.5.1	Problem	104
		6.5.2	Approach	105
		6.5.3	Code	105
		6.5.4	Complexity Analysis	107
		6.5.5	Testing the Code	107
		6.5.6	Expected Output	108
		6.5.7	Explanation of Test Cases	108
7	Sets			111
	7.1	The Basics of Sets		111
		7.1.1	Add Elements	111
		7.1.2	Delete the Element	112
		7.1.3	Union	113
		7.1.4	Intersection	114
8	**Linked Lists**			115
	8.1	Two-pointer Technology		116
	8.2	Example 1: Linked List Cycle?		116
		8.2.1	Problem	116
		8.2.2	Problem Analysis	117
		8.2.3	Approach	117
		8.2.4	Example Walkthrough	117
		8.2.5	Code	118
		8.2.6	Explanation of the Code	118
		8.2.7	Testing the Solution	118
		8.2.8	Test Function	119
		8.2.9	Explanation of the Test Function	120
		8.2.10	Time Complexity Analysis	120
	8.3	Example 2: The Intersection of Two Linked Lists		121
		8.3.1	Problem	121
		8.3.2	Problem Analysis	121
		8.3.3	Solution Approaches	121
		8.3.4	Code	122
		8.3.5	Explanation of the Code	123
		8.3.6	Test Cases	123
		8.3.7	Test Function	124
		8.3.8	Explanation of the Test Function	126
		8.3.9	Time Complexity Analysis	126
	8.4	Example 3: Clone a Random Linked List		126
		8.4.1	Problem	126
		8.4.2	Problem Analysis	127

		8.4.3 Solution Idea	127
		8.4.4 Solution Approach	127
		8.4.5 Code	128
		8.4.6 Explanation of the Code	129
		8.4.7 Time and Space Complexity Analysis	129
		8.4.8 Test Cases	130
		8.4.9 Test Function	130
		8.4.10 Explanation of the Test Function	132
9	**Binary Tree**		133
	9.1	DFS/BFS Traversal	133
	9.2	The Recursive Method	135
		9.2.1 A "Top-down" Solution	136
		9.2.2 A "Bottom-up" Solution	137
	9.3	Example 1: The Lowest Common Ancestor of the Binary Tree	138
		9.3.1 Problem	138
		9.3.2 Solution	139
		9.3.3 Time Complexity	139
		9.3.4 Code Analysis	140
		9.3.5 Explanation of Key Parts	141
		9.3.6 Testing the Code Using a Main Function	141
		9.3.7 Explanation of Test Cases	142
		9.3.8 Conclusion	143
	9.4	Example 2: Serializing and Deserializing Binary Trees	143
		9.4.1 Problem	143
		9.4.2 Approach	144
		9.4.3 Complexity Analysis	144
		9.4.4 Code Analysis	144
		9.4.5 Explanation of Key Parts	146
		9.4.6 Testing the Code with a Main Function	146
		9.4.7 Explanation of the Testing Function	148
		9.4.8 Expected Output	148
		9.4.9 Conclusion	148
	9.5	Example 3: Find the Maximum Path Sum of the Binary Tree	149
		9.5.1 Problem	149
		9.5.2 Solution	149
		9.5.3 Complexity Analysis	150
		9.5.4 Code Analysis	150
		9.5.5 Explanation of Key Parts	152
		9.5.6 Testing the Code with a Main Function	152
		9.5.7 Explanation of the Testing Function	154
		9.5.8 Expected Output	154
		9.5.9 Conclusion	154

9.6		Example 4: Convert a Given Binary Tree to a Doubly Linked List	155
	9.6.1	Problem Analysis	155
	9.6.2	Approach	155
	9.6.3	Code Analysis	156
	9.6.4	Explanation of Key Parts	157
	9.6.5	Complexity Analysis	157
	9.6.6	Test Case and `Node` Class	157
	9.6.7	Explanation of the Test Function	159
	9.6.8	Conclusion	159
10	**Some Other Tree Structures**		**161**
	10.1 Prefix Tree		161
	10.1.1	Why Use a Trie (Prefix Tree) Over Other Data Structures?	161
	10.1.2	Data Structure of the Prefix Tree (Trie)	163
	10.1.3	Example 1: Add and Search for Words	166
	10.2 Segment Tree		170
	10.2.1	Characteristics of Segment Tree	171
	10.2.2	Code Analysis and Explanation	171
	10.2.3	Class `Node`	171
	10.2.4	Class `SegmentTree`	172
	10.2.5	Initialization	172
	10.2.6	Method `get_overlap`	172
	10.2.7	Method `construct_segment_tree`	173
	10.2.8	Method `update_segment_tree`	174
	10.2.9	Range Query Methods (`get_minimum`, `get_maximum`, `get_sum`)	175
	10.2.10	Method `preorder_traversal`	175
	10.2.11	Example Usage	176
	10.2.12	Complexity Analysis	177
	10.2.13	Summary	177
	10.3 Binary Index Tree		177
	10.3.1	Problem Overview	177
	10.3.2	Why Binary Indexed Tree?	177
	10.3.3	How BIT Works	178
	10.3.4	Time Complexity	178
	10.3.5	Core Operations of BIT	178
	10.3.6	Pseudocode Explanation	178
	10.3.7	Code Implementation in Python	179
	10.3.8	Explanation of Code	181
	10.3.9	Output Example	181
	10.3.10	Conclusion	181
	10.4 Example 2: Count of Smaller Numbers After Self		182
	10.4.1	Approach: Binary Indexed Tree (BIT)	182

		10.4.2	Code Implementation	183
		10.4.3	Explanation of the Code	184
		10.4.4	Time Complexity	184
		10.4.5	Test Function	184
		10.4.6	Expected Output	185
		10.4.7	Explanation of Other Solutions	186
		10.4.8	Conclusion	186
11	**Graph**			**187**
	11.1	Representation of the Graph		188
		11.1.1	Adjacency Matrices	188
		11.1.2	Adjacency Table	188
	11.2	Example 1: Clone Graph		191
		11.2.1	Problem	191
		11.2.2	Problem Analysis	191
		11.2.3	BFS Solution	191
		11.2.4	DFS Solution	193
		11.2.5	Complexity Analysis	194
		11.2.6	Test Case and `Node` Class	194
		11.2.7	Explanation of the Test Function	196
		11.2.8	Conclusion	197
	11.3	Example 2: Graph Validation Tree		197
		11.3.1	Problem	197
		11.3.2	DFS Solution	197
		11.3.3	BFS Solution	202
		11.3.4	Union Find solution	206

Part II Algorithmic Part

12	**Binary Search**			**215**
	12.1	Example 1: Find the Square Root		215
		12.1.1	Efficiency	216
	12.2	Example 2: Search in a Rotationally Sorted Array		217
		12.2.1	Efficiency	220
	12.3	Example 3: Search a List of Ranges		220
		12.3.1	Problem	220
		12.3.2	Solution	220
		12.3.3	Efficient Search Strategy	221
		12.3.4	Step-by-Step Process	224
		12.3.5	Example Walkthrough	224
		12.3.6	Time Complexity	225
		12.3.7	Space Complexity	225
		12.3.8	Conclusion	225
13	**Two-Pointer Method**			**227**
	13.1	Example 1: Point Product of a Sparse Vector		227

		13.1.1	Problem	227
		13.1.2	Solutions	227
		13.1.3	Example Solution Using Two Pointers	228
	13.2	Example 2: Minimal Window Substring		231
		13.2.1	Problem	231
		13.2.2	Solutions	231
		13.2.3	Explanation of the Approach	231
		13.2.4	Code Explanation with Comments	232
	13.3	Example 3: Intersecting List of Intersections		237
		13.3.1	Problem	237
		13.3.2	Solution	237
		13.3.3	Code with Comments	238
		13.3.4	Complexity Analysis	238
	13.4	Example 4: The Maximum Number of Consecutive 1		239
		13.4.1	Problem Explanation	239
		13.4.2	Code with Comments	240
		13.4.3	Explanation of Each Step	241
		13.4.4	Example Walkthrough	241
		13.4.5	Complexity Analysis	242
	13.5	Example 5: Find All the Letters in a String		242
		13.5.1	Problem Explanation	242
		13.5.2	Solution	242
		13.5.3	Code with Comments	243
		13.5.4	Explanation of Each Step	244
		13.5.5	Example Walkthrough	245
		13.5.6	Complexity Analysis	245
14	**Dynamic Programming**			**247**
	14.1	Introduction to Dynamic Programming		247
	14.2	Example 1: Best Time to Buy and Sell Stocks		248
		14.2.1	Problem	248
		14.2.2	Explanation of the Code	248
		14.2.3	Code	249
		14.2.4	Explanation of Test Cases	250
	14.3	Example 2: Coin Change		250
		14.3.1	Problem	250
		14.3.2	Dynamic Programming Solution Explanation	251
		14.3.3	Steps	251
		14.3.4	Code with Comments	252
		14.3.5	Example Walkthrough	254
		14.3.6	Complexity Analysis	254
		14.3.7	Summary	254
	14.4	Example 3: Decoding Ways		254
		14.4.1	Problem	254
		14.4.2	Solution	255

		14.4.3	Code Explanation.	255
		14.4.4	Explanation of Key Parts	256
		14.4.5	Complexity.	257
		14.4.6	Example.	257
		14.4.7	Test Cases.	257

15 Depth First Search ... 259
- 15.1 Application for Depth-First Search ... 259
- 15.2 Example 1: Pacific Atlantic Currents. ... 260
  - 15.2.1 Problem ... 260
  - 15.2.2 Solution ... 260
  - 15.2.3 Code. ... 261
  - 15.2.4 Explanation of Key Parts ... 263
  - 15.2.5 Complexity Analysis ... 263
- 15.3 Example 2: Predict the Winner ... 263
  - 15.3.1 Problem ... 263
  - 15.3.2 Solution ... 264
  - 15.3.3 Explanation ... 265
  - 15.3.4 Example Walkthrough ... 266
  - 15.3.5 Complexity Analysis ... 266
- 15.4 Example 3: Expression Plus Operator ... 266
  - 15.4.1 Problem ... 266
  - 15.4.2 Problem Breakdown and Approach ... 267
  - 15.4.3 Key Observations. ... 267
  - 15.4.4 Solution Explanation ... 267
  - 15.4.5 Steps of the Algorithm. ... 268
  - 15.4.6 Code Explanation. ... 269
  - 15.4.7 Complexity Analysis ... 270
  - 15.4.8 Example Walkthrough ... 271
  - 15.4.9 Edge Cases. ... 271
  - 15.4.10 Summary ... 272

16 Backtracking ... 273
- 16.1 Example 1: Sudoku Solves ... 273
  - 16.1.1 Problem ... 273
  - 16.1.2 Solution ... 273
  - 16.1.3 Python Code. ... 275
  - 16.1.4 Complexity Analysis ... 277
- 16.2 Example 2: Robot Vacuum. ... 277
  - 16.2.1 Problem ... 277
  - 16.2.2 Explanation of the Code. ... 279
  - 16.2.3 Code. ... 280
  - 16.2.4 Complexity Analysis ... 281
  - 16.2.5 Explanation of How the Code Works. ... 281
  - 16.2.6 Example Walkthrough ... 282
  - 16.2.7 Key Points ... 282

17	**Breadth-First Search**	283
	17.1 Breadth Traversal	283
	17.1.1 Mechanics of Breadth-First Traversal	283
	17.1.2 Applications of Breadth-First Traversal	284
	17.1.3 Additional Considerations	285
	17.2 Example 1: Walls and Doors	285
	17.2.1 Problem	285
	17.2.2 Solution	286
	17.2.3 Implementation Steps	286
	17.2.4 Explanation of the Code	288
	17.2.5 Complexity	289
	17.3 Example 2: Curriculum	289
	17.3.1 Problem	289
	17.3.2 Solution	289
	17.3.3 Code Implementation	290
	17.3.4 Explanation of Key Parts	292
	17.3.5 Explanation for the Test Cases	293
	17.3.6 Complexity Analysis	293
	17.4 Example 3: Bus Routes	293
	17.4.1 Problem	293
	17.4.2 The Solution	294
	17.4.3 Code Implementation	294
	17.4.4 Explanation	297
	17.4.5 Example Walkthrough	297
	17.4.6 Complexity Analysis	297
	17.5 Example 4: Are Graphs Dichotomy?	298
	17.5.1 Problem	298
	17.5.2 Solution	298
	17.5.3 Code Implementation	298
	17.5.4 Explanation of the Code	301
	17.5.5 Explanation for Test Cases	301
	17.6 Example 5: Word Ladder II	301
	17.6.1 Problem	301
	17.6.2 Problem Summary	302
	17.6.3 Code Analysis	302
	17.6.4 Code Walkthrough	303
	17.6.5 Explanation of Test Cases	306
	17.6.6 Complexity Analysis	306
	17.6.7 Edge Cases	307
	17.6.8 Summary	307
18	**Union-Find**	309
	18.1 Union-Find the Basics	309
	18.1.1 Algorithm Description	309
	18.1.2 Python Code Implementation	310

		18.1.3	Explanation of Key Parts	311

    18.2 Example 1: Circle Number 312
        18.2.1 Problem 312
        18.2.2 Problem Summary 312
        18.2.3 Breadth-First Search (BFS) Solution 312
        18.2.4 Depth-First Search (DFS) Solution 313
        18.2.5 Union-Find Solution 314
        18.2.6 Test Code 315
        18.2.7 Explanation 318
        18.2.8 Summary 319

19 Interview Questions 321
    19.1 Example 1: File System 321
        19.1.1 Problem Summary 322
        19.1.2 Steps and Solution Outline 322
        19.1.3 Key Takeaways for Interview 324
        19.1.4 Full Code Implementation 324
        19.1.5 Explanation of the Code 327
        19.1.6 Usage of DFS for Size Calculation 328
    19.2 Example 2: Longest Significant Word Chain 328
        19.2.1 Problem: Longest Significant Word Chain 328
        19.2.2 Solution 328
        19.2.3 Code Implementation 329
        19.2.4 Analysis of Time Complexity 331
        19.2.5 Test Main Function 332
        19.2.6 Conclusion 333
    19.3 Example 3: Combination of Circles 333
        19.3.1 Problem Overview 333
        19.3.2 Solution Analysis 333
        19.3.3 Code Implementation 334
        19.3.4 Analysis of Time Complexity 337
        19.3.5 Test Function 337
        19.3.6 Expected Output 338

Part III System Design

20 System Design Theory 341
    20.1 Design Steps 341
        20.1.1 Step 1: Define the Use Case, Constraints, and
                Assumptions 341
        20.1.2 Step 2: Develop a High-Level Design 342
        20.1.3 Step 3: Focus on Core Components 342
        20.1.4 Step 4: Address Scalability and Extend the Design 342
    20.2 Basic Knowledge Points of System Design 343
        20.2.1 Domain Name System 344

		20.2.2	Load Balancer	345
	20.3	Distributed Caching System Memcached		346
		20.3.1	LRU: Principle for Efficient Cache Eviction	348
		20.3.2	Memcached Is Distributed	348
		20.3.3	Hash Consistency	350
	20.4	Design a Distributed Cache		352
		20.4.1	The Cache Is Invalid	352
		20.4.2	Cache Eviction Policy	353
		20.4.3	Design a Distributed Key-Value Caching System	353
21	**System Design Practice for Big Data**			**355**
	21.1	Web Crawler Problem		355
		21.1.1	Architectural Design	355
		21.1.2	Crawler Services	357
		21.1.3	Handle Duplicate Links	360
		21.1.4	Determine When to Update Crawl Results	360
		21.1.5	Designed for Scalability	361
	21.2	Encryption and Decryption of TinyURL		362
		21.2.1	Requirements and Objectives of the System	363
		21.2.2	Capacity Estimation and Constraints	363
		21.2.3	System APIs	364
		21.2.4	Core Algorithm Design	365
		21.2.5	Database Design	366
		21.2.6	Data Partitioning and Replication	367
		21.2.7	Cache Design	367
		21.2.8	Load Balancer	368
	21.3	Design Autocomplete		368
		21.3.1	What Is Autocomplete?	368
		21.3.2	Requirements and Objectives of the System	369
		21.3.3	Basic System Design and Algorithms	369
		21.3.4	Data Structure: Trie	370
		21.3.5	Improvements	372
	21.4	Design Twitter		377
		21.4.1	What Is Twitter Search?	377
		21.4.2	System Requirements and Objectives	377
		21.4.3	Capacity Estimation and Constraints	378
		21.4.4	System APIs	378
		21.4.5	Premium Design	379
		21.4.6	Core Algorithm Design	380
		21.4.7	Improvements	381
	21.5	Design Uber/Lyft		384
		21.5.1	Use Case	385
		21.5.2	High-Level Design	385
		21.5.3	What Happens When a User Requests a Ride?	387
		21.5.4	How Is the Driver's Location Updated?	387

22 Multi-threaded Programming ... 389
22.1 Multi-threaded ABC ... 389
22.2 Example 1: Build H2O ... 390
- 22.2.1 Problem ... 390
- 22.2.2 Code Analysis ... 391
- 22.2.3 Test Function ... 392
- 22.2.4 Explanation of the Test ... 393
- 22.2.5 Expected Output ... 394

22.3 Example 2: Print Zero, Even, and Odd Numbers ... 394
- 22.3.1 Problem Overview ... 394
- 22.3.2 Code Analysis ... 395
- 22.3.3 Test Function ... 397
- 22.3.4 Explanation of the Test ... 398
- 22.3.5 Expected Output ... 398

23 Machine Learning System Design ... 399
23.1 Machine Learning Theory ... 399
- 23.1.1 Introduction ... 399
- 23.1.2 What Is Machine Learning? ... 399
- 23.1.3 Supervised and Unsupervised Learning ... 401
- 23.1.4 Classification vs. Regression ... 403
- 23.1.5 Underfitting and Overfitting ... 404
- 23.1.6 Bias and Variance ... 406

23.2 Machine Learning Theory and Practical Interview Questions ... 409
- 23.2.1 Machine Learning Basic Theory Questions ... 409
- 23.2.2 Machine Learning Practical Interview Questions ... 411
- 23.2.3 Deep Learning and Advanced Concepts ... 414

23.3 Machine Learning Scalability ... 415
- 23.3.1 Machine Learning Scalability ... 415
- 23.3.2 General ML Scalability Concepts ... 419
- 23.3.3 Data Scalability ... 420
- 23.3.4 Model Training Scalability ... 421
- 23.3.5 Model Deployment and Serving at Scale ... 421
- 23.3.6 Infrastructure and Resource Management ... 422
- 23.3.7 Model Monitoring and Maintenance at Scale ... 422

23.4 Machine Learning System Design ... 423
- 23.4.1 Machine Learning System Design ... 423
- 23.4.2 Machine Learning Workflows ... 425
- 23.4.3 ML Interview Concepts and Techniques Overview ... 427

23.5 Example 1: Design Google Lens ... 429
- 23.5.1 Technical Questions (Computer Vision and Machine Learning) ... 430
- 23.5.2 System Design and Scalability ... 431
- 23.5.3 Algorithm Optimization and Debugging ... 431
- 23.5.4 Advanced Topics ... 432

		23.5.5	Data Management and Privacy	432
		23.5.6	Metrics and Evaluation	433
		23.5.7	Cross-functional and Product Questions	433
		23.5.8	Final Thought Questions	434
		23.5.9	Summary	434
		23.5.10	General Questions About Google Lens	434
		23.5.11	Technical Questions (Computer Vision and Machine Learning)	435
		23.5.12	System Design and Scalability	435
		23.5.13	Algorithm Optimization and Debugging	436
		23.5.14	Advanced Topics	437
		23.5.15	Data Management and Privacy	437
		23.5.16	Metrics and Evaluation	438
		23.5.17	Cross-functional and Product Questions	438
		23.5.18	Final Thought Questions	438
		23.5.19	Summary	439
	23.6	Example 2: Search Rankings		439
		23.6.1	Problem Statement	439
		23.6.2	Evaluation Metrics	440
		23.6.3	Architectural Components	441
		23.6.4	Training Data Generation	445
		23.6.5	Ranking	447
		23.6.6	Filter the Results	448
	23.7	Example 3: Short Video Recommendation System		449
		23.7.1	High-Level Architecture	449
		23.7.2	System Components	450
		23.7.3	Video Processing and Delivery	452
		23.7.4	Algorithmic Flow for Recommendation	452
		23.7.5	Deep Learning-Based Recommendation Algorithms	453
		23.7.6	Scalability Considerations	457
		23.7.7	Metrics for Measuring Success	458
		23.7.8	Challenges and Solutions	458
		23.7.9	Conclusion	458
24	**Large Language Model System Design**			459
	24.1	Example 1: Building a Text-to-Image Generative AI System		459
		24.1.1	Model Architecture	459
		24.1.2	Data Pipeline and Preprocessing	460
		24.1.3	Model Training and Fine-Tuning	461
		24.1.4	Inference and Real-Time Generation	461
		24.1.5	Scalability and Performance	462
		24.1.6	Refinement and Iterative Generation	462
		24.1.7	Evaluation and Quality Metrics	462
		24.1.8	Handling Unseen Prompts and Out-of-Domain Requests	463

	24.1.9	Ethics and Safety	463
	24.1.10	Bonus Questions	464
24.2	Example 2: Design the ChatGPT Model		464
	24.2.1	Choosing the Right Model Architecture	464
	24.2.2	Gathering Data for Pre-training and Fine-Tuning	465
	24.2.3	Training the Model	465
	24.2.4	Fine-Tuning for Specific Use Cases	466
	24.2.5	Model Evaluation and Testing	466
	24.2.6	Deploying the Model	467
	24.2.7	Real-Time Updates and Feedback Loop	467
	24.2.8	Tools and Resources	467
	24.2.9	Summary of Steps to Build a ChatGPT-Like Model	468

List of Codes

Code 2.1	Create a list	9
Code 2.2	Use the append() function to add a list element	10
Code 2.3	Use the insert() function to add a list element	12
Code 2.4	Use the extend() method to add a list element	12
Code 2.5	Use remove() to remove the list element	13
Code 2.6	Use pop() to delete the element	14
Code 2.7	Python code for findMaxConsecutiveOnes	16
Code 2.8	Test code for findMaxConsecutiveOnes	17
Code 2.9	Python code for addBinary	20
Code 2.10	Test code for AddBinary	21
Code 2.11	Python code for random indexing	24
Code 2.12	Python code for nextPermutation	28
Code 2.13	Python code for isNumber	32
Code 2.14	Test code for isNumber	34
Code 3.1	List-based stack implementation	38
Code 3.2	Stack implementation based on deque	39
Code 3.3	The Python program demonstrates the use of LifoQueueStack implementation of the queue module	40
Code 3.4	Python code for minRemoveToMakeValid	43
Code 3.5	Test code for minRemoveToMakeValid	44
Code 3.6	Python code for exclusiveTime	48
Code 3.7	Test code for exclusiveTime	50
Code 4.1	The Python program demonstrates a queue implementation using lists	54
Code 4.2	The Python program demonstrates a queue implementation using collections.dequeue	55
Code 4.3	The Python program demonstrates a queuing implementation using a queuing module	57
Code 4.4	Python code for MyCircularQueue	60
Code 4.5	Test code for MyCircularQueue	62

xxiii

Code 4.6	Python code for shortestSubarray	65
Code 4.7	Test main function for shortestSubarray	67
Code 5.1	Implement priority queues with lists	70
Code 5.2	Implement priority queues with HEAPQ	71
Code 5.3	1 Make use of queue. PriorityQueue creates a priority queue	72
Code 5.4	Python code for mincostToHireWorkers	74
Code 5.5	Test code for mincostToHireWorkers	76
Code 5.6	Python code for isPossible	78
Code 5.7	Test main for isPossible	80
Code 5.8	Python code for earliest_arrival_time	82
Code 6.1	Use integer keys to create a dictionary	86
Code 6.2	Use dict( ) to create a dictionary	86
Code 6.3	Add an element to the dictionary	87
Code 6.4	How to access elements from a Dictionary	89
Code 6.5	Take advantage of GET()Gets the dictionary element	89
Code 6.6	Use del to delete elements in the dictionary	90
Code 6.7	Use pop() to delete elements	91
Code 6.8	Python code for subarraySum	92
Code 6.9	Test code for subarraySum	93
Code 6.10	Python code for largestValsFromLabels	96
Code 6.11	Test code for largestValsFromLabels	97
Code 6.12	Python code for RandomizedSet	100
Code 6.13	Test code for RandomizedSet	102
Code 6.14	Python code for LRUCache	105
Code 6.15	Test code for LRUCache	107
Code 7.1	Add elements to the set	112
Code 7.2	Remove()Delete the collection element	113
Code 7.3	A Python program demonstrates the union of two collections	113
Code 7.4	The Python program demonstrates the intersection of two collections	114
Code 8.1	Python code for ListNode cycle	118
Code 8.2	Test code for LinkedListWithCycle	119
Code 8.3	Python code for IntersectionNode using the hash table	122
Code 8.4	Python code for IntersectionNode using the two pointers	122
Code 8.5	Test code for Python code for IntersectionNode	124
Code 8.6	Python code for copyRandomList	128
Code 8.7	Test code for copyRandomList	130
Code 9.1	Postorder traversals	134
Code 9.2	Binary tree breadth-first search order traversal	135
Code 9.3	Top-down recursive pseudocode	136
Code 9.4	The maximum depth of the binary tree	137
Code 9.5	"Bottom-up" recursive function pseudocode	137
Code 9.6	Python code for lowestCommonAncestor	140
Code 9.7	Test code for lowestCommonAncestor	141
Code 9.8	Python code for serialize and deserialize	145

List of Codes

Code 9.9	Test code for serialize and deserialize.	147
Code 9.10	Python code for maxPathSum	151
Code 9.11	Test code for maxPathSum	153
Code 9.12	Python code for treeToDoublyList	156
Code 9.13	Test code for treeToDoublyList	158
Code 10.1	Python code for TrieNode	163
Code 10.2	Python code for Trie	165
Code 10.3	Python code for add/search words	167
Code 10.4	Code with optimization for add/search words	169
Code 10.5	Python code for get_overlap	172
Code 10.6	Python code for `construct_segment_tree`	173
Code 10.7	Python code for update_segment_tree	174
Code 10.8	Python code for get_minimum	175
Code 10.9	Python code for `preorder_traversal`	176
Code 10.10	Test code for segment tree	176
Code 10.11	Python implementation of Binary Indexed Tree (BIT)	179
Code 10.12	Python code for countSmaller	183
Code 10.13	Test code for countSmaller	185
Code 11.1	The adjacency table representation of the graph	189
Code 11.2	Python code for cloneGraph using the BFS algorithm	192
Code 11.3	Python code for cloneGraph using the DFS algorithm	194
Code 11.4	Test code for cloneGraph	195
Code 11.5	Python code for graph validation tree	198
Code 11.6	Test code for validTree using the DFS solution	200
Code 11.7	Python code for validTree using the BFS solution	202
Code 11.8	Test code for validTree using the BFS solution	204
Code 11.9	Python code for validTree using the Union-find solution	207
Code 11.10	Test code for validTree using the Union-Find solution	209
Code 12.1	Use the dichotomy to find the square root	216
Code 12.2	Rotate sort search	218
Code 12.3	Search in the intervals	221
Code 13.1	Sparse vector dotProduct	228
Code 13.2	Minimum widnow substring	233
Code 13.3	Interval of the interesection	238
Code 13.4	Maximum number of consecutive 1	240
Code 13.5	Python code for findAnagrams	243
Code 14.1	Python code for maxProfit function	249
Code 14.2	Python code for coinChange	252
Code 14.3	Python implementation for decoding ways	255
Code 14.4	Python implementation for test cases in the decoding	257
Code 15.1	Python implementation for Pacifici-Altantic currents	261
Code 15.2	Python code for predict winner	264
Code 15.3	Python implementation for expression add operator	269
Code 16.1	Python code for sudoku solvers	275
Code 16.2	Python implementation for robot vacuum cleaner	280

Code 17.1	Python implementation for walls and doors	287
Code 17.2	Python implementation for curriculum	290
Code 17.3	Python implemention for bus routes	295
Code 17.4	Python implementation for isBipartite	299
Code 17.5	Python implementation for word ladder II	303
Code 18.1	Python program for the Union-Find algorithm to detect cycles in an undirected graph	310
Code 18.2	BFS to find the circle number	313
Code 18.3	DFS to find the circle number	314
Code 18.4	Union-Find to find the circle number	315
Code 18.5	Test code for the circle number	316
Code 19.1	Python code for file system	325
Code 19.2	Python code for LongestWordChain	329
Code 19.3	Test code for LongestWordChain	332
Code 19.4	Python code for Circle class	334
Code 19.5	Python code for CircleGroup Class	335
Code 19.6	Test code for CircleGroup Class	338
Code 21.1	Pseudocode for the crawler service	358
Code 21.2	How to shorten URLs	366
Code 21.3	The python program implements Trie	371
Code 21.4	Design Twitter	381
Code 22.1	Python code for class H2O	391
Code 22.2	Test code for H2O	392

List of Figures

Fig 8.1	Single-linked lists	115
Fig. 8.2	Doubly linked lists	115
Fig. 8.3	Circular linked lists	116
Fig. 8.4	The intersection of two linked lists	121
Fig. 9.1	Binary tree	139
Fig. 11.1	An example of a graph	187
Fig. 11.2	The adjacency matrix representation of the graph	188
Fig. 11.3	The adjacency linked list representation of the diagram	189
Fig. 16.1	Original image of Sudoko	274
Fig. 16.2	Solution diagram of sudoku	274
Fig. 20.1	General diagram of big data architecture design	343
Fig. 20.2	Domain name system	345
Fig. 20.3	Architectural principles of distributed caches	347
Fig. 20.4	Memcached implements the principle of distributed caching	349
Fig. 20.5	Add a node's hash consistency	351
Fig. 21.1	Crawler design	356
Fig. 21.2	Extended crawler design	362
Fig. 21.3	The database needs to create two tables	367
Fig. 21.4	Based on the query words entered by the user	371
Fig. 21.5	The design of the system for searching for word rankings	374
Fig. 21.6	Design of auto-completion system based on Trie partition design	376
Fig. 21.7	Twitter's high-level design	379
Fig. 21.8	Design the high-level design of the taxi-hailing app	386
Fig. 23.1	Deviation variance model	407
Fig. 23.2	Balance of deviations and variances	408
Fig. 23.3	Application areas for machine learning	423
Fig. 23.4	The process of interviewing machine learning	424
Fig. 23.5	Workflows for machine learning	426
Fig. 23.6	Architectural components of a search engine	442
Fig. 23.7	Hierarchical model approach	445

Chapter 1
Technical Interview Process

A typical technical interview process usually consists of the following stages:

1. **Initial Non-technical Phone Interview**: This is generally conducted by a member of the human resources team and aims to provide a broad overview of your background and expectations.
2. **Technical Phone Interviews**: There may be one or more technical phone interviews, focusing primarily on items listed on your resume. These interviews often include a coding interview to assess the candidate's fundamental programming skills.
3. **On-Site Interview**: The final stage typically involves an on-site interview with about five rounds, covering coding, system design, and behavioral assessments.

For experienced candidates, the on-site interview generally includes two rounds of system design questions, two coding rounds, and one behavioral interview. For recent graduates or early-career engineers, the on-site stage often involves three rounds of coding, one round focused on object-oriented design or research questions related to academic work, and one round assessing company culture fit.

1.1 Non-technical Phone Interview

The first step involves a brief, informal conversation with a recruiter, typically lasting 10–20 min. There are no technical questions during this stage, as recruiters are usually HR personnel or external headhunters, not programmers.

The main goal here is to collect general information about your job search, such as:

- Your background, including any relevant project experience, job skills, or visa status.
- Your availability and preferred start date.

- Key priorities for your next job, like being part of a strong team, flexible hours, technical challenges, or growth potential.
- Specific roles you're interested in, such as front-end, back-end, or machine learning positions.

It's best to answer these questions honestly, as this helps recruiters understand your fit for the role. If asked about salary expectations, it's usually advisable to defer this discussion by stating that you'd like to assess fit with the company first.

1.2 Technical Phone Interviews

After the initial behavioral interview, the process typically moves to one or more technical phone interviews, lasting about an hour each. These interviews are often conducted via phone or video call (e.g., on Skype or Google Meet), with a shared document for coding.

Make sure you have a quiet environment with a stable internet connection. The interviewer will watch you code in real-time using a web-based editor like CoderPad or Collabedit. If you are unfamiliar with these tools, practice using them in advance.

A technical phone interview is typically divided into three parts:

- **Introduction (5 min)**: A brief chat to help you relax and get to know each other's backgrounds.
- **Technical Challenge (30–50 min)**: The core part of the interview, involving one or more coding problems.
- **Questions (5–10 min)**: An opportunity for you to ask questions about the company or role.

1.2.1 Introduction (5 Min)

The initial small talk is meant to set you at ease, but it's still part of the interview. You might be asked open-ended questions like:

- "Tell us a little about yourself."
- "Describe an accomplishment you're proud of."
- "Briefly introduce the items on your resume."

Make sure you're familiar with everything on your resume, as the interviewer may ask about any item or skill listed.

1.2.2 Technical Challenge (30–50 Min)

The technical portion is the most critical part of the phone interview. You may face one long question or multiple shorter ones, depending on the company.

- **Start-Ups**: Often focus on practical coding challenges, such as "Write a function to find if two rectangles overlap."
- **Large Companies**: Usually emphasize data structures and algorithms, asking questions like "Write a function to check if a binary tree is balanced in O(n) time."

The key to success is to communicate your thought process clearly. Discuss your approach and any optimizations with the interviewer as you work through the problem.

If the role requires specific technical knowledge (e.g., Python), some companies may ask language-specific questions, such as "What is a global interpreter lock in Python?"

1.2.3 Asking Questions (5–10 Min)

After the technical segment, the interviewer will usually allow you to ask questions. Take this opportunity to learn about the company and ask questions that show genuine interest in the role.

Once the technical phone interview is completed, the interviewer will typically provide a timeline for next steps. If you perform well, you may be invited to additional phone interviews or an on-site interview.

1.3 On-Site Interviews

The on-site interview is held at the company's office, and if you are not local, the company will typically cover your travel and accommodation expenses. The interview typically involves 2–6 interviewers in a small conference room, each conducting one-on-one technical sessions. Each interview lasts around an hour, beginning with introductions, followed by a technical evaluation, and concluding with an opportunity for you to ask questions.

The primary difference between on-site and phone interviews is that you'll be coding on a whiteboard rather than a computer. Coding on a whiteboard can be challenging, as it lacks the conveniences of a computer, like autocomplete, debugging tools, or easy editing. To prepare, it's essential to practice whiteboard coding extensively. Here are some helpful tips:

- Start writing in the upper left corner of the whiteboard to make the most of your space.
- Leave blank lines between lines of code to allow room for additions or adjustments.
- Take a moment to choose descriptive variable names to avoid confusion as you write the rest of your code.

On-site interviews can be lengthy, so it's best to keep your schedule open and avoid making other plans for the afternoon or evening.

If things go well, the interview might end with a conversation with the CEO or other executives, as companies often aim to leave a positive impression. They might even invite you for a group outing afterward.

A typical on-site interview schedule might look like this:

- **10 a.m. to 12 p.m.**: Two consecutive technical interviews, approximately 1 h each.
- **12 p.m. to 1 p.m.**: Lunch with one or more engineers, possibly at the company cafeteria.
- **1 p.m. to 4 p.m.**: Three consecutive technical interviews, each lasting about an hour.
- **4 p.m. to 5 p.m.**: Meeting with the CEO or a senior executive.
- **5 p.m. to 8 p.m.**: Drinks and dinner with the company team.

Many companies now include behavioral assessments to evaluate whether a candidate fits well with their corporate culture. If the company ends your interview early, it's often a sign they're not interested, and you can consider other opportunities.

The coding portion of the whiteboard interview is usually the most critical, with questions focusing on data structures, algorithms, and system design. To perform well, extensive preparation is necessary, which includes practicing on platforms like LeetCode. Remember: practice, practice, practice!

Here are some additional tips that might help you succeed:

1.3.1 Present Yourself Confidently and Professionally

Interviewers typically begin by discussing your background before diving into technical questions. They'll be assessing your:

- **Coding Skills**: Are you focused on writing clean, efficient code?
- **Ownership and Leadership**: Do you demonstrate responsibility for your work and tackle challenges proactively?
- **Communication Skills**: Are you easy to work with, and can you discuss technical issues effectively?

1.3 On-Site Interviews

Prepare answers to questions like:

- Examples of interesting technical problems you've solved.
- Instances of overcoming interpersonal challenges.
- Situations where you showed leadership or ownership.
- Stories about project challenges and how you addressed them.
- Questions about the company's products and business.
- Inquiries about the company's engineering practices (e.g., testing, Agile methods).

1.3.2 Emphasize Clear Communication

Effective communication is key, especially if you encounter difficulties. Candidates who openly discuss their thought process and seek clarification when needed are often preferred over those who try to tackle questions alone.

- **Coding**: The interviewer wants to see clear, well-structured code.
- **Small Talk**: You may be asked high-level design questions ("How would you build Twitter?") or simpler technical questions ("What does 'static' mean in Java?"). These questions can lead to more complex discussions, so be ready to engage thoughtfully.
- **Collaborative Attitude**: Make the interview feel like a team effort by using inclusive language, such as "we" instead of "I" (e.g., "If we use a breadth-first search, we could achieve an O(n) solution.").
- **Think Aloud**: If you're unsure about an answer, explain your thought process out loud. Share what might work, and evaluate why other approaches may not. This also applies to small talk questions.
- **Admit When You Don't Know**: If you're uncertain about a fact, acknowledge it rather than pretending to know. You could say, "I'm not sure, but I would guess because..." and then reason through why other options don't seem plausible.
- **Slow Down**: Avoid rushing through answers. Even if your solution is correct, take time to explain it. Going too fast can give a negative impression and may lead you to overlook details.

By following these strategies, you'll be better equipped to perform well during an on-site interview and leave a positive impression.

Part I
Data Structures

Chapter 2
List

A list is a collection of elements where the elements may be integers, strings, DVDs, games, books, etc., which are stored in adjacent (contiguous) storage locations. Because the list elements are stored in adjacent locations, it is relatively easy to check the entire collection of list elements.

2.1 The Basics of Lists

2.1.1 Create a List

Simply place the elements in square brackets "[ ]" to create a Python list.

A list can contain duplicate values at different positions. As a result, the locations of multiple duplicate values can be passed as a sequence when creating a list.

Code 2.1: Create a List

```
# Create a list (with duplicate values)
List = [1, 2, 4, 4, 3, 3, 3, 6, 5]
print("\nList with the use of Numbers: ")
print(List)

# Create a list of mixed types
List = [1, 2, 'Geeks', 4, 'For', 6, 'Geeks' ]
print("\nList with the use of Mixed Values: ")
print(List)
```

Results:

```
List using Numbers:
[1, 2, 4, 4, 3, 3, 3, 6, 5]

List using Mixed Values:
[1, 2, 'Geeks', 4, 'For', 6, 'Geeks']
```

2.1.2 Add Elements to the List

There are three ways to add elements to a list: (1) append(), (2) insert(), and (3) extend().

2.1.2.1 Use the append() Function

You can only add one element to the end of the list at a time using the built-in append() function. To add more than one element, you must iterate over the elements using append(), and you can also use append() to add the list to another list.

Code 2.2: Use the append() Function to Add a List Element

```
# Python program demonstrating adding elements to a list
# Create a list
List = []
print("Initial blank List: ")
print(List)

# Add elements to list
List.append(1)
List.append(2)
List.append(4)
print("\nList after adding three elements: ")
print(List)

# Add elements to list using iterator
for i in range(1, 4):
    List.append(i)
print("\nList after  adding elements from 1 to 3: ")
print(List)
```

2.1 The Basics of Lists

```
# Add tuple to list
List.append((5, 6))
print("\nList after Addition of a Tuple: ")
print(List)

# Add the list to the list
List2 = ['For', 'Geeks']
List.append(List2)
print("\nList after Addition of a List: ")
print(List)
```

The result of the code run

```
Initial blank List:
[]

List after Addition of Three elements:
[1, 2, 4]

List after Addition of elements from 1-3:
[1, 2, 4, 1, 2, 3]

List after Addition of a Tuple:
[1, 2, 4, 1, 2, 3, (5, 6)]

List after Addition of a List:
[1, 2, 4, 1, 2, 3, (5, 6), ['For', 'Geeks']]
```

2.1.2.2 Use the insert() Function

The append() function only works for element additions at the end of the list, while for element additions at the desired location, you should use the insert() function. Unlike the append() function, which uses only one parameter, the insert() function requires two arguments (position, value).

Code 2.3: Use the insert() Function to Add a List Element

```
# Python program demonstrating adding elements to a list,
create a list
List = [1,2,3,4]
print("Initial List: ")
print(List)

# using the insert method to add elements to specific
positions
List.insert(3, 12)
List.insert(0, 'Geeks')
print("\nList after performing insert operation: ")
print(List)
```

Results:

```
Initial List:
[1, 2, 3, 4]
List after performing Insert Operation:
['Geeks', 1, 2, 3, 12, 4]
```

2.1.2.3 Use the extend() Function

The extend() function is used to add multiple elements at the end of the list at the same time.

Code 2.4: Use the extend() Method to Add a List Element

```
#Create on List
List = [1,2,3,4]
print("Initial List: ")
print(List)

# using the extension method to add multiple elements to
the end of the list
List.extend([8, 'Geeks', 'Always'])
print("\nList after performing the extend operation: ")
print(List)
```

2.1 The Basics of Lists

Results:

```
Initial List:
[1, 2, 3, 4]
List after performing extend operation:
[1, 2, 3, 4, 8, 'Geeks', 'Always']
```

2.1.3 Delete an Element from the List

There are currently two main ways to delete an element from a list: (1) remove() and (2) pop().

2.1.3.1 Use the remove() Function

Python's built-in remove() function removes the first occurrence of the specified element from the list, and if the element is not in the list, an error will occur. The remove() function deletes the first matched element found, which means you can only delete one element at a time. In order to remove elements within a certain range; thus, it can only remove one element at a time.

Code 2.5: Use remove() to Remove the List Element

```python
# Python program demonstrates deleting elements
from a list
List = [1, 2, 3, 4, 5, 6, 7, 8, 9, 10, 11, 12]
print("Intial List: ")
print(List)

# To remove elements from a list, use the remove() method
List.remove(5)
List.remove(6)
print("\nList after removal of two elements: ")
print(List)

# Remove elements from a list using iterator methods
for i in range(1, 5):
    List.remove(i)
print("\nList after Removing a range of elements: ")
print(List)
```

The result is:

```
Intial List:
[1, 2, 3, 4, 5, 6, 7, 8, 9, 10, 11, 12]

List after Removal of two elements:
[1, 2, 3, 4, 7, 8, 9, 10, 11, 12]

List after Removing a range of elements:
[7, 8, 9, 10, 11, 12]
```

2.1.3.2 Use the pop() Function

The pop() function is used to remove the last element from the list. If a specific position element is removed, it is necessary to give the position of the specific deleted element in the pop() function.

Code 2.6: Use pop() to Delete the Element

```
List = [1,2,3,4,5]

# use the pop() method to delete one element
List.pop()
print("\nList after popping an element: ")
print(List)

# use the pop() method to set up to delete one specific
position element.
List.pop(2)
print("\nList after popping a specific element: ")
print(List)
```

The result is:

```
List after popping an element:
[1, 2, 3, 4]

List after popping a specific element:
[1, 2, 4]
```

2.2 Example 1: The Maximum Number of Consecutive 1

2.2.1 Problem

Given a binary array, find the maximum number of consecutive 1s in this array.

Example 1
Input: [1,1,0,1,1,1]
  Output: 3
  Explanation: The first two or last three digits are consecutive 1s. The maximum number of consecutive 1s is 3.

2.2.2 Approach and Explanation

This problem can be solved with a single pass through the array using two variables:

1. `ones`: Tracks the current count of consecutive 1s.
2. `max_ones`: Tracks the maximum count of consecutive 1s encountered so far.

Steps

1. Initialize `max_ones` and `ones` to 0.
2. Traverse each element in the array:
   - If the current element is 1, increment the `ones` counter by 1.
   - If the current element is 0, it means the streak of consecutive 1s has ended:
     - Update `max_ones` with the maximum of `max_ones` and `ones`.
     - Reset `ones` to 0.
3. After the loop, we perform one last update to `max_ones` because the array might end with a streak of 1's.

This ensures that `max_ones` holds the maximum number of consecutive 1s in the array.

2.2.3 Code Explanation

Here is the code for the solution, along with comments explaining each part.

Code 2.7: Python Code for findMaxConsecutiveOnes

```python
class Solution:
    def findMaxConsecutiveOnes(self, nums):
        max_ones = 0  # This will store the maximum count
        of consecutive 1s
        ones = 0  # This will store the current count of
        consecutive 1s

        # Traverse through each element in the array
        for i in range(len(nums)):
            if nums[i] == 1:
                # If we find a 1, increment the
                consecutive count
                ones += 1
            else:
                # If we find a 0, update max_ones and
                reset ones to 0
                max_ones = max(max_ones, ones)
                ones = 0

        # Final update for the case where the array
        ends with 1s
        return max(max_ones, ones)
```

2.2.4 Complexity Analysis

- **Time Complexity**: O(N), where N is the length of the array `nums`. The array is traversed only once.
- **Space Complexity**: O(1), since we are using only a few variables and no additional data structures.

2.2.5 Explanation of Steps in the Code

1. **Initialization**: We initialize `max_ones` and `ones` to 0. `max_ones` will keep track of the maximum count of consecutive 1's, and `ones` will keep track of the current streak.

2.2 Example 1: The Maximum Number of Consecutive 1

2. **Loop Through Each Element**:
   - If the current element is 1, increment `ones`.
   - If the current element is 0, it means the current streak has ended. We update `max_ones` with the maximum of `max_ones` and `ones`, and reset `ones` to 0.
3. **Final Update**: After the loop, update `max_ones` one last time with `ones` to account for a possible ending streak of 1's.

2.2.6 Testing the Code

Let's create a `main()` function to test the solution using the provided example and additional test cases.

Code 2.8: Test Code for findMaxConsecutiveOnes

```
def main():
    # Create a Solution object
    sol = Solution()

    # Example 1
    nums1 = [1, 1, 0, 1, 1, 1]
    output1 = sol.findMaxConsecutiveOnes(nums1)
    print(f"The maximum number of consecutive 1s in
    {nums1} is: {output1}")  # Expected output: 3

    # Additional Test Cases
    # Case 2: Only 0's in the array
    nums2 = [0, 0, 0, 0]
    output2 = sol.findMaxConsecutiveOnes(nums2)
    print(f"The maximum number of consecutive 1s in
    {nums2} is: {output2}")  # Expected output: 0

    # Case 3: Only 1's in the array
    nums3 = [1, 1, 1, 1, 1]
    output3 = sol.findMaxConsecutiveOnes(nums3)
    print(f"The maximum number of consecutive 1s in
    {nums3} is: {output3}")  # Expected output: 5
```

```
# Case 4: Alternating 1's and 0's
nums4 = [1, 0, 1, 0, 1]
output4 = sol.findMaxConsecutiveOnes(nums4)
print(f"The maximum number of consecutive 1s in
{nums4} is: {output4}")  # Expected output: 1

# Case 5: Array with multiple streaks of
consecutive 1s
nums5 = [1, 1, 0, 1, 1, 1, 0, 1]
output5 = sol.findMaxConsecutiveOnes(nums5)
print(f"The maximum number of consecutive 1s in
{nums5} is: {output5}")  # Expected output: 3

main()
```

2.2.7 Expected Output

The output of the `main()` function should be:

```
The maximum number of consecutive 1s in [1, 1, 0, 1, 1,
1] is: 3
The maximum number of consecutive 1s in [0, 0, 0,
0] is: 0
The maximum number of consecutive 1s in [1, 1, 1, 1,
1] is: 5
The maximum number of consecutive 1s in [1, 0, 1, 0,
1] is: 1
The maximum number of consecutive 1s in [1, 1, 0, 1, 1,
1, 0, 1] is: 3
```

2.2.8 Explanation of Test Cases

1. **Example 1**: The input [1, 1, 0, 1, 1, 1] has a longest streak of three consecutive 1's at the end, so the output is 3.
2. **Case 2**: The input [0, 0, 0, 0] contains no 1's, so the output is 0.
3. **Case 3**: The input [1, 1, 1, 1, 1] contains only 1's, all consecutive, so the output is 5.
4. **Case 4**: The input [1, 0, 1, 0, 1] has only single 1's separated by 0's, so the output is 1.

5. **Case 5**: The input [1, 1, 0, 1, 1, 1, 0, 1] has multiple streaks of consecutive 1's, with the longest streak being 3, so the output is 3.

This test sequence verifies that the solution correctly finds the maximum count of consecutive 1's in various configurations of binary arrays.

2.3 Example 2: Binary Addition

2.3.1 Problem

Given two binary strings, return the sum of them (also a binary string). The input strings are all non-null and contain only the characters 1 or 0.

Example 1
Input: a = "11", b = "1"
Output: "100"

2.3.2 Approach and Explanation

1. **Initialization**:
   - Calculate the lengths of both binary strings, a and b.
   - Initialize carry to 0.
   - An empty list, new_str, is used to accumulate the result in reverse order.

2. **Loop from Right to Left**:
   - Traverse from the last element of both strings to the first, padding with 0 if one string is shorter.
   - For each position:
     - Add the corresponding bits of a and b and the current carry.
     - The value for the current bit is calculated as add % 2, and the carry is updated as add // 2.
   - The resulting bit is inserted at the beginning of new_str.

3. **Final Carry Check**:
   - After the loop, if there's a carry left, prepend it to the result.

4. **Return Result**:
   - Join the list new_str to get the final binary string result.

2.3.3 Code Implementation

Code 2.9: Python Code for addBinary

```python
class Solution:
    def addBinary(self, a: str, b: str) -> str:
        len_a = len(a)  # length of string a
        len_b = len(b)  # length of string b
        max_length = max(len_a, len_b)  # find the maximum length of both strings
        carry = 0  # initialize carry
        new_str = []  # list to store binary result

        # Traverse both strings from right to left
        for i in range(-1, -max_length - 1, -1):
            element_a = int(a[i]) if i >= -len_a else 0
            # digit from a or 0 if out of bounds
            element_b = int(b[i]) if i >= -len_b else 0
            # digit from b or 0 if out of bounds

            # Calculate sum of current bits and carry
            add = element_a + element_b + carry
            value = add % 2  # current binary digit (remainder)
            carry = add // 2  # update carry (quotient)

            # Add the current binary digit to the front of the result list
            new_str.insert(0, str(value))

        # If there's a carry left, add it to the front of the result list
        if carry != 0:
            new_str.insert(0, str(carry))

        # Join the list into a string and return
        return ''.join(new_str)
```

2.3.4 Complexity Analysis

- **Time Complexity**: O(N), where N is the length of the longer string (`max(len(a), len(b))`). We loop over the strings from right to left once.
- **Space Complexity**: O(N), due to the storage of the result in the list `new_str`.

2.3 Example 2: Binary Addition

2.3.5 Explanation of Test Cases

Let's create a `main()` function to test this solution with various cases.

Code 2.10: Test Code for addBinary

```
def main():
    sol = Solution()

    # Example 1
    a1 = "11"
    b1 = "1"
    output1 = sol.addBinary(a1, b1)
    print(f"Binary addition of {a1} and {b1} is:
    {output1}")  # Expected output: "100"

    # Additional Test Cases
    # Case 2: Both inputs are the same length with
    multiple carries
    a2 = "1010"
    b2 = "1011"
    output2 = sol.addBinary(a2, b2)
    print(f"Binary addition of {a2} and {b2} is:
    {output2}")  # Expected output: "10101"

    # Case 3: Different lengths with carry overflow
    a3 = "111"
    b3 = "10"
    output3 = sol.addBinary(a3, b3)
    print(f"Binary addition of {a3} and {b3} is:
    {output3}")  # Expected output: "1001"

    # Case 4: No carry
    a4 = "110"
    b4 = "001"
    output4 = sol.addBinary(a4, b4)
    print(f"Binary addition of {a4} and {b4} is:
    {output4}")  # Expected output: "111"

    # Case 5: Both inputs are zeros
    a5 = "0"
    b5 = "0"
    output5 = sol.addBinary(a5, b5)
    print(f"Binary addition of {a5} and {b5} is:
    {output5}")  # Expected output: "0"

main()
```

2.3.6 Expected Output

The output of the `main()` function should be:

```
Binary addition of 11 and 1 is: 100
Binary addition of 1010 and 1011 is: 10101
Binary addition of 111 and 10 is: 1001
Binary addition of 110 and 001 is: 111
Binary addition of 0 and 0 is: 0
```

2.3.7 Explanation of Test Cases

1. **Example 1**: a = "11" and b = "1". Adding them gives 100, as 1 + 1 + carry leads to a carry-over in the binary addition.
2. **Case 2**: Both strings are of the same length, and we encounter multiple carries during the addition. a = "1010" and b = "1011", producing the result "10101".
3. **Case 3**: Strings of different lengths. a = "111" and b = "10" add to give "1001", as the carry extends to the final addition.
4. **Case 4**: No carry scenario. a = "110" and b = "001" add directly to give "111".
5. **Case 5**: Both inputs are "0", resulting in "0" as there are no 1's to add.

This set of test cases covers different scenarios like no carry, multiple carries, different lengths, and edge cases with zero values

2.4 Example 3: Random Indexing

2.4.1 Problem

Given an array of integers that may be repeated, the index for a given target number is randomly output. It can be assumed that a given target number must exist in the array.

int[] nums = new int[] {1,2,3,3,3};

Solution solution = new Solution(nums);

pick(3) should return either index 2, 3, or 4 randomly. Each index should have equal probability of returning solution.pick(3);pick(1) should return 0. Since in the array only nums[0] is equal to 1 for solution.pick(1).

2.4 Example 3: Random Indexing

2.4.2 Problem Analysis

The problem at hand involves a class `Solution` that allows us to randomly pick the index of a target number from an array of integers that may contain duplicates. The solution efficiently utilizes a hash map (or dictionary) to store the indices of each element, allowing for quick retrieval when picking indices.

2.4.3 Explanation of the Code

1. **Initialization (`__init__` method)**:
   - A `defaultdict` from the `collections` module is used to store indices for each unique number in the list `nums`.
   - The method iterates through the input list using `enumerate`, which provides both the index and the element. For each element, the index is appended to the list of indices corresponding to that element in the hash map.

2. **Picking an Index (`pick` method)**:
   - This method takes a `target` integer and retrieves the list of indices for that integer from the hash map.
   - The `random.choice()` function is used to select a random index from the list of indices, ensuring each index has an equal probability of being selected.

2.4.4 Reservoir Sampling Algorithm

The second part of the code discusses reservoir sampling, which is a technique used for randomly selecting `k` samples from a stream of data where the total number of items (`N`) is unknown.

- **Functionality**:
  - The `selectKItems` function initializes an array called `reservoir` with the first k elements of the stream.
  - For subsequent elements in the stream, a random index is chosen. If this index is less than k, the element at that index in the reservoir is replaced with the current element from the stream.

2.4.5 Code Implementation

Here's a complete implementation of both functionalities, including a main function to test the code:

Code 2.11: Python Code for Random Indexing

```
import collections
import random
from typing import List

class Solution:
    def __init__(self, nums: List[int]):
        # Define one hash map, which stores the index
        position of each element
        self.nums = collections.defaultdict(list)
        # Iterate each element in the array
        for index, ele in enumerate(nums):
            # For each element, add the corresponding
            index position in the hash map.
            self.nums[ele].append(index)

    def pick(self, target: int) -> int:
        # Call python function random.choice()
        return random.choice(self.nums[target])

# Functionality to select K items randomly from a stream
def printArray(stream, n):
    for i in range(n):
        print(stream[i], end=" ")
    print()

def selectKItems(stream, n, k):
    # Reservoir [] is the output array. Initialize it
    with the first k elements of stream[].
    reservoir = [0] * k
    for i in range(k):
        reservoir[i] = stream[i]

    # Iterate the Nth element after k+1 elements.
    for i in range(k, n):
        # Pick up a random index between [0, i+1].
        j = random.randrange(i + 1)
        # If random index is less than k, the elements
        present in the index are replaced with new ones
        in the stream
        if j < k:
            reservoir[j] = stream[i]
```

2.4 Example 3: Random Indexing

```
        print("Following are k randomly selected items:")
        printArray(reservoir, k)

# Main Functions
if __name__ == "__main__":
    # Test the Solution class
    nums = [1, 2, 3, 3, 3]
    solution = Solution(nums)

    # Testing pick method
    print("Picking index for target 3 (should return 2,
    3, or 4):")
    for _ in range(5):
        print(solution.pick(3))

    print("Picking index for target 1 (should
    return 0):")
    print(solution.pick(1))

    # Test reservoir sampling
    stream = [1, 2, 3, 4, 5, 6, 7, 8, 9, 10, 11, 12]
    n = len(stream)
    k = 5
    selectKItems(stream, n, k)
```

2.4.6 Expected Output

When running the main function, you should see output similar to the following:

```
Picking index for target 3 (should return 2, 3, or 4):
3
4
2
2
3
Picking index for target 1 (should return 0):
0
Following are k randomly selected items:
1 4 5 9 11
```

2.4.7 Explanation of the Output

1. **Picking Indices for Target 3**: Since there are three indices (2, 3, 4) that hold the value 3, the output should reflect a random selection from these indices, which may vary each time you run the code due to randomness.
2. **Picking Indices for Target 1**: The output should consistently return 0, as there's only one instance of 1 in the array.
3. **Reservoir Sampling**: The output for the random selection from the stream will vary each time the function is called, demonstrating the reservoir sampling method by printing k randomly selected items from the stream.

2.4.8 Complexity Analysis

- **Time Complexity**:
  - For `Solution`:

    O(N) for initialization, where N is the number of elements in nums.
    O(1) for the `pick` method as it retrieves the index list and performs a random selection.
  - **For Reservoir Sampling**: O(N) where N is the number of elements in the stream, as it requires iterating through the stream once.
- **Space Complexity**:
  - **For `Solution`**: O(N) due to the storage of indices in the hash map.
  - **For Reservoir Sampling**: O(k) for storing the selected items.

2.5 Example 4: The Next Maximum

2.5.1 Problem

Implement the next permutation, which rearranges the numbers on the dictionary to the next larger permutation of the numbers. If this arrangement is not possible, it must be rearranged to the lowest possible order (i.e., in ascending order). Replacement must be in place and only use a constant amount of extra memory. For example, the input is in the left column, and its corresponding output is in the right column.

1,2,3→1,3,2
3,2,1→1,2,3
1,1,5→1,5,1

2.5.2 Problem Analysis

The problem is to implement the "next permutation" function, which rearranges the numbers in an array to produce the next lexicographical permutation. If such a permutation is not possible (i.e., the array is sorted in descending order), it should rearrange the array to the lowest possible order (ascending order).

The following steps are used to achieve the next permutation:

1. **Find the Pivot**:
   - Traverse the array from the end towards the start to find the first pair of consecutive elements `nums[i]` and `nums[i + 1]` where `nums[i] < nums[i + 1]`. This is the "pivot" point where the ascending order breaks.

2. **Find the Successor**:
   - Traverse the array again from the end and find the first element `nums[j]` that is greater than `nums[i]`. This will be the smallest number larger than `nums[i]` on the right side of the array.

3. **Swap the Pivot and Successor**:
   - Swap the values at indices `i` and `j`.

4. **Reverse the Elements After the Pivot**:
   - Reverse the elements after index `i` to get the smallest lexicographical order for the remaining elements.

This algorithm works in-place and has a time complexity of $O(N)$, where N is the number of elements in `nums`.

2.5.3 Code Implementation

Here's the code implementation using the steps outlined above:

Code 2.12: Python Code for nextPermutation

```
from typing import List

def find_pivot(nums: List[int]) -> int:
    m = nums[-1]
    i = len(nums) - 2
    while i >= 0 and nums[i] >= m:
        m = nums[i]
        i -= 1
    return i

def find_successor(nums: List[int], pivot: int) -> int:
    j = len(nums) - 1
    while nums[pivot] >= nums[j]:
        j -= 1
    assert j > pivot
    return j

def reverse(arr: List[int], start: int, end: int)
-> None:
    while start < end:
        arr[start], arr[end] = arr[end], arr[start]
        start += 1
        end -= 1

class Solution:
    def nextPermutation(self, nums: List[int]) -> None:
        if len(nums) < 2:
            return
        # Locate the first index that fell
        i = find_pivot(nums)
        if i < 0:
            nums.sort()
        else:
            # Find the index j where the value is larger
            than nums[i] after index i
```

2.5 Example 4: The Next Maximum

```
                j = find_successor(nums, i)
                # Swap the numbers at index positions i and j
                nums[i], nums[j] = nums[j], nums[i]
                # Array sorting after index position i
                reverse(nums, i + 1, len(nums) - 1)

# Main function to test the code
if __name__ == "__main__":
    # Test cases
    test_cases = [
        [1, 2, 3],
        [3, 2, 1],
        [1, 1, 5],
        [1, 5, 8, 4, 7, 6, 5, 3, 1],
        [1, 3, 2]
    ]

    solution = Solution()
    for nums in test_cases:
        print("Original array:", nums)
        solution.nextPermutation(nums)
        print("Next permutation:", nums)
```

2.5.4 Explanation of the Code

- find_pivot: This function locates the first element from the right that is smaller than the element to its right, returning the index i.
- find_successor: This function finds the smallest element on the right side of the pivot that is larger than nums[i], returning the index j.
- reverse: This function reverses the elements in the list between indices start and end.
- nextPermutation: This method applies the above functions to compute the next permutation, or if the input is the last permutation, it rearranges the list into ascending order.

2.5.5 Expected Output

When running the main function, you should see output similar to the following:

```
Original array: [1, 2, 3]
Next permutation: [1, 3, 2]
Original array: [3, 2, 1]
Next permutation: [1, 2, 3]
Original array: [1, 1, 5]
Next permutation: [1, 5, 1]
Original array: [1, 5, 8, 4, 7, 6, 5, 3, 1]
Next permutation: [1, 5, 8, 5, 1, 3, 4, 6, 7]
Original array: [1, 3, 2]
Next permutation: [2, 1, 3]
```

2.5.6 Explanation of the Output

Each output represents the next lexicographical permutation of the given array:
1. [1, 2, 3] becomes [1, 3, 2].
2. [3, 2, 1] becomes [1, 2, 3] because it is the last permutation, so we reset to the smallest permutation.
3. [1, 1, 5] becomes [1, 5, 1].
4. [1, 5, 8, 4, 7, 6, 5, 3, 1] becomes [1, 5, 8, 5, 1, 3, 4, 6, 7].
5. [1, 3, 2] becomes [2, 1, 3].

2.5.7 Complexity Analysis

- **Time Complexity**: O(N) where N is the number of elements in nums. The algorithm consists of a constant number of linear scans (finding the pivot, finding the successor, and reversing part of the list).
- **Space Complexity**: O(1), as it modifies the list in place and uses only a constant amount of extra memory.

2.6 Example 5: Valid Decimal Number

2.6.1 Problem

Verify that a given string can be interpreted as a decimal number. Some examples:

```
"0" => true" 0.1 " => true"abc" => false"1 a" => false"2e10"
=> true" -90e3    " => true" 1e" => false"e3" => false" 6e-1"
=> true" 99e2.5 " => false"53.5e93" => true" -- 6 " =>
false"-+3" => false"95a54e53" => false
```

2.6.2 Problem Analysis

The task is to determine if a given string can be interpreted as a valid decimal number, which may include integers, decimal numbers, or numbers in scientific notation with an exponent (e.g., "2e10").

The function should return True if the string represents a valid number, and False otherwise.

2.6.3 Rules for Valid Numbers

1. **Integers**: Strings like "0", "123", and "-90" are valid integers.
2. **Decimal Numbers**: Strings with decimal points, such as "0.1", "1.", and ".9", are valid if they contain digits on at least one side of the decimal point.
3. **Scientific Notation**: Numbers with an exponent part represented by "e" or "E", like "2e10" or "-90e3", are valid if:
    - The base (part before e) is a valid integer or decimal number.
    - The exponent (part after e) is an integer, without any decimal points.
4. Leading and Trailing Whitespaces: These should be ignored.
5. **Sign Handling**: The number may start with + or - to indicate its sign.
6. **Invalid Characters**: Letters or symbols that don't contribute to the number format make the string invalid, e.g., "abc", "1a", "--6", "e3".

2.6.4 Code Implementation

The provided code divides the problem into three main steps:

1. **Splitting by 'e'**: First, it checks if the string contains an exponent. If it does, the string is split into two parts: the base (before e) and the exponent (after e).
2. **Checking the Base**: The `decide_num` function validates whether the base part is a valid integer or decimal number.
3. **Checking the Exponent**: The `decide_pow` function checks if the exponent part is a valid integer (with no decimal points).

Here's the provided code with minor corrections (correcting the indentation for `decide_pow` method):

Code 2.13: Python Code for isNumber

```python
class Solution:
    def isNumber(self, s: str) -> bool:
        s = s.strip()  # Remove leading and trailing whitespace
        if not s:
            return False
        ls = s.split('e')  # Split by 'e' to check if it's exponential notation
        if len(ls) == 1:  # No 'e' in the string
            return self.decide_num(ls[0])
        elif len(ls) == 2:  # Contains 'e', so split into base and exponent
            return self.decide_num(ls[0]) and self.decide_pow(ls[1])
        else:
            return False  # More than one 'e' is invalid

    def decide_num(self, s: str) -> bool:
        if not s:
            return False
        if s[0] in ['+', '-']:  # Skip leading '+' or '-'
            s = s[1:]
        ls = s.split('.')  # Split by '.' to check for decimal numbers
        if len(ls) == 1:  # No '.'
            return ls[0].isnumeric()
```

2.6 Example 5: Valid Decimal Number

```
        elif len(ls) == 2:  # Contains '.'
            # Check for valid numbers before and
            after the '.'
            if not ls[0] and ls[1].isnumeric():  # Empty
            before '.'
                return True
            elif not ls[1] and ls[0].isnumeric():  #
            Empty after '.'
                return True
            else:
                return ls[0].isnumeric() and ls[1].
                isnumeric()
    else:
        return False  # More than one '.' is invalid

def decide_pow(self, s: str) -> bool:
    if not s:
        return False
    if s[0] in ['+', '-']:  # Skip leading '+' or '-'
        s = s[1:]
    return s.isnumeric()  # Exponent must be a
    valid integer
```

2.6.5 Explanation of Code

- isNumber:
  - Strips leading/trailing spaces.
  - Splits the string by e. If there's no e, checks if the entire string is a valid number.
  - If there is an e, checks if the part before e is a valid number and the part after e is a valid integer (power).
- decide_num:
  - Validates the number part. It handles positive/negative signs and decimal points, ensuring the format is correct.
- decide_pow:
  - Validates the exponent part. It allows positive/negative signs but requires the rest to be numeric (i.e., no decimal points).

2.6.6 Test Cases

Here's a main function with various test cases based on the examples provided:

Code 2.14: Test Code for isNumber

```
def main():
    solution = Solution()
    test_cases = [
        ("0", True),
        ("0.1", True),
        ("abc", False),
        ("1 a", False),
        ("2e10", True),
        (" -90e3   ", True),
        (" 1e", False),
        ("e3", False),
        (" 6e-1", True),
        (" 99e2.5 ", False),
        ("53.5e93", True),
        (" --6 ", False),
        ("-+3", False),
        ("95a54e53", False),
    ]

    for s, expected in test_cases:
        result = solution.isNumber(s)
        print(f"Input: '{s}' | Expected: {expected} | 
        Result: {result} | {'Pass' if result == expected 
        else 'Fail'}")

if __name__ == "__main__":
    main()
```

2.6.7 Expected Output

```
Input: '0' | Expected: True | Result: True | Pass
Input: '0.1' | Expected: True | Result: True | Pass
Input: 'abc' | Expected: False | Result: False | Pass
Input: '1 a' | Expected: False | Result: False | Pass
```

2.6 Example 5: Valid Decimal Number

```
Input: '2e10' | Expected: True | Result: True | Pass
Input: ' -90e3   ' | Expected: True | Result: True | Pass
Input: ' 1e' | Expected: False | Result: False | Pass
Input: 'e3' | Expected: False | Result: False | Pass
Input: ' 6e-1' | Expected: True | Result: True | Pass
Input: ' 99e2.5 ' | Expected: False | Result: False | Pass
Input: '53.5e93' | Expected: True | Result: True | Pass
Input: ' --6 ' | Expected: False | Result: False | Pass
Input: '-+3' | Expected: False | Result: False | Pass
Input: '95a54e53' | Expected: False | Result: False | Pass
```

Each test case in the `main()` function matches the expected result based on the problem's requirements.

2.6.8 Complexity Analysis

- **Time Complexity**: O(N) where N is the length of the input string. Each check (for e, decimal points, signs, etc.) only traverses the string a constant number of times.
- **Space Complexity**: O(1), as the function uses only a constant amount of additional memory.

This solution efficiently determines if a given string can be interpreted as a valid decimal number, handling various edge cases involving scientific notation, decimal points, signs, and invalid characters.

Chapter 3
Stack

A stack is a linear data structure that follows a specific order of operations. It can be last-in, first-out (LIFO) or first-in, last-out (FILO). There are a few basic operations that are performed in the stack.

- push: Add an element to the stack. Adding an element to a full stack triggers an overflow condition.
- pop: Removes an element from the stack. Removing an element from an empty stack triggers an underflow condition.
- peek/top: Returns the top element of the stack.
- isEmpty: Returns true if the stack is empty, false otherwise.

3.1 Stack Basics

3.1.1 The Time Complexity of Stack Operations

push(), pop(), isEmpty(), and peek() all run in O(1) time, and none of these operations run any loops.

3.1.2 How to Implement the Stack Operations in Python

There are various ways to implement a stack in Python. The stack is implemented using data structures and modules from the Python library. The stack methods implemented in Python are: (1) list; (2) collections.deque; (3) queue.LifoQueue.

3.1.2.1 List-Based Stack Implementation

Python's built-in list data structure, list, can be used as a stack. The function append() is used to add elements to the top of the stack, and pop() removes elements in LIFO order.

The main limitation with lists is that they have speed issues as the data structure grows. The items in the list are stored next to each other in memory. If the size of the stack is larger than the size of the memory block currently stored, Python needs to make some memory allocation. This can cause some append() calls to take longer than others.

Code 3.1: List-Based Stack Implementation

```python
stack = []

# append() function to enter the stack
# element in the stack
stack.append('a')
stack.append('b')
stack.append('c')

print('Initial stack')
print(stack)

#pop() function to eject elements in the stack,
press LIFO
print('\nElements poped from stack:')
print(stack.pop())
print(stack.pop())
print(stack.pop())

print('\nStack after elements are poped:')
print(stack)
```

3.1 Stack Basics

Results:

```
Initial stack
['a', 'b', 'c']

Elements poped from stack:
c
b
a

Stack after elements are poped:
[]
```

3.1.2.2 Stack Implementation Based on Deque

The Python stack can be implemented using the deque class in the collections module. In cases where push and pop operations need to be performed faster from both ends of the container, double-ended queues are preferable over lists, as they offer O(1) time complexity for add and delete operations, compared to lists that provide O(n) time.

Use the same method as the double-ended queue shown in the list, append() and pop().

Code 3.2: Stack Implementation Based on Deque

```
from collections import deque

stack = deque()

# append() function presses elements into the stack
stack.append('a')
stack.append('b')
stack.append('c')

print('Initial stack:')
print(stack)

 # pop() function pops elements from the stack in
 LIFO  order
print('\nElements poped from stack:')
print(stack.pop())
print(stack.pop())
print(stack.pop())

print('\nStack after elements are poped:')
print(stack)
```

Results:

```
Initial stack:
deque(['a', 'b', 'c'])

Elements poped from stack:
c
b
a

Stack after elements are poped:
deque([])
```

3.1.2.3 Stack Implementation Based on LifoQueue

The queue module also has a LIFO queue, which functions as a stack. The put() function inserts data into the queue, and the get() function fetches data. This module provides the following various functions:

- maxsize(): The number of items allowed in the queue.
- empty(): Returns True if the queue is empty, False otherwise.
- full(): Returns True if the queue is full. If the queue is initialized with maxsize = 0 (the default), full() will never return True.
- get(): Removes from the queue and returns an item. If the queue is empty, wait until an item is available.
- get_nowait(): Returns an item if it is immediately available, otherwise throws a QueueEmpty.
- put(item): Queues the item. If the queue is full, wait until a free slot is available before adding items.
- put_nowait (item): Queues the item without blocking.
- qsize(): Returns the number of items in the queue. If there are no free slots available, raise QueueFull.

Code 3.3: The Python Program Demonstrates the Use of LifoQueueStack Implementation of the Queue Module

```
# Python program demonstrates the stack implementation of
using queue module from queue import LifoQueue
# Initialize stack
stack = LifoQueue(maxsize=3)

# qsize() indicates the number of elements in the stack
print(stack.qsize())
```

3.1 Stack Basics

```
# put() function pushes elements into the stack
stack.put('a')
stack.put('b')
stack.put('c')
print("Full: ", stack.full())
print("Size: ", stack.qsize())

# get() function pops elements from the stack
print('\nElements poped from the stack')
print(stack.get())
print(stack.get())
print(stack.get())
print("\ nEmpty: ", stack.empty())
```

Results:

```
0
Full:    True
Size:    3

Elements poped from the stack
c
b
a

Empty:   True
```

3.1.3 Applications

- Symbol balance, such as the 'Valid Parentheses' problem on LeetCode (https://leetcode.com/problems/valid-parentheses/).
- The redo-undo function, (e.g., ctrl-z, Photoshop). https://leetcode.com/ problems/basic-calculator/.
- Forward and backward functionality in a web browser.
- Used in many algorithms, such as the Tower of Hanoi, Tree Traversal (https://leetcode.com/problems/binary-tree-postorder-traversal/), Stock Span Problems (https://www.geeksforgeeks.org/the-stock-span-problem/), histogram problem (https://leetcode.com/problems/largest-rectangle-in-histogram/).
- Other applications such as backtracking problems, knight's journey problems, rats in mazes, N-queen problems, and Sudoku solvers.
- In graph algorithms, such as topological ordering and strongly connected components.

3.2 Example 1: Minimal Removal to Get Valid Parentheses

3.2.1 Problem

Given a string s of parenthesis '(' and ')' alongside lowercase English characters, your task is to remove the minimum number of parentheses ('(' or ')', in any positions) so that the resulting parentheses string is valid and return any valid string.

Formally, a parentheses string is valid if and only if:

- It is the empty string, contains only lowercase characters.
- It can be written as AB (A concatenated with B), where A and B are valid strings.
- It can be written as (A), where A is a valid string.

Example 1

```
Input: s = "lee(t(c)o)de)"
Output: "lee(t(c)o)de"
Explanation: "lee(t(co)de)" , "lee(t(c)ode)" would also
be accepted.
```

Example 2

```
Input: s = "a)b(c)d"
Output: "ab(c)d"
```

Example 3

```
Input: s = "))(("
Output: ""
Explanation: An empty string is also valid.
```

3.2.2 Key Idea

The solution utilizes a stack to identify unmatched parentheses. The stack stores indices of unmatched parentheses, and only the indices of these unmatched parentheses are removed from the original string to produce a valid output.

3.2 Example 1: Minimal Removal to Get Valid Parentheses

3.2.3 Solution Explanation

Here's the code provided with some explanations added:

Code 3.4: Python Code for minRemoveToMakeValid

```python
from collections import deque
class Solution:
    def minRemoveToMakeValid(self, s: str) -> str:
        stk = deque()  # Stack to store indices of
        unmatched parentheses
        for i, ch in enumerate(s):
            if ch == '(':  # If it's an opening
            parenthesis, push index onto the stack
                stk.append(i)
            elif ch == ')':
                # If there's a matching '(', pop it from
                the stack
                if stk and s[stk[-1]] == '(':
                    stk.pop()
                else:
                    # If there's no matching '(', push
                    index onto the stack
                    stk.append(i)

        # Now the stack contains indices of unmatched
        parentheses
        res = ""
        for i in range(len(s)):
            if stk and i == stk[0]:  # If index is in the
            stack, skip it
                stk.popleft()
            else:
                res += s[i]  # Otherwise, add character
                to result

        return res
```

3.2.3.1 Explanation of Code

1. **Stack for Unmatched Parentheses**: We use a stack to store indices of unmatched parentheses.
   - For every (, we add its index to the stack.
   - For every), if the stack is non-empty and the top of the stack is an index of (, we pop it (indicating a match).
   - If there's no matching (, we add the index of) to the stack.
2. **Constructing the Result**: After the loop, the stack will contain indices of all unmatched parentheses (both (and)).
   - The result string is constructed by skipping characters at indices stored in the stack.

This approach has a time complexity of O(N), where N is the length of the string s, because we only traverse the string twice.

3.2.4 Test Function

Here's the main function with test cases as requested:

Code 3.5: Test Code for minRemoveToMakeValid

```
def main():
    solution = Solution()
    test_cases = [
        ("lee(t(c)o)de)", "lee(t(c)o)de"),     # Example 1
        ("a)b(c)d", "ab(c)d"),                  # Example 2
        ("))((", ""),                           # Example 3
        ("(a(b(c)d)", "a(b(c)d)"),              # Additional
        Test Case 1
        ("abc", "abc"),                         # Additional
        Test Case 2 (no parentheses)
        ("", ""),                               # Additional
        Test Case 3 (empty string)
    ]

    for s, expected in test_cases:
        result = solution.minRemoveToMakeValid(s)
        print(f"Input: '{s}' | Expected: '{expected}' |
        Result: '{result}' | {'Pass' if result == expected
        else 'Fail'}")

if __name__ == "__main__":
    main()
```

3.2.5 Expected Output

```
Input: 'lee(t(c)o)de)' | Expected: 'lee(t(c)o)de' |
Result: 'lee(t(c)o)de' | Pass
Input: 'a)b(c)d' | Expected: 'ab(c)d' | Result: 'ab(c)
d' | Pass
Input: '))((' | Expected: '' | Result: '' | Pass
Input: '(a(b(c)d)' | Expected: 'a(b(c)d)' | Result:
'a(b(c)d)' | Pass
Input: 'abc' | Expected: 'abc' | Result: 'abc' | Pass
Input: '' | Expected: '' | Result: '' | Pass
```

Each test case in the `main()` function matches the expected output, ensuring that the solution works for a variety of input cases, including edge cases such as strings without parentheses and empty strings.

3.2.6 Complexity Analysis

- **Time Complexity**: O(N) where N is the length of the string. We perform two passes through the string, one to build the stack and one to construct the result.
- **Space Complexity**: O(N), since we use a stack to store indices of unmatched parentheses and a result string.

This solution efficiently removes the minimum number of parentheses to produce a valid string, handling different types of inputs and edge cases.

3.3 Example 2: The Dedicated Time of the Function

3.3.1 Problem

On a single-threaded CPU, some functions are executed. Each function has a unique ID between 0 and N-1. Logs are stored in chronometric order that describe when a function was entered or exited.

Each log is a string in the format:

"{function_id}:{"start" | "end"}:{timestamp}".

For example, "0:start:3" represents a function with an id of 0, starting at the beginning of timestamp 3.

"1:end:2" represents a function with an id of 1, ending at the end of timestamp 2.

The dedicated time of a function is the unit of time spent by this function. Note that this does not include any recursive calls to subfunctions.

A single-threaded CPU ensures only one function executes at a time.

Returns the exclusive time of each function, sorted by its function ID.

Example 1

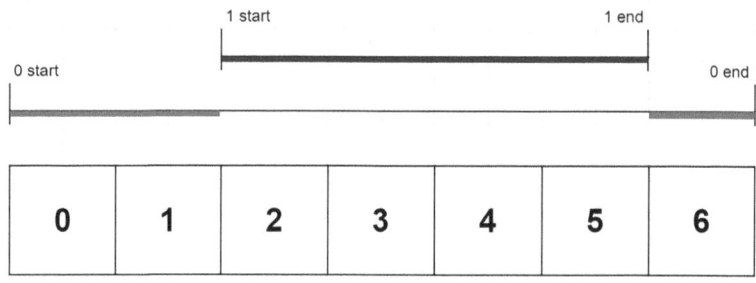

Input: n = 2
log=["0:start:0", "1:start:2", "1:end:5", "0:end:6"]
Output: [3,4]
Explanation:

Function 0 starts at the beginning of time 0 and then executes 2 units of time and reaches the end of time 1.

Now function 1 starts at the beginning of time 2 and executes 4 units of time, ending at time 5.

Function 0 runs again at the beginning of time 6 and ends at the end of time 6, so 1 unit of time is executed.

Therefore, function 0 takes 2 + 1 = 3 units of total execution time, while function 1 takes 4 units of total execution time.

3.3.2 Problem Analysis

The problem involves calculating the exclusive time for each function based on a series of logs in a single-threaded CPU. Each log entry describes when a function is entered (start) or exited (end). Each function has a unique ID in the range of 0 to n-1, and our goal is to determine the exclusive time for each function, which is the time spent by the function alone, excluding time spent in nested sub-functions.

3.3 Example 2: The Dedicated Time of the Function   47

3.3.3 Key Concepts

1. **Single-threaded Execution**:
   - Since the CPU is single-threaded, only one function runs at any given time.

2. **Logs Format**:
   - Logs follow the format "`{function_id}:{startlend}:{timestamp}`".
   - A log like "`0:start:3`" means function 0 starts at timestamp 3.
   - A log like "`1:end:5`" means function 1 ends at timestamp 5.

3. **Exclusive Time**:
   - Exclusive time refers to the time a function executes without including nested calls.

3.3.4 Example Walkthrough

For n = 2 and `logs` = `["0:start:0"`, `"1:start:2"`, `"1:end:5"`, `"0:end:6"]`, the breakdown is as follows:

- **Function 0** starts at time 0 and pauses at time 2 (2 unit of time executed).
- **Function 1** starts at time 2, runs until time 5 (4 units of time), and then ends.
- **Function 0** resumes at time 6 and ends at the same timestamp (1 more unit of time).
- The final exclusive times are `[3, 4]` for functions 0 and 1, respectively.

3.3.5 Approach

1. **Parsing Logs**:
   - Split each log to get `function_id`, `start`/`end`, and `timestamp`.
   - Use a stack to keep track of currently active functions.

2. **Handling Start and End Events**:
   - When encountering a `start` event, push it onto the stack.
   - For an `end` event:
     – Calculate the duration of the function, including both start and end timestamps.
     – Pop the function off the stack.

– Update its exclusive time and. If there's a parent function (remaining in the stack), deduct the time of this function from the parent's exclusive time.

3. **Result Construction**:
   - Each function's exclusive time is stored in an array, indexed by function ID.

3.3.6 Code Implementation

Code 3.6: Python Code for exclusiveTime

```python
from typing import List

class Node:
    def __init__(self, id: int, time_flag: str, time_stamp: int):
        self.id = id
        self.time_flag = time_flag
        self.time_stamp = time_stamp

class Solution:
    def exclusiveTime(self, n: int, logs: List[str]) -> List[int]:
        res = [0] * n    # Array to store exclusive times for each function
        stack = []       # Stack to keep track currently active function calls

        for log in logs:
            # Parse the log into function ID, type (start or end), and timestamp
            func_id, type_flag, timestamp = log.split(":")
            func_id = int(func_id)
            timestamp = int(timestamp)

            if type_flag == "start":
                # Push the start of the function onto the stack
```

3.3 Example 2: The Dedicated Time of the Function   49

```
                stack.append((func_id, timestamp))
        else:
            # Pop the start of the function from
            the stack
            start_func_id, start_time = stack.pop()
            time_duration = timestamp - start_
            time + 1
            # Add the exclusive time to the
            function's result
            res[start_func_id] += time_duration

            # If there is a function on the stack, it
            was paused during this function's execution
            if stack:
                res[stack[-1][0]] -= time_duration

    return res
```

3.3.7 Explanation of Code

1. **Initialization**:
   - `res`: Array to hold exclusive times for each function.
   - `stack`: Stack to manage function calls and their timestamps.
2. **Log Processing**:
   - For each `start` log, push the function ID and timestamp onto the stack.
   - For each `end` log:
     - Pop the top function from the stack and calculate the time spent.
     - Add this duration to the function's total time.
     - If there's another function on the stack, subtract this time from the function on top of the stack.

3.3.8 Testing the Code

The `main()` function tests example and edge cases comprehensively.

Code 3.7: Test Code for exclusiveTime

```
def main():
    solution = Solution()
    test_cases = [
        # Example 1
        (2, ["0:start:0", "1:start:2", "1:end:5",
        "0:end:6"], [3, 4]),

        # Edge Case: Single function starting and ending
        at the same time
        (1, ["0:start:0", "0:end:0"], [1]),

        # Edge Case: Single function with a small
        duration
        (1, ["0:start:0", "0:end:1"], [2]),

        # Nested function calls
        (3, ["0:start:0", "1:start:2", "2:start:3",
        "2:end:4", "1:end:5", "0:end:6"], [3, 2, 2]),

        # Multiple calls for the same function
        (2, ["0:start:0", "1:start:2", "1:end:5",
        "0:end:6", "0:start:7", "0:end:8"], [5, 4])
    ]

    for i, (n, logs, expected) in enumerate(test_cases):
        result = solution.exclusiveTime(n, logs)
        print(f"Test Case {i+1} - Expected: {expected},
        Result: {result}, {'Pass' if result == expected
        else 'Fail'}")

if __name__ == "__main__":
    main()
```

3.3.9 Expected Output

```
Test Case 1 - Expected: [3, 4], Result: [3, 4], Pass
Test Case 2 - Expected: [1], Result: [1], Pass
Test Case 3 - Expected: [2], Result: [2], Pass
Test Case 4 - Expected: [3, 2, 2], Result: [3, 2,
2], Pass
Test Case 5 - Expected: [5, 4], Result: [5, 4], Pass
```

3.3.10 Complexity Analysis

- **Time Complexity**: O(N), where N is the number of logs. We iterate over the logs once, processing each log in constant time.
- **Space Complexity**: O(N), as the stack may store all active functions in the worst-case scenario.

This solution effectively calculates the exclusive time for each function by utilizing a stack to manage the function call hierarchy, allowing us to handle nested and sequential calls accurately.

Chapter 4
Queue

A queue is a linear structure that follows a specific sequence of operations, with the order of first-in, first-out (FIFO). A good example of a queue is in a line of people buying items, the person at the front of the line gets to buy the items first. The key difference between a stack and a queue lies in their deletion operations: stacks remove the most recently added element, while queues delete the oldest added element. Queues are commonly utilized in breadth-first search (BFS) algorithms.

4.1 Basic Knowledge of Queues

4.1.1 How Queues are Implemented

There are several ways to implement queues in Python, using data structures and modules from Python libraries:

1. list
2. collections.deque
3. queue.Queue

4.1.2 Implement Queues with Lists

"list" is a built-in data structure in Python that can be used as an implementation queue. The `append()` and `pop(0)` methods act as substitutes for `enqueue()` and `dequeue()`, respectively. The list is very slow because inserting or deleting an element at the beginning requires all the other elements to be shifted by one, which takes O(n) time.

Code 4.1: The Python Program Demonstrates a Queue Implementation Using Lists

```
# Python program implemented using a list demo queue
# Initialize queue
   queue = []

# Add element to queue
queue.append('a')
queue.append('b')
queue.append( 'c')

print("Initial queue")
   print(queue)

# Remove elements from the queue
   print("\nElements dequeued from queue")
   print(queue.pop(0))
   print(queue.pop(0))
   print(queue.pop(0))

print("\nQueue after removing elements")
   print(queue)
```

Results:

```
Initial queue
['a', 'b', 'c']

Elements dequeued from queue
a
b
c

Queue after removing elements
[]
```

4.1.2.1 Implement the Queue Using collections.deque

Queues can be implemented in Python using the deque class in the collections module. In cases where append and delete operations need to be performed faster from both ends of the container, double-ended queues are preferable to lists, as double-ended queues provide O(1) time complexity for append and eject operations compared to lists that provide O(n) time complexity. The `append()` and `popleft()` methods correspond to `enqueue()` and `dequeue()` operations in queues.

Code 4.2: The Python Program Demonstrates a Queue Implementation Using collections.dequeue

```python
# The Python program demonstrates the queue
# implementation using collections.dequeue
from collections import deque

# Initialize the queue
q = deque()

# Add elements to the queue
q.append('a')
q.append('b')
q.append('c')

print("Initial queue")
print(q)

# Remove elements from the queue
print("\nElements dequeued from the queue")
print(q.popleft())
print(q.popleft())
print(q.popleft())

print("\nQueue after removing elements")
print(q)
```

The result is:

```
Initial queue
deque(['a', 'b', 'c'])

Elements dequeued from the queue
a
b
c

Queue after removing elements
deque([])
```

4.1.2.2 Use queue.Queue Implements Queues

queue.Queue() is a built-in module in Python that can be used to implement queues. queue.Queue(maxsize) initializes the maximum size of the queue to maxsize, the maximum value is 0, and "0" means infinite queues. This queue follows FIFO rules. This module provides the following various features:

- maxsize: Specifies the maximum number of elements allowed in the queue.
- empty(): Returns True if the queue is empty, False otherwise.
- full(): Returns True if the queue is full, and never returns True if the queue is initialized with maxsize = 0 (the default).
- get(): Removes from the queue and returns an element, if the queue is empty, wait until an item is available.
- get_nowait(): Returns the element if it is immediately available, otherwise throws a QueueEmpty.
- put(item): Adds an element to the queue, blocking until a free slot becomes available if the queue is full.
- put_nowait (item): Queues the item without blocking.
- qsize(): Returns the number of items in the queue, if there are no free slots available, increase the QueueFull.

4.1 Basic Knowledge of Queues

Code 4.3: The Python Program Demonstrates a Queuing Implementation Using a Queuing Module

```python
# Python program demonstrating queue implementation using
queue module


from queue import Queue

# Initialize the queue
q = Queue(maxsize = 3)

# qsize() gives the queue size
print(q.qsize())

# Add elements to the queue
q.put('a')
q.put('b')
q.put('c')

# Is the testing queue full?
print("\nFull: ", q.full())

# Remove elements from the queue
print("\nElements dequeued from the queue")
print(q.get())
print(q.get())
print(q.get())

# Check if the current queue is empty?
print("\nEmpty: ", q.empty())

q.put(1)
print("\nEmpty: ", q.empty())
print("Full: ", q.full())
```

Results:

```
0
Full: True
Elements dequeued from the queue
a
b
c
Empty: True
Empty: False
Full: False
```

4.2 Example 1: Design a Circular Queue

4.2.1 Problem

A circular queue is a linear data structure in which operations are performed on a FIFO (first-in, first-out) basis, with the last position connected to the first position to form a circle, also known as a "ring buffer."

One of the benefits of looping queues is that you can take advantage of the space in front of the queue. In a normal queue, once the queue is full, the next element cannot be inserted. But with a circular queue, you can use the front space to store the new value.

Issue: The circular queue should be designed to support the following actions:

- MyCircularQueue(k): Constructor that sets the size of the queue to k.
- Front(): Retrieves the previous item from the queue. If the queue is empty, -1 is returned.
- Rear(): Returns the last item in the queue. If the queue is empty, -1 is returned.
- enQueue(value): Inserts the element into the circular queue. If the operation succeeds, true is returned.
- deQueue(): Removes an element from the loop queue. If the operation succeeds, true is returned.
- isEmpty(): Checks whether the loop queue is empty.
- isFull(): Checks whether the recurrence queue is full.

4.2.2 Problem Analysis

The problem involves designing a **circular queue** (also known as a circular buffer or ring buffer). In a circular queue, when you reach the end of the buffer, the next element wraps around to the beginning of the buffer. This allows for efficient use of space and makes it ideal for scenarios where the buffer is repeatedly filled and emptied.

4.2 Example 1: Design a Circular Queue

A circular queue should support the following actions:

1. **MyCircularQueue(k)**: Initialize the queue with a fixed capacity k.
2. **enQueue(value)**: Insert an element at the end of the queue. Return True if successful, otherwise False.
3. **deQueue()**: Remove the front element from the queue. Return True if successful, otherwise False.
4. **Front()**: Get the front element of the queue without removing it. Return -1 if the queue is empty.
5. **Rear()**: Get the last element of the queue without removing it. Return -1 if the queue is empty.
6. **isEmpty()**: Check if the queue is empty.
7. **isFull()**: Check if the queue is full.

4.2.3 Key Concepts

1. **Array and Pointers**:
   - We use an array of size k to store the elements.
   - head pointer keeps track of the front of the queue.
   - tail pointer keeps track of the next available position for inserting an element.

2. **Conditions**:
   - **Empty Condition**: The queue is empty if head == tail.
   - **Full Condition**: The queue is full if (tail - head) == k.

3. **Index Calculation**:
   - Since the queue is circular, the head and tail indexes need to wrap around to the start of the array when they exceed the array length. We achieve this using modulo operations.

4.2.4 Example Walkthrough

For a queue of size 3:

1. **enQueue(1)**: Insert 1, tail moves forward.
2. **enQueue(2)**: Insert 2, tail moves forward.
3. **enQueue(3)**: Insert 3, tail moves forward.
4. **isFull()**: Returns True, as the queue is full.
5. **deQueue()**: Removes the front element (1), head moves forward.
6. **Front()**: Returns 2, which is now at the front.
7. **Rear()**: Returns 3, which is at the rear.
8. **enQueue(4)**: Inserts 4, tail wraps around due to the circular structure.

4.2.5 Code Implementation

Code 4.4: Python Code for MyCircularQueue

```
class MyCircularQueue:
    def __init__(self, k: int):
        """
        Initialize your data structure here. Set the size of
        the queue to k.
        """
        self.data = [0] * k
        self.head = 0
        self.tail = 0
        self.size = 0  # Tracks the current number of
        elements in the queue
        self.capacity = k

    def enQueue(self, value: int) -> bool:
        """
        Inserts elements into a circular queue. If the
        operation succeeds, true is returned.
        """
        if self.isFull():
            return False
        self.data[self.tail] = value
        self.tail = (self.tail + 1) % self.capacity
        self.size += 1
        return True

    def deQueue(self) -> bool:
        """
        Deletes an element from the loop queue. If the
        operation succeeds, true is returned.
        """
        if self.isEmpty():
            return False
        self.head = (self.head + 1) % self.capacity
        self.size -= 1
        return True
```

4.2 Example 1: Design a Circular Queue

```
def Front(self) -> int:
    """
Get the top item from the queue.
    """
    if self.isEmpty():
        return -1
    return self.data[self.head]

def Rear(self) -> int:
    """
Get the last item from the queue.
    """
    if self.isEmpty():
        return -1
    return self.data[(self.tail - 1 + self.capacity) % self.capacity]

def isEmpty(self) -> bool:
    """
Check if the recurrence queue is empty.
    """
    return self.size == 0

def isFull(self) -> bool:
    """
Check if the recurring queue is full.
    """
    return self.size == self.capacity
```

4.2.6 Explanation of Code

1. **Initialization**:
   - `data`: Array to hold elements.
   - `head` and `tail`: Pointers to manage the circular nature of the queue.
   - `size`: Keeps track of the current number of elements.
   - `capacity`: Stores the fixed size k of the queue.

2. **Methods**:
   - **enQueue(value)**: Adds `value` to the queue if it's not full, and updates `tail` and `size`.

- **deQueue()**: Removes the front element if it's not empty, and updates `head` and `size`.
- **Front()** and **Rear()**: Return the front and rear values, respectively, or -1 if the queue is empty.
- **isEmpty()** and **isFull()**: Check if the queue is empty or full based on the `size` variable.

4.2.7 Testing the Code

Here's the main function to test various cases, including edge cases.

Code 4.5: Test Code for MyCircularQueue

```python
def main():
    queue = MyCircularQueue(3)
    print(queue.enQueue(1))     # Expected: True
    print(queue.enQueue(2))     # Expected: True
    print(queue.enQueue(3))     # Expected: True
    print(queue.enQueue(4))     # Expected: False (Queue is full)
    print(queue.Rear())         # Expected: 3
    print(queue.isFull())       # Expected: True
    print(queue.deQueue())      # Expected: True
    print(queue.enQueue(4))     # Expected: True
    print(queue.Rear())         # Expected: 4

    # Additional test cases
    print(queue.Front())        # Expected: 2
    print(queue.deQueue())      # Expected: True
    print(queue.deQueue())      # Expected: True
    print(queue.isEmpty())      # Expected: False
    print(queue.deQueue())      # Expected: True
    print(queue.isEmpty())      # Expected: True
    print(queue.deQueue())      # Expected: False (Queue is already empty)

if __name__ == "__main__":
    main()
```

4.2.8 Expected Output

```
True
True
True
False
3
True
True
True
4
2
True
True
False
True
False
```

4.2.9 Complexity Analysis

- **Time Complexity**: All operations (`enQueue`, `deQueue`, `Front`, `Rear`, `isEmpty`, `isFull`) have a time complexity of O(1), as they only involve simple index calculations and condition checks.
- **Space Complexity**: O(k), where k is the capacity of the queue. We allocate an array of size k to store the elements in the queue.

This implementation is efficient for real-time applications where we need to manage data in a fixed-size buffer, such as streaming applications, buffering data, or implementing rate-limited queues.

4.3 Example 2: The Shortest Subarray That is Summed is Greater Than K

4.3.1 Problem

Returns the length of the shortest non-empty continuous subarray whose sum is at least K for subarray A. Return −1 if no non-empty subarray meets the sum requirement.

```
Example 1:
Input: A = [1], K = 1
Output 1
Example 2:
Input: A = [1,2], K = 4
Output: -1
Example 3:
Input: A = [2,-1,2], K = 3
Output 3
```

4.3.2 Solution Approach: Sliding Window with Deque

An efficient solution employs a sliding window approach utilizing a deque. Here are the steps involved:

1. **Prefix Sum Array**: Calculate cumulative (prefix) sums up to each index. This helps in determining the sum of any subarray by subtracting the prefix sums at two indices.
2. **Deque for Monotonic Queue**:
   - We use a deque to keep track of indices of the prefix sums in an increasing order.
   - The elements in the deque represent potential start points for subarrays that might have a sum of at least KKK.
3. **Minimizing Subarray Length**:
   - For each prefix sum `cumsum` at index `j`, we check if the difference between `cumsum` and the prefix sum at the front of the deque is at least KKK. If yes, this represents a subarray with a sum of at least KKK.
   - We update the minimum subarray length whenever we find a valid subarray, and then remove the front element of the deque because it will not contribute to a smaller subarray in future iterations.
4. **Maintain Monotonicity**:
   - To ensure that the deque remains in increasing order of prefix sums, we remove elements from the back of the deque if they have a prefix sum greater than or equal to the current `cumsum`. This keeps only potential candidates for the starting indices of future subarrays.

4.3.3 Code Implementation

Code 4.6: Python Code for shortestSubarray

```
from typing import List
from collections import deque

class Solution:
    def shortestSubarray(self, A: List[int], K:
    int) -> int:
        # Initialize a deque to store indices and their
        respective prefix sums
        q = deque()
        q.append((-1, 0))  # Start with (-1, 0) for easier
        subarray calculations
        min_size = float("inf")  # Initialize minimum size
        to infinity
        cumsum = 0  # Cumulative sum for the current prefix

        # Iterate through each element in the array
        for j in range(len(A)):
            cumsum += A[j]  # Update cumulative sum with
            the current element

            # Check if there's any valid subarray by
            comparing cumsum and deque's front
            while q and cumsum - q[0][1] >= K:
                min_size = min(min_size, j - q[0][0])  #
                Update minimum subarray length
                q.popleft()  # Remove the element from the
                front of the deque

            # Maintain monotonicity by removing elements
            from the back
            while q and q[-1][1] >= cumsum:
                q.pop()

            # Add the current index and cumulative sum to
            the deque
            q.append((j, cumsum))

        # If min_size is still infinity, it means no valid
        subarray was found
        return -1 if min_size == float("inf") else min_size
```

4.3.4 Explanation of Code

- **Initialize** the deque with (-1, 0) to simplify subarray sum calculations.
- **Loop through A**:
  - Update cumsum with the current element.
  - **Front Checking**: While the difference between cumsum and the front of the deque is at least KKK, update min_size and remove the front.
  - **Monotonic Queue**: Ensure the deque remains in increasing order by removing elements from the back if they have a greater prefix sum than cumsum.
  - Append (index, cumsum) to the deque for future checks.
- **Return** min_size or -1 if no valid subarray is found.

4.3.5 Complexity Analysis

- **Time Complexity**: O(N)
  - Each element is added to and removed from the deque at most once.
- **Space Complexity**: O(N)
  - The deque stores at most NNN elements.

4.3.6 Test Cases and Main Function

Let's add a main function with various test cases, including edge cases, to ensure correctness.

4.3 Example 2: The Shortest Subarray That is Summed is Greater Than K

Code 4.7: Test Main Function for shortestSubarray

```python
def main():
    # Create an instance of the Solution class
    solution = Solution()

    # Test cases
    test_cases = [
        ([84, -37, 32, 40, 95], 167, 3),   # Expected output: 3
        ([2, -1, 2], 3, 3),                # Expected output: 3
        ([1, 2], 4, -1),                   # Expected output: -1
        ([1], 1, 1),                       # Expected output: 1
        ([1, 2, 3, 4, 5], 15, 5),          # Expected output: 5
        ([1, -1, 6, -1, 2, 5], 7, 2),      # Expected output: 2
        ([84, 10, -10, 70, 20], 100, 2)    # Expected output: 2
    ]

    # Run test cases
    all_passed = True
    for i, (A, K, expected) in enumerate(test_cases):
        result = solution.shortestSubarray(A, K)
        if result != expected:
            print(f"Test case {i + 1} failed: Input (A={A}, K={K}) - Expected {expected}, got {result}")
            all_passed = False
        else:
            print(f"Test case {i + 1} passed.")

    if all_passed:
        print("All test cases passed!")

if __name__ == "__main__":
    main()
```

4.3.7 Expected Output

```
Test case 1 passed.
Test case 2 passed.
Test case 3 passed.
Test case 4 passed.
Test case 5 passed.
Test case 6 passed.
Test case 7 passed.
All test cases passed!
```

This main function tests various cases, including:

- Single element arrays.
- Arrays with positive and negative elements.
- Cases where no subarray meets the condition.
- Cases with subarrays of different lengths that meet the condition.

This ensures that our function is well-tested and robust for a variety of inputs.

Chapter 5
Priority Queues

The queue has a FIFO (first-in, first-out) order, where elements are taken out or accessed on a first-come, first-served basis. An example of a queue includes a line at a movie box office. But what is a priority queue?

A priority queue is an abstract data structure (a data structure defined by its behavior) that is similar to a normal queue, but each item has a special "key" to quantify its "priority". For example, if a movie theater decides to serve loyal customers first, it will order them based on their loyalty (points or the number of tickets purchased). In this case, the ticket queue will no longer be on a first-come, first-served basis, but on its priority level. The customer will be an element in this priority queue, and the "priority" is their loyalty.

5.1 Implementation of Priority Queues

Consider that we want to have a priority customer queue based on customer loyalty. The higher the score, the higher the priority. There are several ways to implement priority queues in Python, and we mainly introduced three approaches here.

5.1.1 Implement Priority Queues with Lists

A very simple and straightforward way to do this is to use a normal list but sort it every time you add items. Here are some examples:

Code 5.1: Implement Priority Queues with Lists

```
customers = []
customers.append((2, "Harry"))
customers.append((3, "Charles"))
customers.sort(reverse=True)
# Sort is required to maintain position
customers.append((1, "Riya"))
customers.sort(reverse=True)
# Sort is needed to keep the position
customers.append((4, "Stacy")).
customers.sort(reverse=True)
while customers:
print(customers.pop(0))
# Will print names in the order: Stacy, Charles,
Harry, Riya.
```

Results:

```
(4, 'Stacy')
(3, 'Charles')
(2, 'Harry')
(1, 'Riya')
```

When adding items to a list, it takes O(n log n) time to maintain the order. Therefore, the above method is only used when very little insertion is required.

5.1.2 Implement Priority Queues Using HEAPQ

In Python, it is also possible to use the heapq module to implement the priority queue, which has an implementation time complexity of O(log n) and can be used for the insertion and extraction of the smallest elements. Note that heapq only has a minimal heap implementation.

5.1 Implementation of Priority Queues

For example:

Code 5.2: Implement Priority Queues with HEAPQ

```
import heapq
customers = []
heapq.heappush(customers, (2, "Harry"))
heapq.heappush(customers, (3, "Charles"))
heapq.heappush(customers, (1, "Riya"))
heapq.heappush( customers, (4, "Stacy"))
while customers:
print(heapq.heappop(customers))
      #Will print names in the order: Riya, Harry,
      Charles, Stacy.
```

Results:

```
(1, 'Riya')
(2, 'Harry')
(3, 'Charles')
(4, 'Stacy')
```

5.1.3 Use queue.PriorityQueue Implements Priority Queues

queue.PriorityQueue internally uses the same heapq implementation in Sect. 4.1.2 and therefore has the same time complexity. However, it differs in two key ways. First, it is synchronous, so it supports concurrent processes. Second, it is a class-based interface, not a function-based interface for heapq. As such, PriorityQueue is the classic OOP style for implementing and using Priority Queues.

Let's build a priority queue for movie fans:

Code 5.3: 1 Make Use of queue.PriorityQueue Creates a Priority Queue

```
from queue import PriorityQueue
customers = PriorityQueue()
# We initialize the PQ class instead of using functions
to manipulate the list.
customers.put((2, "Harry"))
customers.put((3, "Charles"))
customers.put((1, "Riya"))
customers.put((4, "Stacy"))
while customers:
      print(customers.get())
      #Will print names in the order: Riya, Harry,
      Charles, Stacy.
```

Results:

```
(1, 'Riya')
(2, 'Harry')
(3, 'Charles')
(4, 'Stacy')
```

5.2 Example 1: Minimum Cost of Employing K Workers

5.2.1 Problem

There are n workers. You are given two integer arrays *quality* and *wage* where quality[i] is the quality of the ith worker and wage[i] is the minimum wage expectation for the ith worker.

We want to hire exactly k workers to form a paid group. To hire a group of k workers, we must pay them according to the following rules:

1. Every worker in the paid group must be paid at least their minimum wage expectation.
2. In the group, each worker's pay must be directly proportional to their quality. This means that if a worker's quality is double that of another worker in the group, then they must be paid twice as much as the other worker.

5.2 Example 1: Minimum Cost of Employing K Workers

Given the integer k, return the least amount of money needed to form a paid group satisfying the above conditions.

Example 1

```
Inputs: Quality = [10,20,5], Salary = [70,50,30], K = 2
Output: 105.00000
Explanation: Pay 0 to the 70th worker and 2 to the
35th worker.
```

Example 2

```
Inputs: Quality = [3,1,10,1,1], Salary =
[4,8,2,2,7], K = 3
Output: 30.66667
Note: Salaries were paid to workers 4 and 0,
respectively, and $13.33333 was paid to workers 2 and 3.
```

5.2.2 Approach and Explanation

To solve this problem:

1. **Calculate Wage-to-Quality Ratio**: For each worker, compute the ratio of wage[i] / quality[i]. This ratio represents how much the worker demands per unit of quality. Workers with a lower ratio are more cost-effective.
2. **Sort by Ratio**: Sort all workers by their wage-to-quality ratio in ascending order. By doing this, we aim to form groups where all workers are paid according to the highest wage-to-quality ratio in the group (i.e., the most expensive worker determines the rate for everyone in the group).
3. **Use a Max-Heap to Maintain K Smallest Qualities**:
   - As we iterate through the sorted list of workers, we maintain a heap of size K that stores the qualities of the selected workers.
   - Track the sum of the qualities (qSum) in the current group.
   - Each time the group size exceeds K, remove the worker with the highest quality from the heap (to minimize the cost) and adjust qSum.
4. **Calculate Minimum Cost**:
   - For each group of KKK workers, calculate the total cost as ratioxqSum, where ratio is the current worker's wage-to-quality ratio.
   - Update the result if the calculated cost is lower than the previous minimum.

5.2.3 Code Explanation

Let's go through the code with detailed comments:

Code 5.4: Python Code for mincostToHireWorkers

```python
from typing import List
import heapq

class Solution:
    def mincostToHireWorkers(self, quality: List[int],
    wage: List[int], K: int) -> float:
        # Step 1: Calculate the wage-to-quality ratio and
        pair it with each worker's quality.
        wq = sorted([(w / q, q) for w, q in zip(wage,
        quality)])  # Sort by ratio

        # Initialize the result with infinity (as we want
        the minimum).
        res = float('inf')

        # Initialize a max-heap to keep track of the
        highest quality workers in the group.
        heap = []
        qSum = 0  # Sum of qualities of current K workers

        # Step 2: Iterate over the sorted list and form
        groups of size K
        for ratio, q in wq:
            # Add the current worker's quality to the sum
            and push it to the heap (negated to simulate
            max-heap)
            qSum += q
            heapq.heappush(heap, -q)

            # If we exceed the number of K workers,
            remove the worker with the highest quality
            if len(heap) > K:
                qSum += heapq.heappop(heap)  # `heapq.
                heappop(heap)` returns the smallest
                (negative) quality, so we add it
                to `qSum`
```

5.2 Example 1: Minimum Cost of Employing K Workers

```
        # If we have exactly K workers, calculate the
        minimum cost for this configuration
        if len(heap) == K:
            res = min(res, ratio * qSum)

# Return the minimum cost found
return res
```

5.2.4 Complexity Analysis

- Time Complexity:
    - Sorting the workers by wage-to-quality ratio takes O(nlogn).
    - The loop through the workers has O(nlogK) time complexity due to pushing and popping operations on the heap (with at most K elements in the heap).
    - Therefore, the overall time complexity is O(nlogn).
- Space Complexity:
    - We use a heap to store up to K elements, so the space complexity is O(K).

5.2.5 Explanation of Steps in the Code

1. **Calculate wage-to-quality ratio**: For each worker, compute `w / q` and pair it with their quality `q`.
2. **Sort**: Sort the workers by their wage-to-quality ratio to ensure that each group's ratio is determined by the most expensive worker.
3. **Maintain a Max-Heap for Quality**: Use a max-heap to keep track of the qualities of the current K workers. By using a max-heap, we ensure that we can easily remove the worker with the highest quality if we exceed K workers, minimizing the total cost.
4. **Calculate the Minimum Cost for Each Group**: For each group of K workers, calculate the total cost and update `res` if this configuration provides a lower cost.

5.2.6 Testing the Code

Let's create a `main()` function to test the solution using the provided examples.

Code 5.5: Test Code for mincostToHireWorkers

```
def main():
    # Create a Solution object
    sol = Solution()

    # Example 1
    quality1 = [10, 20, 5]
    wage1 = [70, 50, 30]
    K1 = 2
    output1 = sol.mincostToHireWorkers(quality1,
    wage1, K1)
    print(f"Minimum cost for example 1: {output1:.5f}")
    # Expected output: 105.00000

    # Example 2
    quality2 = [3, 1, 10, 1, 1]
    wage2 = [4, 8, 2, 2, 7]
    K2 = 3
    output2 = sol.mincostToHireWorkers(quality2,
    wage2, K2)
    print(f"Minimum cost for example 2: {output2:.5f}")
    # Expected output: 30.66667

main()
```

5.2.7 Expected Output

The output of the `main()` function should match the examples given in the problem statement:

```
Minimum cost for example 1: 105.00000
Minimum cost for example 2: 30.66667
```

5.2.8 Explanation of Test Cases

1. Example 1
   - Workers: [(10, 70), (20, 50), (5, 30)]
   - Wage-to-quality ratios: [(7.0, 10), (2.5, 20), (6.0, 5)]
   - Sorted by ratio: [(2.5, 20), (6.0, 5), (7.0, 10)]
   - The optimal way to hire two workers is to choose workers with qualities 20 and 5, resulting in a cost of 105.00000.

2. Example 2
   - Workers: [(3, 4), (1, 8), (10, 2), (1, 2), (1, 7)]
   - Wage-to-quality ratios: [(1.333, 3), (8.0, 1), (0.2, 10), (2.0, 1), (7.0, 1)]
   - Sorted by ratio: [(0.2, 10), (1.333, 3), (2.0, 1), (7.0, 1), (8.0, 1)]
   - The optimal way to hire three workers is to select the workers with qualities 3, 1, and 1, resulting in a cost of 30.66667.

This test sequence verifies that the solution correctly computes the minimum cost to hire K workers while adhering to the specified proportional payment requirements.

5.3 Example 2: Split an Array into Consecutive Subsequences

5.3.1 Problem

Given an array num sorted in ascending order, it can be split into 1 or more subsequences, returning true only if each subsequence consists of consecutive integers and is at least 3 in length.

Example 1
Input: [1,2,3,3,4,5]
   Output: True
   Description: You can divide them into two sequential subsequences:

   1 2 3
   3 4 5

5.3.2 Approach and Explanation

To solve this problem, we use a hash table and **priority queues** (min-heaps). The main idea is to keep track of subsequences ending at each integer. For each integer:
- If it can extend an existing subsequence, we add it to that subsequence.
- Otherwise, we start a new subsequence.

Steps
1. **Initialize Priority Queues for Each Integer**: Create a hash table `heaps` where `heaps[x]` stores a min-heap of lengths of subsequences ending at integer x.
2. **Process Each Integer in the Array**:
    - For each integer n:
        - If there's a subsequence ending at n-1 (i.e., `heaps[n-1]` is not empty), extend that subsequence by popping the shortest subsequence from `heaps[n-1]`, increasing its length by 1, and pushing it to `heaps[n]`.
        - If no subsequence ends at n-1, start a new subsequence of length 1 ending at n.
3. **Verify the Result**:
    - After processing all elements, check each subsequence. If any subsequence has a length less than 3, return `False` because it doesn't satisfy the requirement.

5.3.3 Code Explanation

Let's go through the code with detailed comments:

Code 5.6: Python Code for isPossible

```
from typing import List
import heapq

class Solution:
    def isPossible(self, nums: List[int]) -> bool:
        # Step 1: Initialize the hash table for
        min-heaps.
        heaps = {}

        # Step 2: Populate the heaps dictionary with
        empty lists for all elements in nums.
```

```
                # This will store min-heaps for sequences ending
                at each integer.
                for n in range(nums[0] - 1, nums[-1] + 1):
                    heaps[n] = []

                # Step 3: Process each number in the array.
                for n in nums:
                    if heaps[n - 1]:
                        # If there is a subsequence ending at
                        n-1, extend it by adding n.
                        length = heapq.heappop(heaps[n - 1]) + 1
                    else:
                        # Otherwise, start a new subsequence of
                        length 1.
                        length = 1
                    # Push the updated subsequence length into
                    the min-heap for subsequences ending at n.
                    heapq.heappush(heaps[n], length)

        # Step 4: Check if all subsequences have a length
        of at least 3.
        for n in nums:
            if heaps[n] and heaps[n][0] < 3:
                return False
        return True
```

5.3.4 Complexity Analysis

- **Time Complexity**:
  - The outer loop iterates through each element in nums, resulting in O(n) time.
  - The heappop and heappush operations on the priority queues take O(logk), where k is the maximum number of subsequences ending at a particular integer.
  - The overall time complexity is therefore O(nlogk), which is efficient for large inputs.

- **Space Complexity**:
  - The space complexity is O(n) due to storing min-heaps in the dictionary heaps.

5.3.5 Explanation of Steps in the Code

1. **Initialization**: The hash table `heaps` is initialized with empty lists for each integer from the smallest to the largest integer in `nums`. This ensures that we have a place to store subsequences ending at each integer.
2. **Process Each Number**: For each number in `nums`, either extend an existing subsequence or start a new one. By using a min-heap, we always extend the shortest subsequence, which minimizes the risk of having subsequences shorter than 3 in length.
3. **Validation**: After processing all numbers, check each subsequence's length. If any subsequence has a length less than 3, return `False`; otherwise, return `True`.

5.3.6 Testing the Code

Let's create a `main()` function to test the solution using the provided example.

Code 5.7 Test Main for isPossible

```python
def main():
    # Create a Solution object
    sol = Solution()

    # Example 1
    nums1 = [1, 2, 3, 3, 4, 5]
    output1 = sol.isPossible(nums1)
    print(f"Is it possible to split array {nums1} into
consecutive subsequences? {output1}")  # Expected
output: True

    # Additional Example 2
    nums2 = [1, 2, 3, 4, 4, 5, 6]
    output2 = sol.isPossible(nums2)
    print(f"Is it possible to split array {nums2} into
consecutive subsequences? {output2}")  # Expected
output: False

    # Additional Example 3
    nums3 = [1, 2, 3, 4, 5, 6]
    output3 = sol.isPossible(nums3)
    print(f"Is it possible to split array {nums3} into
consecutive subsequences? {output3}")  # Expected
output: True

main()
```

5.3.7 Expected Output

The output of the `main()` function should be:

```
Is it possible to split array [1, 2, 3, 3, 4, 5] into
consecutive subsequences? True
Is it possible to split array [1, 2, 3, 4, 4, 5, 6] into
consecutive subsequences? False
Is it possible to split array [1, 2, 3, 4, 5, 6] into
consecutive subsequences? True
```

5.3.8 Explanation of Test Cases

1. Example 1
   - Input: [1, 2, 3, 3, 4, 5]
   - Possible split: [1, 2, 3] and [3, 4, 5]. Each subsequence is consecutive and of length at least 3, so the output is True.

2. Example 2
   - Input: [1, 2, 3, 4, 4, 5, 6]
   - It is impossible to split this into consecutive subsequences of length at least 3 without breaking one of the subsequences, so the output is False.

3. Example 3
   - Input: [1, 2, 3, 4, 5, 6]
   - Possible split: [1, 2, 3] and [4, 5, 6]. Each subsequence is consecutive and of length at least 3, so the output is True.

This test sequence verifies that the solution correctly determines if it's possible to split an array into consecutive subsequences of at least length 3.

5.4 Example 3: Traffic Light

5.4.1 Problem

You are programming for a self-driving car system. The system is given a 2D map of a city, where each point represents a traffic light. All the traffic lights are RED at the beginning, which means the car cannot pass through them. The number of each point represents the time after which a light will turn GREEN, meaning the car can pass through it.

The car is asked to drive from the top-left corner to the right-bottom corner. The car can only drive in the right or down direction. Please find the earliest time that the car can get to the destination.

Sample Input:

1 2 0 3
4 6 5 1
9 2 5 7
5 4 2 2

Sample Output:

5

Explanation: The best route is

1 2 0
5
5
2 2

5.4.2 Solution

To solve this problem, we can use a priority queue (min-heap) with Dijkstra's algorithm to explore paths from the top-left corner of the grid to the bottom-right corner. The priority queue helps us to always consider the path that allows the car to pass the traffic light at the earliest possible time.

For each point, we can only move right or down, and we need to wait until the light turns green before proceeding to the next point. We maintain a minimum waiting time for each cell, and only visit each cell once.

Here's the Python code to solve this problem:

Code 5.8: Python Code for earliest_arrival_time

```
import Heapq


def earliest_arrival_time(city_map):
    rows = len(city_map)
    cols = len(city_map[0])

    # Priority queue to store (time, row, col)
    pq = [(city_map[0][0], 0, 0)]

    # To keep track of the minimum time to reach each cell
    min_time = [[float('inf')] * cols for _ in
    range(rows)]
    min_time[0][0] = city_map[0][0]
```

5.4 Example 3: Traffic Light

```
        # Directions (right, down)
        directions = [(0, 1), (1, 0)]

        while pq:
            time, r, c = heapq.heappop(pq)

            # If we reach the bottom-right corner, return
            the time
            if r == rows - 1 and c == cols - 1:
                return time

            # Explore the next cells in the right and down
            directions
            for dr, dc in directions:
                nr, nc = r + dr, c + dc
                if 0 <= nr < rows and 0 <= nc < cols:
                    # Wait until the traffic light turns green
                    next_time = max(time, city_map[nr][nc])

                    # If we found a faster time to reach this
                    cell, update it and add to the queue
                    if next_time < min_time[nr][nc]:
                        min_time[nr][nc] = next_time
                        heapq.heappush(pq, (next_time,
                        nr, nc))

        # If we can't reach the destination
        return -1

# Sample input
city_map = [
    [1, 2, 0, 3],
    [4, 6, 5, 1],
    [9, 2, 5, 7],
    [5, 4, 2, 2]
]

# Output the earliest arrival time
print(earliest_arrival_time(city_map))   # Expected
Output: 5
```

5.4.3 Explanation

1. **Priority Queue**: We use a priority queue to explore paths based on the minimum time required to reach each cell. This ensures that we always consider the shortest (earliest possible) paths first.
2. **Waiting Time Calculation**: For each cell, the car has to wait until the traffic light turns green, which is indicated by the cell's value. So, the `next_time` to enter a cell is the maximum of the current time and the cell's value.
3. **Updating Minimum Time**: If the calculated `next_time` is less than the previously recorded minimum time for the cell, we update it and push the cell into the priority queue.
4. **Return Result**: Once we reach the bottom-right corner, we return the time, which is the earliest possible arrival time.

5.4.4 Complexity Analysis

- **Time Complexity**: O(NlogN), where is the number of cells in the grid, because we are using Dijkstra's algorithm with a min-heap.
- **Space Complexity**: O(N), where N is the number of cells in the grid for the `min_time` array and the priority queue.

This solution is efficient and works well for large grids. The use of Dijkstra's algorithm ensures that we get the optimal (earliest) time to reach the destination.

Chapter 6
Dictionary

A dictionary in Python is an unordered collection of data values that is used to store key-value pairs (such as maps), and unlike other data types that only have a single value as an element, key-value pairs, making them more optimized.

6.1 Basic Knowledge of Dictionaries

6.1.1 Create a Dictionary

In Python, you can create a dictionary by placing a sequence of elements in curly braces {} separated by a commas. The dictionary contains two elements: a key and its associated value. The value in the dictionary can be any data type and can be repeated, but the key cannot be repeated and must be immutable.

Note Keys in dictionaries are case-sensitive.

Code 6.1: Use Integer Keys to Create a Dictionary

```
# Create a dictionary with integer keys
Dict = {1: 'Geeks', 2: 'For', 3: 'Geeks'}
print("\nDictionary with the use of Integer Keys: ")
print(Dict)

# Create a dictionary with a blend key
Dict = {'Name': 'Geeks', 1: [1, 2, 3, 4]}
print("\nDictionary with the use of Mixed Keys: ")
print(Dict)
```

Result of the code run:

```
Dictionary with the use of Integer Keys:
{1: 'Geeks', 2: 'For', 3: 'Geeks'}

Dictionary with the use of Mixed Keys:
{'Name': 'Geeks', 1: [1, 2, 3, 4]}
```

Dictionaries can also be created with the built-in function dict(). Just put curly braces {} to create an empty dictionary.

Code 6.2: Use dict( ) to Create a Dictionary

```
#Create one empty dictionary
Dict = {}
print("Empty Dictionary: ")
print(Dict)

#use dict () method to create a dictionary
Dict = dict({1: 'Geeks', 2: 'For', 3:'Geeks'})
print("\nDictionary with the use of dict(): ")
print(Dict)

#Create one dictionary, each item appears in pairs
Dict = dict([(1, 'Geeks'), (2, 'For')])
print("\nDictionary with each item as a pair: ")
print(Dict)
```

6.1 Basic Knowledge of Dictionaries

Results:

```
Empty Dictionary:
{}

Dictionary with the use of dict():
{1: 'Geeks', 2: 'For', 3: 'Geeks'}

Dictionary with each item as a pair:
{1: 'Geeks', 2: 'For'}
```

6.1.2 Dictionary

In Python, there are several ways to add elements to a dictionary. You can add one value at a time to the dictionary by defining the value along with the key, Dict[key]= 'value', as shown in Code 6.3. You can use the built-in update() method to update existing values in Dictionary. Nested key values can also be added to existing dictionaries.

Note When adding a value, if the key already exists, its value will be updated; otherwise, a new key-value pair will be added to the dictionary.

Code 6.3: Add an Element to the Dictionary

```
# Create an empty dictionary
Dict = {}
print("Empty Dictionary: ")
print(Dict)

# Add the element
Dict[0] = 'Geeks'
Dict[2] = 'For'
Dict[3] = 1
print("\nDictionary after adding 3 elements: ")
print(Dict)

# Add a set of elements to the dictionary
Dict['Value_set'] = 2, 3, 4
print("\nDictionary after adding 3 elements: ")
print(Dict)
```

```
# Update the healthy value in the dictionary
Dict[2] = 'Welcome'
print("\nUpdated key value: ")
print(Dict)

# Add the embedded dictionary to the healthy value of the
dictionary
Dict[5] = {'Nested' :{'1' : 'Life', '2' : 'Geeks'}}
print("\nAdding a Nested Key: ")
print(Dict)
```

Results:

```
Empty Dictionary:
{}

Dictionary after adding 3 elements:
{0: 'Geeks', 2: 'For', 3: 1}

Dictionary after adding 3 elements:
{0: 'Geeks', 2: 'For', 3: 1, 'Value_set': (2, 3, 4)}

Updated key value:
{0: 'Geeks', 2: 'Welcome', 3: 1, 'Value_set': (2, 3, 4)}

Adding a Nested Key:
{0: 'Geeks', 2: 'Welcome', 3: 1, 'Value_set': (2, 3, 4),
5: {'Nested': {'1': 'Life', '2': 'Geeks'}}}
```

6.1.3 Access Elements from the Dictionary

To access an item in a dictionary, use its key. Keys are enclosed in square brackets.

6.1 Basic Knowledge of Dictionaries

Code 6.4: How to Accesses Elements from a Dictionary

```
# Python program demonstrates how to access elements from
Dictionary
# Creating a Dictionary
Dict = {1: 'Geeks', 'name': 'For', 3: 'Geeks'}

# accessing a element using key
print("Accessing a element using key:")
print(Dict['name'])

# accessing a element using key
print("Accessing a element using key:")
print(Dict[1])
```

You can also use the get() function to retrieve elements from a dictionary.

Code 6.5: Take Advantage of GET()Gets the Dictionary Element

```
# Create a dictionary
Dict = {1: 'Geeks', 'name': 'For', 3: 'Geeks'}

# Use the get() function to get the element
print("Accessing a element using get:")
print(Dict.get(3))
```

6.1.4 Remove an Element from the Dictionary

6.1.4.1 Use the del Keyword

In a Python dictionary, you can use the del keyword to remove keys. With the del keyword, you can delete specific values in the dictionary as well as in the dictionary as a whole; you can also delete items in a nested dictionary by using the del keyword and providing a specific nested key and a specific key to remove from that nested dictionary.

Code 6.6: Use del to Delete Elements in the Dictionary

```
# initialization dictionary
dict = { 5 : 'welcome', 6 : 'to', 7 : 'geeks', 'A' : {1 :
'geeks', 2 : 'for', 3 : 'geeks'}, 'B' : {1 : 'geeks', 2 :
'life'}}
print("initial dictionary: ")
print(dict)

# Delete a healthy value in the dictionary
 del Dict[6]
print("\nDeleting a specific key: ")
print(Dict)

# Delete the embedded healthy value
del Dict['A'][2]
print("\nDeleting a key from Nested Dictionary: ")
print(Dict)
```

Running results:

```
Initial Dictionary:
{5: 'Welcome', 6: 'To', 7: 'Geeks', 'A': {1: 'Geeks', 2:
'For', 3: 'Geeks'}, 'B': {1: 'Geeks', 2: 'Life'}}

Deleting a specific key:
{5: 'Welcome', 7: 'Geeks', 'A': {1: 'Geeks', 2: 'For', 3:
'Geeks'}, 'B': {1: 'Geeks', 2: 'Life'}}

Deleting a key from Nested Dictionary:
{5: 'Welcome', 7: 'Geeks', 'A': {1: 'Geeks', 3: 'Geeks'},
'B': {1: 'Geeks', 2: 'Life'}}
```

6.1.4.2 Use the pop() Method

The pop() method is used to return and delete the value of the specified key.

Code 6.7: Use pop() to Delete Elements

```
# Create a dictionary
Dict = {1: 'Geeks', 'name': 'For', 3: 'Geeks'}

# Use the pop() function to delete the health value
pop_ele = Dict.pop(1)
print('\nDictionary after deletion: ' + str(Dict))
print('Value associated to poped key is: ' +
str(pop_ele))
```

The result is:

```
Dictionary after deletion: {3: 'Geeks', 'name': 'For'}
Value associated to poped key is: Geeks
```

6.2 Example 1: The Sum of the Subarrays is Equal to K

6.2.1 Problem

Given an array of integers and an integer k, determine the total number of contiguous subarrays whose sum equals to k.
  Input: nums = [1,1,1], k = 2
  Output: 2

6.2.2 Solution Approach: Prefix Sum with Hash Table

This approach is efficient because it requires only a single pass through the array, resulting in an O(N) time complexity. Here's the step-by-step explanation:

1. **Prefix Sum**: As we iterate through the array, we calculate the prefix sum (cumulative sum) up to each element. This prefix sum helps in determining if a subarray sum up to the current index equals k.
2. **Hash Table (Dictionary)**: We maintain a dictionary `table` where:
   - Keys are prefix sums observed so far.
   - Values are the number of times each prefix sum has occurred.
3. **Subarray Sum Calculation**: For each prefix sum (`presum`):
   - Check if (`presum - k`) exists in the hash table.

- If it exists, add the frequency of (presum - k) in the hash table to the result, as it represents the number of subarrays ending at the current index that sum to k.

4. **Update the Hash Table**: After checking, increment the frequency of the current prefix sum in the hash table. This helps in tracking all possible subarrays that could sum to k as we move forward in the array.
5. **Initialization**: The dictionary table is initialized with 0: 1, as a prefix sum of 0 means that the subarray starting from the beginning can itself be equal to k.

6.2.3 Code Explanation

Here's the implementation based on the provided code:

Code 6.8: Python Code for subarraySum

```python
from typing import List
from collections import defaultdict

class Solution:
    def subarraySum(self, nums: List[int], k: int) -> int:
        # Dictionary to store the frequency of each prefix sum
        table = defaultdict(int)
        # Initialize result and prefix sum
        res = 0
        presum = 0
        # Initialize with a prefix sum of zero
        table[0] = 1

        # Traverse each element in nums
        for num in nums:
            # Update prefix sum
            presum += num
            # If (presum - k) is in the table, add its
            count to the result
            if presum - k in table:
                res += table[presum - k]
            # Update the frequency of the current prefix sum
            table[presum] += 1

        return res
```

6.2.4 Complexity Analysis

- **Time Complexity**: O(N), where N is the number of elements in nums, as we are iterating over the array once.
- **Space Complexity**: O(N), due to the hash table storing prefix sums.

6.2.5 Extension: Two-Pointer Method for Positive Numbers

If all numbers in the array are positive, we can use a two-pointer (sliding window) approach. However, this method is not applicable to arrays with negative numbers, as it would not guarantee valid subarrays with a fixed sum.

6.2.6 Test Cases

Let's write a `main` function to test the solution on different cases:

Code 6.9: Test Code for subarraySum

```python
def main():
    # Test Case 1
    nums1 = [1, 1, 1]
    k1 = 2
    solution = Solution()
    result1 = solution.subarraySum(nums1, k1)
    print(f"Input: nums = {nums1}, k = {k1}")
    print(f"Output: {result1}")
    print(f"Expected Output: 2\n")

    # Test Case 2: Mixed positive and negative numbers
    nums2 = [1, 2, 3, -2, 1, 4]
    k2 = 5
    result2 = solution.subarraySum(nums2, k2)
    print(f"Input: nums = {nums2}, k = {k2}")
    print(f"Output: {result2}")
    print(f"Expected Output: 3\n")

    # Test Case 3: All elements are zeros
    nums3 = [0, 0, 0, 0]
    k3 = 0
    result3 = solution.subarraySum(nums3, k3)
```

```
        print(f"Input: nums = {nums3}, k = {k3}")
        print(f"Output: {result3}")
        print(f"Expected Output: 10\n")

        # Test Case 4: Array with both positive and
        negative numbers
        nums4 = [-1, -1, 1]
        k4 = 0
        result4 = solution.subarraySum(nums4, k4)
        print(f"Input: nums = {nums4}, k = {k4}")
        print(f"Output: {result4}")
        print(f"Expected Output: 1\n")

        # Test Case 5: No subarrays with sum k
        nums5 = [1, 2, 3]
        k5 = 7
        result5 = solution.subarraySum(nums5, k5)
        print(f"Input: nums = {nums5}, k = {k5}")
        print(f"Output: {result5}")
        print(f"Expected Output: 0\n")

main()
```

6.2.7 *Expected Output*

```
Input: nums = [1, 1, 1], k = 2
Output: 2
Expected Output: 2

Input: nums = [1, 2, 3, -2, 1, 4], k = 5
Output: 3
Expected Output: 3

Input: nums = [0, 0, 0, 0], k = 0
Output: 10
Expected Output: 10

Input: nums = [-1, -1, 1], k = 0
Output: 1
Expected Output: 1

Input: nums = [1, 2, 3], k = 7
Output: 0
Expected Output: 0
```

6.2.8 Explanation of Each Test Case

1. **Test Case 1**: Standard case with multiple subarrays summing to k.
2. **Test Case 2**: Mixed positive and negative numbers with subarrays that sum to k.
3. **Test Case 3**: All zero elements where subarrays of various lengths sum to zero.
4. **Test Case 4**: Negative and positive numbers, a single subarray that sums to zero.
5. **Test Case 5**: No subarrays add up to k, result should be zero.

6.2.9 Conclusion

This solution is efficient and handles both positive and negative numbers due to the prefix sum and hash table combination. The test cases above should provide good coverage for verifying the implementation.

6.3 Example 2: The Maximum Value from the Labels

6.3.1 Problem

There is a set of items: the ith item has the value value [i] and the label label [i]. Then, select a subset of these items, such as | S | < = num_wanted, for each label L, the number of items in S with label L is < = use_limit. Returns the maximum possible sum of subset S.

Example 1
Input: Value = [5,4,3,2,1], Label = [1,1,2,2,3], num_wanted = 3, use_limit = 1
  Output: 9
  Description: The subsets selected are the first, third, and fifth terms.

6.3.2 Solution Approach

The solution uses a greedy approach with sorting and a hash table for label counting. Here's the step-by-step approach:

1. **Pairing Values and Labels**: Zip the `values` and `labels` lists together, creating pairs of `(value, label)`.
2. **Sorting**: Sort these pairs in descending order based on the values. This ensures that when we start selecting items, we always pick the highest value available first.

3. **Using a Counter for Labels**: Use a hash table (or a `Counter`) to keep track of the number of items selected for each label. This ensures that we don't exceed `use_limit` for any label.
4. **Selecting Values**: Iterate through the sorted list, and for each item:
   - Check if adding it would exceed the label's `use_limit`.
   - If it doesn't, add the item's value to the result list and update the label count.
   - Stop when we've selected `num_wanted` items.
5. **Returning the Result**: Sum up the values in the result list and return the total as the maximum possible sum.

6.3.3 Code Implementation

Here is the provided code with explanations as comments:

Code 6.10: Python Code for largestValsFromLabels

```python
from typing import List
from collections import Counter

class Solution:
    def largestValsFromLabels(self, values: List[int],
    labels: List[int], num_wanted: int, use_limit:
    int) -> int:
        # Zip values and labels, then sort them in
        descending order based on values.
        options = sorted(zip(values, labels),
        reverse=True)  # Sorts by value descending

        # Counter to track how many times each label
        is used.
        used_labels = Counter()

        # List to keep the selected values
        res = []

        # Iterate through sorted options and pick items
        based on constraints.
        for value, label in options:
            # Stop if we've already selected the desired
            number of items
            if len(res) >= num_wanted:
                break
```

6.3 Example 2: The Maximum Value from the Labels

```
            # Only add the value if the label's count is
            below the use limit
            if used_labels[label] < use_limit:
                used_labels[label] += 1
                res.append(value)

    # Return the sum of selected values
    return sum(res)
```

6.3.4 Complexity Analysis

- **Time Complexity**: O(NlogN), where N is the number of items. Sorting the list takes O(NlogN) time.
- **Space Complexity**: O(N), for storing the sorted items and the label counter.

6.3.5 Testing the Code

Here's a `main` function that tests the code with multiple cases to verify correctness:

Code 6.11: Test Code for largestValsFromLabels

```
def main():
    solution = Solution()

    # Test Case 1
    values1 = [5, 4, 3, 2, 1]
    labels1 = [1, 1, 2, 2, 3]
    num_wanted1 = 3
    use_limit1 = 1
    result1 = solution.largestValsFromLabels(values1,
    labels1, num_wanted1, use_limit1)
    print(f"Test Case 1 Result: {result1} (Expected: 9)")

    # Test Case 2: Multiple items with the same label
    values2 = [9, 8, 8, 7, 6]
    labels2 = [1, 1, 2, 2, 2]
```

```
num_wanted2 = 3
use_limit2 = 2
result2 = solution.largestValsFromLabels(values2,
labels2, num_wanted2, use_limit2)
print(f"Test Case 2 Result: {result2}
(Expected: 25)")

# Test Case 3: No restrictions (use_limit higher than
number of items)
values3 = [5, 4, 3, 2, 1]
labels3 = [1, 1, 1, 1, 1]
num_wanted3 = 5
use_limit3 = 10
result3 = solution.largestValsFromLabels(values3,
labels3, num_wanted3, use_limit3)
print(f"Test Case 3 Result: {result3}
(Expected: 15)")

# Test Case 4: Single item wanted
values4 = [5, 4, 3]
labels4 = [1, 1, 2]
num_wanted4 = 1
use_limit4 = 1
result4 = solution.largestValsFromLabels(values4,
labels4, num_wanted4, use_limit4)
print(f"Test Case 4 Result: {result4} (Expected: 5)")

# Test Case 5: Edge case with num_wanted = 0
values5 = [5, 4, 3, 2]
labels5 = [1, 2, 3, 4]
num_wanted5 = 0
use_limit5 = 1
result5 = solution.largestValsFromLabels(values5,
labels5, num_wanted5, use_limit5)
print(f"Test Case 5 Result: {result5} (Expected: 0)")

main()
```

6.3.6 Expected Output

```
Test Case 1 Result: 9 (Expected: 9)
Test Case 2 Result: 25 (Expected: 25)
Test Case 3 Result: 15 (Expected: 15)
Test Case 4 Result: 5 (Expected: 5)
Test Case 5 Result: 0 (Expected: 0)
```

6.3.7 Explanation of Test Cases

1. **Test Case 1**: Standard example given in the problem statement. It should return 9.
2. **Test Case 2**: Tests multiple items with the same label and a use limit higher than 1. The expected result is 25 (selecting values 9, 8, and 8).
3. **Test Case 3**: No restriction on use limit or number of items, effectively summing all items. The result should be 15.
4. **Test Case 4**: Only one item needed, so we select the highest value 5.
5. **Test Case 5**: Edge case with num_wanted = 0, meaning no items are selected, so the result should be 0.

This main function verifies the code's correctness for various edge cases and ensures it performs as expected.

6.4 Example 3: Insert/Delete/Get Random Value O(1)

6.4.1 Problem

Design a data structure that supports all of the following operations with an average O(1) time.

- insert(val): Inserts a val item into the collection if it doesn't already exist.
- remove(val): Removes the item val from the collection, if it exists.
- getRandom: Returns a random element from the current set of elements (guaranteed to have at least one element present when this method is called). Each element must have an equal probability of being returned.

To achieve O(1) for each operation, we need to use both a list (array) and a hash table:

- **List (self.data)**: Used to store the elements of the set.
- **Hash table (self.table)**: Used to store the index of each element in the list.

6.4.2 Approach

1. Insert Operation:

   - Check if the value exists in the hash table (self.table). If it exists, return False as it's already in the set.
   - If it doesn't exist, add it to the end of the list (self.data) and store its index in the hash table.
   - Return True to indicate successful insertion.

2. Remove Operation:

   - Check if the value exists in the hash table. If it doesn't exist, return False as it's not in the set.
   - Get the index of the element to be removed (removed_idx) and the last index of the list (last_idx).
   - Swap the element to be removed with the last element in the list. This way, the element we want to delete is at the end of the list.
   - Update the hash table for the element that was moved.
   - Pop the last element from the list and delete its entry in the hash table.
   - Return True to indicate successful removal.

3. GetRandom Operation:

   - Generate a random index within the bounds of the list and return the element at that index.

6.4.3 Code

Here is the code with comments explaining each section:

Code 6.12: Python Code for RandomizedSet

```
import random
from collections import defaultdict
from typing import List

class RandomizedSet:

    def __init__(self):
        """
        Initialize your data structure here.
        """
        self.data = []   # List to store elements
        self.table = {}  # Dictionary to store the index
                         of each element in the list
```

6.4 Example 3: Insert/Delete/Get Random Value O(1)

```python
def insert(self, val: int) -> bool:
    """
    Inserts a value to the set. Returns true if the
    set did not already contain the specified element.
    """
    if val in self.table:
        return False  # Value already exists
        in the set
    # Insert value into the list and store its index
    in the table
    self.data.append(val)
    self.table[val] = len(self.data) - 1
    return True

def remove(self, val: int) -> bool:
    """
    Removes a value from the set. Returns true if the
    set contained the specified element.
    """
    if val not in self.table:
        return False  # Value not found in the set
    # Get the index of the element to remove and the
    last element in the list
    removed_idx = self.table[val]
    last_idx = len(self.data) - 1
    last_element = self.data[last_idx]

    # Move the last element to the place of the
    element to be removed
    self.data[removed_idx] = last_element
    self.table[last_element] = removed_idx

    # Remove the last element from the list and
    delete the element from the table
    self.data.pop()
    del self.table[val]
    return True

def getRandom(self) -> int:
    """
    Get a random element from the set.
    """
    idx = random.randint(0, len(self.data) - 1)  #
    Generate a random index
    return self.data[idx]
```

6.4.4 Complexity Analysis

- **Time Complexity**: Each operation (insert, remove, and getRandom) has $O(1)$ time complexity on average.
- **Space Complexity**: $O(n)$, where nnn is the number of elements in the set, since we store each element in both the list and the hash table.

6.4.5 Testing the Code

To test the `RandomizedSet` class, let's create a function `main()` that demonstrates various scenarios, including insertion, deletion, and retrieving random elements.

Code 6.13: Test Code for RandomizedSet

```
def main():
    # Create an instance of RandomizedSet
    randomized_set = RandomizedSet()

    # Test Case 1: Insertions
    print("Insert 1:", randomized_set.insert(1))   # Expected: True
    print("Insert 2:", randomized_set.insert(2))   # Expected: True
    print("Insert 3:", randomized_set.insert(3))   # Expected: True
    print("Insert 2 (again):", randomized_set.insert(2))
    # Expected: False (already exists)

    # Test Case 2: Removals
    print("Remove 2:", randomized_set.remove(2))   # Expected: True
    print("Remove 2 (again):", randomized_set.remove(2))
    # Expected: False (already removed)

    # Test Case 3: GetRandom
    print("Random Element:", randomized_set.getRandom())
    # Should return a random element from [1, 3]
```

6.4 Example 3: Insert/Delete/Get Random Value O(1)

```
    # Test Case 4: Edge Case - Single Element
    print("Remove 3:", randomized_set.remove(3))   #
    Expected: True
    print("Random Element with one element left (1):",
    randomized_set.getRandom())   # Expected: 1

    # Test Case 5: Empty after Removal
    print("Remove 1:", randomized_set.remove(1))   #
    Expected: True
    # At this point, the set should be empty; inserting
    new elements should work as expected
    print("Insert 4:", randomized_set.insert(4))   #
    Expected: True
    print("Random Element:", randomized_set.getRandom())
    # Expected: 4

main()
```

6.4.6 Explanation of Test Cases

1. Insertions:
   - Insert values 1, 2, and 3. The first insertions should return `True`.
   - Re-inserting 2 should return `False` as it's already in the set.
2. Removals:
   - Remove 2, which should return `True`.
   - Attempt to remove 2 again, which should return `False` as it was already removed.
3. GetRandom:
   - With elements [1, 3] remaining, calling `getRandom()` should return either 1 or 3 randomly.
4. Single Element Edge Case:
   - After removing 3, only 1 should remain. `getRandom()` should always return 1.
5. Empty After Removal:
   - After removing all elements, the set is empty. Inserting a new element (4) should work normally, and `getRandom()` should return 4.

6.4.7 Expected Output

The output of the test cases may vary due to the randomness in the `getRandom()` function, but it should resemble the following structure:

```
Insert 1: True
Insert 2: True
Insert 3: True
Insert 2 (again): False
Remove 2: True
Remove 2 (again): False
Random Element: 1 or 3 (random)
Remove 3: True
Random Element with one element left (1): 1
Remove 1: True
Insert 4: True
Random Element: 4
```

This test verifies that each operation performs as expected and that the random element selection provides a fair distribution among the elements.

6.5 Example 4: Least Recently Used (LRU) Cache

6.5.1 Problem

The goal is to design a Least Recently Used (LRU) Cache that supports the following operations:

1. **get(key)**: Retrieve the value associated with the key if it exists in the cache. If the key does not exist, return -1.
2. **put(key, value)**: Insert or update the value associated with the key. If the cache reaches its capacity, it should evict the least recently used item before inserting the new item.

The LRU cache is designed to keep track of recently accessed items. The most recently accessed item should always be at the end of the data structure, while the least recently used item is kept at the beginning. When capacity is exceeded, the first item (least recently used) should be removed.

6.5 Example 4: Least Recently Used (LRU) Cache

6.5.2 Approach

To implement an LRU cache efficiently, we can use:

- **Hash Table** (`self.items`): Stores the key-value pairs for constant-time access to items.
- **Doubly Linked List** (`self.list`): Stores the order of keys to track the least and most recently used keys. With a doubly linked list, we can remove nodes from any position in constant time, and the `deque` data structure from Python's collections library can help simulate a doubly linked list for this purpose.

For **constant time O(1)** operations:

1. The `get()` operation needs to:
   - Retrieve the value from the hash table.
   - Move the key to the end of the list (to mark it as recently used).

2. The `put()` operation needs to:
   - Insert or update the key-value pair in the hash table.
   - Move the key to the end of the list.
   - If the capacity is exceeded, evict the least recently used item (from the beginning of the list).

6.5.3 Code

Let's go through the code for the `LRUCache` class with detailed comments.

Code 6.14: Python Code for LRUCache

```
from collections import deque

class LRUCache:
    def __init__(self, capacity: int) -> None:
        """
        Initialize the LRUCache with a given capacity.
        """
        self.capacity = capacity  # Maximum number of items the cache can hold
        self.list = deque(maxlen=capacity)  # Doubly-ended queue to keep track of usage order
        self.items = {}  # Dictionary to store key-value pairs for constant-time access
```

```python
def get(self, key: int) -> int:
    """
    Retrieve the value of the key if it exists in the
    cache; otherwise, return -1.
    If the key exists, it is moved to the end to mark
    it as recently used.
    """
    if key not in self.items:
        return -1  # Key not found in cache

    # Remove the key from its current position in the
    # list and append it to the end
    self.list.remove(key)
    self.list.append(key)

    return self.items[key]  # Return the value
    # associated with the key

def put(self, key: int, value: int) -> None:
    """
    Insert or update the value for the given key.
    If the cache reaches its capacity, the least
    recently used item is removed.
    """
    if key in self.items:
        # If the key is already in the cache, update
        # its value and move it to the end
        self.list.remove(key)
        self.list.append(key)
        self.items[key] = value
        return

    # If the cache is at full capacity, remove the
    # least recently used item
    if len(self.items) == self.capacity:
        lru_key = self.list.popleft()  # Remove the
        # least recently used item (first item in
        # the list)
        del self.items[lru_key]  # Delete it from the
        # hash table

    # Add the new key-value pair to the cache
    # and list
    self.list.append(key)
    self.items[key] = value
```

6.5.4 Complexity Analysis

- **Time Complexity**:
  - `get(key)`: O(n) in the worst case due to `self.list.remove(key)`, which has O(n) complexity because `deque` lacks indexed access.
  - `put(key, value)`: O(n) in the worst case due to `self.list.remove(key)`.
- **Space Complexity**: O(N), where N is the cache capacity, because we store up to N items in both the `items` dictionary and the `list` deque.

Note The above implementation has some inefficiencies due to `self.list.remove(key)`, which is O(n). For optimal O(1) performance, a doubly linked list and dictionary combination (rather than `deque`) would be ideal.

6.5.5 Testing the Code

To test the `LRUCache` class, let's create a function `main()` that demonstrates the example scenario provided in the problem statement.

Code 6.15: Test Code for LRUCache

```
def main():
    # Initialize the LRUCache with a capacity of 2
    cache = LRUCache(2)

    # Perform operations as described in the example
    cache.put(1, 1)  # Cache: {1:1}
    cache.put(2, 2)  # Cache: {1:1, 2:2}

    # Get the value for key 1; expect 1
    print("Get 1:", cache.get(1))  # Returns 1; Cache:
    {2:2, 1:1}

    # Insert key 3 with value 3; evicts key 2
    cache.put(3, 3)  # Cache: {1:1, 3:3}

    # Get the value for key 2; expect -1 as it
    was evicted
    print("Get 2:", cache.get(2))  # Returns -1
    (not found)
```

```
                # Insert key 4 with value 4; evicts key 1
                cache.put(4, 4)   # Cache: {3:3, 4:4}

                # Get the value for key 1; expect -1 as it
                was evicted
                print("Get 1:", cache.get(1))  # Returns -1
                (not found)

                # Get the value for key 3; expect 3
                print("Get 3:", cache.get(3))  # Returns 3; Cache:
                {4:4, 3:3}

                # Get the value for key 4; expect 4
                print("Get 4:", cache.get(4))  # Returns 4; Cache:
                {3:3, 4:4}

        main()
```

6.5.6 Expected Output

The output of the main() function should match the example given in the problem statement:

```
        Get 1: 1
        Get 2: -1
        Get 1: -1
        Get 3: 3
        Get 4: 4
```

6.5.7 Explanation of Test Cases

1. **Initial Insertion**:

    - Insert (1, 1) and (2, 2). The cache now has {1:1, 2:2}.
2. **Accessing Key 1**:

    - Calling get(1) returns 1 and moves key 1 to the end to mark it as recently used. Cache now has {2:2, 1:1}.

6.5 Example 4: Least Recently Used (LRU) Cache

3. **Inserting Key 3**:
    - Calling `put(3, 3)` causes the cache to exceed its capacity. Therefore, the least recently used key 2 is evicted, resulting in the cache `{1:1, 3:3}`.
4. **Accessing Key 2**:
    - Calling `get(2)` returns `-1` since key 2 was evicted in the previous step.
5. **Inserting Key 4**:
    - Calling `put(4, 4)` again exceeds the capacity, so the least recently used key 1 is evicted, resulting in `{3:3, 4:4}`.
6. **Accessing Keys 1, 3, and 4**:
    - `get(1)` returns `-1` since key 1 was evicted.
    - `get(3)` returns 3.
    - `get(4)` returns 4.

This test sequence confirms that the `LRUCache` class behaves as expected, maintaining the correct eviction policy and offering O(1) access (despite the inefficiencies in this implementation).

Chapter 7
Sets

A set is an unordered data type that is iterable, mutable, and has no repeating elements. Python's set class represents the mathematical concept of a set. Unlike lists, sets are highly optimized for checking whether they contain specific elements, thanks to their underlying hash table structure. Since sets are unordered, you cannot access items by index as you would in a list.

7.1 The Basics of Sets

7.1.1 Add Elements

The set.add() function allows you to add elements to the sets, creating the appropriate record values in the sets to store in the hash table. Adding elements to a set typically has an average time complexity of $O(1)$, but in the worst case, it can become $O(n)$.

Code 7.1: Add Elements to the Set

```
# A Python program demonstrating adding elements to a set
# Create a set
people = {"Jay", "Idrish", "Archi"}

print("People:", end = " ")
print(people)

# Add Daxit to the sets
people.add("Daxit")

# Use iterators to add elements to a set
for i in range(1, 6):
    people.add(i)

print("\nSet after adding element:", end = " ")
print(people)
```

Output:

```
People: {'Idrish', 'Archi', 'Jay'}

Set after adding element: {1, 2, 3, 4, 5, 'Idrish',
'Archi', 'Jay', 'Daxit'}
```

7.1.2 Delete the Element

The remove() method removes the specified element from the set and updates it. This method does not return a value. If the element passed to remove() does not exist, a KeyError exception is thrown.

7.1 The Basics of Sets

Code 7.2: remove()Delete the Collection Element

```
# language set
language = {'English', 'French', 'German'}

# removing 'German' from language
language.remove('German')

# Updated language set
print('Updated language set:', language)
```

7.1.3 Union

You can use the `union()` method or the | operator to merge two sets. This process accesses and combines the hash table values of both sets while removing duplicates. The time complexity is O(len(s1)+len(s2)), where s1 and s2 are the two sets being merged.

Code 7.3: A Python Program Demonstrates the Union of Two Collections

```
# Python program demonstrates the union of two sets
people = {"Jay", "Idrish", "Archil"}
vampires = {"Karan", "Arjun"}
dracula = {"Deepanshu", "Raju"}

# Union using union() function
population = people.union(vampires)

print("Union using union() function")
print(population)

# Union using "|" operator
population = people|dracula

print("\nUnion using '|' operator")
print(population)
```

Results:

```
Union using union() function
{'Karan', 'Idrish', 'Jay', 'Arjun', 'Archil'}

Union using '|' operator
{'Deepanshu', 'Idrish', 'Jay', 'Raju', 'Archil'}
```

7.1.4 Intersection

Intersection can be done with the "()" or "&" operators. Choose common elements, which are similar to iterating on a hash table and combining the same values on both tables. The time complexity is O(min(len(s1), len(s2))), where `s1` and `s2` are the two sets being intersected.

Code 7.4: The Python Program Demonstrates the Intersection of Two Collections

```
# Python program demonstrates the intersection of
two sets
set1 = set()
set2 = set()

for i in range(5):
    set1.add(i)

for i in range(3,9):
    set2.add(i)

# Intersection using intersection() function
set3 = set1.intersection(set2)

print("Intersection using intersection() function")
print(set3)

# Intersection using
# "&" operator
set3 = set1 & set2

print("\nIntersection using '&' operator")
print(set3)
```

Chapter 8
Linked Lists

A linked list, as the name suggests, is a list of links. Similar to arrays, a linked list is a linear data structure. For example:

As shown in Fig. 8.1, each element in the linked list is actually a separate object, and all objects are linked together by a reference field in each element. There are two types of linked lists: singly linked lists and doubly linked lists. The example in Fig. 8.1 is a singly linked list, and the example in Fig. 8.2 is a doubly linked list.

Fig 8.1 Single-linked lists

Fig. 8.2 Doubly linked lists

8.1 Two-pointer Technology

There are two scenarios for using the two-pointer technique:

1. The two pointers start in different positions: one from the beginning and the other from the end.
2. The two pointers move at different speeds: one is faster, while the other may be slower.

For singly linked lists, the first option does not work because the linked list can only be traversed in one direction. However, the second option, also known as the slow pointer technique and fast pointer technique, is very useful. This chapter will focus on the slow and fast pointer techniques in linked lists and show you how to solve the problem.

8.2 Example 1: Linked List Cycle?

8.2.1 Problem

Given head, the head of a linked list, determine if the linked list has a cycle in it.

There is a cycle in a linked list if there is some node in the list that can be reached again by continuously following the next pointer. Internally, pos is used to denote the index of the node that tail's next pointer is connected to. Note that pos is not passed as a parameter.

Return True if there is a cycle in the linked list. Otherwise, return False.

Example 1
Input: head = [3, 2, 0, −4], pos = 1
    Output: True
    Description: There is a loop in the linked list with the tail connected to the second node (Fig. 8.3).

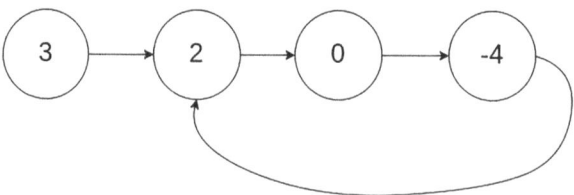

Fig. 8.3 Circular linked lists

8.2 Example 1: Linked List Cycle?

8.2.2 Problem Analysis

The problem requires determining whether a linked list has a cycle. In a cycle, a node in the linked list can be revisited by continuously following the next pointer. To solve this, we can use the **two-pointer (Floyd's Tortoise and Hare) technique**, where one pointer moves one step at a time (slow pointer), and the other pointer moves two steps at a time (fast pointer). If there's a cycle in the linked list, the two pointers will eventually meet.

8.2.3 Approach

1. **Initialize Two Pointers**:
   - Use slow and fast pointers, both initialized to the head of the linked list.
2. **Traverse the Linked List**:
   - Move the slow pointer one step at a time (slow = slow.next).
   - Move the fast pointer two steps at a time (fast = fast.next.next).
3. **Cycle Detection**:
   - If fast and slow pointers meet at any point (i.e., slow == fast), it means there's a cycle in the list, so return True.
   - If fast reaches the end of the list (either fast or fast.next becomes None), it means there is no cycle, so return False.

8.2.4 Example Walkthrough

Consider the example provided in this problem:

- **Input**: head = [3, 2, 0, -4], with the last node pointing back to the second node (index 1).
- **Expected Output**: True (because there is a cycle).

When traversing with two pointers, they will eventually meet within the cycle, confirming its presence.

8.2.5 Code

Here's the code that implements the above approach:

Code 8.1: Python Code for ListNode Cycle

```
class ListNode:
    def __init__(self, val=0, next=None):
        self.val = val
        self.next = next

class Solution:
    def hasCycle(self, head: ListNode) -> bool:
        slow = head
        fast = head

        while fast and fast.next:
            slow = slow.next              # Move slow pointer
                                          by 1 step
            fast = fast.next.next         # Move fast pointer
                                          by 2 steps
            if slow == fast:              # Check if they meet
                return True               # Cycle detected
        return False                      # No cycle detected
```

8.2.6 Explanation of the Code

- `slow` pointer moves by one node at a time.
- `fast` pointer moves by two nodes at a time.
- If there is a cycle, `slow` and `fast` will eventually point to the same node, thus confirming a cycle exists.
- If `fast` or `fast.next` becomes `None`, it means the list has reached the end, so there's no cycle.

8.2.7 Testing the Solution

To test this code, we need to set up different scenarios:

1. **Cycle Test Case**:
    - Input: [3, 2, 0, -4] with `pos` = 1 (cycle from tail to the second node)
    - Expected Output: `True`

8.2 Example 1: Linked List Cycle?

2. **No Cycle Test Case**:
   - Input: `[1, 2, 3, 4]` with no cycle
   - Expected Output: `False`

3. **Single Node with Cycle**:
   - Input: `[1]` where the node points to itself (cycle)
   - Expected Output: `True`

4. **Single Node without Cycle**:
   - Input: `[1]` with no cycle
   - Expected Output: `False`

8.2.8 Test Function

Below is a test function that creates the linked list structure and checks the output.

Code 8.2: Test Code for LinkedListWithCycle

```python
def test_hasCycle():
    # Helper function to create a cycle in the
    linked list
    def createLinkedListWithCycle(values, pos):
        head = ListNode(values[0])
        current = head
        cycle_node = None

        # Creating the linked list
        for i in range(1, len(values)):
            new_node = ListNode(values[i])
            current.next = new_node
            current = new_node
            if i == pos:
                cycle_node = new_node

        # Creating the cycle
        if cycle_node:
            current.next = cycle_node

        return head
```

```
# Test Case 1: Cycle exists
head = createLinkedListWithCycle([3, 2, 0, -4], 1)
solution = Solution()
assert solution.hasCycle(head) == True, "Test Case 1 Failed"

# Test Case 2: No cycle
head = createLinkedListWithCycle([1, 2, 3, 4], -1)
assert solution.hasCycle(head) == False, "Test Case 2 Failed"

# Test Case 3: Single node with a cycle
head = createLinkedListWithCycle([1], 0)
assert solution.hasCycle(head) == False, "Test Case 3 Failed"

# Test Case 4: Single node without a cycle
head = createLinkedListWithCycle([1], -1)
assert solution.hasCycle(head) == False, "Test Case 4 Failed"

print("All test cases passed!")

# Run the test function
test_hasCycle()
```

8.2.9 Explanation of the Test Function

1. **Helper Function**: `createLinkedListWithCycle` builds a linked list with a possible cycle based on the `values` list and the `pos` (index to which the last node should point to create a cycle).
2. **Test Cases**: We create linked lists for each test case and use assertions to check if `hasCycle` returns the expected result.
3. **Execution**: Running `test_hasCycle()` should print "All test cases passed!" if all tests succeed.

8.2.10 Time Complexity Analysis

- **Time Complexity**: O(n) where nnn is the number of nodes in the linked list. In the worst case, we traverse each node once.
- **Space Complexity**: O(1) as only two pointers (slow and fast) are used, regardless of the input size.

8.3 Example 2: The Intersection of Two Linked Lists

8.3.1 Problem

Write a program to find the node where the intersection of two singly linked lists begins.

For example, the following two linked lists (Fig. 8.4):

8.3.2 Problem Analysis

The problem requires finding the intersection node of two singly linked lists. In other words, we need to identify the node at which the two lists merge.

8.3.3 Solution Approaches

There are two common approaches to solve this problem:

1. **Using a Hash Table**:
   - Traverse the first linked list and store each node in a hash set.
   - Then, traverse the second linked list. If any node from the second list exists in the hash set, it means this is the intersection node.
   - This solution has O(n + m) time complexity, where n and m are the lengths of the two linked lists, and O(n) space complexity due to the hash set.

2. **Using Two Pointers**:
   - First, calculate the lengths of both linked lists.
   - Adjust the starting position of the pointer for the longer list so that both pointers traverse the same number of nodes in the remaining portion of the lists.
   - Traverse both lists simultaneously until the pointers meet. If they meet, this is the intersection node; otherwise, there's no intersection.
   - This solution has O(n + m) time complexity but only O(1) space complexity.

The code implementations for both approaches are provided below.

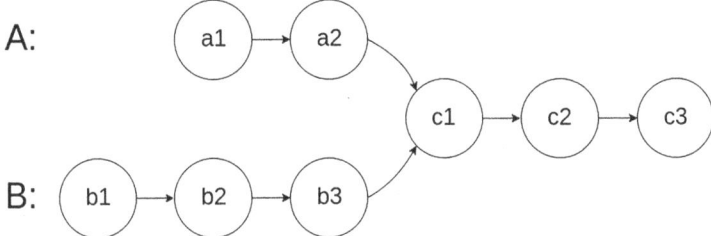

Fig. 8.4 The intersection of two linked lists

8.3.4 Code

8.3.4.1 Approach 1: Using Hash Table

Code 8.3: Python Code for IntersectionNode Using the Hash Table

```python
class ListNode(object):
    def __init__(self, x):
        self.val = x
        self.next = None

class Solution:
    def getIntersectionNode(self, headA: ListNode, headB: ListNode) -> ListNode:
        nodes_in_listA = set()

        # Traverse the first linked list and store each node in the set
        while headA:
            nodes_in_listA.add(headA)
            headA = headA.next

        # Traverse the second linked list to find the intersection
        while headB:
            if headB in nodes_in_listA:
                return headB   # Found the intersection node
            headB = headB.next

        return None   # No intersection found
```

8.3.4.2 Approach 2: Using Two Pointers

Code 8.4: Python Code for IntersectionNode Using the Two Pointers

```
class Solution:
    def getIntersectionNode(self, headA: ListNode, headB:
    ListNode) -> ListNode:
        # Helper function to calculate the length of a
        linked list
        def get_length(head):
            length = 0
            while head:
                length += 1
                head = head.next
            return length

        # Get lengths of both linked lists
        lenA = get_length(headA)
        lenB = get_length(headB)
```

8.3 Example 2: The Intersection of Two Linked Lists

```
# Align the start of the two lists by skipping
nodes in the longer list
while lenA > lenB:
    headA = headA.next
    lenA -= 1
while lenB > lenA:
    headB = headB.next
    lenB -= 1

# Traverse both lists to find the intersection
while headA != headB:
    headA = headA.next
    headB = headB.next

return headA  # Either the intersection node or
None if no intersection
```

8.3.5 Explanation of the Code

1. **Hash Table Approach**:
   - The `nodes_in_listA` set is used to store nodes from the first linked list.
   - If a node from the second linked list is found in `nodes_in_listA`, it is the intersection node.

2. **Two Pointers Approach**:
   - First, compute the lengths of both linked lists.
   - We then align the two pointers to ensure they traverse the same number of nodes to the end of the lists.
   - Both pointers are advanced together until they meet at the intersection node or reach the end (indicating no intersection).

8.3.6 Test Cases

Let's create some test cases to validate the code.

1. **Intersection Case**:
   - Input: Two lists [4, 1, 8, 4, 5] and [5, 0, 1, 8, 4, 5] intersect at node with value 8.
   - Expected Output: Node with value 8.

2. **No Intersection Case**:
   - Input: Two lists [1, 2, 3] and [4, 5, 6] with no intersection.
   - Expected Output: None.
3. **One List is Empty**:
   - Input: First list is [1, 2, 3], and the second list is empty.
   - Expected Output: None.
4. **Same List**:
   - Input: Both lists are [1, 2, 3] (pointing to the same list).
   - Expected Output: Node with value 1.

8.3.7 Test Function

Code 8.5: Test Code for Python Code for IntersectionNode

```python
def test_getIntersectionNode():
    # Helper function to create linked lists with
    intersection
    def create_linked_lists_with_
    intersection(intersection_val, listA_vals,
    listB_vals):
        intersect_node = None
        headA = ListNode(0)
        currentA = headA

        # Create the first list
        for val in listA_vals:
            new_node = ListNode(val)
            currentA.next = new_node
            currentA = new_node
            if val == intersection_val:
                intersect_node = new_node

        headB = ListNode(0)
        currentB = headB

        # Create the second list
        for val in listB_vals:
            if val == intersection_val:
                currentB.next = intersect_node
                break
```

8.3 Example 2: The Intersection of Two Linked Lists

```
                new_node = ListNode(val)
                currentB.next = new_node
                currentB = new_node

        return headA.next, headB.next, intersect_node

    solution = Solution()

    # Test Case 1: Lists intersect
    headA, headB, intersect_node = create_linked_lists_
    with_intersection(8, [4, 1, 8, 4, 5], [5, 0, 1,
    8, 4, 5])
    assert solution.getIntersectionNode(headA, headB) ==
    intersect_node, "Test Case 1 Failed"

    # Test Case 2: No intersection
    headA, headB, _ = create_linked_lists_with_
    intersection(-1, [1, 2, 3], [4, 5, 6])
    assert solution.getIntersectionNode(headA, headB) ==
    None, "Test Case 2 Failed"

    # Test Case 3: One list is empty
    headA = ListNode(1)
    headA.next = ListNode(2)
    headA.next.next = ListNode(3)
    headB = None
    assert solution.getIntersectionNode(headA, headB) ==
    None, "Test Case 3 Failed"

    # Test Case 4: Same list
    headA = ListNode(1)
    headA.next = ListNode(2)
    headA.next.next = ListNode(3)
    headB = headA
    assert solution.getIntersectionNode(headA, headB) ==
    headA, "Test Case 4 Failed"

    print("All test cases passed!")

# Run the test function
test_getIntersectionNode()
```

8.3.8 Explanation of the Test Function

1. **Helper Function**: `create_linked_lists_with_intersection` constructs two linked lists with a possible intersection.
2. **Test Cases**:
   - We set up multiple scenarios, including cases where the lists intersect, do not intersect, have one empty list, and are the same list.
3. **Execution**: Running `test_getIntersectionNode()` should print "All test cases passed!" if all assertions succeed.

8.3.9 Time Complexity Analysis

- **Hash Table Approach**:
  - **Time Complexity**: O(n+m) where nnn and mmm are the lengths of the two linked lists.
  - **Space Complexity**: O(n) due to the hash table storing nodes of the first list.
- **Two Pointers Approach**:
  - **Time Complexity**: O(n + m) since we traverse both lists.
  - **Space Complexity**: O(1) as only two pointers are used.

8.4 Example 3: Clone a Random Linked List

8.4.1 Problem

A linked list of length n is given such that each node contains an additional random pointer, which could point to any node in the list, or null.

Construct a deep copy of the list. The deep copy should consist of exactly n brand new nodes, where each new node has its value set to the value of its corresponding original node. Both the next and random pointer of the new nodes should point to new nodes in the copied list such that the pointers in the original list and copied list represent the same list state. None of the pointers in the new list should point to nodes in the original list.

For example, if there are two nodes X and Y in the original list, where X.random --> Y, then for the corresponding two nodes x and y in the copied list, x.random --> y.

Return the head of the copied linked list.

8.4 Example 3: Clone a Random Linked List

The linked list is represented in the input/output as a list of n nodes. Each node is represented as a pair of [val, random_index] where:

- val: an integer representing Node.val
- random_index: the index of the node (range from 0 to n-1) that the random pointer points to, or null if it does not point to any node.

Your code will only be given the head of the original linked list.

8.4.2 Problem Analysis

The problem requires creating a deep copy of a linked list where each node has two pointers:

1. `next` pointer that points to the next node in the list.
2. `random` pointer that may point to any node in the list or `null`.

In a deep copy, we need to create entirely new nodes and ensure that the `next` and `random` pointers in the copied list refer to the copied nodes, not the original nodes.

8.4.3 Solution Idea

The solution leverages a hash table to keep track of nodes that have already been copied. This approach allows you to:

1. Create each node only once.
2. Retrieve previously created nodes quickly to assign their `next` and `random` pointers in the copied list.

8.4.4 Solution Approach

1. **Hash Table for Cloning**:
   - Traverse the original linked list, copying each node and storing it in a hash table where the key is the original node, and the value is the copied node.
   - During traversal, handle both the `next` and `random` pointers for each node. If a node's `next` or `random` target has already been copied, use the hash table to retrieve the copy.

2. **Steps**:

    - Initialize a hash table `table` to map each original node to its copy.
    - For each node in the original list:
        - If the `next` pointer is not `None`, set the `next` pointer in the copied node.
        - If the `random` pointer is not `None`, set the `random` pointer in the copied node.
    - Finally, return the copied head node from the hash table.

8.4.5 Code

Here's the solution code implementing the hash table approach.

Code 8.6: Python Code for copyRandomList

```
class Node:
    def __init__(self, val: int, next: 'Node' = None,
    random: 'Node' = None):
        self.val = val
        self.next = next
        self.random = random

class Solution:
    def copyRandomList(self, head: 'Node') -> 'Node':
        if not head:
            return None

        # Hash table to store the mapping from original
        nodes to their copies
        table = {}

        # Create the copy of the head node
        table[head] = Node(head.val)

        # Initialize the current node pointer
        curr = head

        # Iterate through the list and copy the nodes
        while curr:
            copy = table[curr]
```

8.4 Example 3: Clone a Random Linked List

```
            # Copy the next pointer
            if curr.next is not None:
                if curr.next not in table:
                    table[curr.next] = Node(curr.
                    next.val)
                copy.next = table[curr.next]

            # Copy the random pointer
            if curr.random is not None:
                if curr.random not in table:
                    table[curr.random] = Node(curr.
                    random.val)
                copy.random = table[curr.random]

            # Move to the next node in the original list
            curr = curr.next

        # Return the copied head node
        return table[head]
```

8.4.6 Explanation of the Code

1. **Hash Table Setup**: A hash table `table` is used to map each node in the original list to its copied node.
2. **Node Creation**:
   - For each node in the original list, check if its `next` and `random` pointers have been copied.
   - If not, create a new node and store it in the hash table.
   - Set the `next` and `random` pointers for the copied node accordingly.
3. **Return the Copied List**: The copied head node is accessed via `table[head]`, which is returned as the result.

8.4.7 Time and Space Complexity Analysis

- **Time Complexity**: O(n) where nnn is the number of nodes in the linked list. We visit each node once and perform O(1) operations for each node.
- **Space Complexity**: O(n) as we use a hash table to store the mapping from original nodes to copied nodes.

8.4.8 Test Cases

Let's write some test cases to validate the code.

1. **Standard Case**:
   - Input: A list with nodes having both `next` and `random` pointers.
   - Expected Output: A deep copy of the list.
2. **Single Node with `random` Pointer to Itself**:
   - Input: `[7]` with `random` pointing to itself.
   - Expected Output: A copy of this node where `random` in the copy points to itself in the copy.
3. **Empty List**:
   - Input: `None`
   - Expected Output: `None`
4. **All `random` Pointers as `None`**:
   - Input: A list where each node's `random` pointer is `None`.
   - Expected Output: A deep copy where all `random` pointers are `None`.

8.4.9 Test Function

Code 8.7: Test Code for copyRandomList

```
def test_copyRandomList():
    # Helper function to create a linked list with random
    pointers
    def create_linked_list_with_random_pointers(values,
    random_indices):
        if not values:
            return None

        nodes = [Node(val) for val in values]
        head = nodes[0]

        # Set the next pointers
        for i in range(len(nodes) - 1):
            nodes[i].next = nodes[i + 1]
```

8.4 Example 3: Clone a Random Linked List

```python
        # Set the random pointers
        for i, random_index in enumerate(random_indices):
            nodes[i].random = nodes[random_index] if
            random_index is not None else None

        return head


# Helper function to compare two linked lists with
random pointers
def compare_linked_lists(head1, head2):
    while head1 and head2:
        if head1.val != head2.val or (head1.random
        and head2.random and head1.random.val !=
        head2.random.val):
            return False
        if (head1.random is None) != (head2.random is
        None):  # one random is None and the
        other is not
            return False
        head1 = head1.next
        head2 = head2.next
    return head1 is None and head2 is None

solution = Solution()


# Test Case 1: Standard Case
head = create_linked_list_with_random_pointers([7,
13, 11, 10, 1], [None, 0, 4, 2, 0])
copied_head = solution.copyRandomList(head)
assert compare_linked_lists(head, copied_head), "Test
Case 1 Failed"

# Test Case 2: Single Node with random pointer
to itself
head = create_linked_list_with_random_
pointers([7], [0])
copied_head = solution.copyRandomList(head)
assert compare_linked_lists(head, copied_head), "Test
Case 2 Failed"
```

```
            # Test Case 3: Empty List
            head = None
            copied_head = solution.copyRandomList(head)
            assert copied_head == None, "Test Case 3 Failed"

            # Test Case 4: All random pointers as None
            head = create_linked_list_with_random_pointers([1, 2,
            3, 4], [None, None, None, None])
            copied_head = solution.copyRandomList(head)
            assert compare_linked_lists(head, copied_head), "Test
            Case 4 Failed"

            print("All test cases passed!")

        # Run the test function
        test_copyRandomList()
```

8.4.10 Explanation of the Test Function

1. **Helper Functions**:

    - `create_linked_list_with_random_pointers`: Creates a linked list based on given values and random pointer indices.
    - `compare_linked_lists`: Compares two linked lists by checking both `val` and `random` pointers.

2. **Test Cases**:

    - **Test Case 1**: A list with multiple nodes and random pointers set to different nodes.
    - **Test Case 2**: A single node with `random` pointing to itself.
    - **Test Case 3**: An empty list (expected to return `None`).
    - **Test Case 4**: A list where all `random` pointers are `None`.

3. **Execution**: Running `test_copyRandomList()` should print "All test cases passed!" if all assertions succeed.

Chapter 9
Binary Tree

Trees are common data structures that represent a hierarchical structure. Each node of the tree will have a root value and a list of references to other nodes called child nodes. From a graph point of view, a tree can also be defined as a directed acyclic graph with N nodes and N-1 edges.

Binary trees are one of the most typical tree structures. As the name suggests, a binary tree is a tree data structure in which each node has at most two child nodes, called left and right child nodes. This chapter explains how to traverse binary trees and how to use recursion to solve problems related to binary trees.

9.1 DFS/BFS Traversal

Traversal methods include preorder, inorder, and postorder traversals. Code 9.1 demonstrates a postorder traversal for the binary tree.

Code 9.1: Postorder Traversals

```
class Solution:
    def postorderTraversal(self, root: TreeNode) ->
List[int]:
        curr = root
        stack = []
        s = []
        while True:
            if curr is not None:
                s.append(curr.val)
                stack.append(curr)
                curr = curr.right
            elif (stack):
                curr = stack.pop(-1)
                curr = curr.left
            else:
                break
        return s[::-1]
```

Layer-ordered traversal is essentially a breadth-first search algorithm, where the tree is traversed step by step. Starting at the root node, it visits the node itself, followed by its neighbors, second-order neighbors, and so on. When performing a breadth-first search in a tree, the order in which nodes are accessed is in layer order.

Code 9.2: Binary Tree Breadth-First Search Order Traversal

```python
from queue import Queue
class Solution:
  def levelOrder(self, root: TreeNode) -> List[List[int]]:

    result = []
    if root == None:
       return

    # Queues using python
    q = Queue ()
    # add the root
    q.put (root)

    while q.empty () != True :
      # Travers the number of elements in the queue
      temp = []
      for i in range (q.qsize()):
        # Take out the first value
        node = q.get()
        temp.append(node.val)

        if node.left != None:
          q.put(node.left)
        if node.right != None:
          q.put(node.right)

      result.append(temp)
    return result
```

9.2 The Recursive Method

As we all know, a tree can be defined recursively as a node (root node) that includes a list of values and references to child nodes, so recursion is one of the most powerful and commonly used techniques for solving tree problems. Each recursive function call focuses on the problem of the current node, and then recursively calls the function to solve its child nodes. In general, tree problems can be solved recursively using either a top-down approach or a bottom-up approach.

9.2.1 A "Top-down" Solution

"Top-down" means that in each recursive call, the node is first accessed to provide some values, and then those values are passed to its children when the function is recursively called. Therefore, a "top-down" solution can be thought of as a kind of pre-traversal. Specifically, the recursive function top_down (root, params) works like this:

```
1. return specific value for null node
2. update the answer if needed    // answer <-- params
3. left_ans = top_down(root.left, left_params)  // left_
   params <-- root.val, params
4. right_ans = top_down(root.right, right_params) //
   right_params <-- root.val, params
5. return the answer if needed    // answer <-- left_ans,
   right_ans
```

Example Given a binary tree, find its maximum depth.

The depth of the root node is 1. For each node, if its depth is known, the depth of its child nodes will be known. So, if you pass the depth of a node as a parameter when calling a function recursively, all nodes will know its depth. For leaf nodes, depth can be used to update the final answer.

Below is the pseudocode for the top-down recursive function maximum_depth (root, depth):

Code 9.3: Top-down Recursive Pseudocode

```
2. if root is a leaf node:
3. answer = max(answer, depth) // update the answer
   if needed
4. maximum_depth(root.left, depth + 1) // call the
   function recursively for left child
5. maximum_depth(root.right, depth + 1)// call the
   function recursively for right child
```

9.2 The Recursive Method

Here's the code:

Code 9.4: The Maximum Depth of the Binary Tree

```
class Solution:
    def maxDepth(self, root: TreeNode) -> int:
        if root==None:
            return 0
        return 1+max(self.maxDepth(root.left),self.
        maxDepth(root.right))
```

9.2.2 A "Bottom-up" Solution

"Bottom-up" is another recursive solution, in which the function is first recursively called on all child nodes in each recursive call, and then the answer is derived based on the value returned and the value of the current node itself, a process that can be thought of as a kind of post-traversal. In general, the "bottom-up" recursive function bottom_up (root) pseudocode is as follows.

Code 9.5: "Bottom-up" Recursive Function Pseudocode

```
1. return specific value for null node
2. left_ans = bottom_up(root.left)    // call function
   recursively for left child
3. right_ans = bottom_up(root.right)  // call function
   recursively for right child
4. return answers                     // answer <-- left_ans,
   right_ans, root.val
```

Moving on to the question about maximum depth, but using another way of thinking: for a single node of the tree, what is the maximum depth x of a subtree rooted in itself?

If we know the maximum depth of the subtree with its left child as the root l and the maximum depth r of the subtree with its right child as the root, we can choose the maximum between them and then add 1 to get the maximum depth of the subtree rooted in the current node, i.e., $x = \max(l,r) + 1$.

This means that for each node, an answer can be obtained after solving the problem for its child nodes. So, a "bottom-up" solution can be used to solve this problem. Here's the pseudocode for the recursive function maximum_depth (root):

```
1. return 0 if root is null     // return 0 for null node
2. left_depth = maximum_depth(root.left)
3. right_depth = maximum_depth(root.right)
4. return max(left_depth, right_depth) + 1   // return
   depth of the subtree rooted at root
```

The specific code is as follows:

```
int maximum_depth(TreeNode* root) {
    if (!root) {
        return 0;      #return 0 for null node
    }
    int left_depth = maximum_depth(root->left);
    int right_depth = maximum_depth(root->right);
    return max(left_depth, right_depth) + 1;   #return depth
    of the subtree rooted at root
}
```

Understanding recursion and finding a recursive solution to the problem is not easy and requires a lot of practice.

When you have a tree problem, ask yourself two questions: Is it possible to determine some parameters to help the node know its answer? Can you use these parameters and the value of the node itself to determine what parameters to pass to its children? If the answer is yes, try using a "top-down" recursive solution to solve the problem.

Alternatively, consider this: for a node in the tree, if the answers for its children are known, can you compute the answer for that node? If so, a bottom-up recursive approach is applicable.

9.3 Example 1: The Lowest Common Ancestor of the Binary Tree

9.3.1 Problem

Given a binary tree, the lowest common ancestor (LCA) of two given nodes is found in the tree.

9.3 Example 1: The Lowest Common Ancestor of the Binary Tree

According to the definition of LCA on Wikipedia: "The lowest common ancestor is defined as the relationship between two nodes p and q, which is the lowest node in the tree that has both p and q as offspring (here, allowing a node to become its own offspring)."

Example Given the following binary tree, the lowest common ancestor of a node is given. As shown in Fig. 9.1, root = [3,5,1,6,2,0,8,null,null,7,4].

```
Input: root = [3,5,1,6,2,0,8,null,null,7,4], p = 5, q = 1
Output: 3
Result: The LCA of nodes 5 and 1 is 3
```

9.3.2 Solution

We can solve this problem using a Depth-First Search (DFS) traversal in a bottom-up approach:

1. Traverse the tree from the root node down to the leaf nodes.
2. When a node is encountered that matches either ppp or qqq, return that node to its parent call.
3. If both the left and right child of a node return a non-null value, it indicates that one of ppp or qqq is in the left subtree and the other is in the right subtree. Therefore, the current node is the LCA.
4. If only one of the child calls returns a non-null value, propagate that result upwards.

9.3.3 Time Complexity

- **Time Complexity**: O(N), where N is the number of nodes in the tree, as we traverse each node once.
- **Space Complexity**: O(H), where H is the height of the tree. This is because of the recursive call stack in DFS.

Fig. 9.1 Binary tree

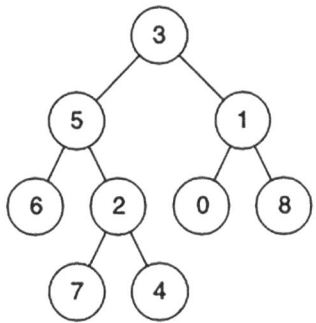

9.3.4 Code Analysis

Here's the code with comments to explain each part:

Code 9.6: Python Code for lowestCommonAncestor

```python
class Solution:
  def lowestCommonAncestor(self, root: 'TreeNode', p: 'TreeNode', q: 'TreeNode') -> 'TreeNode':
    # Base Case: If root is None, return None (no ancestor found here)
    if root is None:
      return None

    # If the current node is either p or q, we return this node
    if root is p or root is q:
      return root

    # Recursively search the left subtree for p or q
    left = self.lowestCommonAncestor(root.left, p, q)

    # Recursively search the right subtree for p or q
    right = self.lowestCommonAncestor(root.right, p, q)

    # If both left and right are non-null, it means p and q are found in
    # different subtrees, so root is their lowest common ancestor
    if left and right:
      return root

    # If only one side (left or right) is non-null, return that side's result
    # This indicates that both p and q are found on the same side
    elif left:
      return left
    else:
      return right
```

9.3.5 Explanation of Key Parts

1. **Base Case**: If the current node (root) is None, return None because there's no node to process here.
2. **Check for Match**: If the current node is either p or q, return it, as it may be the potential LCA.
3. **Left and Right Traversals**: Recursively search for ppp and qqq in the left and right subtrees.
4. **Determine LCA**:
   - If both left and right are non-null, it means ppp and qqq are found in different subtrees, so the current node is the LCA.
   - If only one of left or right is non-null, return that value because it represents the subtree where both nodes reside.

9.3.6 Testing the Code Using a Main Function

To test this code, we'll need to set up a binary tree with the structure shown in the example, and then verify the output of the function.

Here's how we could set up the testing function:

Code 9.7: Test Code for lowestCommonAncestor

```
class TreeNode:
    def __init__(self, x):
        self.val = x
        self.left = None
        self.right = None

def test_lowest_common_ancestor():
    # Create nodes for the binary tree
    root = TreeNode(3)
    root.left = TreeNode(5)
    root.right = TreeNode(1)
    root.left.left = TreeNode(6)
    root.left.right = TreeNode(2)
    root.left.right.left = TreeNode(7)
    root.left.right.right = TreeNode(4)
    root.right.left = TreeNode(0)
    root.right.right = TreeNode(8)

    # Create an instance of the Solution class
    solution = Solution()
```

```
# Test Case 1: LCA of nodes 5 and 1 should be 3
p, q = root.left, root.right   # Nodes 5 and 1
lca = solution.lowestCommonAncestor(root, p, q)
assert lca.val == 3, f"Expected LCA: 3, Got: {lca.val}"
print(f"LCA of {p.val} and {q.val} is {lca.val}")

# Test Case 2: LCA of nodes 5 and 4 should be 5
p, q = root.left, root.left.right.right   #
Nodes 5 and 4
lca = solution.lowestCommonAncestor(root, p, q)
assert lca.val == 5, f"Expected LCA: 5, Got: {lca.val}"
print(f"LCA of {p.val} and {q.val} is {lca.val}")

# Test Case 3: LCA of nodes 7 and 8 should be 3
p, q = root.left.right.left, root.right.right   #
Nodes 7 and 8
lca = solution.lowestCommonAncestor(root, p, q)
assert lca.val == 3, f"Expected LCA: 3, Got: {lca.val}"
print(f"LCA of {p.val} and {q.val} is {lca.val}")

# Run the test function
test_lowest_common_ancestor()
```

9.3.7 Explanation of Test Cases

1. **Test Case 1**:
   - Input: $p = 5, q = 1$
   - Expected Output: 3 (Root node)
   - Explanation: Node 3 is the LCA because it is the lowest node that has both 5 and 1 as descendants.

2. **Test Case 2**:
   - Input: $p = 5, q = 4$
   - Expected Output: 5
   - Explanation: Node 5 is the LCA because 4 is a descendant of 5, so 5 is the lowest node containing both 5 and 4.

3. **Test Case 3**:
   - Input: $p = 7, q = 8$
   - Expected Output: 3
   - Explanation: Node 3 is the LCA because it is the lowest node that has both 7 (left subtree) and 8 (right subtree) as descendants.

9.3.8 Conclusion

This problem is a classic application of tree traversal using DFS to find the Lowest Common Ancestor in O(N) time. The `lowestCommonAncestor` function is implemented recursively to handle each subtree, and the main function (`test_lowest_common_ancestor`) provides test cases to validate correctness. Each test case checks a specific aspect of LCA and verifies that the function provides the correct node based on the tree structure.

9.4 Example 2: Serializing and Deserializing Binary Trees

9.4.1 Problem

Serialization is the process of converting a data structure or object into a sequence of bits so that it can be stored in a file or memory buffer, or transferred over a network link to be reconstructed later in the same or another computer environment.

An algorithm for serializing and deserializing binary trees was designed. There are no restrictions on how the serialization/deserialization algorithm works. Just make sure that you can serialize the binary tree as a string and that you can deserialize that string into the original tree structure.

Example You can use the following binary tree:

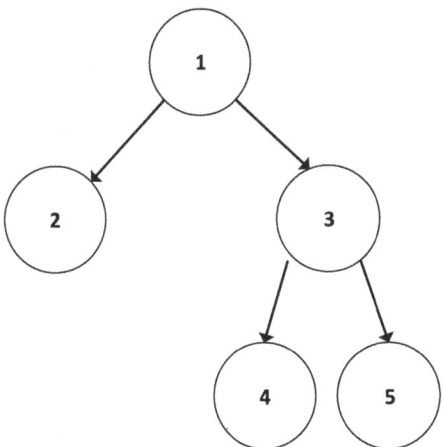

Serialized as "[1,2,3,null,null,4,5]".

9.4.2 Approach

The approach used here is preorder traversal (root, left, right).

1. **Serialization**:
   - Use a **depth-first search (DFS)** to traverse the tree in a preorder fashion.
   - Append each node's value to a string separated by commas.
   - Use # to indicate NULL nodes (when a node doesn't have a left or right child).
   - For example, for the above binary tree, serialization yields "1,2,#,#,3,4,#,#,5,#,#".

2. **Deserialization**:
   - Split the serialized string by commas to get a list of values.
   - Use DFS to reconstruct the tree:
     - Each time we encounter #, we return None, representing a NULL node.
     - For each other value, we create a new TreeNode.
     - Recur for the left and right children.

9.4.3 Complexity Analysis

- **Time Complexity**: O(N) where N is the number of nodes in the tree. Each node is visited once during both serialization and deserialization.
- **Space Complexity**: O(N), due to the storage required for the serialized string and the recursive call stack in DFS.

9.4.4 Code Analysis

Here's the provided code with comments to clarify each part:

9.4 Example 2: Serializing and Deserializing Binary Trees

Code 9.8: Python Code for Serialize and Deserialize

```python
class Codec:
    def dfs(self, s):
        # Pop the first element in the list
        first = s.pop(0)

        # If it's "#", it represents a NULL node, so
        return None
        if first == "#":
            return None

        # Create a new TreeNode with the current value
        root = TreeNode(int(first))

        # Recursively set the left and right children
        root.left = self.dfs(s)
        root.right = self.dfs(s)

        return root

    def serialize(self, root):
        # Base case for a null node
        if root is None:
            return "#,"

        # Convert the root value to a string and recursively
        serialize left and right children
        return str(root.val) + "," + self.serialize(root.
        left) + self.serialize(root.right)

    def deserialize(self, data):
        # Split the serialized data into a list of
        node values
        s = data.split(',')

        # Start the DFS deserialization process
        root = self.dfs(s)

        return root
```

9.4.5 Explanation of Key Parts

1. **DFS Helper Function (Line 2–12)**:

   - The dfs function is used during **deserialization**. It reconstructs the tree by popping elements from the list s.
   - If an element is #, it represents a NULL node.
   - Otherwise, create a TreeNode with the current value and recursively set its left and right children.

2. **Serialize Function (Line 14–18)**:

   - Converts the tree to a comma-separated string using **preorder traversal**.
   - For each NULL node, "#," is added to indicate an absent child.

3. **Deserialize Function (Line 20–23)**:

   - Converts the serialized string into a list and calls the dfs function to reconstruct the tree.

9.4.6 Testing the Code with a Main Function

To test this code, we'll create a binary tree, serialize it, then deserialize it, and finally verify if the deserialized tree matches the original structure.

Here's a main function to test the serialization and deserialization process:

9.4 Example 2: Serializing and Deserializing Binary Trees

Code 9.9: Test Code for Serialize and Deserialize

```python
class TreeNode:
    def __init__(self, x):
        self.val = x
        self.left = None
        self.right = None

def test_codec():
    # Create a binary tree
    #     1
    #    / \
    #   2   3
    #      /\
    #     4 5
    root = TreeNode(1)
    root.left = TreeNode(2)
    root.right = TreeNode(3)
    root.right.left = TreeNode(4)
    root.right.right = TreeNode(5)

    # Initialize Codec
    codec = Codec()

    # Test Serialization
    serialized = codec.serialize(root)
    print("Serialized Tree:", serialized)  # Expected: "1,2,#,#,3,4,#,#,5,#,#"

    # Test Deserialization
    deserialized_root = codec.deserialize(serialized)

    # Helper function to validate the tree structure by serializing again
    serialized_again = codec.serialize(deserialized_root)
    print("Serialized Again after Deserialization:", serialized_again)

    # Check if the serialized string before and after deserialization is the same
    assert serialized == serialized_again, "Error: The tree structure does not match after deserialization."
    print("The tree structure is preserved after deserialization.")

# Run the test function
test_codec()
```

9.4.7 Explanation of the Testing Function

1. **Tree Creation**:
   - We manually create a binary tree with the structure shown above.
2. **Serialization**:
   - We serialize the tree and print the result. This serialized string should match our expectations.
3. **Deserialization**:
   - We deserialize the serialized string to reconstruct the tree.
   - To confirm that the tree structure is preserved, we serialize the deserialized tree again and compare it with the original serialized string.
4. **Validation**:
   - If the serialized string before and after deserialization is the same, then the deserialization successfully reconstructs the original tree structure.

9.4.8 Expected Output

For the tree in the example, the expected output would be:

```
Serialized Tree: 1,2,#,#,3,4,#,#,5,#,#
Serialized Again after Deserialization:
1,2,#,#,3,4,#,#,5,#,#
The tree structure is preserved after deserialization.
```

9.4.9 Conclusion

The Codec class efficiently serializes and deserializes binary trees using preorder traversal, with # representing NULL nodes. The `test_codec` function confirms that the original and deserialized trees have the same structure, demonstrating that the algorithm works as expected.

9.5 Example 3: Find the Maximum Path Sum of the Binary Tree

9.5.1 Problem

Given a non-empty binary tree, find the maximum sum of paths. For this problem, a path is defined as a sequence of parent-child connections from a starting node to any node in the tree. The path must contain at least one node and does not need to go through the root.

Example

```
Input: [1,2,3]
    1
   / \
  2   3
Output: 6
```

9.5.2 Solution

The solution uses a recursive approach to compute the maximum path sum, leveraging **postorder traversal** (bottom-up traversal). The key points of the approach are as follows:

1. **Helper Function (Recursive Traversal)**:
   - A recursive helper function `maxPath` is defined to calculate the maximum contribution of each subtree to its parent.
   - This function returns the maximum path sum starting from a given node `v` to any of its descendants.
   - **Return Value**: At each node, the function returns the maximum sum of a path that extends either to the left or right subtree, including the current node. If extending either branch results in a negative sum, we discard it by returning 0 instead.

2. **Tracking Global Maximum Sum**:
   - A variable `best_sum` is maintained to track the highest path sum encountered during traversal.
   - At each node, we compute a **local maximum path sum** using:

     ```
     best_sum = max(best_sum, v.val + L + R)
     ```

where L and R are the maximum contributions from the left and right subtrees, respectively. This includes the possibility of using both left and right branches simultaneously.

3. **Recursive Return**:

    - The recursive function returns the **maximum path sum that can be extended** from the current node to its parent. This value is calculated as:

    ```
    return max(0, v.val + L, v.val + R)
    ```

    - Here, max(0, ...) ensures that if adding either branch results in a negative sum, we ignore that branch (return 0 instead).

9.5.3 Complexity Analysis

- **Time Complexity**: O(N), where N is the number of nodes in the binary tree. Each node is visited once.
- **Space Complexity**: O(H), where H is the height of the binary tree, due to the recursive call stack.

9.5.4 Code Analysis

Here's the provided code with comments explaining each part:

9.5 Example 3: Find the Maximum Path Sum of the Binary Tree   151

Code 9.10: Python Code for maxPathSum

```python
class Solution:
    def maxPathSum(self, root: 'TreeNode') -> int:
        best_sum = -float('inf')        # Initialize tracker
                                        for the best sum

        def maxPath(v: 'vertex') -> int:        # Helper
        function
            nonlocal best_sum           # Reference our tracker
            if v is None:               # Base case
                return 0

            L = maxPath(v.left)         # Recurse on left child
            R = maxPath(v.right)        # Recurse on right child

            # Update the tracker with the sum of the current
            node and both subtrees
            best_sum = max(best_sum, v.val + L + R)

            # Return the best path sum of either subtree plus
            the current node
            return max(0, v.val + L, v.val + R)

        maxPath(root)           # Run recursive traversal
        from root
        return best_sum         # Return the maximum path
        sum found
```

9.5.5 Explanation of Key Parts

1. **Helper Function** `maxPath`:
   - `maxPath` computes the maximum path sum contribution for each subtree.
   - It returns the maximum contribution of either the left or right subtree, including the current node.
   - If the maximum path sum contribution from either subtree is negative, it returns 0 to disregard that branch.
2. **Tracking Maximum Path Sum**:
   - `best_sum` is updated with the sum of the current node's value and the maximum contributions from both left and right subtrees, allowing paths that use both branches.
3. **Return Statement** :
   - The maximum path sum, `best_sum`, is returned as the result of the function.

9.5.6 Testing the Code with a Main Function

To test this code, create a binary tree, compute its maximum path sum, and print the result.

Here is a `TreeNode` class definition and a main function to test the solution:

9.5 Example 3: Find the Maximum Path Sum of the Binary Tree

Code 9.11: Test Code for maxPathSum

```
class TreeNode:
    def __init__(self, x):
        self.val = x
        self.left = None
        self.right = None

def test_max_path_sum():
    # Create a binary tree as follows:
    #          -10
    #         /   \
    #        9    20
    #            /  \
    #           15   7
    root = TreeNode(-10)
    root.left = TreeNode(9)
    root.right = TreeNode(20)
    root.right.left = TreeNode(15)
    root.right.right = TreeNode(7)

    # Initialize Solution
    solution = Solution()

    # Test the max path sum function
    max_sum = solution.maxPathSum(root)
    print("Maximum Path Sum:", max_sum)  # Expected Output: 42

# Run the test function
test_max_path_sum()
```

9.5.7 Explanation of the Testing Function

1. **Tree Creation**:
   - We manually create a binary tree with the following structure:

   ```
       -10
       / \
      9   20
         / \
        15  7
   ```

   - For this tree, the maximum path sum is 42 (from nodes 15 -> 20 -> 7).

2. **Testing**:
   - We initialize an instance of Solution and call maxPathSum with the tree's root.
   - We then print the result.

9.5.8 Expected Output

For the tree example given, the expected output would be:

```
Maximum Path Sum: 42
```

9.5.9 Conclusion

The Solution class calculates the maximum path sum in a binary tree efficiently using recursive postorder traversal. The helper function returns the maximum path sum that can be extended to the parent node, and best_sum keeps track of the highest path sum encountered. The test_max_path_sum function confirms that the solution works as expected.

9.6 Example 4: Convert a Given Binary Tree to a Doubly Linked List

9.6.1 Problem Analysis

We are given a Binary Search Tree (BST) and need to convert it to a sorted circular doubly linked list. This means:

- The nodes should be connected in ascending order.
- Each node should have a `left` pointer to its previous node and a `right` pointer to its next node.
- The last node in the list should point back to the first node, forming a circular linked list.

For example, given the BST:

The resulting doubly linked list should look like this:

```
1 <-> 2 <-> 3 <-> 4 <-> 5
^                 ^
|                 |
+-----------------+
```

9.6.2 Approach

To convert the BST to a sorted circular doubly linked list, we can perform the following steps:

1. Inorder Traversal:
    - Traverse the BST using inorder traversal (left-root-right) to ensure the nodes are accessed in ascending order.
    - During traversal, append each node to a list to keep track of the nodes in sorted order.
2. Linking Nodes:
    - After collecting the nodes in an ordered list, iterate through the list to set each node's `right` pointer to the next node and each node's `left` pointer to the previous node.
    - The first node's `left` pointer should point to the last node, and the last node's `right` pointer should point to the first node, making the list circular.

9.6.3 Code Analysis

Here is the provided code with additional comments explaining each part:

Code 9.12: Python Code for treeToDoublyList

```python
class Solution:
    def treeToDoublyList(self, root: 'Node') -> 'Node':
        if not root:
            return root

        # Step 1: Perform in-order traversal and collect nodes
        in a list
        res = []

        def inorder(node):
            if node is None:
                return
            inorder(node.left)
            res.append(node)
            inorder(node.right)

        inorder(root)   # Start in-order traversal from the root

        # Step 2: Link nodes to form a circular doubly
        linked list
        for i in range(len(res) - 1):
            res[i].right = res[i + 1]    # Point current node's
            right to next node
            res[i + 1].left = res[i]    # Point next node's left
            to current node

        # Step 3: Connect the head and tail to form a
        circular list
        res[-1].right = res[0]        # Last node's right points
        to the first node
        res[0].left = res[-1]         # First node's left points
        to the last node

        return res[0]                 # Return the head of the
        circular doubly linked list
```

9.6.4 Explanation of Key Parts

1. Inorder Traversal:

   - The `inorder` function recursively traverses the tree in an inorder manner.
   - Each node visited is appended to the `res` list, which will contain nodes in sorted order.

2. Linking Nodes:

   - After the traversal, a loop iterates through the list `res` and links each node with its next and previous nodes.
   - Finally, we connect the last node's `right` pointer to the first node and the first node's `left` pointer to the last node, making the list circular.

3. Return the Head Node:

   - The head of the doubly linked list (first node in `res`) is returned as the output.

9.6.5 Complexity Analysis

- **Time Complexity**: O(N), where N is the number of nodes in the BST. The inorder traversal and the linking process both take linear time.
- **Space Complexity**: O(N), due to the `res` list that stores all nodes of the BST.

9.6.6 Test Case and Node Class

To test the code, we need a `Node` class definition and a test function that creates a BST, calls `treeToDoublyList`, and verifies the structure of the doubly linked list.

Code 9.13: Test Code for treeToDoublyList

```python
class Node:
    def __init__(self, val=0, left=None, right=None):
        self.val = val
        self.left = left
        self.right = right

def print_doubly_linked_list(head):
    # Helper function to print the doubly linked list in a
    circular manner
    if not head:
        return "Empty list"
    result = []
    current = head
    while True:
        result.append(current.val)
        current = current.right
        if current == head:
            break
    return " <-> ".join(map(str, result))

def test_tree_to_doubly_list():
    # Create a BST
    #         4
    #        / \
    #       2   5
    #      / \
    #     1   3
    root = Node(4)
    root.left = Node(2)
    root.right = Node(5)
    root.left.left = Node(1)
    root.left.right = Node(3)

    # Initialize Solution
    solution = Solution()

    # Convert BST to sorted circular doubly linked list
    head = solution.treeToDoublyList(root)

    # Print the result in a circular linked list format
    print("Doubly Linked List:",
    print_doubly_linked_list(head))

# Run the test function
test_tree_to_doubly_list()
```

9.6.7 Explanation of the Test Function

1. Tree Creation:
   - We create a BST with nodes 4, 2, 5, 1, and 3.
   - The structure is as follows:

2. Testing:
   - We create an instance of `Solution` and call `treeToDoublyList` with the root of the BST.
   - The function `print_doubly_linked_list` is a helper to print the circular doubly linked list by traversing it in a circular fashion.

3. Expected Output:
   - For the above tree, the expected output of the doubly linked list is:
     Doubly Linked List: 1 <-> 2 <-> 3 <-> 4 <-> 5
   - Since it's a circular list, the head's left pointer should point to the last node (5), and the last node's right pointer should point back to the head (1).

9.6.8 Conclusion

The provided code effectively converts a BST into a sorted circular doubly linked list using inorder traversal. The test function confirms that the solution accuracy, and the helper function `print_doubly_linked_list` allows us to verifies the circular structure of the linked list.

Chapter 10
Some Other Tree Structures

10.1 Prefix Tree

A Trie, or prefix tree, is a tree data structure designed to retrieve keys in a string dataset. This highly efficient data structure has a variety of applications, such as: Autocomplete, Spell check and IP Route (Longest Prefix Matching).

10.1.1 Why Use a Trie (Prefix Tree) Over Other Data Structures?

While balanced trees and hash tables allow efficient search operations, a Trie (or prefix tree) offers unique advantages in specific scenarios, especially in handling strings. Here are the primary reasons:

1. **Efficiently Finding All Keys with a Common Prefix**
   - **Hash Table Limitation**: Hash tables are efficient in finding exact keys with $O(1)$ time complexity on average. However, finding all keys that share a common prefix is challenging and inefficient with hash tables.
   - **Trie Advantage**: With a Trie, finding all keys that share a common prefix can be done in $O(m)$ time complexity, where mmm is the length of the prefix. The Trie structure inherently supports prefix-based search, making it ideal for applications like autocomplete or prefix matching.
2. **Enumerating Strings in Lexicographic Order**
   - **Balanced Tree Limitation**: While balanced trees can also enumerate strings in lexicographic order, they may not be as space-efficient when dealing with a large number of strings with similar prefixes.

- **Trie Advantage**: A Trie naturally supports lexicographic ordering of strings by traversing its nodes in a preorder manner. This allows for easy enumeration of strings in sorted order, which is useful in applications like dictionary implementations.

3. **Handling Hash Conflicts in Large Datasets**
   - **Hash Table Limitation**: As the size of a hash table grows, the risk of hash collisions increases. Collisions can degrade the time complexity of searches, potentially leading to O(n) time complexity, where nnn is the number of keys inserted. This can be problematic in cases where there are many keys with similar prefixes.
   - **Trie Advantage**: Tries avoid hash conflicts entirely. The tree structure inherently organizes words based on their character sequences, eliminating the need for hash functions and reducing the risk of performance degradation as the dataset grows.

4. **Space Efficiency for Keys with Common Prefixes**
   - **Hash Table Limitation**: Hash tables store each key separately, which can lead to higher memory usage, especially when many keys share common prefixes. For example, keys like "apple," "app," and "application" are stored independently in a hash table, leading to redundant storage.
   - **Trie Advantage**: Tries can be more space-efficient for storing keys with common prefixes. They use a shared path for keys that begin with the same characters, saving memory and reducing redundancy. In such cases, the time complexity for insertion and search remains O(m)O(m)O(m), where mmm is the length of the key.

Overall, while balanced trees and hash tables are suitable for many applications, a Trie is more efficient for:

- Searching for keys with a common prefix
- Enumerating strings in lexicographic order
- Avoiding hash conflicts and providing consistent performance as the dataset grows
- Saving space when storing many keys with common prefixes

In summary, the Trie offers advantages in scenarios where prefix matching, lexicographic ordering, or space-efficient storage of similar keys are important. Its time complexity for operations is O(m), where m is the length of the key, making it efficient for string-based applications.

10.1.2 Data Structure of the Prefix Tree (Trie)

A prefix tree, also known as a Trie, is a specialized tree-like data structure used to store and manage a large set of strings efficiently. It is particularly useful for searching words based on prefixes and storing keys that share similar prefixes, making it an optimal choice for applications like autocomplete and dictionary search.

10.1.2.1 Structure of a Trie Node

Each node in the Trie has the following properties:

1. **Children**: Each node can have up to **R links** to its child nodes, where each link corresponds to one of the **R character values** in the dataset's alphabet. Here, we assume **R = 26**, representing each lowercase letter in the Latin alphabet (a to z). The child nodes are stored in a dictionary, with keys as characters and values as Trie nodes.
2. **End of Word** Marker (`isWord`): A Boolean field that specifies whether the node represents the end of a valid word in the Trie. If `isWord` is `True`, then the path from the root to this node represents a complete word. Otherwise, it only represents a prefix of one or more words.

10.1.2.2 Code Representation of the Trie Node

Below is a Python code implementation for a Trie node:

Code 10.1: Python Code for TrieNode

```python
class TrieNode:
    def __init__(self):
        # Dictionary to store children where each key is
        a character and each value is a TrieNode
        self.children = {} # e.g., {'a': TrieNode(),
        'b': TrieNode()}

        # Boolean to indicate if the node marks the end
        of a word
        self.isWord = False
```

10.1.2.3 Common Operations in a Trie

The two most common operations in a Trie are inserting a word and searching for a word. Let's look at each of these operations briefly:

10.1.2.4 Insert a Word

To insert a word into a Trie, start from the root node and follow the path represented by each character in the word:

- For each character in the word, check if it already exists as a child of the current node.
  - If it doesn't exist, create a new node for that character.
  - Move to the child node corresponding to the character.
- Once all characters are processed, mark the last node as the end of a word by setting isWord = True.

10.1.2.5 Search for a Word

To search for a word in a Trie, you start from the root and follow the path represented by each character in the word:

- For each character in the word, check if it exists as a child of the current node.
  - If it doesn't exist, return False (word not found).
  - If it exists, move to the child node corresponding to the character.
- After processing all characters, check if the last node is marked as an end of a word (isWord = True). If so, return True (word found), otherwise return False.

10.1.2.6 Example of Trie Implementation

Here is a basic example of a Trie class with insert and search methods:

Code 10.2: Python Code for Trie

```python
class Trie:
    def __init__(self):
        # Initialize the root node
        self.root = TrieNode()

    def insert(self, word):
        node = self.root
        for char in word:
            # Check if the character exists in the
            current node's children
            if char not in node.children:
                # Create a new node for the character if
                it does not exist
                node.children[char] = TrieNode()
            # Move to the next node
            node = node.children[char]
        # Mark the last node as the end of a word
        node.isWord = True

    def search(self, word):
        node = self.root
        for char in word:
            # Check if the character exists in the
            current node's children
            if char not in node.children:
                return False  # Word not found
            # Move to the next node
            node = node.children[char]
        # Return True if the last node is the end
        of a word
        return node.isWord
```

10.1.2.7 Summary

- **Trie Nodes** have a dictionary for children nodes and a boolean to mark the end of a word.
- The **Insert Operation** involves traversing or creating nodes along the path of the word and marking the final node as an end of the word.
- The **Search Operation** involves traversing nodes based on the characters of the word and checking if the final node is marked as the end of a word.

Using a Trie allows efficient storage and lookup of words, especially for operations involving prefixes and lexicographic order. This makes it highly effective for applications like autocompletion, spell-checking, and word validation in large datasets.

10.1.3 Example 1: Add and Search for Words

10.1.3.1 Problem

Design a data structure that supports the following two operations:
- Void addWord(word);
- Bool search(word);

You can search for only the letters a-z or ". A literal word or regular expression string. Indicates that it can represent any letter.

Example

```
addWord("bad")
addWord("dad")
addWord("mad")
search("pad") -> false
search("bad") -> true
search(".ad") -> true
search("b..") -> true
```

10.1.3.2 Solution Using Trie

To solve this, we will use a Trie structure with some modifications:

1. Each node will have a dictionary to store its children, where keys are characters and values are Trie nodes.
2. A boolean `isWord` in each node will indicate if a particular node represents the end of a valid word.
3. In the `search` function, we use Depth-First Search (DFS) to traverse nodes when encountering the . wildcard, allowing us to explore all possible paths for matching.

10.1 Prefix Tree

10.1.3.3 Code Implementation

Code 10.3: Python Code for add/search Words

```python
class TrieNode:
    def __init__(self):
        # Dictionary to hold children nodes where keys
        # are characters
        self.children = {}
        # Boolean flag to mark end of a word
        self.isWord = False

class WordDictionary:
    def __init__(self):
        """
        Initialize your data structure here.
        """
        # Root of the Trie
        self.root = TrieNode()

    def addWord(self, word: str) -> None:
        """
        Adds a word into the data structure.
        """
        cur = self.root
        for c in word:
            # Create a new TrieNode if character is
            # not present
            if c not in cur.children:
                cur.children[c] = TrieNode()
            # Move to the next node
            cur = cur.children[c]
        # Mark the end of the word
        cur.isWord = True

    def search(self, word: str) -> bool:
        """
        Search a literal word or a regex pattern with '.'
        as any character.
        """
        # Depth-First Search function for matching
        # patterns
```

```
def dfs(i, cur):
    # If we've checked all characters in 'word'
    if i == len(word):
        return cur.isWord
    # If current character is '.'
    if word[i] == '.':
        # Try all possible paths
        for child in cur.children.values():
            if dfs(i + 1, child):
                return True
        return False
    else:
        # If current character is in children,
        continue down that path
        if word[i] not in cur.children:
            return False
        return dfs(i + 1, cur.children[word[i]])

return dfs(0, self.root)
```

10.1.3.4 Explanation of `search` Function

- The `search` method uses DFS to handle cases where the character is a ..
- If we encounter . in the search word, we recursively search all possible child nodes at that position, simulating any possible letter.
- If the character is not . and is not in the children of the current node, the search fails for that path.
- If we reach the end of the word (all characters processed) and the current node's `isWord` is `True`, we return `True`.

10.1.3.5 Optimization Suggestion: Adding . Markers

The suggestion to add . markers at each level during insertion could theoretically speed up searches involving wildcards by reducing the number of recursive calls during searches. Here's how it might work:

- When adding a word like "cat", in addition to inserting "`c`", "`a`", and "`t`" at each level, we also add a "`.`" entry at each level:
  - First level: `c`, .
  - Second level: `a`, .
  - Third level: `t`, .

10.1 Prefix Tree

This way, when a . is encountered in the search, we can directly follow the . marker if it exists, reducing the need to explore all children.

10.1.3.6 Code with Optimization

The optimized version includes additional . markers during insertion.

Code 10.4: Code with Optimization for add/search Words

```python
class TrieNode:
    def __init__(self):
        self.children = {}
        self.isWord = False

class WordDictionary:
    def __init__(self):
        self.root = TrieNode()

    def addWord(self, word: str) -> None:
        cur = self.root
        for c in word:
            # Add both the character and the "." marker
            at each level
            if c not in cur.children:
                cur.children[c] = TrieNode()
            if '.' not in cur.children:
                cur.children['.'] = TrieNode()
            cur = cur.children[c]
        cur.isWord = True

    def search(self, word: str) -> bool:
        def dfs(i, cur):
            if i == len(word):
                return cur.isWord
            if word[i] == '.':
                # Directly follow the "." marker if
                it exists
                if '.' in cur.children and dfs(i + 1,
                cur.children['.']):
                    return True
                # Otherwise, explore all other
                child paths
```

```
                for child in cur.children.values():
                    if dfs(i + 1, child):
                        return True
                return False
            else:
                if word[i] not in cur.children:
                    return False
                return dfs(i + 1, cur.children[word[i]])

        return dfs(0, self.root)
```

10.1.3.7 Explanation of Optimization

In the optimized version:

- Each node also includes a "." child, so that when a wildcard search for . is performed, the search can quickly follow the "." path if available, without needing to try all paths.
- This can potentially reduce the number of recursive calls, making the search operation faster when . wildcards are heavily used.

10.1.3.8 Summary

This Trie-based solution, combined with the optional optimization, allows efficient handling of add and search operations, even with the wildcard . feature. The optimization improves performance by using "." markers during insertion to streamline wildcard searches, making this approach more efficient for applications with a high frequency of wildcard search queries.

10.2 Segment Tree

The segment tree is a powerful data structure that allows efficient range queries and updates on an array. This includes operations like finding the sum, minimum, or maximum value in a given range, and updating an element within that range. Below is a detailed analysis of the segment tree structure, along with comments on each function in the provided code.

10.2 Segment Tree

10.2.1 Characteristics of Segment Tree

1. **Efficient Range Queries**: Segment trees enable efficient range queries (like sum, min, max) with a time complexity of O(logn).
2. **Efficient Updates**: They allow efficient point and range updates with O(logn) complexity.
3. **Memory Efficiency**: Segment trees use O(n) memory space.
4. **Recursive Structure**: Segment trees are built using recursive divide-and-conquer techniques, dividing the array into segments and building a tree structure based on these segments.

10.2.2 Code Analysis and Explanation

The code provided is a class-based implementation of a segment tree, with functionalities to construct the tree, perform range queries (sum, minimum, maximum), and update the tree nodes.

10.2.3 Class Node

The Node class represents a single node in the segment tree. Each node has the following properties:

- **left and right**: References to the left and right children of the node.
- **min, max, and sum**: Store the minimum, maximum, and sum of values within the segment represented by the node.
- **leftEdge and rightEdge**: Represent the range of the array segment this node covers.

```
class Node:
    def __init__(self):
        self.left = None
        self.right = None
        self.min = float("inf")
        self.max = float("-inf")
        self.sum = float("inf")
        self.leftEdge = None
        self.rightEdge = None
```

10.2.4 Class `SegmentTree`

The `SegmentTree` class provides the functionality for constructing the segment tree, updating values, and querying the range (sum, min, max).

10.2.5 Initialization

```
class SegmentTree:
    def __init__(self):
        self.partial_overlap = "Partial overlap"
        self.no_overlap = "No overlap"
        self.complete_overlap = "Complete overlap"
```

The `SegmentTree` class initializes with three types of overlap labels to identify the type of overlap between the query range and the node range:

1. **Complete Overlap**: The node range completely falls within the query range.
2. **No Overlap**: The node range and query range do not intersect.
3. **Partial Overlap**: The node range and query range partially overlap.

10.2.6 Method `get_overlap`

This function determines the type of overlap between the current node's range and the query range.

Code 10.5: Python Code for get_overlap

```python
def get_overlap(self, x1, y1, x2, y2):
    if (x1 == x2 and y1 == y2) or (x1 >= x2 and y1 <= y2):
        overlap = self.complete_overlap
    elif (y1 < x2) or (x1 > y2):
        overlap = self.no_overlap
    else:
        overlap = self.partial_overlap
    return overlap
```

10.2 Segment Tree

This method helps optimize query performance by avoiding unnecessary recursion when there is no overlap.

10.2.7 Method `construct_segment_tree`

The `construct_segment_tree` function recursively builds the segment tree from the input array.

Code 10.6: Python Code for `construct_segment_tree`

```python
def construct_segment_tree(self, array, start, end):
    if end - start <= 0 or len(array) == 0:
        return None
    if end - start == 1:
        # Leaf node representing a single element
        node = Node()
        node.min = array[start]
        node.max = array[start]
        node.sum = array[start]
        node.leftEdge = start
        node.rightEdge = end - 1
        return node
    else:
        # Internal node with recursive construction of
        left and right children
        node = Node()
        mid = start + (end - start) // 2
        node.left = self.construct_segment_tree(array,
        start=start, end=mid)
        node.right = self.construct_segment_tree(array,
        start=mid, end=end)

        # Setting node properties based on children
        if node.left and node.right:
            node.min = min(node.left.min, node.right.min)
            node.max = max(node.left.max, node.right.max)
            node.sum = node.left.sum + node.right.sum
        elif node.left:
            node.min = node.left.min
            node.max = node.left.max
            node.sum = node.left.sum
```

```
        elif node.right:
            node.min = node.right.min
            node.max = node.right.max
            node.sum = node.right.sum

        node.leftEdge = start
        node.rightEdge = end - 1
        return node
```

- **Leaf Nodes**: Represent individual elements of the array.
- **Internal Nodes**: Represent aggregated values (min, max, sum) of segments by combining information from child nodes.

10.2.8 Method `update_segment_tree`

This method updates the segment tree when an element in the array is modified.

Code 10.7: Python Code for update_segment_tree

```
def update_segment_tree(self, head, index, new_
value, array):
    if index == head.leftEdge == head.rightEdge:
        head.max = new_value
        head.min = new_value
        head.sum = new_value
        array[index] = new_value
        return head
    elif head.leftEdge <= index <= head.rightEdge:
        left_node = self.update_segment_tree(head=head.
        left, index=index, new_value=new_value,
        array=array)
        right_node = self.update_segment_tree(head=head.
        right, index=index, new_value=new_value,
        array=array)
        head.sum = left_node.sum + right_node.sum
        head.min = min(left_node.min, right_node.min)
        head.max = max(left_node.max, right_node.max)
        return head
    return head
```

10.2 Segment Tree

- The function uses recursion to locate the node corresponding to the updated index and modifies its min, max, and sum values.
- After updating the specific leaf node, the changes propagate back up to the root, ensuring the segment tree remains accurate.

10.2.9 Range Query Methods (get_minimum, get_maximum, get_sum)

These methods perform range queries on the segment tree:

- **get_minimum**: Finds the minimum value within a given range.
- **get_maximum**: Finds the maximum value within a given range.
- **get_sum**: Computes the sum of values within a given range.

Each of these methods leverages the get_overlap function to determine the overlap type and optimize the query.

Code 10.8: Python Code for get_minimum

```python
def get_minimum(self, head, left, right):
    overlap = self.get_overlap(head.leftEdge, head.rightEdge, left, right)
    if overlap == self.complete_overlap:
        return head.min
    elif overlap == self.no_overlap:
        return float("inf")
    else:
        left_min = self.get_minimum(head=head.left,
            left=left, right=right)
        right_min = self.get_minimum(head=head.right,
            left=left, right=right)
        return min(left_min, right_min)
```

Similarly, get_maximum and get_sum follow the same structure.

10.2.10 Method preorder_traversal

This method performs a preorder traversal to print the contents of each segment.

Code 10.9: Python Code for `preorder_traversal`

```
def preorder_traversal(self, head, array):
    if head is None:
        return
    print("Array = {} Min = {}, Max = {}, Sum = {}".
    format(array[head.leftEdge:head.rightEdge + 1],
    head.min,
                    head.max, head.sum))
    self.preorder_traversal(head=head.left, array=array)
    self.preorder_traversal(head=head.right, array=array)
```

10.2.11 Example Usage

The main function demonstrates how to construct the tree, perform updates, and execute range queries.

Code 10.10: Test Code for Segment Tree

```
if __name__ == "__main__":
    arr = [10, 20, 30, 40, 50, 60, 70]
    st = SegmentTree()
    root = st.construct_segment_tree(array=arr, start=0,
    end=len(arr))
    left_index = 0
    right_index = 4
    update_index = 0
    update_value = 200
    print(st.get_sum(head=root, left=left_index,
    right=right_index))
    print(st.get_minimum(head=root, left=left_index,
    right=right_index))
    st.update_segment_tree(head=root, index=update_index,
    new_value=update_value, array=arr)
    print(st.get_maximum(head=root, left=left_index,
    right=right_index))
    st.preorder_traversal(root, arr)
```

10.2.12 Complexity Analysis

- **Time Complexity for Queries and Updates**: O(logn) for each operation due to the recursive nature of segment trees and halving the array at each step.
- **Space Complexity**: O(n) as each segment requires a node in the tree.

10.2.13 Summary

This implementation provides a flexible segment tree that supports efficient range queries and updates, with clear recursive logic for both construction and query handling. It's ideal for scenarios that require frequent updates and range-based calculations, such as competitive programming and real-time analytics.

10.3 Binary Index Tree

10.3.1 Problem Overview

Given an array `arr[0..n-1]`, we need to:

1. Calculate the sum of elements from the beginning of the array up to a specified index `i`.
2. Update the value of an element at a specified index `i` to a new value `x`.

We are aiming to perform these operations efficiently:

- **Query operation** (sum of elements): Ideally, this should be faster than the naive approach of iterating through elements, which takes `O(n)`.
- **Update operation**: Ideally, this should also be faster than re-computing prefix sums after each update.

10.3.2 Why Binary Indexed Tree?

A Binary Indexed Tree (BIT), also known as a Fenwick Tree, is a data structure that allows us to perform both update and prefix sum operations in `O(log n)` time. This is achieved by leveraging the binary representation of indices to store and retrieve cumulative sums for efficiently computed ranges.

A BIT is generally simpler to implement and requires less space compared to other data structures like Segment Trees for similar tasks.

10.3.3 How BIT Works

The BIT array `BITree[]` is an auxiliary structure where each index `i` in `BITree[]` stores the sum of a specific range of elements in `arr[]`. Each element of `BITree[]` only keeps track of a partial sum, which is enough to retrieve any prefix sum efficiently.

The range that each `BITree[i]` covers can be understood based on the binary representation of `i`. Specifically:

- **Adding** an index `i` to the BITree involves incrementing values in specific ancestor nodes.
- **Querying** for a prefix sum involves combining values from specific ancestor nodes.

10.3.4 Time Complexity

- **Space Complexity**: `O(N)`, where n is the size of the input array `arr[]`.
- **Update Operation**: `O(logN)`.
- **Query Operation**: `O(logN)`.

10.3.5 Core Operations of BIT

1. **Update**: Adds a value to the element at index `i` in `arr[]` and updates the necessary nodes in `BITree`.
2. **Query** (Prefix Sum): Computes the sum of elements from the beginning of the array up to index `i` by aggregating values in `BITree`.

10.3.6 Pseudocode Explanation

10.3.6.1 getSum() Operation

The `getSum(x)` function calculates the sum of `arr[0]` to `arr[x]`:

1. Initialize `sum = 0`.
2. Set `index = x + 1` (since BIT indices are 1-based).
3. While `index > 0`:
    - Add `BITree[index]` to `sum`.
    - Move to the parent node by updating `index = index - (index & -index)` (removes the last set bit).
4. Return `sum`.

10.3 Binary Index Tree

10.3.6.2 updateBIT() Operation

The `updateBIT(x, val)` function updates `arr[x]` by adding `val`:

1. Set `index = x + 1`.
2. While `index <= n`:
   - Add `val` to `BITree[index]`.
   - Move to the next node by updating `index = index + (index & -index)` (adds the last set bit).

10.3.6.3 Range Sum

To get the sum of elements in a range `[l, r]`, use:

```
rangeSum(l, r) = getSum(r) - getSum(l - 1)
```

10.3.7 Code Implementation in Python

Here's a Python implementation of Binary Indexed Tree using the above logic:

Code 10.11: Python Implementation of Binary Indexed Tree (BIT)

```python
# Python implementation of Binary Indexed Tree (BIT)

# Function to get the sum of arr[0] to arr[index]
def getSum(BITree, index):
    sum = 0  # Initialize the result
    index += 1  # BITree is 1-based index

    # Traverse ancestors in BITree
    while index > 0:
        sum += BITree[index]   # Add current element in
        BITree to sum
        index -= index & (-index)  # Move to parent node
    return sum

# Function to update the BITree with value 'val' at
index 'i'
```

```python
def updateBIT(BITree, n, index, val):
    index += 1  # BITree is 1-based index

    # Traverse all ancestors and add 'val'
    while index <= n:
        BITree[index] += val
        index += index & (-index)  # Move to the
        next node

# Function to construct and return a BITree for a
given array
def constructBITree(arr, n):
    BITree = [0] * (n + 1)  # Create and
    initialize BITree
    # Store the actual array values in BITree
    using update
    for i in range(n):
        updateBIT(BITree, n, i, arr[i])
    return BITree

# Function to get the sum of a range [l, r]
def rangeSum(BITree, l, r):
    return getSum(BITree, r) - getSum(BITree, l - 1)

# Example usage
arr = [2, 1, 1, 3, 2, 3, 4, 5, 6, 7, 8, 9]
n = len(arr)
BITree = constructBITree(arr, n)

print("Sum of elements in arr[0..5] is",
getSum(BITree, 5))

# Update arr[3] by adding 6 to it
arr[3] += 6
updateBIT(BITree, n, 3, 6)

print("Sum of elements in arr[0..5] after update is",
getSum(BITree, 5))

# Get the sum of elements from index 3 to 8
print("Sum of elements in arr[3..8] is",
rangeSum(BITree, 3, 8))
```

10.3.8 Explanation of Code

1. **getSum()**:
   - This function computes the sum from `arr[0]` to `arr[index]`.
   - It traverses up the tree from `index` by removing the last set bit to move to the parent node.

2. **updateBIT()**:
   - This function updates the `BITree` by adding a value `val` to `arr[index]`.
   - It traverses up the tree from `index` by adding the last set bit to move to the next node, ensuring that all affected nodes are updated.

3. **constructBITree()**:
   - Constructs a BITree by initializing all nodes to zero and then using `updateBIT` for each element in `arr`.

4. **rangeSum()**:
   - Calculates the sum in a given range `[l, r]` using the formula `getSum(r) - getSum(l - 1)`.

10.3.9 Output Example

The output for the example array `arr = [2, 1, 1, 3, 2, 3, 4, 5, 6, 7, 8, 9]` will be:

```
Sum of elements in arr[0..5] is 12
Sum of elements in arr[0..5] after update is 18
Sum of elements in arr[3..8] is 27
```

10.3.10 Conclusion

Binary Indexed Trees offer an efficient way to perform both update and query operations on cumulative sums with `O(log n)` complexity, making them suitable for use cases with frequent updates and range queries. The code implementation shows the simplicity and efficiency of BIT operations, and they are especially useful in problems related to cumulative sums and frequency counting.

10.4 Example 2: Count of Smaller Numbers After Self

You will get an array of integers nums, and you will have to return a new array of counts. The counts array has the following property: counts[i] is the number of smaller elements to the right of nums[i].

Example 1
Input: nums = [5,2,6,1]
  Output: [2,1,1,0]
  Illustrate:

- To the right of 5 there are 2 smaller elements (2 and 1).
- To the right of 2 there is only 1 smaller element (1).
- To the right of 6 there is 1 smaller element (1).
- There are 0 smaller elements to the right of 1.

This problem can indeed be efficiently solved using different approaches such as a Binary Indexed Tree (BIT), Binary Search, and a Segment Tree. Below, I'll analyze and explain the Binary Indexed Tree (BIT) approach in detail, as well as provide a test function to demonstrate the code implementation. I'll also briefly explain the binary search and segment tree approaches.

10.4.1 Approach: Binary Indexed Tree (BIT)

We can leverage a BIT for this problem due to its efficient handling of prefix sums and updates. This approach involves several steps:

1. **Coordinate Compression**: Map each element in nums to an index in a sorted unique array. This step is necessary because BIT requires indices that are consecutive integers starting from 1.
2. **BIT Operations**:
    - **Query (`sum_query`)**: Get the prefix sum up to a given index. This allows us to count how many elements are smaller than the current element.
    - **Update (`update`)**: Update the BIT when we encounter a new element, increasing the count of elements observed so far.
3. **Processing from Right to Left**: By processing elements from right to left, we can build the BIT as we go, and use the `sum_query` to get the count of smaller elements to the right efficiently.

10.4.2 Code Implementation

Here is the Python implementation using a BIT:

Code 10.12: Python Code for countSmaller

```
from typing import List

class BIT:
    def __init__(self, size):
        self.tree = [0] * (size + 1)

    def sum_query(self, i):
        # Get the sum of all elements from index 0 to i
        result = 0
        i += 1
        while i > 0:
            result += self.tree[i]
            i -= i & -i
        return result

    def update(self, i, delta):
        # Update the BIT by adding delta at index i
        i += 1
        while i < len(self.tree):
            self.tree[i] += delta
            i += i & -i

class Solution:
    def countSmaller(self, nums: List[int]) -> List[int]:
        # Step 1: Coordinate Compression
        sorted_unique_nums = sorted(set(nums))
        rank_map = {val: idx for idx, val in
        enumerate(sorted_unique_nums)}

        # Initialize BIT
        bit = BIT(len(rank_map))

        # Step 2: Traverse from right to left and
        compute counts
        result = []
        for num in reversed(nums):
```

```
                # Get the compressed index for the
                current number
                rank = rank_map[num]
                # Query BIT to find count of elements less
                than the current number
                result.append(bit.sum_query(rank - 1))
                # Update BIT for the current number
                bit.update(rank, 1)

        return result[::-1]
```

10.4.3 Explanation of the Code

1. **Coordinate Compression**: `rank_map` is a dictionary that maps each unique element in `nums` to an index based on its position in the sorted list. This is used to compress the values so they can be indexed in BIT.
2. **BIT Initialization**: We create a BIT of size `len(rank_map)`, which represents the number of unique elements in `nums`.
3. **Counting and Updating**:
    - For each `num` in `nums` (processed from right to left), we:
        - Use `bit.sum_query(rank - 1)` to get the count of elements smaller than `num` that have been encountered so far.
        - Use `bit.update(rank, 1)` to add the current `num` to the BIT.
4. **Result Reversal**: We reverse `result` at the end to get the answer in the correct order, as we processed `nums` from right to left.

10.4.4 Time Complexity

- The coordinate compression step has a time complexity of O(nlogn) due to sorting and dictionary creation.
- BIT operations (`sum_query` and `update`) are each O(logn), and we perform these for each element in `nums`, resulting in an overall time complexity of O(nlogn).

10.4.5 Test Function

Here's a test function to verify the implementation:

10.4 Example 2: Count of Smaller Numbers After Self

Code 10.13: Test Code for countSmaller

```
def main():
    # Example 1
    nums1 = [5, 2, 6, 1]
    solution = Solution()
    result1 = solution.countSmaller(nums1)
    print(f"Input: {nums1}")
    print(f"Output: {result1}")
    print(f"Expected Output: [2, 1, 1, 0]\n")

    # Example 2: Additional test cases
    nums2 = [1, 0, 2, 0]
    result2 = solution.countSmaller(nums2)
    print(f"Input: {nums2}")
    print(f"Output: {result2}")
    print(f"Expected Output: [2, 0, 1, 0]\n")

    # Example 3: Larger input
    nums3 = [7, 8, 5, 2, 1]
    result3 = solution.countSmaller(nums3)
    print(f"Input: {nums3}")
    print(f"Output: {result3}")
    print(f"Expected Output: [3, 3, 2, 1, 0]\n")

main()
```

10.4.6 Expected Output

The output of the `main` function should be:

```
Input: [5, 2, 6, 1]
Output: [2, 1, 1, 0]
Expected Output: [2, 1, 1, 0]

Input: [1, 0, 2, 0]
Output: [2, 0, 1, 0]
Expected Output: [2, 0, 1, 0]

Input: [7, 8, 5, 2, 1]
Output: [3, 3, 2, 1, 0]
Expected Output: [3, 3, 2, 1, 0]
```

10.4.7 Explanation of Other Solutions

1. **Binary Search Solution**:
   - This approach involves maintaining a sorted list and inserting each number in reverse order. The insertion position in this sorted list indicates the number of smaller elements to the right.
   - This solution has a time complexity of $O(n^2)$ due to list insertion.
2. **Segment Tree Solution**:
   - Similar to BIT, but we use a segment tree to handle range queries and updates.
   - It also provides $O(\log n)$ complexity for both updates and range queries, but segment trees are often more complex to implement compared to BIT.

10.4.8 Conclusion

The BIT approach provides an efficient $O(n \log n)$ solution to this problem and balances simplicity with performance. It's particularly useful when handling prefix sums and range updates efficiently.

Chapter 11
Graph

Graphs are used to solve many problems in real life. Graphs can be used to represent networks, which can include city networks, telephone networks, or circuit networks. Graphs can also be used for social networks such as LinkedIn and Facebook. For example, in Facebook, each user is represented by a node, which stores information such as ID, name, gender, and locale.

A graph is a nonlinear data structure composed of nodes and edges, sometimes called vertices, which are lines or arcs that connect any two nodes in a graph. A graph can be thought of as consisting of a finite set of vertices (or nodes) and a set of edges that connect a pair of nodes. For example, in Fig. 11.1, vertex set V = {0,1,2,3,4} and edge set E = {01,12,23,34,04,14,13}.

The most commonly used representations of graph representations are: (1) Adjacency matrix, (2) Adjacency table. There are also other representations, such as the Event Matrix and the Event List. The choice of graph representation depends on the situation, mainly on the type of operation performed and the ease of use.

Fig. 11.1 An example of a graph

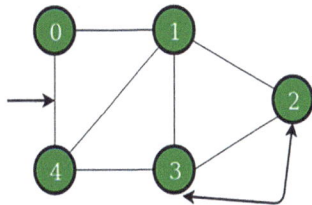

11.1 Representation of the Graph

11.1.1 Adjacency Matrices

An adjacency matrix is a two-dimensional array of size V×V, where V is the number of vertices in the graph. Assuming that the two-dimensional array is adj[][], then the slot adj[i][j] = 1 means that there is an edge from vertex i to vertex j. The adjacency matrices of undirected graphs are always symmetrical. Adjacency matrices are also used to represent weighted graphs, for example: if adj[i][j] = w, then the weight from vertex i to vertex j is the edge of w (Fig. 11.2).

Pros: This notation is easier to implement and follow, and it takes O(1) time to remove edges. For example, the query for the existence of edges from vertex "u" to vertex "v" is valid, and it takes time to execute O(1).

Cons: Takes up more space O(V2). Even if the graph is sparse (contains fewer edges), it will take up the same amount of space. Adding a vertex is O(V2) time.

11.1.2 Adjacency Table

Use a linked list array, where the size of the array is equal to the number of vertices. Let the array be array[], and the array[i] represents the linked list of vertices adjacent to the i-th vertex. This representation can also be used to represent weighted charts. The weights of edges can be expressed as pairwise linked lists. Figure 11.3 shows the adjacency table in Fig. 11.2.

Fig. 11.2 The adjacency matrix representation of the graph

	0	1	2	3	4
0	0	1	0	0	1
1	1	0	1	1	1
2	0	1	0	1	0
3	0	1	1	0	1
4	1	1	0	1	0

11.1 Representation of the Graph

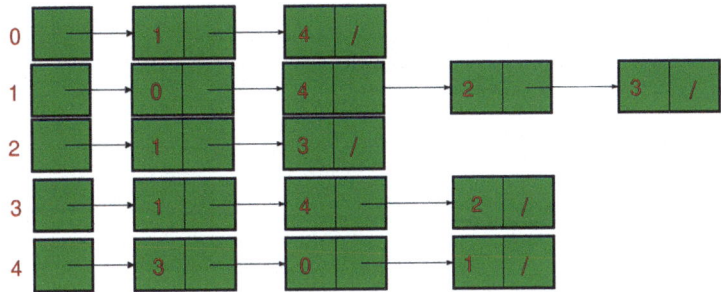

Fig. 11.3 The adjacency linked list representation of the diagram

Code 11.1: The Adjacency Table Representation of the Graph

```
"""
A list representation of a Python program diagram that
demonstrates adjacencies
"""

# Represents a class of node adjacency tables
class AdjNode:
    def __init__(self, data):
        self.vertex = data
        self.next = None

# A graph is a list of adjacency tables. The size of the
array will be the number of vertices "V".
class Graph:
    def __init__(self, vertices):
        self.V = vertices
        self.graph = [None] * self.V

    # The ability to add edges to undirected graphs
    def add_edge(self, src, dest):
        # Add the node to the source node
        node = AdjNode(dest)
        node.next = self.graph[src]
        self.graph[src] = node

        # Add the source node as a target
        node = AdjNode(src)
        node.next = self.graph[dest]
        self.graph[dest] = node
```

```python
        # The ability to print graphics
        def print_graph(self):
            for i in range(self. V):
                print("Adjacency list of vertex {}\n head".
                    format(i), end="")
                temp = self.graph[i]
                while temp:
                    print(" -> {}".format(temp.
                        vertex), end="")
                    temp = temp.next
                print(" \n")
# Drivers of the above picture
if __name__ == "__main__":
    V = 5
    graph = Graph(V)
    graph.add_edge(0, 1)
    graph.add_edge(0, 4)
    graph.add_edge(1, 2)
    graph.add_edge(1, 3)
    graph.add_edge(1, 4)
    graph.add_edge(2, 3)
    graph.add_edge(3, 4)

    graph.print_graph()
```

Results:

```
Adjacency list of vertex 0
 head -> 4 -> 1

Adjacency list of vertex 1
 head -> 4 -> 3 -> 2 -> 0

Adjacency list of vertex 2
 head -> 3 -> 1

Adjacency list of vertex 3
 head -> 4 -> 2 -> 1

Adjacency list of vertex 4
 head -> 3 -> 1 -> 0
```

11.2 Example 1: Clone Graph

11.2.1 Problem

Given a reference to a node in the undirected graph that joins the connection, a deep copy (clone) of the graph is returned.

11.2.2 Problem Analysis

The input is a **reference to a node in an undirected graph**, and the goal is to return a **deep copy** of the graph. This means that:

1. Each node in the cloned graph should have the same value as the corresponding node in the original graph.
2. Each node in the cloned graph should have the same neighbors as the corresponding node in the original graph.
3. The structure of the graph should be maintained, so the cloned graph should be a true copy of the original.

Key Challenges
- The graph is **undirected**.
- There can be cycles in the graph.
- Each node can have multiple neighbors, and multiple nodes may refer to the same neighbor.

To solve this problem, we need to maintain a **mapping** between nodes in the original graph and nodes in the cloned graph. This mapping helps ensure that:

- Each node is only cloned once.
- We can efficiently retrieve the cloned node when establishing connections in the new graph.

11.2.3 BFS Solution

Using Breadth-First Search (BFS) allows us to iteratively clone each node layer by layer.

11.2.3.1 BFS Algorithm

1. Initialize a **queue** with the input node and a **hash table** (`vis`) to map each original node to its clone.
2. For each node in the queue:
   (a) Pop the node from the queue and get its neighbors.
   (b) For each neighbor:
   - If the neighbor has not been cloned (not in `vis`), create a clone of the neighbor and add it to the hash table.
   - Add the cloned neighbor to the cloned node's neighbors list.
   - Enqueue the original neighbor if it hasn't been processed yet.
3. Continue this until all nodes are processed and return the clone of the input node.

Here is the BFS code with comments explaining each step:

Code 11.2: Python Code for cloneGraph Using the BFS Algorithm

```python
from collections import deque, defaultdict

class Node:
    def __init__(self, val=0, neighbors=None):
        self.val = val
        self.neighbors = neighbors if neighbors is not None else []

class Solution:
    def cloneGraph(self, node: 'Node') -> 'Node':
        if node is None:
            return None

        # Queue to perform BFS traversal
        q = deque()
        q.append(node)

        # Hash table to store the mapping of original
        node to the cloned node
        vis = defaultdict()
        vis[node] = Node(node.val)
```

11.2 Example 1: Clone Graph

```
            # BFS traversal
            while q:
                front = q.popleft()   # Pop the first element
                for child in front.neighbors:
                    # If the neighbor has not been cloned yet
                    if child not in vis:
                        vis[child] = Node(child.val)    #
                        Create a new node (clone)
                        q.append(child)                  # Add
                        neighbor to queue
                    vis[front].neighbors.append(vis[child])
                    # Append cloned neighbor to the cloned
                    node's neighbors

            return vis[node]   # Return the clone of the
            input node
```

11.2.4 *DFS Solution*

The DFS approach uses recursion to perform a deep copy of the graph. It is useful for graphs with a structure that can be easily traversed in a depth-first manner.

11.2.4.1 DFS Algorithm

1. Use a **hash table** (`table`) to map each original node to its clone.
2. Define a recursive **DFS function** that:
    (a) Checks if the node has been cloned. If it has, return the cloned node.
    (b) If not, clone the node and store it in the hash table.
    (c) Recursively process each neighbor, cloning and linking them to the current node's neighbors.
3. Call the DFS function with the input node to start cloning.

    Here is the DFS code with comments explaining each step:

Code 11.3: Python Code for cloneGraph Using the DFS Algorithm

```python
class Solution:
    def cloneGraph(self, node: 'Node') -> 'Node':
        # Hash table to store cloned nodes
        table = {}

        def dfs(node):
            if not node:  # Base case for empty node
                return node
            elif node in table:  # If node is already cloned
                return table[node]
            else:
                ans = Node(node.val)  # Create a new node (clone)
                table[node] = ans     # Store in hash table
                for n in node.neighbors:  # Recursively clone neighbors
                    ans.neighbors.append(dfs(n))
                return ans

        return dfs(node)  # Start DFS traversal
```

11.2.5 Complexity Analysis

Both BFS and DFS solutions have:

- **Time Complexity**: O(N+E), where N is the number of nodes and E is the number of edges in the graph. This is because each node and edge is processed once.
- **Space Complexity**: O(N), for the hash table that stores the cloned nodes.

11.2.6 Test Case and Node Class

To test the code, we need a function that creates a graph, invokes `cloneGraph`, and verifies the cloned structure.

11.2 Example 1: Clone Graph

Code 11.4: Test Code for cloneGraph

```python
def build_graph():
    # Create a sample graph with the following structure:
    #     1 -- 2
    #     |    |
    #     4 -- 3
    node1 = Node(1)
    node2 = Node(2)
    node3 = Node(3)
    node4 = Node(4)
    node1.neighbors = [node2, node4]
    node2.neighbors = [node1, node3]
    node3.neighbors = [node2, node4]
    node4.neighbors = [node1, node3]
    return node1  # Return the reference to node 1

def print_graph(node):
    # Print the graph in a BFS manner for verification
    visited = set()
    q = deque([node])
    result = []
    while q:
        curr = q.popleft()
        if curr in visited:
            continue
        visited.add(curr)
        result.append((curr.val, [neighbor.val for
        neighbor in curr.neighbors]))
        for neighbor in curr.neighbors:
            if neighbor not in visited:
                q.append(neighbor)
    return result

def test_cloneGraph():
    # Build a sample graph
    original_graph = build_graph()

    # Print the original graph structure
    print("Original graph:", print_graph(original_graph))

    # Initialize Solution
    solution = Solution()
```

```
# Clone the graph using BFS or DFS solution
cloned_graph = solution.cloneGraph(original_graph)

# Print the cloned graph structure
print("Cloned graph:", print_graph(cloned_graph))

# The structures of the original and cloned graphs
should match
assert print_graph(original_graph) == print_
graph(cloned_graph), "The cloned graph structure does
not match the original."

# Run the test function
test_cloneGraph()
```

11.2.7 Explanation of the Test Function

1. **Graph Creation**:

    (a) We create a small undirected graph with four nodes.

    (b) The graph structure is:

    ```
            1 -- 2
            |    |
            4 -- 3
    ```

2. **Testing**:

    (a) The `build_graph` function constructs this graph.

    (b) We then use the `print_graph` function to verify the graph structure by printing each node and its neighbors in a BFS manner.

    (c) The `test_cloneGraph` function clones the graph using `Solution.cloneGraph()` and checks if the structure of the cloned graph matches the original graph.

3. **Expected Output**:

    (a) The output should confirm that the cloned graph has the same structure as the original graph.

11.2.8 Conclusion

Both the BFS and DFS solutions are efficient for cloning undirected graphs and handle cycles and repeated nodes properly. The test function ensures that the cloned graph has the correct structure, verifying the integrity of the clone.

11.3 Example 2: Graph Validation Tree

11.3.1 Problem

Given n nodes labeled from 0 to n − 1 and a series of undirected edges (each edge is a pair of nodes), write a function to check if these edges form a valid tree.

Example 1
Input: n = 5, edge = [[0,1],[0,2],[0,3],[1,4]].
  Output: True

Example 2
Input: n = 5, edge = [[0, 1],[1, 2],[2, 3],[1, 3],[1, 4]].
  Output: False
  Note: It can be assumed that there will be no duplicates in the edges. Since all edges are undirectional, [0,1] is the same as [1,0], and [0,1] and [1,0] do not appear in the edges at the same time.

There are three different methods that can be used to solve this problem: DFS, BFS, and Union Find.

11.3.2 DFS Solution

The main steps involved are:

1. **Building the Adjacency List**: We start by representing the graph using an adjacency list. Each node points to a list of its neighboring nodes.
2. **Using DFS for Cycle Detection and Connectivity**:
   (a) We start DFS from node 0. If we encounter any node that has already been visited, it means there is a cycle, so we return `False`.
   (b) We use a `visited` array to keep track of visited nodes.
   (c) We also use a `parent` parameter in the DFS helper function to keep track of the previous node. This helps us avoid incorrectly identifying the immediate parent node as part of a cycle.

3. **Check if All Nodes are Visited**:
   (a) After the DFS completes, we check if all nodes are visited. If any node remains unvisited, it means the graph is not fully connected, so we return `False`.
   (b) If all nodes are visited and no cycle is found, we return `True`, indicating that the graph is a valid tree.

   Let's add comments to the provided code to improve readability and clarity.

11.3.2.1 Updated Code with Detailed Comments

Code 11.5: Python Code for Graph Validation Tree

```python
class Solution(object):
    # Function to check if a graph with 'n' nodes and
    edges is a valid tree
    def validTree(self, n, edges):
        # Step 1: Create an adjacency list from the edges
        lookup = collections.defaultdict(list)
        for edge in edges:
            # Add each edge to the adjacency list for
            both nodes
            lookup[edge[0]].append(edge[1])
            lookup[edge[1]].append(edge[0])

        # Step 2: Initialize the visited array to track
        visited nodes
        visited = [False] * n  # Initially, all nodes are
        unvisited

        # Step 3: Use DFS to check for cycles and
        connectivity starting from node 0
        if not self.helper(0, -1, lookup, visited):
            return False  # If a cycle is detected,
            return False

        # Step 4: Check if all nodes are visited (i.e.,
        the graph is fully connected)
        for v in visited:
            if not v:  # If any node is unvisited, it
            means the graph is disconnected
                return False
```

11.3 Example 2: Graph Validation Tree

```
            # If no cycles are found and the graph is
            connected, return True
            return True

        # Helper function for DFS traversal
        # 'curr' is the current node, 'parent' is the
        previous node, 'lookup' is the adjacency list,
        # 'visited' is an array to track visited nodes
        def helper(self, curr, parent, lookup, visited):
            # If the current node is already visited, a cycle
            is detected
            if visited[curr]:
                return False

            # Mark the current node as visited
            visited[curr] = True

            # Recursively visit all neighboring nodes
            for i in lookup[curr]:
                # Skip the parent node to avoid going back
                in the DFS
                if i != parent:
                    # If DFS on the neighbor returns False, a
                    cycle is detected
                    if not self.helper(i, curr, lookup,
                    visited):
                        return False

            # If no cycles are detected, return True
            return True
```

11.3.2.2 Explanation of Each Section

1. **Adjacency List Construction**:

   (a) We use a `defaultdict` to create an adjacency list. This list stores the connections for each node, making it easier to traverse the graph.

2. **Visited Array**:

   (a) We initialize an array called `visited` with `False` values. Each index represents a node, and the value indicates whether the node has been visited.

3. **DFS Traversal (Helper Function)**:
   (a) The `helper` function performs DFS traversal.
   (b) If a node is already visited when we try to visit it again, it means there is a cycle, so we return `False`.
   (c) For each node, we recursively check its neighbors, skipping the immediate parent node to prevent backtracking.
   (d) If we complete DFS without detecting a cycle, we return `True`.

4. **Final Connectivity Check**:
   (a) After DFS completes, we check if all nodes have been visited by inspecting the `visited` array. If any node is unvisited, it means the graph is not fully connected.

11.3.2.3 Test Main Function

Here's a main function to test this DFS-based solution with different test cases:

Code 11.6: Test Code for validTree Using the DFS Solution

```
def main():
    # Instantiate the Solution class
    solution = Solution()

    # Test Case 1: A simple tree (valid tree)
    n1 = 5
    edges1 = [[0, 1], [0, 2], [0, 3], [3, 4]]
    print("Test Case 1:", solution.validTree(n1, edges1))
    # Expected Output: True

    # Test Case 2: A graph with a cycle (not a tree)
    n2 = 5
    edges2 = [[0, 1], [0, 2], [0, 3], [3, 4], [1, 4]]
    print("Test Case 2:", solution.validTree(n2, edges2))
    # Expected Output: False

    # Test Case 3: Disconnected graph (not a tree)
    n3 = 5
    edges3 = [[0, 1], [1, 2], [3, 4]]
    print("Test Case 3:", solution.validTree(n3, edges3))
    # Expected Output: False
```

11.3 Example 2: Graph Validation Tree

```
# Test Case 4: Only one node with no edges
(valid tree)
n4 = 1
edges4 = []
print("Test Case 4:", solution.validTree(n4, edges4))
# Expected Output: True

# Test Case 5: Two nodes connected by one edge
(valid tree)
n5 = 2
edges5 = [[0, 1]]
print("Test Case 5:", solution.validTree(n5, edges5))
# Expected Output: True

# Test Case 6: Two nodes with no edge (not a tree)
n6 = 2
edges6 = []
print("Test Case 6:", solution.validTree(n6, edges6))
# Expected Output: False

# Test Case 7: Multiple nodes with a single line
connection (valid tree)
n7 = 4
edges7 = [[0, 1], [1, 2], [2, 3]]
print("Test Case 7:", solution.validTree(n7, edges7))
# Expected Output: True

# Test Case 8: Multiple nodes with an extra edge
creating a cycle (not a tree)
n8 = 4
edges8 = [[0, 1], [1, 2], [2, 3], [3, 0]]
print("Test Case 8:", solution.validTree(n8, edges8))
# Expected Output: False

# Run the main function to execute test cases
main()
```

11.3.2.4 Explanation of Test Cases

1. **Test Case 1**: A valid tree with no cycles and all nodes connected.
2. **Test Case 2**: A graph with a cycle, which is not a valid tree.
3. **Test Case 3**: A disconnected graph, not all nodes are reachable, so it's not a valid tree.

4. **Test Case 4**: A single node with no edges, which is considered a valid tree.
5. **Test Case 5**: Two nodes connected by one edge, forming a valid tree.
6. **Test Case 6**: Two nodes with no edge, making it disconnected and thus not a valid tree.
7. **Test Case 7**: Multiple nodes connected in a line, which is a valid tree.
8. **Test Case 8**: Multiple nodes with a cycle, which is not a valid tree.

This main function tests the DFS-based solution with various configurations, checking for cycles, connectivity, and edge cases.

11.3.3 BFS Solution

This is a Breadth-First Search (BFS) approach to check if an undirected graph is a valid tree. In this algorithm, we use a queue to facilitate the BFS traversal, and a hash table (`visited`) to keep track of whether a node has already been visited, which helps detect cycles. Additionally, we check that the number of edges is exactly n - 1, which is a necessary condition for the graph to be a tree with n nodes.

Here's a breakdown of each part of the code with comments for clarity:

11.3.3.1 Updated BFS Code with Detailed Comments

Code 11.7: Python Code for validTree Using the BFS Solution

```python
import collections

class Solution(object):
    # Function to check if a graph with 'n' nodes and
    edges is a valid tree
    def validTree(self, n, edges):
        # Condition 1: For a graph to be a tree, it must
        have exactly n - 1 edges.
        if len(edges) != n - 1:
            return False

        # Step 1: Build an adjacency list (neighbors) to
        represent the graph
        neighbors = collections.defaultdict(list)
        for u, v in edges:
```

11.3 Example 2: Graph Validation Tree

```
            neighbors[u].append(v)   # Add 'v' to the
            adjacency list of 'u'
            neighbors[v].append(u)   # Add 'u' to the
            adjacency list of 'v'

    # Step 2: Initialize a dictionary to mark
    visited nodes
    visited = {}

    # Step 3: Initialize a queue for BFS and add the
    starting node (0)
    q = collections.deque([0])

    # Step 4: Perform BFS to detect cycles and ensure
    full connectivity
    while q:
        # Get the current node from the front of
        the queue
        curr = q.popleft()

        # Traverse all neighboring nodes of the
        current node
        for node in neighbors[curr]:
            # If 'node' has not been visited, mark it
            as visited and add it to the queue
            if node not in visited:
                visited[node] = True
                q.append(node)
            else:
                # If 'node' is already in 'visited',
                a cycle is detected
                return False

    # Step 5: Check if all nodes were visited
    # If the number of visited nodes equals 'n', the
    graph is fully connected
    return len(visited) == n
```

11.3.3.2 Explanation of Each Section

1. **Edge Count Check**:
   (a) For an undirected graph to be a tree, it must contain exactly n - 1 edges, where n is the number of nodes. If the edge count is different from n - 1, the graph cannot be a valid tree, so we return False.

2. **Building the Adjacency List**:
   (a) We create an adjacency list (`neighbors`) using a `defaultdict` of lists, where each node points to a list of its connected nodes. This allows easy traversal of each node's neighbors.

3. **Visited Dictionary**:
   (a) We use a dictionary (`visited`) to mark nodes as visited. Unlike a list, a dictionary allows efficient lookups and handles cases where the nodes are non-sequential integers or sparsely populated.

4. **BFS Traversal**:
   (a) We initialize a queue with the starting node (0) and perform BFS traversal.
   (b) For each node (`curr`) we dequeue, we check all its neighbors. If a neighbor (`node`) is not in `visited`, it means it hasn't been visited, so we mark it as visited and enqueue it.
   (c) If a neighbor has already been visited, it means there's a cycle (since it was reached from two different paths), so we return `False`.

5. **Final Check**:
   (a) After BFS traversal, we check if the size of the `visited` dictionary is equal to n. If all nodes were visited, the graph is fully connected, so we return `True`. If not, it means there are disconnected nodes, so we return `False`.

11.3.3.3 Test Main Function

To test this BFS-based solution, here's a main function with some test cases:

Code 11.8: Test Code for validTree Using the BFS Solution

```
def main():
    # Instantiate the Solution class
    solution = Solution()

    # Test Case 1: A simple tree (valid tree)
    n1 = 5
    edges1 = [[0, 1], [0, 2], [0, 3], [3, 4]]
    print("Test Case 1:", solution.validTree(n1, edges1))
    # Expected Output: True

    # Test Case 2: A graph with a cycle (not a tree)
    n2 = 5
    edges2 = [[0, 1], [0, 2], [0, 3], [3, 4], [1, 4]]
    print("Test Case 2:", solution.validTree(n2, edges2))
    # Expected Output: False
```

11.3 Example 2: Graph Validation Tree

```
    # Test Case 3: Disconnected graph (not a tree)
    n3 = 5
    edges3 = [[0, 1], [1, 2], [3, 4]]
    print("Test Case 3:", solution.validTree(n3, edges3))
    # Expected Output: False

    # Test Case 4: Only one node with no edges
    (valid tree)
    n4 = 1
    edges4 = []
    print("Test Case 4:", solution.validTree(n4, edges4))
    # Expected Output: True

    # Test Case 5: Two nodes connected by one edge
    (valid tree)
    n5 = 2
    edges5 = [[0, 1]]
    print("Test Case 5:", solution.validTree(n5, edges5))
    # Expected Output: True

    # Test Case 6: Two nodes with no edge (not a tree)
    n6 = 2
    edges6 = []
    print("Test Case 6:", solution.validTree(n6, edges6))
    # Expected Output: False

    # Test Case 7: Multiple nodes with a single line
    connection (valid tree)
    n7 = 4
    edges7 = [[0, 1], [1, 2], [2, 3]]
    print("Test Case 7:", solution.validTree(n7, edges7))
    # Expected Output: True

    # Test Case 8: Multiple nodes with an extra edge
    creating a cycle (not a tree)
    n8 = 4
    edges8 = [[0, 1], [1, 2], [2, 3], [3, 0]]
    print("Test Case 8:", solution.validTree(n8, edges8))
    # Expected Output: False

# Run the main function to execute test cases
main()
```

11.3.3.4 Explanation of Test Cases

- **Test Case 1**: A valid tree with no cycles and all nodes connected.
- **Test Case 2**: A graph with a cycle, which is not a valid tree.
- **Test Case 3**: A disconnected graph, so it's not a valid tree.
- **Test Case 4**: A single node with no edges, which is considered a valid tree.
- **Test Case 5**: Two nodes connected by one edge, forming a valid tree.
- **Test Case 6**: Two nodes with no edge, making it disconnected and not a valid tree.
- **Test Case 7**: A straight line of nodes (chain structure), which is a valid tree.
- **Test Case 8**: Multiple nodes with a cycle, which is not a valid tree.

This main function tests the BFS-based solution with various configurations, checking for cycles, connectivity, and edge cases. This approach ensures that we are accurately verifying whether the graph meets the conditions to be a valid tree.

11.3.4 Union Find solution

The Union-Find algorithm, also known as Disjoint Set Union (DSU), is often used for solving graph-related problems involving connectivity. In this context, it can help us determine if a given undirected graph is a valid tree by checking for cycles and ensuring the graph is fully connected.

11.3.4.1 Steps in Union-Find

1. **Initialize Parent Array**: We initialize an array called `root` (or `parent`) where each element is its own root. This means every node is initially its own set, representing itself.
2. **Union Operation**: For every edge, we perform the union operation. If two nodes are connected by an edge, we connect their root nodes by updating the `root` array.
3. **Cycle Detection**: When processing an edge between two nodes, if both nodes have the same root, it indicates they are already connected, meaning a cycle exists. Therefore, the graph cannot be a tree in this case, as a valid tree cannot contain cycles.
4. **Find Operation**: The `find` function is used to get the root of a node. It's typically implemented with **path compression** to optimize the union-find algorithm by flattening the structure of the tree, so all nodes point directly to the root node of their set.
5. **Tree Verification**: After iterating through all edges, if there are no cycles and the number of edges is exactly `n-1` (where n is the number of nodes), then the graph is a valid tree.

11.3.4.2 Python Code

Code 11.9: Python Code for validTree Using the Union-Find Solution

```
class Solution:
    # @param {int} n an integer representing the number
    of nodes
    # @param {int[][]} edges a list of undirected edges,
    where each edge is represented as a pair of nodes
    # @return {boolean} true if the graph is a valid
    tree, false otherwise
    def validTree(self, n, edges):
        # Initialize the root array, where each node is
        initially its own parent (disjoint set)
        root = [i for i in range(n)]

        # Iterate through each edge in the graph
        for i in edges:
            # Find the root parent of the first node in
            the edge
            root1 = self.find(root, i[0])
            # Find the root parent of the second node in
            the edge
            root2 = self.find(root, i[1])

            # If both nodes have the same root, it means
            they are already connected,
            # forming a cycle. Therefore, the graph is
            not a tree.
            if root1 == root2:
                return False
            else:
                # Union operation: connect the components
                by setting the root of one
                # component to be the root of the other
                component
                root[root1] = root2

        # A valid tree should have exactly 'n - 1' edges
        for 'n' nodes to ensure
        # that all nodes are connected and there are
        no cycles.
        return len(edges) == n - 1
```

```
# Helper function to find the root parent of a given
node 'e' using path compression
def find(self, root, e):
    # If the node is its own root, return it as
    the root
    if root[e] == e:
        return e
    else:
        # Path compression optimization: set the root
        of the node directly to
        # the result of finding its root, which helps
        speed up future queries
        root[e] = self.find(root, root[e])
        return root[e]
```

11.3.4.3 Explanation of Key Parts

1. **Initialization**:

   (a) `root = [i for i in range(n)]`: Initializes the `root` array where each node is initially its own parent. This is the initial setup for the Union-Find (disjoint-set) data structure.

2. **Union-Find Operations**:

   (a) **Finding Roots**:

   - `root1 = self.find(root, i[0])` and `root2 = self.find(root, i[1])`: For each edge, we find the root parent of each of the nodes connected by the edge.

   (b) **Cycle Detection**:

   - `if root1 == root2`: If both nodes in the edge have the same root parent, it means they are already in the same connected component, indicating a cycle. A cycle would mean that the graph is not a valid tree.

   (c) **Union**:

   - `root[root1] = root2`: If the two nodes are in different components, we perform a union operation by connecting the root of one component to the root of the other component.

3. **Edge Count Check**:

   (a) `return len(edges) == n - 1`: For a graph to be a valid tree, it should have exactly $n - 1$ edges where n is the number of nodes. This ensures that the graph is fully connected and has no cycles.

   (a) **Path Compression in Find Operation**:

11.3 Example 2: Graph Validation Tree

(b) `root[e] = self.find(root, root[e])`: This is a path compression technique that optimizes the Union-Find data structure. By setting the root of a node directly to its root parent, we speed up future queries by reducing the tree height.

The code checks if the given graph with n nodes and `edges` is a valid tree by using the Union-Find data structure with path compression.

11.3.4.4 Test Code

Here's a test main function to verify the `validTree` method of the `Solution` class. This function will create various test cases and check if the `validTree` function correctly identifies whether the given graph is a valid tree.

Code 11.10: Test Code for validTree Using the Union-Find Solution

```python
def main():
    # Instantiate the Solution class
    solution = Solution()

    # Test Case 1: A simple tree (valid tree)
    n1 = 5
    edges1 = [[0, 1], [0, 2], [0, 3], [3, 4]]
    print("Test Case 1:", solution.validTree(n1, edges1))
    # Expected Output: True

    # Test Case 2: A graph with a cycle (not a tree)
    n2 = 5
    edges2 = [[0, 1], [0, 2], [0, 3], [3, 4], [1, 4]]
    print("Test Case 2:", solution.validTree(n2, edges2))
    # Expected Output: False

    # Test Case 3: Disconnected graph (not a tree)
    n3 = 5
    edges3 = [[0, 1], [1, 2], [3, 4]]
    print("Test Case 3:", solution.validTree(n3, edges3))
    # Expected Output: False

    # Test Case 4: Only one node with no edges
    (valid tree)
    n4 = 1
    edges4 = []
```

```
    print("Test Case 4:", solution.validTree(n4, edges4))
    # Expected Output: True

    # Test Case 5: Two nodes connected by one edge
    (valid tree)
    n5 = 2
    edges5 = [[0, 1]]
    print("Test Case 5:", solution.validTree(n5, edges5))
    # Expected Output: True

    # Test Case 6: Two nodes with no edge (not a tree)
    n6 = 2
    edges6 = []
    print("Test Case 6:", solution.validTree(n6, edges6))
    # Expected Output: False

    # Test Case 7: Multiple nodes with a single line
    connection (valid tree)
    n7 = 4
    edges7 = [[0, 1], [1, 2], [2, 3]]
    print("Test Case 7:", solution.validTree(n7, edges7))
    # Expected Output: True

    # Test Case 8: Multiple nodes with an extra edge
    creating a cycle (not a tree)
    n8 = 4
    edges8 = [[0, 1], [1, 2], [2, 3], [3, 0]]
    print("Test Case 8:", solution.validTree(n8, edges8))
    # Expected Output: False

# Run the main function to execute test cases
main()
```

11.3.4.5 Explanation of Test Cases

1. **Test Case 1**: A valid tree with five nodes connected in a way that forms a tree structure. Expected result is True.
2. **Test Case 2**: A graph with a cycle formed by the edge [1, 4]. Expected result is False because of the cycle.
3. **Test Case 3**: A disconnected graph with two separate components (0-1-2 and 3-4). Expected result is False because it is not connected.

11.3 Example 2: Graph Validation Tree

4. **Test Case 4**: A single node with no edges, which is considered a valid tree. Expected result is `True`.
5. **Test Case 5**: Two nodes connected by one edge, which forms a valid tree. Expected result is `True`.
6. **Test Case 6**: Two nodes without any edge, which is not a connected graph, hence not a tree. Expected result is `False`.
7. **Test Case 7**: A line graph with nodes connected sequentially (a valid tree). Expected result is `True`.
8. **Test Case 8**: A line graph with an additional edge to form a cycle, making it not a valid tree. Expected result is `False`.

This test main function will help validate the correctness of the `validTree` method.

Part II
Algorithmic Part

Chapter 12
Binary Search

Binary search operates by dividing the search interval into two halves. It starts with an interval that covers the entire array. If the value of the search key is less than the middle element, narrow the interval to the lower half. Otherwise shrink it down to the upper half. Repeat this process until until the value is found or the interval becomes empty.

Binary search is one of the basic algorithms in computer science, which is generally used for sorted arrays, and its computational complexity is O(logN). Let's take a look at some of the more common dichotomous interview questions, so you can get a good idea of how to use the dichotomous approach.

12.1 Example 1: Find the Square Root

Implement int sqrt(int x). Calculates and returns the square root of x, where x is guaranteed to be a non-negative integer. Since the return type is an integer, the decimal digits will be truncated and only the integer portion of the result will be returned.

Idea
1. Idea: **Initial Edge Case Handling**:
    (a) If x is either 0 or 1, the function immediately returns x, as the square root of these numbers is trivial.

2. **Binary Search Setup**:
    (a) A binary search approach is used to find the integer square root. The search space is initialized between `left = 0` and `right = x`.

3. **Binary Search Execution**:
    (a) In each iteration, the midpoint `mid` of the current search space is calculated.

(b) The code checks if mid * mid is greater than x:
- If true, it means that the square root is smaller than mid, so it moves the search space to the left (right = mid - 1).
- If false, it means the square root could be larger, so it moves the search space to the right (left = mid + 1).

(c) The value variable keeps track of the current mid, which is a candidate for the integer square root.

4. **Final Adjustment**:

(a) After the binary search ends, the code checks if the value's square is greater than x. If so, it returns value - 1 because the exact square root has been surpassed.

(b) Otherwise, the value itself is returned.

12.1.1 Efficiency

- The binary search runs in O(log x) time, making it very efficient for large numbers compared to a brute force approach, which would take O(sqrt(x)) or more.

Code 12.1: Use the Dichotomy to Find the Square Root

```
class Solution:
    def mySqrt(self, x: int) -> int:
        # If the number is 0, the square root is 0.
        if x == 0:
            return 0

        # If the number is 1, the square root is 1.
        if x == 1:
            return 1

        # Initialize the left boundary of the binary
        search to 0.
        left = 0

        # Initialize the right boundary of the binary
        search to the given number 'x'.
        right = x
```

```
# 'value' will store the closest integer square
root found.
value = -1

# Start binary search until left surpasses right.
while left <= right:
    # Find the midpoint between left and right.
    mid = (left + right) // 2

    # If the square of 'mid' is greater than 'x',
    move the search to the left.
    if mid * mid > x:
        value = mid   # Store the current mid as a
        candidate value.
        right = mid - 1   # Adjust the right
        boundary to mid-1 to search
        smaller values.
    else:
        # If 'mid' squared is less than or equal
        to 'x', move the search to the right.
        left = mid + 1

# Check if the current candidate value's square
exceeds 'x'.
if value * value > x:
    return value - 1   # If so, return one less
    than the candidate value.

return value   # Otherwise, return the
candidate value.
```

12.2 Example 2: Search in a Rotationally Sorted Array

Suppose an array sorted in ascending order rotates at some unknown pivot, such as [0, 1, 2, 4, 5, 6, 7] may become [4, 5, 6, 7, 0, 1, 2], search for the target value in that array, and return its index if the target value is found in the array, otherwise −1 is returned. It can be assumed that there are no duplicates in the array, and the running time complexity of the algorithm must be on the order of $O(\log n)$.

Idea: Use the dichotomy to solve. If the middle element is larger than the one on the left, the left part is ordered; otherwise, the right part is ordered.

Code 12.2: Rotate Sort Search

```
class Solution:
    def search(self, nums: List[int], target:
    int) -> int:
        # Initialize the left (l) and right (r)
        boundaries of the array
        l, r = 0, len(nums) - 1

        # Continue searching as long as the left boundary
        is less than or equal to the right boundary
        while l <= r:
            # Find the middle index of the current
            search space
            mid = (l + r) // 2

            # If the target is at the mid index, return
            the index
            if target == nums[mid]:
                return mid

            # Check if the left side (from l to mid)
            is sorted
            if nums[l] <= nums[mid]:
                # If the target is greater than mid or
                less than the value at l, the target is
                not on the left side
                if target > nums[mid] or target <
                nums[l]:
                    # Move the left boundary to mid + 1
                    to search the right side
                    l = mid + 1
                else:
                    # Otherwise, continue searching on
                    the left by moving the right boundary
                    to mid - 1
                    r = mid - 1
            # If the right side (from mid to r) is sorted
            else:
                # If the target is less than mid or
                greater than the value at r, the target
                is not on the right side
```

12.2 Example 2: Search in a Rotationally Sorted Array

```
                if target < nums[mid] or target >
            nums[r]:
                    # Move the right boundary to mid - 1
                    to search the left side
                    r = mid - 1
                else:
                    # Otherwise, continue searching on
                    the right by moving the left boundary
                    to mid + 1
                    l = mid + 1

    # If the target is not found in the array,
    return -1
    return -1
```

1. **Initial Setup**:
   (a) The function takes an array `nums` (which is rotated and sorted) and a `target` integer to search.
   (b) The left (`l`) and right (`r`) pointers are initialized to the start (`0`) and end (`len(nums) - 1`) of the array.

2. **Binary Search Loop**:
   (a) The while loop continues as long as `l <= r`, meaning there's still a portion of the array left to search.
   (b) The middle index is calculated as `(l + r) // 2` (integer division).

3. **Target Check**:
   (a) If `target == nums[mid]`, the function immediately returns `mid`, as the target is found.

4. **Checking if Left or Right Half is Sorted**:
   (a) Since the array is rotated but still sorted in portions, the function needs to check which half (left or right) is sorted in order to know where to search.

   Left Side Sorted Check:
   (a) If `nums[l] <= nums[mid]`, it means the left portion (from index `l` to `mid`) is sorted.
   (b) If the target isn't in the sorted left portion (i.e., `target > nums[mid]` or `target < nums[l]`), the search continues in the right portion by adjusting `l = mid + 1`.
   (c) Otherwise, the target must be on the left side, so the search continues there by adjusting `r = mid - 1`.

Right Side Sorted Check:

(a) If nums[mid] <= nums[r], it means the right portion (from index mid to r) is sorted.
(b) If the target isn't in the sorted right portion (i.e., target < nums[mid] or target > nums[r]), the search continues in the left portion by adjusting r = mid - 1.
(c) Otherwise, the target must be on the right side, so the search continues there by adjusting l = mid + 1.

5. **Return Value**:

(a) If the while loop completes without finding the target, it returns -1 to indicate that the target is not in the array.

12.2.1 Efficiency

- The time complexity is O(log n) since this uses a modified binary search technique.
- This method is efficient for searching in a rotated sorted array, leveraging the fact that one half of the array is always sorted, even if the array has been rotated.

12.3 Example 3: Search a List of Ranges

12.3.1 Problem

Given a list of timestamp ranges representing the usage of a Google service by different users, the goal is to return the indices of users using the service at a given query timestamp.

12.3.2 Solution

We need a function that efficiently handles multiple queries over a static set of timestamp ranges. The most straightforward solution involves:

1. **Preprocessing** the ranges: We can preprocess the ranges in a way that makes querying faster.
2. **Querying** efficiently for a given timestamp.

12.3 Example 3: Search a List of Ranges

12.3.3 Efficient Search Strategy

A **brute-force** solution would involve iterating over all the ranges for each query, checking if the query timestamp falls within the range [start, end]. However, this has a time complexity of $O(N)$ per query, which can be inefficient for large datasets with repeated queries.

We want to efficiently find which intervals contain a specific query point. For this, the code builds a **lookup table** of intervals and their start and end points and uses **binary search** to quickly query which intervals contain a specific point.

Code 12.3: Search in the Intervals

```python
class RangeTable:
    def __init__(self, intervals: list[list]):
        # Step 1: Initialize with the list of intervals.
        # Each interval is assumed to be inclusive on
        both ends.
        self.intervals = intervals
        self.points = self.read_intervals()  # Sort all
        interval start and end points
        self.range_table = self.build_range_table()  # Build
        a lookup table for query points

    def read_intervals(self) -> list[tuple[int, int]]:
        points = []
        # Step 2: For each interval, store both the start
        and end points along with index.
        # We increment end points by 1 because intervals are
        inclusive, and we treat [start, end] as
        inclusive ranges.
        for index, interval in enumerate(self.intervals):
            points.append((interval[0], index))  # Store
            start point with index
            points.append((interval[1] + 1, index))  # Store
            end point + 1 to manage inclusivity

        points.sort()  # Sort points based on the interval
        boundaries
        return points

    def build_range_table(self) -> dict[int, set]:
        range_table = {}  # Dictionary to store ranges for
        each point
```

```python
        current_range = set()  # Set of indices that
        represent the intervals covering the current point

        # Step 3: Loop over each point (sorted) and build
        the lookup table.
        # Add or remove intervals from the 'current_range'
        set as points are processed.
        for point, index in self.points:
            if index not in current_range:
                current_range.add(index)  # Add interval to
                current range (start of interval)
            else:
                current_range.remove(index)  # Remove
                interval from range (end of interval)

            # Create a copy of the current set and associate
            it with the point
            range_table[point] = current_range.copy()  #
            Copy is required since sets are mutable

        return range_table

    def query(self, query_point: int) -> list[list]:
        # If the query point is smaller than the smallest
        interval's start point, no intervals contain it.
        if query_point < self.points[0][0]:
            return []

        # Step 4: Use binary search to find the closest point
        in the range table.
        low = 0
        high = len(self.points) - 1

        # Perform binary search for the query point
        while low < high:
            m = (low + high + 1) // 2
            if self.points[m][0] > query_point:
                high = m - 1  # Narrow the range to the left
            else:
                low = m  # Move towards the right
```

12.3 Example 3: Search a List of Ranges

```python
        # Step 5: After the binary search, 'low' points to
        the closest point <= query_point
        closest_point = self.points[low][0]

        # Step 6: Return the intervals (based on original
        indices) that contain the query point
        return [self.intervals[i] for i in self.range_table
        [closest_point]]

def main():
    # Example input list of intervals (each represents a
    user's usage)
    intervals = [
        [0, 5],
        [6, 8],
        [2, 9],
        [4, 10],
        [3, 5]
    ]

    # Query timestamp
    query_timestamp = 6

    # Initialize the RangeTable with the given intervals
    range_table = RangeTable(intervals)

    # Perform the query
    result = range_table.query(query_timestamp)

    # Print the result (should print indices of intervals
    covering the query_timestamp)
    print(f"Users active at timestamp {query_timestamp}:
    {result}")

if __name__ == "__main__":
    main()
```

12.3.4 Step-by-Step Process

1. **read_intervals()**:
   (a) Extract all start and end points from the intervals and store them as tuples `(point, index)` where `index` represents the interval's index in the original list.
   (b) Increment end points by 1 to handle the fact that intervals are inclusive.
   (c) After processing all intervals, the list of points is sorted by value.

2. **build_range_table()**:
   (a) Using the sorted points, a range table is built which keeps track of the active intervals at each point.
   (b) As we encounter a start point of an interval, we add it to the `current_range` set, and as we encounter an end point, we remove it from the set.
   (c) We store a copy of the `current_range` set at each point in a dictionary called `range_table`.

3. **query()**:
   (a) For each query, we perform a **binary search** on the sorted points to find the closest point $\leq$ query point.
   (b) Once the closest point is found, the corresponding set of intervals (stored in `range_table`) is returned.
   (c) The binary search ensures that the query is fast, taking $O(\log N)$ time.

12.3.5 Example Walkthrough

Let's walk through the example given in the problem:
- Intervals: `[[0, 5], [6, 8], [2, 9], [4, 10], [3, 5]]`
- Query: 3

1. **read_intervals()**:
   (a) We process each interval, converting it to points:

   $$(0, 0), (6, 1), (2, 2), (4, 3), (3, 4)$$

   (Note that we also add `end + 1` as another point for the closing boundary).

2. **build_range_table()**:
   (a) We iterate over the sorted points and maintain the `current_range` set of active intervals.

3. **query()**:
   (a) Using binary search, we find the closest point ≤3 and return the corresponding intervals that cover this point.

12.3.6 Time Complexity

- **Preprocessing** (`read_intervals` **and** `build_range_table`):
  - `read_intervals`: We traverse all intervals, which takes $O(N)$ where N is the number of intervals. Sorting the points takes $O(N \log N)$.
  - `build_range_table`: For each of the 2N points (start and end), we add or remove elements from the set. Since copying a set takes $O(N)$, this leads to an overall complexity of $O(N^2)$ for building the range table.
- **Query**:
  - Binary search takes $O(\log N)$ and retrieving the set of intervals takes $O(K)$ where K is the number of intervals active at the queried point.

12.3.7 Space Complexity

- The space complexity is $O(N^2)$ due to the need to store a copy of the current set for each point in the `range_table`.

12.3.8 Conclusion

This solution preprocesses the intervals into a lookup table to make querying efficient. The lookup table provides $O(\log N)$ time complexity for each query thanks to binary search, making it well-suited for scenarios where you have a large number of queries to handle after preprocessing the intervals.

Chapter 13
Two-Pointer Method

13.1 Example 1: Point Product of a Sparse Vector

13.1.1 *Problem*

Suppose there are very large sparse vectors, where most elements in the vector are zero.

1. Find a data structure to store them.
2. Calculate the dot product.

   Further discussion: What if one of the vectors is small?

13.1.2 *Solutions*

The problem revolves around **efficient multiplication of two sparse vectors**. In a typical scenario, when vectors are sparse (i.e., many elements are zero), iterating over all elements and multiplying corresponding positions is inefficient. The goal is to optimize the multiplication by focusing only on non-zero elements. Two-pointer techniques or hash tables can help to skip the zeroes.

- **Sparse Vector**: A vector where many of the elements are zero, so storing all values wastes space.
- **Efficient Multiplication**: Instead of multiplying all elements, we only multiply non-zero elements, which can be identified by their indices.

13.1.2.1 Commonly Used Approaches

1. **Hash Table (Dictionary) Approach**
   (a) We can store non-zero elements in a hash table, where the keys are the indices of the non-zero elements and the values are the non-zero elements themselves.
   (b) Then, for multiplication, iterate over the non-zero entries of one vector and check if those indices also exist in the other vector. If they do, multiply them and sum up the result.

2. **Two Pointers Approach**
   (a) If the sparse vectors are represented in a compact format where only non-zero values and their indices are stored, you can use two pointers to traverse both vectors simultaneously.
   (b) If the indices of both pointers match, multiply the values and add the result to the final sum. If they don't match, advance the pointer with the smaller index.

13.1.3 Example Solution Using Two Pointers

Let's assume each sparse vector is represented as a list of tuples where each tuple is (index, value) for non-zero elements.

Code 13.1: Sparse Vector dotProduct

```
from typing import List

# SparseVector class as provided
class SparseVector:
    def __init__(self, nums: List[int]):
        # Store only non-zero elements as (index, value)
        self.elements = [(i, num) for i, num in
        enumerate(nums) if num != 0]

    def dotProduct(self, vec: 'SparseVector') -> int:
        # Use two pointers to traverse both
        sparse vectors
        p1 = p2 = 0
        result = 0
        elements1, elements2 = self.elements, vec.
        elements
```

13.1 Example 1: Point Product of a Sparse Vector

```
            while p1 < len(elements1) and p2 <
            len(elements2):
                index1, value1 = elements1[p1]
                index2, value2 = elements2[p2]

                if index1 == index2:
                    # If indices match, multiply values and
                    add to result
                    result += value1 * value2
                    p1 += 1
                    p2 += 1
                elif index1 < index2:
                    # Move pointer 1 if its index is smaller
                    p1 += 1
                else:
                    # Move pointer 2 if its index is smaller
                    p2 += 1

            return result

# Main function to test the SparseVector class
def main():
    # Example input lists
    nums1 = [1, 0, 0, 2, 3]
    nums2 = [0, 3, 0, 4, 0]

    # Create two sparse vectors
    vec1 = SparseVector(nums1)
    vec2 = SparseVector(nums2)

    # Calculate the dot product of vec1 and vec2
    result = vec1.dotProduct(vec2)

    # Print the result
    print(f"The dot product of vec1 and vec2 is:
    {result}")

# Run the main function
if __name__ == "__main__":
    main()
```

13.1.3.1 Explanation

1. We define two lists, `nums1` and `nums2`, representing the input vectors. These lists contain both zero and non-zero elements.
2. We create two instances of the `SparseVector` class, `vec1` and `vec2`, initialized with `nums1` and `nums2`, respectively.
3. We call the `dotProduct` method of `vec1` with `vec2` as the argument. This computes the dot product of `vec1` and `vec2`.
4. Finally, we print the result of the dot product.

1. **Initialization**

   (a) The `SparseVector` class is initialized with a list of numbers (the vector), and it only stores the non-zero elements as tuples (`index, value`).

2. **Dot Product Method**:

   (a) Two pointers, `p1` and `p2`, are used to traverse the non-zero elements of two sparse vectors.

   (b) If the indices of both vectors match, their values are multiplied, and the result is added to the final sum.

   (c) If the indices do not match, the pointer with the smaller index is moved forward to try and find a match.

13.1.3.2 Example

```
# Suppose we have the following sparse vectors:
v1 = SparseVector([1, 0, 0, 2, 3])
v2 = SparseVector([0, 3, 0, 4, 0])

# Compute the dot product
result = v1.dotProduct(v2)
print(result)   # Output will be 8 (because 2 * 4 = 8)
```

13.1.3.3 Why This Is Efficient

- Instead of iterating over all the elements (including the zeroes), we only focus on non-zero elements, reducing the time complexity significantly when the vectors are sparse.
- The two-pointer technique ensures that we only compare elements at matching indices, making it efficient for computing the dot product of sparse vectors.

13.1.3.4 Time Complexity

- Let n be the number of non-zero elements in the first vector and m the number of non-zero elements in the second vector.
- The time complexity is O(n + m) since we only traverse the non-zero elements once using the two pointers.

13.2 Example 2: Minimal Window Substring

13.2.1 Problem

Given a string S and a string T, find the smallest window in S, which will contain all the characters in T with a time complexity of O(n).
Input: S = "ADOBECODEBANC", T = "ABC".
Output: "BANC".

13.2.2 Solutions

The problem can be solved by using the sliding window technique, which employs a two-pointer approach combined with a hash table (or a dictionary in Python). The main goal is to find the smallest substring in a given string s that contains all characters of another string t. Here's a breakdown of how to solve this problem:

13.2.3 Explanation of the Approach

1. **Hash Table (Dictionary) for Frequency Count**
    (a) First, create a hash table for the string t to store the count of each character required in the substring.
    (b) Keep a variable figures that counts the number of unique characters in t. This will help us determine if we have all required characters in the current window of s.

2. **Two Pointers**
    (a) Use two pointers (left and right) to create a sliding window.
    (b) The right pointer will expand the window by moving to the right.
    (c) The left pointer will contract the window by moving to the right.

3. **Expand Window with the Right Pointer**

    (a) For each character at the `right` pointer, check if it's in the hash table (i.e., if it's a required character).
    (b) If it's in the hash table, decrement the count for that character in the table.
    (c) If the count for a character in the hash table reaches zero, this means that the character count requirement for this character has been met, so decrement figures.
    (d) If figures becomes zero, it indicates that the current window contains all characters of t.

4. **Contract Window with the Left Pointer**

    (a) When figures is zero (meaning the window contains all required characters), check if the current window length is smaller than the minimum found so far.
    (b) Move the `left` pointer to see if the window can be contracted (minimized) while still containing all characters of t.
    (c) For each character removed by moving the `left` pointer, if it's in the hash table, increment its count in the table.
    (d) If the character count for any character goes above zero, increment figures because we're missing a required character again.

5. **Result**

    (a) Keep track of the minimum length window that contains all characters.
    (b) Once done, return the substring corresponding to the minimum window.

13.2.4 Code Explanation with Comments

This code solves the **minimum window substring** problem using the **sliding window technique**. The goal of this problem is to find the smallest substring in s that contains all the characters from string t. Here's a step-by-step explanation of how the code works, with detailed comments:

13.2 Example 2: Minimal Window Substring

Code 13.2: Minimum Window Substring

```
import collections

# Solution class as provided
class Solution:
    def minWindow(self, s: str, t: str) -> str:
        s += "@"  # Append "@" to the end of the string 's'.
        This acts as a sentinel to prevent out-of-
        bound errors.

        # Define a dictionary to store the character counts
        of the target string 't'.
        # This is a Counter object that tracks the frequency
        of each character in 't'.
        dict_t = collections.Counter(t)

        # Initialize two pointers 'l' (left) and 'r'
        (right), which will be used to create a
        sliding window.
        # Initialize 'figures' to the number of distinct
        characters in 't' that need to be matched in 's'.
        l, r, figures = 0, 0, len(dict_t.keys())

        # Initialize a 'res' list to store the starting and
        ending indices of the smallest window.
        # The result starts with a size larger than the
        length of 's' to ensure any valid window can
        replace it.
        res = [0, len(s) + 1]

        # While the right pointer 'r' is within bounds of
        string 's':
        while r < len(s):
            # If 'figures' is 0, it means the current window
            contains all the required characters.
            if figures == 0:
                # Check if the current window length (r - l)
                is smaller than the best result
                found so far.
                if r - l < res[1] - res[0]:
```

```python
                    # If so, update 'res' with the current
                    window's start and end indices.
                    res = [l, r]
                
                # If the character at the left pointer 'l'
                is part of 'dict_t':
                if s[l] in dict_t:
                    # Increment its count back (since we are
                    shrinking the window from the left).
                    dict_t[s[l]] += 1
                    # If its count becomes positive, it
                    means we are missing this character in
                    the window.
                    if dict_t[s[l]] > 0:
                        # Increase 'figures' since we now
                        need to find this character again.
                        figures += 1
                # Move the left pointer to the right,
                shrinking the window.
                l += 1
            else:
                # If 'figures' is not 0, we haven't found all
                the characters yet.
                # Check if the character at the right
                pointer 'r' is part of 'dict_t':
                if s[r] in dict_t:
                    # Decrement its count since it's now
                    part of the window.
                    dict_t[s[r]] -= 1
                    # If its count becomes 0, it means we
                    have matched this character fully.
                    if dict_t[s[r]] == 0:
                        # Decrease 'figures' since this
                        character is now satisfied.
                        figures -= 1
                # Move the right pointer to the right,
                expanding the window.
                r += 1
        
        # After the loop, if no valid window was found,
        return an empty string.
        if res == [0, len(s) + 1]:
            return ""
```

13.2 Example 2: Minimal Window Substring

```python
            # Otherwise, return the smallest window
            found in 's'.
        else:
            return s[res[0]:res[1]]

# Main function to test the Solution class
def main():
    # Test cases
    test_cases = [
        ("ADOBECODEBANC", "ABC"),   # Expected output: "BANC"
        ("a", "a"),                  # Expected output: "a"
        ("a", "aa"),                 # Expected output: ""
        ("thisisateststring", "tist"),  # Expected
        output: "tstri"
    ]

    # Create an instance of Solution
    solution = Solution()

    # Test each case
    for s, t in test_cases:
        result = solution.minWindow(s, t)
        print(f"minWindow('{s}', '{t}') -> '{result}'")

# Run the main function
if __name__ == "__main__":
    main()
```

13.2.4.1 Detailed Explanation

1. **Initial Setup**

    (a) The function adds "@" to the end of s to avoid issues with out-of-bound errors (since we don't want to accidentally go past the end of the string).

    (b) A dictionary (dict_t) is created using the Counter class from the collections module to store the frequency of each character in t. This dictionary helps track which characters are still needed in the current window.

2. **Sliding Window Technique**

    (a) The window is represented by two pointers, l (left) and r (right). Initially, both pointers are at the start of the string s.

    (b) The variable figures keeps track of how many distinct characters from t still need to be found in the window.

(c) `res` keeps track of the start and end indices of the smallest window found so far.

3. **While Loop**

    (a) **Case 1**: If all the required characters from t are present in the current window (i.e., `figures == 0`), the code checks if this window is the smallest one found so far. If it is, the `res` array is updated.

    - The code then tries to shrink the window by moving the left pointer l to the right. If the character at l is part of t, its count is increased in the dictionary (`dict_t`), and if the count becomes positive, it means this character is now missing, so `figures` is increased.

    (b) **Case 2**: If not all the characters are present (`figures != 0`), the code tries to expand the window by moving the right pointer r to the right. If the character at r is part of t, its count is decreased in the dictionary (`dict_t`), and if the count becomes zero, it means this character is fully matched, so `figures` is decreased.

4. **Result**

    (a) After the loop ends, the code checks if any valid window was found by comparing the `res` array to its initial value. If no window was found, an empty string is returned. Otherwise, the smallest window is returned as a substring of s.

13.2.4.2 Time Complexity

- The time complexity is **O(n)** where n is the length of string s. This is because both pointers (l and r) traverse the string once.
- The space complexity is **O(m)** where m is the length of string t, which is the size of the dictionary used to store the frequency of characters.

13.2.4.3 Example

```
s = "ADOBECODEBANC"
t = "ABC"
solution = Solution()
print(solution.minWindow(s, t))   # Output: "BANC"
```

Here, the smallest window in s that contains all the characters from t is "BANC".

13.3 Example 3: Intersecting List of Intersections

13.3.1 Problem

Given two closed interval lists, each interval list does not intersect in pairs and is arranged in sort order. Returns the intersection of these two interval lists. In general, the closed interval [a,b] (where a≤b) represents the set of real numbers x, where a≤x≤b. The intersection of two closed intervals is either a set of real numbers, or can be expressed as a closed interval, or is empty. For example, the intersection of [1, 3] and [2, 4] is [2, 3].

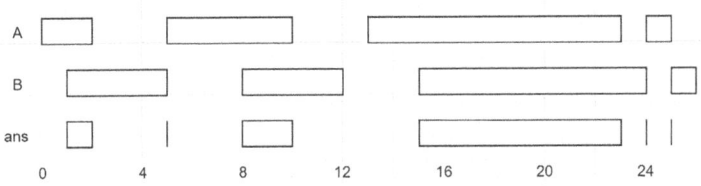

```
Input: A = [[0,2],[5,10],[13,23],[24,25]], B = [[1,5],[8,12],[15,24],[25,26]]
Output: [[1,2],[5,5],[8,10],[15,23],[24,24],[25,25]]
```

13.3.2 Solution

In the interval [a, b], the point **b** is referred to as the "endpoint." When considering the intervals, let's focus on **A[0]**, the interval with the smallest endpoint within a given interval (as a general rule, this interval exists in array A). Now, within the intervals of array B, **A[0]** can only intersect with one such interval in B. If two intervals in B were to intersect with **A[0]**, they would both share the endpoint of **A[0]**. However, this contradicts the assumption that the intervals in B are disjoint.

Since **A[0]** has the smallest endpoint, it can only intersect with **B[0]**. Once this intersection is considered, **A[0]** can be discarded, as it cannot intersect with any other interval. Similarly, if **B[0]** has the smallest endpoint, it can only intersect with **A[0]**, and afterward, **B[0]** can also be discarded because it cannot intersect with any other interval.

To manage this process efficiently, two pointers, **i** and **j**, are used to iteratively discard intervals by comparing their endpoints between the two arrays, A and B.

13.3.3 Code with Comments

Here is the corresponding code:

Code 13.3: Interval of the intersection

```
class Solution:
    def intervalIntersection(self, A: List[List[int]], B:
    List[List[int]]) -> List[List[int]]:
        ans = []
        i = j = 0

        while i < len(A) and j < len(B):
            # Check if A[i] intersects with B[j]
            # lo - Starting point of the intersection
            # hi - End point of the intersection
            lo = max(A[i][0], B[j][0])
            hi = min(A[i][1], B[j][1])

            if lo <= hi:
                ans.append([lo, hi])

            # Remove the interval with the smaller
            endpoint
            if A[i][1] < B[j][1]:
                i += 1
            else:
                j += 1

        return ans
```

13.3.4 Complexity Analysis

- **Time Complexity**: O(N), where N is the total number of intervals across both arrays A and B. The algorithm only iterates through each interval once.
- **Space Complexity**: O(1), excluding the space used to store the result, since no additional data structures are used other than the output list.

This approach efficiently handles the intersection of two sets of intervals using a two-pointer technique, minimizing both time and space complexity.

13.4 Example 4: The Maximum Number of Consecutive 1

Problem: Given that the array A is 0 and 1, we can change the K value from 0 to 1 at most. Returns the length of the longest (consecutive) subarray containing only 1.

Example 1
Input: A = [1,1,1,0,0,0,1,1,1,1,0], K = 2
  Output: 6
  Description: [1,1,1,0,0,1,1,1,1,1,1], bold numbers are flipped from 0 to 1, and the longest subarray is underscored.

Example 2
Input: A = [0,0,1,1,0,0,1,1,1,0,1,1,0,1,0,0,1,1,1,1,1,1], K = 3
  Output: 10
  Description: [0,0,1,1,1,1,1,1,1,1,1,1,0,0,0,1,1,1,1,1,1], the bold number is flipped from 0 to 1, and the longest subarray is underscored.

  Idea: Here is the explanation and comments for the provided code that solves the problem of finding the longest consecutive sequence of 1's in an array, allowing up to K flips (turning 0's into 1's):

13.4.1 Problem Explanation

The task is to find the longest subarray that consists of only 1's by flipping at most K zeros into 1's. This can be efficiently done using a sliding window (two-pointer) approach where:

1. We maintain a window between two pointers, **left** and **right**.
2. The variable **flip** keeps track of how many zeros have been flipped into ones within the current window.
3. If **flip** exceeds **K**, it means the window has too many zeros, and we need to move the left pointer to shrink the window.
4. Throughout the process, the code updates the maximum length of 1's found.

13.4.2 Code with Comments

Code 13.4: Maximum Number of Consecutive 1

```
class Solution:
    def longestOnes(self, A: List[int], K: int) -> int:
        # Initialize the maximum length of
        consecutive ones
        max_len = -1
        # Define two pointers (left and right) to
        represent the sliding window
        left, right = 0, 0
        # Define the variable to count the number of zeros
        encountered (i.e., flips)
        flip = 0

        # Iterate through the array using the
        right pointer
        for right, item in enumerate(A):
            # If we encounter a zero, we increment the
            flip count
            if item == 0:
                flip += 1

            # If the number of zeros (flips) exceeds K,
            move the left pointer
            while flip > K:
                # When the left pointer encounters a
                zero, decrement the flip count
                if A[left] == 0:
                    flip -= 1
                # Move the left pointer to shrink
                the window
                left += 1

            # Update the maximum length of the valid
            window (right - left + 1)
            max_len = max(max_len, right - left + 1)

        # Return the maximum length of the consecutive
        ones (with at most K flips)
        return max_len
```

13.4 Example 4: The Maximum Number of Consecutive 1

13.4.3 Explanation of Each Step

1. **Initialization**
   (a) `max_len` is set to -1 initially to store the length of the longest subarray.
   (b) Two pointers, `left` and `right`, are used to represent the sliding window. Both are initialized to 0.
   (c) `flip` keeps track of how many zeros have been flipped to 1's. It is initialized to 0.

2. **Iterate through the array**
   (a) For each element `item` in array A, the **right** pointer moves from left to right.
   (b) If the current element is 0, the **flip** count is incremented because we are "flipping" the zero into a one.

3. **Check if the number of flips exceeds K**
   (a) If the number of zeros (flips) exceeds **K**, we need to reduce the window by moving the **left** pointer. We do this until the number of flips is less than or equal to **K**.
   (b) If the element at the **left** pointer is 0, it means this zero was counted as a flip, so we reduce the **flip** count as we move the pointer.

4. **Update the maximum length**:
   (a) After adjusting the window, we calculate the current length of the window (`right - left + 1`), and update `max_len` if this window is larger than the previous maximum.

5. **Return the result**
   (a) The final value of `max_len` is returned, which represents the longest sequence of 1's that can be obtained by flipping at most **K** zeros.

13.4.4 Example Walkthrough

Let's assume **A = [1,1,0,0,1,1,1,0,1,1,0,0]** and **K = 2**

1. **Step 1**: Encounter 1, flip=0, max_len=1.
2. **Step 2**: Encounter another 1, flip=0, max_len=2.

3. **Step 3**: Encounter two 0's, flip=2, max_len=4.
4. **Step 4**: Encounter another 0, flip=3, and since flip > K, move the left pointer until flip=2. The new max_len is 5.
5. **Step 5**: Continue with similar steps until the end of the array, tracking the maximum length of consecutive 1's by moving the pointers and maintaining the flip count.

13.4.5 Complexity Analysis

- **Time Complexity**: O(N), where N is the length of array A. Each element in the array is processed at most twice (once by the right pointer and once by the left pointer).
- **Space Complexity**: O(1), since no additional data structures are used apart from a few variables for pointers and counts.

This solution effectively finds the longest subarray of 1's by using the sliding window technique while maintaining a count of flipped zeros.

13.5 Example 5: Find All the Letters in a String

13.5.1 Problem Explanation

Given two strings, s (a long string) and p (a smaller string), the goal is to find all the starting indices in s where the substring is an anagram of p. An anagram of p is any rearrangement of the characters of p.

13.5.2 Solution

This problem can be solved using a **sliding window** technique and hash maps (or counters) to keep track of the frequency of characters in the current window of the string s and compare it with the frequency of characters i90okn string p. The idea is to slide a window over the string s with the same length as p and check whether the current window is an anagram of p.

13.5 Example 5: Find All the Letters in a String

13.5.3 Code with Comments

Code 13.5: Python Code for findAnagrams

```python
class Solution:
    def findAnagrams(self, s: str, p: str) -> List[int]:
        # Use Counter to store the frequency of
        characters in the target string p
        p_counter = Counter(p)
        # Define a counter for the sliding window in the
        string s
        s_counter = Counter()

        # List to store the result (starting indices of
        anagrams)
        ans = []
        # Length of string p and s
        np = len(p)
        ns = len(s)

        # Use the sliding window technique with left and
        right pointers
        left = 0  # This will represent the left pointer
        of the window

        # Iterate over the string s using the
        right pointer
        for i in range(ns):
            # Add the character at the right pointer to
            the sliding window's counter
            s_counter[s[i]] += 1

            # If the current window size equals the
            length of p
            if i - left + 1 == np:
                # Compare the frequency counters of s
                (current window) and p
                if s_counter == p_counter:
                    # If they are equal, add the starting
                    index (left pointer) to the result
                    ans.append(left)
```

```
                    # Before moving the left pointer, adjust
                    the s_counter for the character at left
                    if s_counter[s[left]] == 1:
                        # If there is only one instance of
                        the left character, remove it
                        del s_counter[s[left]]
                    else:
                        # Otherwise, decrement the count of
                        the left character
                        s_counter[s[left]] -= 1
                    # Move the left pointer to the right,
                    shrinking the window
                    left += 1

            # Return the result containing all the starting
            indices of p's anagrams in s
            return ans
```

13.5.4 Explanation of Each Step

1. **Initial Setup**

    (a) `p_counter` is a frequency counter (hash map) that stores the character count of string p.

    (b) `s_counter` is a frequency counter that will keep track of the characters in the current sliding window of string s.

    (c) `ans` will store the starting indices where an anagram of p is found.

    (d) We also define the lengths of p (np) and s (ns), as these will be useful later.

2. **Sliding Window**

    (a) We use a sliding window over string s. The window size is equal to the length of string p (np).

    (b) The **right pointer** i iterates through each character in s, adding it to s_counter.

3. **Window Size Check**

    (a) When the window size (i - left + 1) becomes equal to the length of p, we compare the two frequency counters (s_counter and p_counter).

    (b) If they are the same, it means the current window is an anagram of p, and we append the starting index (left) to the ans list.

4. **Adjust the Window**

   (a) After processing the current window, we need to slide the window to the right. To do this, we remove the character at the **left pointer** from s_counter and move the **left pointer** to the right by 1.

5. **Final Result**

   (a) After the loop, ans contains all the starting indices where anagrams of p occur in s.

13.5.5 Example Walkthrough

Example 1
- **Input**: s = "cbaebabacd", p = "abc".
- **Output**: [0,6].

   Explanation:

- The substring starting at index 0 is "cba", which is an anagram of "abc".
- The substring starting at index 6 is "bac", which is another anagram of "abc".
- Both substrings are found using the sliding window approach, and the starting indices [0, 6] are returned.

13.5.6 Complexity Analysis

- **Time Complexity**: O(N), where N is the length of string s. We use a sliding window, so both the right pointer and the left pointer traverse the string s once. Each operation inside the loop (updating counters, comparing) takes constant time.
- **Space Complexity**: O(1), because the size of the frequency counters (p_counter and s_counter) is constant and bounded by the number of distinct characters (which is at most 26 for lowercase English letters).

This solution efficiently finds all anagrams of p in s using the sliding window technique and frequency counting.

Chapter 14
Dynamic Programming

The main idea of Dynamic Programming (DP) is to decompose a complex problem into multiple sub-problems, combining their solutions to form the solution to the original problem. Problem-solving skills can be greatly improved by using dynamic programming, making this chapter a crucial step in solving problems through this approach.

14.1 Introduction to Dynamic Programming

Dynamic Programming (DP) is an algorithmic technique that relies on a recursive formula and one or more initial states. This technique builds solutions to complex problems by assembling solutions to smaller, previously solved sub-problems. The polynomial time complexity of DP solutions typically results in faster execution than methods like backtracking and exhaustive search.

To illustrate the core concept of DP, consider an example where you are given a list of N coin denominations, each with a specific value, and you need to find the minimum number of coins required to achieve a target sum S. You can use any denomination of coins as many times as needed. If it's impossible to reach the target sum with the given denominations, the solution should indicate this.

To develop a DP solution, you need to define a "state," find the optimal solution for that state, and use it to build the optimal solution for the next state.

Key questions to address include:

1. **What is a "state"?** A "state" is a way of describing a sub-problem of the overall solution. For example, in this problem, a state could represent a specific sum that can be achieved using a combination of coins. Let's say `state(i)` represents the minimum number of coins needed to sum up to `i`. To determine the solution for `state(i)`, you must first know the solutions for all smaller states (i.e., all sums less than `i`).

2. **How do you find each state?** For each coin denomination j where $V\_j \le i$, look at the minimum number of coins needed to achieve the sum $i - V\_j$ (which should already be calculated for a smaller state). Let this minimum be m. If $m + 1$ (i.e., adding one more coin) is less than the current recorded minimum for i, update the result for `state(i)` accordingly.

By using these smaller sub-problems and incrementally building up, you can efficiently find the minimum number of coins required for the target sum.

14.2 Example 1: Best Time to Buy and Sell Stocks

14.2.1 Problem

Consider an array where the i-th element represents the price of a stock on day i. If only one transaction is allowed to be completed (i.e., buying and selling one share), an algorithm aims to find the maximum profit. Additionally, a stock cannot be sold before it is bought.

Example 1
Input: [7,1,5,3,6,4]
   Output: 5

14.2.2 Explanation of the Code

This algorithm iterates through the list of prices and keeps track of two variables:

1. `min_price`: the lowest price encountered so far (the best day to buy).
2. `profit`: the maximum profit that can be achieved by selling at the current day's price and buying at the lowest price seen before this day.

   On each day:

- `min_price` is updated with the minimum of the current `min_price` and today's price.
- `profit` is updated with the maximum of the current `profit` and the difference between today's price and `min_price`.

   At the end of the iteration, `profit` contains the maximum possible profit.

14.2.3 Code

Here is the Python code to test the `maxProfit` function:

Code 14.1: Python Code for maxProfit Function

```python
from typing import List

class Solution:
    def maxProfit(self, prices: List[int]) -> int:
        min_price, profit = float('inf'), 0
        for price in prices:
            min_price = min(min_price, price)
            profit = max(profit, price - min_price)
        return profit

# Main function to test the code
if __name__ == "__main__":
    solution = Solution()

    # Test case 1
    prices = [7, 1, 5, 3, 6, 4]
    print("Test Case 1")
    print("Prices:", prices)
    print("Maximum Profit:", solution.maxProfit(prices))  #
    Expected Output: 5

    # Test case 2
    prices = [7, 6, 4, 3, 1]
    print("\nTest Case 2")
    print("Prices:", prices)
    print("Maximum Profit:", solution.maxProfit(prices))  #
    Expected Output: 0 (no profit possible)

    # Test case 3
    prices = [1, 2, 3, 4, 5]
    print("\nTest Case 3")
    print("Prices:", prices)
    print("Maximum Profit:", solution.maxProfit(prices))  #
    Expected Output: 4
```

```
# Test case 4
prices = [3, 2, 6, 1, 4]
print("\nTest Case 4")
print("Prices:", prices)
print("Maximum Profit:", solution.maxProfit(prices))   #
Expected Output: 3
```

14.2.4 Explanation of Test Cases

1. **Test Case 1**: Prices fluctuate, allowing for a maximum profit of 5 by buying on day 2 (price = 1) and selling on day 5 (price = 6).
2. **Test Case 2**: Prices consistently decrease, so no profit can be made, resulting in a profit of 0.
3. **Test Case 3**: Prices continuously increase, so buying on the first day and selling on the last yields the maximum profit of 4.
4. **Test Case 4**: Prices fluctuate, with the optimal solution to buy on day 4 (price = 1) and sell on day 3 (price = 4) for a profit of 3.

This main function will test the solution with different price lists and print out the maximum profit for each case.

14.3 Example 2: Coin Change

14.3.1 Problem

The system provides coins of different denominations and a total amount, writes a function to calculate the minimum number of coins needed to compose that total amount, and returns −1 if the money cannot be done with any combination of coins.

Example 1
Input: Coin = [1, 2, 5], Total Coin Value = 11
   Output: 3
   Description: 11 = 5 + 5 + 1

Example 2
Input: Coin = [2], Coin Total Value = 3
   Output: −1

14.3 Example 2: Coin Change 251

14.3.2 Dynamic Programming Solution Explanation

This problem can be solved using dynamic programming. We define a dp array where each element at index i represents the minimum number of coins needed to make up the amount i. The idea is to fill up this dp array by calculating the minimum coins required for each value from 0 to amount.

14.3.3 Steps

1. **Initialization**:
   (a) Create a dp array of size amount + 1.
   (b) Initialize dp[0] to 0 because zero coins are needed to make up an amount of zero.
   (c) Initialize other elements of dp to a large number (maxsize), since initially, we assume it's impossible to reach those amounts.

2. **Iterate Through Each Coin**:
   (a) For each coin, update the dp array to reflect the minimum number of coins required for each amount from 1 to amount.
   (b) For each amount i, if the current amount i is greater than or equal to the coin's value, then we calculate the minimum coins required by considering the current coin (dp[i - coin] + 1) and comparing it to the current value dp[i].

3. **Return Result**:
   (a) After filling up the dp array, if dp[amount] is still greater than amount, it means that it's not possible to form that amount, so return -1.
   (b) Otherwise, return dp[amount] as the minimum number of coins needed.

14.3.4 Code with Comments

Code 14.2: Python Code for coinChange

```python
from typing import List
from sys import maxsize

class Solution:
    def coinChange(self, coins: List[int], amount: int) -> int:
        # Initialize a dp array where dp[i] means the
        minimum coins needed for amount i.
        # Set all values to a large number initially, as
        we want to minimize this later.
        dp = [maxsize] * (amount + 1)

        # Base case: 0 coins are needed to make the
        amount of 0.
        dp[0] = 0

        # Iterate over each coin
        for coin in coins:
            # Update the dp array for all amounts from 1
            to 'amount'
            for i in range(1, amount + 1):
                # Only update if the current amount is at
                least as large as the coin's value
                if i >= coin:
                    # dp[i] is updated to the minimum of
                    its current value or
                    # dp[i - coin] + 1, which represents
                    taking this coin.
                    dp[i] = min(dp[i], dp[i - coin] + 1)

        # If dp[amount] is still set to maxsize, it means
        we can't form this amount
        # Return -1 in that case. Otherwise, return
        dp[amount].
        return -1 if dp[amount] == maxsize else
        dp[amount]

def main():
    # Instantiate the Solution class
    solution = Solution()
```

14.3 Example 2: Coin Change

```
    # Test cases
    test_cases = [
        # Basic cases
        {"coins": [1, 2, 5], "amount": 11, "expected": 3},
        # 11 = 5 + 5 + 1
        {"coins": [2], "amount": 3, "expected": -1},  #
        Cannot make 3 with only 2s
        {"coins": [1], "amount": 0, "expected": 0},  #
        Amount is 0, no coins needed
        {"coins": [1], "amount": 2, "expected": 2},  #
        2 = 1 + 1

        # Edge cases
        {"coins": [1, 3, 4], "amount": 6, "expected": 2},  #
        6 = 3 + 3
        {"coins": [2, 4], "amount": 7, "expected": -1},  #
        Impossible to make 7 with [2, 4]
        {"coins": [5, 10, 25], "amount": 30, "expected": 2},
        # 30 = 25 + 5
        {"coins": [2, 5, 10, 1], "amount": 27, "expected":
        4},  # 27 = 10 + 10 + 5 + 2

        # Large case
        {"coins": [186, 419, 83, 408], "amount": 6249,
        "expected": 20},
    ]

    # Test each case
    for i, test_case in enumerate(test_cases):
        coins = test_case["coins"]
        amount = test_case["amount"]
        expected = test_case["expected"]

        # Get the result from the coinChange function
        result = solution.coinChange(coins, amount)

        # Print the results
        print(f"Test case {i + 1}: coins = {coins}, amount =
        {amount}")
        print(f"Expected: {expected}, Got: {result}")
        print("Pass" if result == expected else "Fail")
        print("------")
# Run the main test function
if __name__ == "__main__":
    main()
```

14.3.5 Example Walkthrough

Example 1

(a) Input: `coins = [1, 2, 5]`, `amount = 11`
(b) `dp` array after processing:
    dp = [0, 1, 1, 2, 2, 1, 2, 2, 3, 3, 2, 3]
(c) Output: `dp[11] = 3`
(d) Explanation: $11 = 5 + 5 + 1$, so it takes three coins.

Example 2

(a) Input: `coins = [2]`, `amount = 3`
(b) `dp` array after processing:
    dp = [0, maxsize, 1, maxsize]
(c) Output: `-1`
(d) Explanation: It is not possible to make an amount of 3 with only coin 2.

14.3.6 Complexity Analysis

- **Time Complexity**: $O(N \times M)$ where N is the number of coins and M is the target amount. This is because we iterate through each coin for each value up to `amount`.
- **Space Complexity**: $O(M)$ where M is the target amount, as we use a `dp` array of size `amount + 1`.

14.3.7 Summary

This solution uses a dynamic programming approach to find the minimum number of coins needed to form a given amount. The `dp` array is built up from 0 to `amount` using previously computed results, making it efficient and optimal for this type of problem. If the value at `dp[amount]` remains a large number, it implies that the given coins cannot form the amount, and `-1` is returned. Otherwise, `dp[amount]` gives the minimum number of coins needed.

14.4 Example 3: Decoding Ways

14.4.1 Problem

Use the following mapping to encode a message containing A–Z letters as a number:
    'A' -> 1

14.4 Example 3: Decoding Ways

'B' -> 2

...

'Z' -> 26

Given a non-empty string containing only numbers, determine the total number of decodes it.

Example 1
Enter: "12".
  Output: 2.
  Explanation: It can be decoded as "AB" (1 2) or "L" (12).

Example 2
Enter: "226".
  Output: 3.

14.4.2 Solution

This problem can be solved using dynamic programming. The idea is to build an array dp where dp[i] represents the number of ways to decode the string up to the i-th position.

14.4.3 Code Explanation

Code 14.3: Python Implementation for Decoding Ways

```
class Solution:
    def numDecodings(self, s: str) -> int:
        n = len(s)

        # Define a list of length n+1 to store the ways to
        decode up to each point
        dp = [0] * (n + 1)

        # Base cases
        dp[0] = 1   # One way to decode an empty string
        dp[1] = 0 if s[0] == '0' else 1   # If the first
        character is '0', no valid decoding

        # Fill in the dp array
```

```
for i in range(2, n + 1):
    # 'first' represents the single digit at the
    current position
    first = int(s[i - 1:i])

    # 'second' represents the two digits formed
    by the current and previous position
    second = int(s[i - 2:i])

    # If the single digit is valid (1-9), add the
    ways from dp[i-1]
    if 1 <= first <= 9:
        dp[i] += dp[i - 1]

    # If the two-digit number is valid (10-26),
    add the ways from dp[i-2]
    if 10 <= second <= 26:
        dp[i] += dp[i - 2]

# The last element of dp will contain the total
number of ways to decode the full string
return dp[n]
```

14.4.4 Explanation of Key Parts

1. **Base Case Initialization**:
   (a) `dp[0] = 1`: There's one way to decode an empty string.
   (b) `dp[1] = 0 if s[0] == '0' else 1`: If the first character is '0', there's no valid decoding, so set `dp[1]` to 0. Otherwise, there's one way to decode it.

2. **Loop Through the String**:
   (a) For each position `i` from 2 to n:
   - Check if the single digit at position `i-1` (i.e., `first`) is between 1 and 9. If it is, add `dp[i-1]` to `dp[i]`.
   - Check if the two digits ending at position `i` (i.e., `second`) are between 10 and 26. If they are, add `dp[i-2]` to `dp[i]`.

3. **Return Result**:
   (a) `dp[n]` contains the total number of ways to decode the entire string.

14.4.5 Complexity

- **Time Complexity**: O(n) where nnn is the length of the input string.
- **Space Complexity**: O(n) due to the dp array.

14.4.6 Example

Let's go through the example with s = "226":

1. Initialize dp = [1, 1, 0, 0] (since len(s) + 1 = 4).
2. For i = 2:

    (a) first = 2 (valid single digit), so dp[2] += dp[1] → dp[2] = 1.
    (b) second = 22 (valid two-digit), so dp[2] += dp[0] → dp[2] = 2.

3. For i = 3:

    (a) first = 6 (valid single digit), so dp[3] += dp[2] → dp[3] = 2.
    (b) second = 26 (valid two-digit), so dp[3] += dp[1] → dp[3] = 3.

4. Final dp = [1, 1, 2, 3]. Therefore, dp[3] = 3.

Thus, there are three ways to decode "226".

14.4.7 Test Cases

Code 14.4: Python Implementation for Test Cases in the Decoding

```python
def main():
    solution = Solution()

    # Test cases
    print(solution.numDecodings("12"))      # Output: 2
    print(solution.numDecodings("226"))     # Output: 3
    print(solution.numDecodings("06"))      # Output: 0
    print(solution.numDecodings("10"))      # Output: 1
    print(solution.numDecodings("27"))      # Output: 1
    print(solution.numDecodings("11106"))   # Output: 2

if __name__ == "__main__":
    main()
```

This test code will print the expected results for different test cases, helping validate the implementation of the numDecodings function.

Chapter 15
Depth First Search

Graph traversal commonly utilizes depth-first search/breadth-first search (DFS/BFS) algorithms, and many interview questions can be solved using this idea.

DFS is an algorithm for traversing or searching a tree or graph data structure, starting with the root node (or any arbitrary node) and exploring along each branch as much as possible before backtracking. So, the basic idea is to start with the root node or any node, mark that node, move to an adjacent untagged node, and continue the cycle until there are no untagged neighbors. Finally, backtrack and inspect other unvisited nodes and iterate through them.

The key points of using depth-first search to solve the problem are: (1) setting the initial conditions, (2) using variables to prevent loops or visited nodes, and (3) determining which nodes need to be traversed in the next stage.

15.1 Application for Depth-First Search

Depth-first search (DFS) is an algorithm (or technique) used to traverse a graph. There are a number of problems that can be solved with DFS:

1. For weighted graphs, the depth-first traversal can generate the minimum spanning tree and the shortest path tree for all pairs. See https://leetcode.com/problems/path-sum/.
2. Detect cycles in the graph, and the graph loops if and only if the back edge is seen during a depth-first search. As a result, you can run a depth-first search for the graph and check the back edges. Please refer to https://leetcode.com/problems/graph-valid-tree/.
3. Wayfinding. A depth-first search algorithm can be used specifically to find a path between two given vertices, you and z. (a) Call DFS (G,u) with u as the starting vertex. (b) Use stack S to trace the path between the starting vertex and the

current vertex. (c) Once the target vertex z is encountered, the path is returned as the stack contents.
4. Topological sorting. Topological ordering is mainly used to schedule jobs based on given dependencies between jobs, and in computer science, this type of application appears in instruction scheduling, when recalculating the value of a formula in a spreadsheet, evaluating the order of formula cells, logical synthesis, determining the order of compilation tasks to be executed in a makefile, serialization of data, and parsing symbolic dependencies in linkers. Please refer to https://leetcode.com/problems/course-schedule/.
5. Test whether the chart is a bipartite diagram. When a new vertex is discovered for the first time, you can enhance BFS or DFS by coloring its corresponding edges, and for each other's edges, checking that it does not link two vertices of the same color. The first vertex in any connected component can be red or black! see https://leetcode.com/problems/is-graph-bipartite/.
6. Labyrinth problems. By including only the nodes on the current path in the access set, DFS can be applied to all solutions for finding mazes. Please refer to https://leetcode.com/problems/the-maze-ii/.

15.2 Example 1: Pacific Atlantic Currents

15.2.1 Problem

Given a non-negative integer matrix of m×n representing the height of each unit unit in a continent, the "Pacific Ocean" touches the left and upper edges of the matrix, and the "Atlantic Ocean" touches the right and lower edges.

Water can only flow from one cell to another with a height equal to or lower from four cells (up, down, left, or right). Find a list of grid coordinates where water flows to the Pacific and Atlantic Oceans.

15.2.2 Solution

The solution uses depth-first search (DFS) to explore reachable cells from the edges touching each ocean.

1. Initialization:

    (a) Let R and C represent the number of rows and columns in the matrix, respectively.
    (b) `pacific` and `atlantic` are sets that store cells reachable from the Pacific and Atlantic oceans, respectively.

2. DFS Function:

15.2 Example 1: Pacific Atlantic Currents

(a) The DFS function marks all reachable cells starting from a given cell (r, c).
(b) If a cell (r, c) has already been seen, the function exits to avoid redundant processing.
(c) For each cell, it checks its four neighbors. If the neighbor has a height greater than or equal to the current cell, DFS continues from that neighbor.

3. Exploration:

   (a) For the Pacific Ocean, DFS starts from all cells on the left edge (column 0) and top edge (row 0).
   (b) For the Atlantic Ocean, DFS starts from all cells on the right edge (last column) and bottom edge (last row).

4. Intersection of Reachable Cells:

   (a) The cells that can reach both oceans are the intersection of the pacific and atlantic sets.

15.2.3 Code

Here's the solution as extracted from the image:

Code 15.1: Python Implementation for Pacifici-Altantic Currents

```python
from typing import List, Set, Tuple

class Solution:
    def pacificAtlantic(self, matrix: List[List[int]]) -> List[List[int]]:
        if not matrix or not matrix[0]:
            return []

        R, C = len(matrix), len(matrix[0])
        pacific, atlantic = set(), set()

        def dfs(r: int, c: int, seen: Set[Tuple[int, int]]):
            if (r, c) in seen:
                return
            seen.add((r, c))
            for nr, nc in [(r, c+1), (r, c-1), (r+1, c),
            (r-1, c)]:
```

```
                    # Check boundaries and flow condition
                    if 0 <= nr < R and 0 <= nc < C and
                    matrix[nr][nc] >= matrix[r][c]:
                        dfs(nr, nc, seen)

            # Start DFS from cells touching the Pacific Ocean
            (top and left edges)
            for r in range(R):
                dfs(r, 0, pacific)   # left edge
            for c in range(C):
                dfs(0, c, pacific)   # top edge

            # Start DFS from cells touching the Atlantic
            Ocean (bottom and right edges)
            for r in range(R):
                dfs(r, C - 1, atlantic)   # right edge
            for c in range(C):
                dfs(R - 1, c, atlantic)   # bottom edge

            # Intersection of cells that can reach
            both oceans
            return list(pacific & atlantic)
def main():
    solution = Solution()
    matrix = [
        [1, 2, 2, 3, 5],
        [3, 2, 3, 4, 4],
        [2, 4, 5, 3, 1],
        [6, 7, 1, 4, 5],
        [5, 1, 1, 2, 4]
    ]
    result = solution.pacificAtlantic(matrix)
    print(result)   # Expected output: [[0,4],[1,3],[1,4]
    ,[2,2],[3,0],[3,1],[4,0]]

if __name__ == "__main__":
    main()
```

15.3 Example 2: Predict the Winner

Here's how you would call the function with an example matrix:

For the given `matrix`:

- The cells with coordinates like [0,4], [1,3], and so on can flow to both the Pacific and Atlantic oceans, satisfying the problem requirement.

This solution efficiently finds all such cells using DFS and set intersection.

15.2.4 Explanation of Key Parts

1. DFS Traversal:
    (a) The `dfs` function explores cells from a starting point and marks all reachable cells that can flow to the respective ocean.
2. Initialization of Ocean-Accessible Cells:
    (a) The cells touching the Pacific and Atlantic oceans are identified as starting points for DFS.
3. Finding Common Cells:
    (a) The intersection `pacific & atlantic` gives cells that can flow to both oceans.

15.2.5 Complexity Analysis

- **Time Complexity**: O(m×n), where m is the number of rows and n is the number of columns because each cell is visited at most once during the DFS.
- **Space Complexity**: O(m×n) for storing the `pacific` and `atlantic` sets and the recursion stack in DFS.

15.3 Example 2: Predict the Winner

15.3.1 Problem

Given an array of fractions, these fractions are non-negative integers. Player 1 chooses a number from either end of the array, followed by Player 2, then Player 1, and so on. Whenever a player chooses a number, that number will not be available for the next player. Continue until all scores are selected, and the player with the highest score wins.

Input: [1, 5, 2].
Output: False.

15.3.2 Solution

The solution uses a recursive function with the minimax strategy to simulate the optimal decisions each player would make. Here's the code:

Code 15.2: Python Code for Predict Winner

```python
from typing import List

class Solution:
    def PredictTheWinner(self, nums: List[int]) -> bool:
        total_sum = sum(nums)
        player1_score = self.dfs(nums, 0, len(nums) - 1)
        player2_score = total_sum - player1_score
        return player1_score >= player2_score

    def dfs(self, nums: List[int], s: int, e: int) -> int:
        if s > e:
            return 0
        # If Player 1 chooses the start element
        start = nums[s] + min(self.dfs(nums, s + 1,
        e - 1), self.dfs(nums, s + 2, e))
        # If Player 1 chooses the end element
        end = nums[e] + min(self.dfs(nums, s + 1, e - 1),
        self.dfs(nums, s, e - 2))
        # Player 1 maximizes their score
        return max(start, end)

def main():
    solution = Solution()

    # Test cases
    test_cases = [
        ([1, 5, 2], False),         # Example 1: Player 1
        cannot win
        ([1, 5, 233, 7], True),     # Example 2: Player
        1 can win
```

```
                ([1, 2, 3, 4], True),      # Player 1 can at
        least tie
                ([1, 5, 2, 4, 6], True),   # Player 1 can win with
        optimal strategy
                ([7, 8, 8, 9], True),      # Player 1 can win with
        an equal number of values
                ([5], True),               # Edge case: Only one
        element, Player 1 wins by default
                ([2, 2], True),            # Edge case: Two equal
        elements, Player 1 can at least tie
        ]

        # Run each test case
        for i, (nums, expected) in enumerate(test_cases):
            result = solution.PredictTheWinner(nums)
            print(f"Test Case {i + 1}: Input: {nums}")
            print(f"Expected: {expected}, Got: {result}")
            print("Pass" if result == expected else "Fail")
            print("")

    # Run the main function
    if __name__ == "__main__":
        main()
```

15.3.3 *Explanation*

1. **Recursive DFS with Minimax**:

    (a) The dfs function takes the array nums, start index s, and end index e as parameters and returns the maximum score Player 1 can achieve if they play optimally.

    (b) **Base Case**: If s > e, the recursion ends, and 0 is returned because no more elements are left to choose.

2. **Optimal Choice Calculation**:

    (a) If Player 1 chooses the first element nums[s], then the next possible score for Player 1 will be nums[s] + min(...), where the minimum represents Player 2's optimal choice to minimize Player 1's score.

    (b) If Player 1 chooses the last element nums[e], the possible score for Player 1 will be nums[e] + min(...), applying the same minimax strategy.

    (c) Finally, max(start, end) ensures that Player 1 picks the option that maximizes their score.

3. **Winning Condition**:
   (a) In PredictTheWinner, we calculate the total sum of the array (total_sum) and the score Player 1 can achieve (player1_score).
   (b) Player 1 wins if their score is at least half of the total sum, which is checked by player1_score >= player2_score.

15.3.4 Example Walkthrough

For the input [1, 5, 2]:
1. Player 1 can start by picking either 1 or 2.
2. If Player 1 picks 1, Player 2 will pick 5, leaving Player 1 with 2.
3. If Player 1 picks 2, Player 2 will pick 5, leaving Player 1 with 1.
4. In both cases, Player 2 ends up with a higher score, and hence Player 1 cannot win with optimal play.

Thus, for this example, the output is False.

15.3.5 Complexity Analysis

- **Time Complexity**: $O(2^n)$ due to the recursive approach and overlapping subproblems.
- **Space Complexity**: $O(n)$ due to recursion stack depth.

The current recursive solution can be improved with memoization or dynamic programming to avoid recalculating subproblems, making it more efficient for larger inputs.

15.4 Example 3: Expression Plus Operator

15.4.1 Problem

Given a string containing only the numbers 0–9 and the target value, all possibilities of adding a binary operator (non-unary) +, − or * between the numbers are returned in order to get the target value by the operator.

Example 1
Input: num="123", target=6.
  Output: ["1+2+3","1*2*3"].

Example 2
Input: num="232", target=8.
   Output: ["2*3+2","2+3*2"].

Example 3
Input: num="105", target=5.
   Output: ["1*0+5", "10-5"].

This problem is known as "Expression Add Operators," where we need to find all possible ways to insert binary operators (+, −, *) between the digits in a string (representing numbers) such that the expression evaluates to a given target value. This problem is typically solved using a recursive approach known as Depth-First Search (DFS) with backtracking.

15.4.2 *Problem Breakdown and Approach*

Given:

1. num—a string containing only the digits 0-9.
2. target—an integer value.

Objective: Generate all possible expressions by inserting binary operators +, −, or * between the numbers in the num string, such that the expression evaluates to the target.

15.4.3 *Key Observations*

1. **Non-Unary Operators**: The operators +, −, and * are binary, meaning they operate on two operands. For example, 1+2, 3-4, 5*6.
2. **No Leading Zeros**: We need to ensure that any number we take from the num string doesn't have leading zeros (except for the number "0" itself). For example, in "105", the number "05" should not be treated as valid.
3. **Multiplication Complexity**: The * operator has higher precedence than + and −. This means that in expressions like 2+3*4, the multiplication must be evaluated before the addition. To handle this, we must track the last operand when multiplication is involved.

15.4.4 *Solution Explanation*

The solution is implemented using DFS with backtracking. We maintain several parameters at each step:

- `fstr`—The current expression string being built.
- `fval`—The current evaluated result of the expression.
- `flast`—The last operand's value, which is necessary to handle multiplication properly.

The key challenge is to handle the multiplication operator (*) because it requires us to "undo" the last addition or subtraction in the current evaluation when a multiplication is encountered.

15.4.5 Steps of the Algorithm

1. **Initial DFS Call**: Start by dividing the `num` string into possible initial numbers (from 1 to `len(num)` characters). For each initial number, we make recursive DFS calls to explore further possibilities.
2. **Recursive DFS**:
   (a) If we have reached the end of the string and the current evaluated value (`fval`) matches the target, then we add the current expression string (`fstr`) to the result list.
   (b) For each substring `val` in `num`:
   - If `val` has more than one digit and starts with 0, we skip it (e.g., `"05"` is invalid).
   - **Addition** (+): Add `val` to `fstr`, add its value to `fval`, and update `flast` to `int(val)`.
   - **Subtraction** (-): Add `val` to `fstr` with a - sign, subtract its value from `fval`, and update `flast` to `-int(val)`.
   - **Multiplication** (*): Handle multiplication by updating `fval` to undo the last addition/subtraction, then apply multiplication. Update `flast` to `flast * int(val)`.
3. **Backtracking**: As we explore each operator, we recursively build expressions, and if the expression doesn't yield the target, we backtrack to explore alternative operator placements.

15.4.6 Code Explanation

Here's a code breakdown:

Code 15.3 Python Implementation for Expression Add Operator

```
from typing import List

class Solution:
    def addOperators(self, num: str, target: int) ->
    List[str]:
        res = []
        self.target = target

        for i in range(1, len(num) + 1):
            if i == 1 or (i > 1 and num[0] != '0'):
                self.dfs(num[i:], num[:i], int(num[:i]),
                int(num[:i]), res)
        return res

    def dfs(self, num, fstr, fval, flast, res):
        # fstr = string of current formula
        # fval = value of current formula
        # flast = last value for +- and last computing
        result for * in formula.
        if not num:
            if fval == self.target:
                res.append(fstr)
            return

        for i in range(1, len(num) + 1):
            val = num[:i]
            if i == 1 or (i > 1 and num[0] != '0'):
                self.dfs(num[i:], fstr + '+' + val, fval
                + int(val), int(val), res)
                self.dfs(num[i:], fstr + '-' + val,
                fval - int(val), -int(val), res)
                self.dfs(num[i:], fstr + '*' + val,
                fval - flast + flast * int(val), flast *
                int(val), res)

    def main():
```

```python
solution = Solution()

# Test cases
test_cases = [
    ("123", 6, ["1+2+3", "1*2*3"]),       # Example 1
    ("232", 8, ["2*3+2", "2+3*2"]),       # Example 2
    ("105", 5, ["1*0+5", "10-5"]),        # Example 3
    ("00", 0, ["0+0", "0-0", "0*0"]),     # Edge case: All zeroes, target 0
    ("3456237490", 9191, []),             # Edge case: No solution exists
    ("123456789", 45, ["12+34-5+6-7+8+9"]), # Large input case
]

# Run each test case
for i, (num, target, expected) in enumerate(test_cases):
    result = solution.addOperators(num, target)
    result.sort()    # Sort the result to match the sorted expected for comparison
    expected.sort()  # Sort the expected as the order of expressions does not matter
    print(f"Test Case {i + 1}: Input: num='{num}', target={target}")
    print(f"Expected: {expected}")
    print(f"Got: {result}")
    print("Pass" if result == expected else "Fail")
    print("")

# Run the main function
if __name__ == "__main__":
    main()
```

15.4.7 Complexity Analysis

1. **Time Complexity**: The worst-case time complexity is exponential, approximately $O(4^n)$, where nnn is the length of the num string. This is because for each digit in num, we make up to three recursive calls (one for each operator). Additionally, we need to check and construct valid expressions, which can lead to a large number of combinations.

15.4 Example 3: Expression Plus Operator

2. **Space Complexity**: The space complexity is also $O(4^n)$, as we need to store the results of each valid expression that matches the target. Recursive stack space can also contribute to space complexity, as each recursive call adds to the call stack.

15.4.8 Example Walkthrough

15.4.8.1 Example 1

- Input: num="123", target=6.
- Possible expressions: "1+2+3" and "1*2*3" both evaluate to 6.

15.4.8.2 Example 2

- Input: num="232", target=8.
- Possible expressions: "2*3+2" and "2+3*2" both evaluate to 8.

15.4.8.3 Example 3

- Input: num="105", target=5.
- Possible expressions: "1*0+5" and "10-5" both evaluate to 5.

15.4.9 Edge Cases

1. **Leading Zeros**: Expressions like "05" or "01" are not allowed, so they must be skipped.
2. **Empty String**: If num is an empty string, there are no possible expressions.
3. **No Valid Expressions**: If there are no expressions that match the target, the function should return an empty list.
4. **Single-Digit Target**: If the target is a single digit, the solution should be able to handle it, including cases where only one number achieves the target.

15.4.10 Summary

This problem is a complex recursive problem involving DFS and backtracking to explore all possible combinations of numbers and operators. The multiplication operator requires special handling to maintain correct precedence. While the time complexity is exponential, the solution effectively explores all possible combinations to find valid expressions that match the target value.

Chapter 16
Backtracking

Backtracking is an algorithmic technique for solving problems by exploring all potential solutions to find those meeting specific criteria. Backtracking incrementally builds solution candidates, abandoning ("backtracking") paths that cannot yield valid solutions. This approach is especially useful for combinatorial problems, such as generating permutations, solving mazes, or handling recursive problems with multiple decision points. By systematically exploring each option and pruning unfeasible paths early, backtracking narrows the solution space efficiently, minimizing exhaustive searching.

16.1 Example 1: Sudoku Solves

16.1.1 Problem

Write a program to solve the sudoku puzzle by filling in blank cells. The Sudoku solution must satisfy these rules: each number from 1 to 9 must appear exactly once in each row. Each number 1–9 must appear once in each column. In the 9 3×3 sub-boxes of the grid, each number 1–9 must appear exactly once. Empty cells are defined by characters "." Instructions.

After filling in the spaces in Fig. 16.1, the result is as follows in Fig. 16.2.

16.1.2 Solution

The solution to solving a Sudoku puzzle using backtracking is an elegant application of recursive depth-first search (DFS). In this approach, we locate each empty cell in the board and attempt to fill it with a digit (1 through 9) that adheres to the

Fig. 16.1 Original image of Sudoko

5	3			7				
6			1	9	5			
	9	8					6	
8				6				3
4			8		3			1
7				2				6
	6					2	8	
			4	1	9			5
				8			7	9

Fig. 16.2 Solution diagram of sudoku

5	3	4	6	7	8	9	1	2
6	7	2	1	9	5	3	4	8
1	9	8	3	4	2	5	6	7
8	5	9	7	6	1	4	2	3
4	2	6	8	5	3	7	9	1
7	1	3	9	2	4	8	5	6
9	6	1	5	3	7	2	8	4
2	8	7	4	1	9	6	3	5
3	4	5	2	8	6	1	7	9

Sudoku rules. If we successfully fill all cells while following the rules, then we have a solution. If a dead-end is reached (no valid number fits in a cell), we backtrack by clearing previously filled cells and trying different numbers.

Here's an explanation of each part of the code:

1. `isValid` **Function**: This function verifies if placing a certain number (`digit`) in a given cell (`board[x][y]`) is valid. It ensures that:

    (a) The number does not appear in the same row.
    (b) The number does not appear in the same column.
    (c) The number does not appear in the 3×3 subgrid that contains this cell.

2. `emptySlots` **Function**: This function identifies all the empty cells (marked by '.') and stores their coordinates in a list. This allows us to focus only on the empty cells while solving the puzzle.

3. `DFS` **Function**: This is the core backtracking function that iterates over each empty cell and tries to place numbers 1 through 9. For each number, it:

    (a) Checks if placing the number is valid using `isValid`.
    (b) Places the number if valid and recursively tries to fill the next cell.
    (c) If it reaches the end of the list of empty cells (`start >= N`), it returns `True`, indicating that the puzzle is solved.
    (d) If placing a number leads to a dead-end, it resets the cell to '.' and backtracks, trying the next possible number.

16.1 Example 1: Sudoku Solves

4. `solveSudoku` **Function**: This function initializes the board by calculating the rows, columns, and empty cells, then invokes the DFS function to start solving the puzzle.

16.1.3 Python Code

Here is the code with a test example to run the solution:

Code 16.1: Python Code for Sudoku Solvers

```python
class Solution(object):
    def isValid(self, board, x, y, rows, cols, digit):
        # Detect columns
        for j in range(cols):
            if board[x][j] == digit:
                return False

        # Detect rows
        for i in range(rows):
            if board[i][y] == digit:
                return False

        # Detect 3x3 blocks
        boundary_x = x - x % 3
        boundary_y = y - y % 3

        for i in range(boundary_x, boundary_x + 3):
            for j in range(boundary_y, boundary_y + 3):
                if board[i][j] == digit:
                    return False

        return True


    def emptySlots(self, board, rows, cols):
        empty = []

        # Record empty cell coordinates
        for i in range(rows):
            for j in range(cols):
                if board[i][j] == '.':
```

```python
            empty.append((i, j))

    return empty


def DFS(self, board, empty, start, N, rows, cols):
    # N is the number of empty slots
    if start >= N:
        return True

    # Get the coordinates of the current space
    position
    x = empty[start][0]
    y = empty[start][1]

    # Try all digits from 1 to 9
    for k in range(1, 10):
        # Check whether the current value meets the
        requirements
        if self.isValid(board, x, y, rows, cols,
        str(k)):
            board[x][y] = str(k)   # Assign value
            if self.DFS(board, empty, start + 1, N,
            rows, cols):
                return True
            # Backtrack
            board[x][y] = '.'

    return False


def solveSudoku(self, board):
    """
    :type board: List[List[str]]
    :rtype: None Do not return anything, modify board
    in-place instead.
    """
    rows = len(board)
    cols = len(board[0])

    empty = self.emptySlots(board, rows, cols)
    self.DFS(board, empty, 0, len(empty), rows, cols)
```

16.2 Example 2: Robot Vacuum

```
# Example Usage
if __name__ == "__main__":
    board = [
        ["5", "3", ".", ".", "7", ".", ".", ".", "."],
        ["6", ".", ".", "1", "9", "5", ".", ".", "."],
        [".", "9", "8", ".", ".", ".", ".", "6", "."],
        ["8", ".", ".", ".", "6", ".", ".", ".", "3"],
        ["4", ".", ".", "8", ".", "3", ".", ".", "1"],
        ["7", ".", ".", ".", "2", ".", ".", ".", "6"],
        [".", "6", ".", ".", ".", ".", "2", "8", "."],
        [".", ".", ".", "4", "1", "9", ".", ".", "5"],
        [".", ".", ".", ".", "8", ".", ".", "7", "9"]
    ]

    solution = Solution()
    solution.solveSudoku(board)
    for row in board:
        print(row)
```

16.1.4 Complexity Analysis

- **Time Complexity**: The time complexity is approximately $O(9^M)$, where MMM is the number of empty cells. For each empty cell, we have nine possible numbers to check. While backtracking prunes invalid choices, the worst-case complexity remains high due to the vast number of possibilities.
- **Space Complexity**: The space complexity is $O(M)$ because we store the coordinates of empty cells in a list and use recursion, which has a stack size proportional to the number of empty cells.

This solution is efficient enough to solve a standard Sudoku puzzle due to the constraints of 9×9 grid size.

16.2 Example 2: Robot Vacuum

16.2.1 Problem

Given a robot cleaner in a room that is simulated as a grid. Each cell in the grid can be empty or blocked. A robot cleaner with four given APIs can go forward, turn left or turn right. Each revolution is 90°. When it tries to move into an occupied cell, its sensors detect an obstacle and stay on the current cell.

Design an algorithm to clean the entire room using only the four given APIs shown below.

```
interface Robot {
    returns true if next cell is open and robot moves into
    the cell.
    returns false if next cell is obstacle and robot stays
    on the current cell.
    boolean move();

    //robot will stay on the same cell after calling
    turnLeft/turnright, each turn will be 90 degrees.
    void turnLeft();
    void turnRight();

    //Clean the current cell.
    void clean();
}
```

Example
Input: room = [

```
    [1,1,1,1,1,0,1,1],
    [1,1,1,1,1,0,1,1],
    [1,0,1,1,1,1,1,1],
    [0,0,0,1,0,0,0,0],
    [1,1,1,1,1,1,1,1]
],
Row = 1,
col = 3
```

Illustrate:
All grids in the room are marked with 0 or 1.
0 means the unit is blocked, while 1 means the unit is accessible.
The robot initially starts from a position where row = 1, col = 3. Starting from the top left corner, it is placed in the lower row and in the right three columns.

16.2.2 Explanation of the Code

This problem involves programming a robot to clean an entire room with obstacles, where the room is represented as a 2D grid. The robot can use only a set of limited APIs: `move()`, `turnLeft()`, `turnRight()`, and `clean()`. We do not have direct access to the room layout, so we rely on depth-first search (DFS) and backtracking to ensure that the robot covers every accessible cell while avoiding obstacles.

The solution is implemented using a recursive DFS approach with backtracking to clean the room effectively.

16.2.2.1 Step-by-Step Explanation

1. **Direction Handling**:
   (a) We define four possible movement directions for the robot in the `directions` list: `[(0, 1), (1, 0), (0, -1), (-1, 0)]`.
   (b) Each tuple represents a movement in the grid (right, down, left, up), corresponding to moving in four directions.
   (c) The variable d represents the robot's current direction.

2. `goBack()` **Function**:
   (a) This helper function allows the robot to return to its previous position after exploring a direction.
   (b) To go back, the robot turns around by making two left turns (`turnLeft` twice), moves one step back (`move`), and then turns back to its original orientation (`turnRight` twice).

3. `dfs()` **Function**:
   (a) This is the core function that performs DFS to clean the room.
   (b) `pos`: The current position of the robot.
   (c) d: The direction in which the robot is currently facing.
   (d) `lookup`: A set to keep track of visited positions to avoid redundant work.
   (e) The function first checks if the current position `pos` is already cleaned (in `lookup`). If so, it returns to avoid re-cleaning.
   (f) The robot cleans the current cell and adds the position to `lookup`.
   (g) For each of the four possible directions, it attempts to move forward.
   - If `move()` returns `True`, indicating an accessible cell, it recursively calls `dfs()` to explore further.
   - After exploring in a particular direction, it uses `goBack()` to return to the original position and orientation.
   (h) The robot then turns right to change direction and continues with the next direction.

(i) `d = (d + 1) % len(directions)` updates the direction index, ensuring it rotates through all four directions.

4. **Starting the Cleaning Process**:
   (a) The cleaning process is initiated by calling `dfs()` with the robot starting at the position `(0, 0)` and facing "upward" (initial direction `d = 0`).
   (b) A `set()` is used to keep track of visited cells, so the robot does not re-clean cells or revisit paths unnecessarily.

16.2.3 Code

Here's the full code implementation for the robot vacuum cleaner:

Code 16.2: Python Implementation for Robot Vacuum Cleaner

```python
class Solution(object):
    def cleanRoom(self, robot):
        """
        :type robot: Robot
        :rtype: None
        """
        directions = [(0, 1), (1, 0), (0, -1), (-1, 0)]
        # Right, Down, Left, Up

        def goBack(robot):
            robot.turnLeft()
            robot.turnLeft()
            robot.move()
            robot.turnRight()
            robot.turnRight()

        def dfs(pos, robot, d, lookup):
            # If the position is already cleaned, return
            if pos in lookup:
                return

            # Mark the position as cleaned
            lookup.add(pos)
            robot.clean()
```

16.2 Example 2: Robot Vacuum

```
            # Attempt to move in each of the 4 possible
            directions
            for _ in range(4):
                new_x, new_y = pos[0] + directions[d][0],
                pos[1] + directions[d][1]

                if robot.move():
                    dfs((new_x, new_y), robot, d, lookup)
                    goBack(robot)

                # Rotate the robot to the next direction
                robot.turnRight()
                d = (d + 1) % 4

    # Start DFS from the initial position (0, 0) with
    the initial direction facing "up" (index 0)
    dfs((0, 0), robot, 0, set())
```

16.2.4 Complexity Analysis

- **Time Complexity**: The time complexity is $O(N - K)$, where NNN is the number of cells in the room and KKK is the number of obstacles. This is because, in the worst case, we need to visit every accessible cell exactly once.
- **Space Complexity**: The space complexity is $O(N - K)$ as well, due to the `lookup` set that stores the positions of all accessible cells. Additionally, the recursive stack can reach a depth of up to $O(N - K)$ in the worst case if the robot has to explore all cells.

16.2.5 Explanation of How the Code Works

1. **Traversal**:
   (a) The robot starts from its initial position and explores each direction recursively.

(b) For each direction, if it encounters an obstacle, it does not move. If the path is clear, it moves forward, cleans the cell, and then calls `dfs()` to continue exploring from this new cell.

2. **Backtracking**:

   (a) After fully exploring a direction, the robot uses `goBack()` to return to its previous position.

   (b) This allows it to clean each cell once and only once, avoiding redundant moves and ensuring all reachable cells are eventually cleaned.

3. **Direction Rotation**:

   (a) The robot attempts each direction in a clockwise manner. After finishing all four directions from a cell, it completes the DFS call and returns to the previous cell to continue cleaning from there.

16.2.6 Example Walkthrough

For a given room with obstacles and the robot starting at $(1, 3)$, the robot will:

1. Clean the starting cell.
2. Check all four directions (right, down, left, up).
3. Move to any accessible cell and repeat the process.
4. If it reaches a dead-end, it backtracks using `goBack()`.
5. Continue until all reachable cells are cleaned.

16.2.7 Key Points

- **DFS with Backtracking** ensures that all reachable cells are cleaned without needing knowledge of the room layout.
- **Avoiding Infinite Loops**: By marking visited cells, we avoid cleaning the same cell multiple times.
- **Clockwise Rotation** enables efficient exploration in all four directions without unnecessary movements.

Chapter 17
Breadth-First Search

17.1 Breadth Traversal

Breadth-first traversal (BFT) is a fundamental graph traversal algorithm widely used in computer science for various applications. Below, I'll elaborate on the key aspects of BFT, its mechanics, and specific applications, as well as additional details regarding its behavior in different scenarios.

17.1.1 Mechanics of Breadth-First Traversal

1. **Queue-Based Approach**:
   (a) Starting at the source node, BFS marks it as visited and enqueues it. Nodes are dequeued one at a time, processed, and their unvisited neighbors are added to the queue.

2. **State Management**:
   (a) During the traversal, it's crucial to manage the state of nodes to avoid revisiting them. This is achieved by maintaining a set of visited nodes.
   (b) If a newly encountered node has already been visited or falls outside predefined bounds (like graph boundaries), it is not enqueued for further exploration.

3. **Distance Calculation**:
   (a) When finding the shortest path in an unweighted graph, BFT guarantees that the first time a node is visited, it is reached via the shortest path (minimum edges).
   (b) Additional data structures (like arrays or maps) may be used to keep track of distances from the source node to other nodes.

17.1.2 Applications of Breadth-First Traversal

1. **Shortest Path in Unweighted Graphs**:
   (a) BFT is optimal for finding the shortest path by the number of edges from a starting node to other nodes in an unweighted graph. The traversal inherently explores all paths layer by layer.

2. **Smallest Spanning Tree (SST)**:
   (a) Any spanning tree obtained from an unweighted graph can be considered a smallest spanning tree since all edges are of equal weight. BFT effectively explores these edges.

3. **Peer-to-Peer Networks**:
   (a) In networks like BitTorrent, BFT finds all neighbor nodes efficiently, enabling resource sharing and connectivity checks.

4. **Web Crawlers**:
   (a) Search engine crawlers utilize BFT for indexing. They start from a source page, follow all links, and index pages layer by layer, which helps in managing the depth of the search.

5. **Social Networking**:
   (a) Social networks use BFS to identify users within a specified distance kkk, aiding in friend recommendations and connections.

6. **GPS Navigation Systems**:
   (a) BFT helps in identifying nearby locations or points of interest by exploring the network of roads or paths.

7. **Network Broadcasting**:
   (a) In networking, BFT is used to disseminate packets efficiently, ensuring that all nodes receive messages through layer-wise traversal.

8. **Garbage Collection**:
   (a) Algorithms like Cheney's use BFT for memory management, ensuring that objects are reachable and minimizing overhead by prioritizing citation positions.

9. **Loop Detection in Graphs**:
   (a) BFT can identify cycles in directed graphs and loops in undirected graphs by tracking the nodes and their visitation status.

10. **Ford-Fulkerson Algorithm**:
    (a) Used for computing maximum flow in networks, BFT is preferred for finding augmenting paths, as it optimizes time complexity to $O(VE^2)$.

17.2 Example 1: Walls and Doors

11. **Bipartite Graph Testing**:

    (a) BFT can be employed to determine if a graph is bipartite by attempting to color the graph using two colors and checking for conflicts.

12. **Pathfinding**:

    (a) BFT is useful for pathfinding between two vertices, confirming the existence of a path through level-wise exploration.

13. **Connected Component Detection**:

    (a) BFT can find all nodes in a connected component starting from a given node, marking all reachable nodes.

17.1.3 *Additional Considerations*

- **Time Complexity**: BFT runs in O(V+E) where V is the number of vertices and EEE is the number of edges, making it efficient for sparse graphs.
- **Space Complexity**: The space complexity is also O(V) due to the storage required for the queue and visited set.
- **Depth vs. Breadth**: While depth-first traversal (DFT) may be used in similar applications, BFT is often favored when the shortest path or minimum distance is required due to its systematic layer-wise exploration.

In summary, breadth-first traversal is a versatile and efficient algorithm used in various applications, especially in scenarios where the shortest path, connectivity, or exhaustive exploration of nodes is required. Its queue-based approach and systematic exploration make it particularly suitable for unweighted graphs and practical applications like networking and search indexing.

17.2 Example 1: Walls and Doors

17.2.1 *Problem*

For an m × n 2D mesh, initialize with three possible values. 1: Walls or barriers, 0: Doors, INF-Infinity: Indicates an empty room.

The value 2147483647 represents INF, assuming distances are less than this value. Each empty room is filled with its shortest distance to a door. Unreachable rooms retain INF.

For example, given the following 2D mesh:

INF −1 0 INF

INF INF INF −1

INF −1 INF −1

0 −1 INF INF

When the function is executed, the mesh becomes:

3 −1 0 1

2 2 1 −1

1 −1 2 −1

0 −1 3 4

To solve the problem where you want to identify the best positions for a rat to stay as far away from a cat as possible on a 2D board, we can approach it by calculating the distance from each empty space to the nearest cat and then selecting the positions that maximize this distance.

17.2.2 Solution

1. **Board Representation**:

    (a) **Empty Space**: Represented as 0.
    (b) **Obstacle**: Represented as −1.
    (c) **Cat**: Represented as 1.

2. **Distance Calculation**:

    (a) We'll use **Breadth-First Search (BFS)** to calculate the distance from each cat to every reachable empty space. This ensures that we find the shortest distance from each cat to each empty space efficiently.

3. **Maximizing Distance**:

    (a) After calculating the distances, we will find the maximum distance and collect all empty spaces that have this maximum distance.

17.2.3 Implementation Steps

1. Initialize a queue with the positions of all cats.
2. Use BFS to propagate the distances from the cats to the empty spaces.
3. After BFS, determine the maximum distance found and return all positions that have this distance.

    Here's how you can implement this solution in Python:

17.2 Example 1: Walls and Doors

Code 17.1: Python Implementation for Walls and Doors

```
from collections import deque


def farthest_positions(board):
    if not board or not board[0]:
        return []

    rows, cols = len(board), len(board[0])
    directions = [(-1, 0), (1, 0), (0, -1), (0, 1)]  #
    Up, Down, Left, Right
    queue = deque()

    # Initialize queue with positions of cats and set
    distances
    distance = [[float('inf')] * cols for _ in
    range(rows)]

    for r in range(rows):
        for c in range(cols):
            if board[r][c] == 1:  # Cat found
                queue.append((r, c))
                distance[r][c] = 0  # Distance to
                itself is 0

    # Perform BFS from all cats
    while queue:
        x, y = queue.popleft()

        for dx, dy in directions:
            nx, ny = x + dx, y + dy

            if 0 <= nx < rows and 0 <= ny < cols:
                if board[nx][ny] == 0 and distance[nx]
                [ny] == float('inf'):
                    distance[nx][ny] = distance[x][y] + 1
                    queue.append((nx, ny))

    # Find the maximum distance and corresponding
    positions
    max_distance = -1
    result = []
```

```
            for r in range(rows):
                for c in range(cols):
                    if board[r][c] == 0:   # Only check
                    empty spaces
                        if distance[r][c] > max_distance:
                            max_distance = distance[r][c]
                            result = [(r, c)]
                        elif distance[r][c] == max_distance:
                            result.append((r, c))

    return result

# Example Usage
board = [
    [0, -1, 1, 0],
    [0, 0, 0, -1],
    [0, -1, 0, -1],
    [1, -1, 0, 0]
]

farthest_spots = farthest_positions(board)
print(f"The positions farthest from the cats are:
{farthest_spots}")
```

17.2.4 Explanation of the Code

1. **Input Board**: The `board` variable is defined, representing empty spaces, obstacles, and cats.
2. **Distance Initialization**: A 2D list `distance` is initialized to infinity for each cell, representing the minimum distance from each cat to the empty spaces.
3. **BFS**:
   (a) All cats are added to a queue, and their distances are initialized to 0.
   (b) For each position, we check its neighbors. If an empty space (0) is found and its distance hasn't been set (still infinity), we update its distance and add it to the queue.
4. **Max Distance Calculation**:
   (a) After BFS, we iterate through the `distance` list to find the maximum distance and the corresponding positions that have this distance.
5. **Output**: The positions are returned as a list of tuples.

17.2.5 Complexity

- **Time Complexity**: O(R×C), where RRR is the number of rows and CCC is the number of columns, because we process each cell in the board once.
- **Space Complexity**: O(R×C) for the distance grid and the queue used in BFS.

This implementation effectively ensures the rat can identify the best spots to stay away from the cats while considering the obstacles on the board.

17.3 Example 2: Curriculum

17.3.1 Problem

You must take a total of numCourses courses, marked from 0 to numCourses-1. Some courses may have prerequisites, for example, to take course 0, you must first take course 1, which is represented by a pair: [0,1]. Given the total number of courses and the list of prerequisite pairs, can you complete all the courses?

17.3.2 Solution

This can be done by using a topological sort approach, where the courses and their prerequisites form a Directed Acyclic Graph (DAG). If the graph contains a cycle, it's impossible to complete all courses, since some courses will have circular dependencies. The Breadth-First Search (BFS) algorithm, specifically Kahn's Algorithm for topological sorting, can help solve this.

Here's a breakdown of the solution:

1. **Graph Representation**:
   (a) Each course is a node.
   (b) Each prerequisite pair [a,b] represents a directed edge from course b to course a, meaning you must complete course b before course aaa.

2. **In-Degree Array**:
   (a) We use an in-degree array to keep track of the number of prerequisites each course has.
   (b) Courses with `in-degree = 0` (no prerequisites) can be taken immediately.

3. **Queue and BFS**:
   (a) All courses with `in-degree = 0` are added to the queue initially.

(b) Each time a course is taken (dequeued), it reduces the in-degree of its dependent courses. If any dependent course's in-degree reaches zero, it is also added to the queue.
(c) This process continues until there are no more courses with zero in-degree left.

4. **Cycle Detection**:
   (a) If we're able to "unlock" all courses (meaning `count == numCourses`), then it's possible to complete all courses. Otherwise, there's a cycle, making it impossible to finish.

17.3.3 Code Implementation

Here's the Python code implementing this logic:

Code 17.2: Python Implementation for Curriculum

```python
from collections import deque
from typing import List

class Solution:
    def canFinish(self, numCourses: int, prerequisites: List[List[int]]) -> bool:
        if numCourses == 0:
            return True

        # Initialize adjacency list and in-degree array
        adj = [[] for _ in range(numCourses)]
        indegree = [0] * numCourses

        # Build the graph and in-degree array
        for course, prereq in prerequisites:
            adj[prereq].append(course)
            indegree[course] += 1

        # Initialize the queue with courses that have no
        prerequisites
        q = deque([i for i in range(numCourses) if indegree[i] == 0])
        count = len(q)  # Start count with number of
        courses with no prerequisites
```

17.3 Example 2: Curriculum

```python
        # Process the queue using BFS
        while q:
            current_course = q.popleft()
            for next_course in adj[current_course]:
                indegree[next_course] -= 1  # Reduce the
                in-degree for each neighboring course
                if indegree[next_course] == 0:  # If
                in-degree is 0, add it to the queue
                    q.append(next_course)
                    count += 1  # Increase the count of
                    courses that can be taken

        # If count matches numCourses, all courses can be
        finished
        return count == numCourses
def main():
    solution = Solution()

    # Test cases
    test_cases = [
        # Basic cases
        (2, [[1, 0]], True),             # Possible to
        finish: Course 1 depends on course 0.
        (2, [[1, 0], [0, 1]], False),    # Impossible to
        finish: Circular dependency between course 0 and
        course 1.
        (3, [[1, 0], [2, 1]], True),     # Possible to
        finish: Chain dependency 0 -> 1 -> 2.

        # Edge cases
        (1, [], True),                   # Only one
        course, no prerequisites, possible to finish.
        (5, [], True),                   # Multiple
        courses, no prerequisites, all are independent.
        (0, [], True),                   # No courses,
        trivially possible to "finish".

        # More complex cases
        (4, [[1, 0], [2, 1], [3, 2]], True),    # Chain
        of dependencies, possible to finish.
        (4, [[1, 0], [2, 1], [3, 2], [1, 3]], False),  #
        Circular dependency introduced.
```

```
    # Larger input with no cycles
    (6, [[1, 0], [2, 0], [3, 1], [4, 2], [5,
    3]], True),

    # Larger input with a cycle
    (6, [[1, 0], [2, 0], [3, 1], [4, 2], [5, 3], [0,
    5]], False),
]

# Running each test case
for i, (numCourses, prerequisites, expected) in
enumerate(test_cases):
    result = solution.canFinish(numCourses,
    prerequisites)
    assert result == expected, f"Test case {i+1}
    failed: Expected {expected}, got {result}"
    print(f"Test case {i+1} passed")

if __name__ == "__main__":
    main()
```

17.3.4 Explanation of Key Parts

1. **Graph Initialization**:

    (a) We create an adjacency list adj to represent dependencies and an indegree array to keep track of the number of prerequisites for each course.

2. **Building Graph and Indegree**:

    (a) Each prerequisite pair [a, b] updates the adjacency list (adj[b].append(a)) and increments indegree[a] since a depends on b.

3. **Queue Initialization**:

    (a) Courses with in-degree = 0 are enqueued as they have no prerequisites, making them immediately available to be taken.

4. **BFS Traversal**:

    (a) Each time a course is taken (popped from the queue), we "unlock" its dependent courses by reducing their in-degree. If a course's in-degree reaches zero, it's added to the queue.

5. **Completion Check**:

    (a) If count equals numCourses, it means we successfully took all courses; otherwise, there's a dependency cycle preventing completion.

17.3.5 Explanation for the Test Cases

- **Test Cases**:
  - A mix of small cases, edge cases (e.g., zero courses, no prerequisites), and more complex examples with and without cycles.
  - Each test includes the expected result to verify correctness.
- **Assertions**:
  - Each test compares the actual output of `canFinish` to the expected result. If it fails, it will output the test case number and expected vs. actual results.
- **Execution**:
  - `main()` runs all test cases. If all assertions pass, each case prints `"Test case X passed"`. If any fail, an assertion error is raised with details.

This approach will allow you to confirm the code's correctness across a range of scenarios.

17.3.6 Complexity Analysis

- **Time Complexity**: $O(V+E)$, where V is the number of courses (nodes) and E is the number of prerequisites (edges).
- **Space Complexity**: $O(V+E)$ for storing the graph and the queue.

This BFS approach efficiently determines if it's possible to complete all courses by ensuring all prerequisites are accounted for in the correct order.

17.4 Example 3: Bus Routes

17.4.1 Problem

Question: There is a list of bus routes. Each route [i] is a bus route that the ith bus repeats forever. For example, if routes [0] = [1, 5, 7], it means that the first bus (index 0) runs in the order of 1-> 5-> 7-> 1-> 5-> 7-> 1-> ... Forever.

Start at station S (not on the bus at first) and want to go to station T. What is the minimum number of buses needed to reach the destination while traveling by bus? If unreachable, return −1.

Example
Input: route = [[1, 2, 7], [3, 6, 7]]; S = 1, T = 6.
  Output: 2.
  Explanation: The best strategy is to take the first bus to bus stop 7 and then take the second bus to bus stop 6.

17.4.2 The Solution

To solve this problem, we use a Breadth-First Search (BFS) approach to find the shortest path (minimum number of buses) from the starting station S to the target station T. Here's an explanation of how the code works and the BFS approach used.

1. **Early Return**:
   (a) If the starting station S is the same as the target station T, we return 0 immediately, as no buses are needed.

2. **Mapping Stops to Routes**:
   (a) We use a `stop_bus` dictionary where each stop points to a list of bus routes that stop there. This helps to quickly find all routes accessible from any stop.

3. **BFS Initialization**:
   (a) A queue is used to explore each stop along with the count of buses taken so far. We start by enqueuing the starting station S with 1 (indicating the first bus).
   (b) A `bus_visited` set tracks the buses that have already been used to prevent redundant traversals.

4. **BFS Traversal**:
   (a) For each stop dequeued, we check all bus routes available from that stop.
   (b) If a route has not been visited, mark it as visited.
   (c) For each stop on that bus route:
   - If the stop is the target T, return the count of buses, as this is the minimum found.
   - Otherwise, enqueue the stop with an incremented bus count.

5. **End of BFS**:
   (a) If the queue is exhausted without reaching the target, return −1, indicating it's not possible to reach the target station.

17.4.3 Code Implementation

Code 17.3: Python Implemention for Bus Routes

17.4 Example 3: Bus Routes

```python
from collections import defaultdict, deque
from typing import List

class Solution:
    def numBusesToDestination(self, routes: List[List[int]], S: int, T: int) -> int:
        if S == T:
            return 0

        # Map each stop to the list of buses (routes)
        # that visit that stop
        stop_bus = defaultdict(list)
        for i, route in enumerate(routes):
            for stop in route:
                stop_bus[stop].append(i)

        # Initialize BFS
        bus_visited = set()  # Tracks which bus routes have been taken
        queue = deque([(S, 1)])  # Queue with (current stop, number of buses taken)

        # BFS loop
        while queue:
            stop, buses = queue.popleft()
            for bus in stop_bus[stop]:  # Check all bus routes passing through current stop
                if bus in bus_visited:
                    continue
                bus_visited.add(bus)

                # Traverse each stop in the current bus route
                for s in routes[bus]:
                    if s == T:
                        return buses
                    queue.append((s, buses + 1))

        return -1  # If the target cannot be reached


def main():
    solution = Solution()
```

```python
    # Test cases
    test_cases = [
        # Basic case
        ([[1, 2, 7], [3, 6, 7]], 1, 6, 2),  # Expected output: 2

        # Edge case: Start and target are the same
        ([[1, 2, 7], [3, 6, 7]], 1, 1, 0),  # Expected output: 0

        # Case with multiple bus options but shortest path is direct
        ([[1, 2, 3], [3, 4, 5], [5, 6, 7]], 1, 7, 3),  # Expected output: 3

        # Edge case: Destination unreachable
        ([[1, 2, 7], [3, 6, 7]], 1, 8, -1),  # Expected output: -1

        # Case with overlapping routes and multiple choices
        ([[1, 2, 7], [7, 8, 9], [8, 3, 6]], 1, 6, 3),  # Expected output: 3

        # Case with one route covering start and destination
        ([[1, 2, 3, 4, 5, 6]], 1, 6, 1),  # Expected output: 1

        # Large case with chain dependencies
        ([[i, i+1] for i in range(100)], 0, 99, 99),  # Expected output: 99
    ]

    # Running each test case
    for i, (routes, S, T, expected) in enumerate(test_cases):
        result = solution.numBusesToDestination(routes, S, T)
        assert result == expected, f"Test case {i+1} failed: Expected {expected}, got {result}"
        print(f"Test case {i+1} passed")

if __name__ == "__main__":
    main()
```

17.4.4 *Explanation*

- **Test Cases**:
  - **Basic cases** with direct routes and expected bus transfers.
  - **Edge cases** including starting at the destination and unreachable destinations.
  - **Overlapping routes** to test the algorithm's efficiency in handling multiple path options.
  - A **large test case** to check performance with numerous stops and buses.
- **Assertions**:
  - Each test checks if `result` matches the expected output and raises an error with details if it fails.
  - If all assertions pass, the function will output "Test case X passed" for each test.

17.4.5 *Example Walkthrough*

For `routes = [[1, 2, 7], [3, 6, 7]]`, `S = 1`, and `T = 6`:

1. **Mapping Creation**: `stop_bus = {1: [0], 2: [0], 7: [0, 1], 3: [1], 6: [1]}`
2. **BFS Process**:
   (a) Start at stop 1 with 1 bus.
   (b) Stop 1 has route 0, so visit stops 1, 2, and 7.
   (c) Enqueue stops 2 and 7 with 2 buses.
   (d) Stop 7 has route 1, so visit stops 3, 6, and 7.
   (e) Upon reaching stop 6, return 2 as the minimum number of buses needed.

17.4.6 *Complexity Analysis*

- **Time Complexity**: O(N×M), where N is the number of bus routes and M is the average number of stops per route. We visit each stop on each route at most once.
- **Space Complexity**: O(N+M) due to the space needed for the `stop_bus` mapping, `bus_visited`, and the BFS queue.

This BFS solution finds the minimum buses needed to reach the target efficiently.

17.5 Example 4: Are Graphs Dichotomy?

17.5.1 Problem

Given an undirected graph, determine if it is a bipartite graph. A graph is bipartite if its nodes can be split into two independent subsets, A and B, so that every edge connects a node in A with a node in B.

The graph is represented such that `graph[i]` contains a list of all nodes j that are connected to node i. Each node is an integer between 0 and `graph.length - 1`, and there are no self-loops or multiple edges (i.e., `graph[i]` will not contain i or duplicate nodes).

Input:

```
[[1,3],[0,2],[1,3],[0,2]]
```

Output:

```
True
```

Explanation:
The graph can be split into two groups: {0, 2} and {1, 3}.

Input:

```
[[1,2,3],[0,2],[0,1,3],[0,2]]
```

Output:

```
False
```

Explanation:
There is no way to split the nodes into two independent sets.

17.5.2 Solution

To solve this problem, use a breadth-first search (BFS) to attempt to color each node. If at any point two connected nodes have the same color, the graph is not bipartite. Otherwise, it is bipartite.

17.5.3 Code Implementation

Code 17.4: Python Implementation for isBipartite

17.5 Example 4: Are Graphs Dichotomy?

```python
from collections import deque
from typing import List

class Solution:
    def isBipartite(self, graph: List[List[int]])
    -> bool:
        size = len(graph)
        colors = [None] * size  # None = unvisited, "red"
        and "green" for two colors

        for i in range(size):
            if colors[i] is not None:  # Node
            already colored
                continue

            # Start BFS from the unvisited node
            queue = deque([i])
            colors[i] = "red"  # Start coloring the first
            node as "red"

            while queue:
                node = queue.popleft()
                current_color = colors[node]
                next_color = "green" if current_color ==
                "red" else "red"

                # Visit all neighbors
                for neighbor in graph[node]:
                    if colors[neighbor] is None:  # If
                    unvisited
                        colors[neighbor] = next_color
                        queue.append(neighbor)
                    elif colors[neighbor] == current_
                    color:  # Conflict in coloring
                        return False

        return True


def main():
    solution = Solution()
```

```
# Test cases
test_cases = [
    # Basic bipartite case
    ([[1, 3], [0, 2], [1, 3], [0, 2]], True),  # Expected output: True

    # Non-bipartite case
    ([[1, 2, 3], [0, 2], [0, 1, 3], [0, 2]], False),  # Expected output: False

    # Bipartite case with disconnected nodes
    ([[1], [0, 3], [3], [1, 2]], True),  # Expected output: True

    # Single node (trivially bipartite)
    ([[]], True),  # Expected output: True

    # Empty graph (no edges, so it's bipartite)
    ([], True),  # Expected output: True

    # Bipartite case with complex structure
    ([[1, 4], [0, 2, 3], [1, 5], [1, 5], [0, 5], [2, 3, 4]], True),  # Expected output: True

    # Larger bipartite case
    ([[1, 2], [0, 3], [0, 3], [1, 2]], True),  # Expected output: True
]

# Running each test case
for i, (graph, expected) in enumerate(test_cases):
    result = solution.isBipartite(graph)
    assert result == expected, f"Test case {i+1} failed: Expected {expected}, got {result}"
    print(f"Test case {i+1} passed")

if __name__ == "__main__":
    main()
```

17.5.4 Explanation of the Code

1. **Initialization**: A `colors` array keeps track of each node's color, with `None` indicating unvisited nodes.
2. **BFS Traversal**: For each unvisited node, we perform BFS. Starting with "red," we alternate colors for each node's neighbors.
3. **Conflict Check**: If we encounter a neighbor with the same color as the current node, the graph is not bipartite, and we return `False`.
4. **Completion**: If no conflicts are found, we return `True`, indicating the graph is bipartite.

17.5.5 Explanation for Test Cases

- **Test Cases**:
  - **Basic cases** to check simple bipartite and non-bipartite graphs.
  - **Edge cases** with a single node and no nodes at all, which should both return `True` as they meet bipartite criteria.
  - **Complex and larger cases** to test the algorithm's ability to handle various graph configurations.
- **Assertions**:
  - Each test verifies that the `result` matches `expected` and raises an error with details if it fails.
  - Passing tests output "Test case X passed" for each case.

17.6 Example 5: Word Ladder II

17.6.1 Problem

Given two words (beginWord and endWord) and a dictionary of words, find all the shortest conversion sequences from beginWord to endWord, for example: (1) Only one letter can be changed at a time; (2) Each converted word must be present in the word list. Note that beginWord is not a converted word.

Example 1
Input:

```
beginWord ="hit",
endWord =" cog",
wordList = ["hot", " dot", " dog", " lot", " log", " cog"]
```

Output:

```
[
    [" hit", " hot", " dot", " dog", " cog"],
    [" hit", " hot", " lot", " log", " cog"]
]
```

Example 2
Input:

```
beginWord ="hit"
endWord ="cog"
wordList = [" hot", " dot", " dog", " lot", " log"]
```

Output:

[ ]

Explanation: endWord "cog" is not in wordList, so it can't be converted.

17.6.2 Problem Summary

The problem is to find all shortest transformation sequences from a `beginWord` to an `endWord`, where:

1. Only one letter can be changed at a time.
2. Each intermediate word in the sequence must be in a given `wordList`.
3. The sequence length must be minimized.

The transformation can be viewed as finding the shortest paths in an unweighted graph, where:

- Each word is a node.
- An edge exists between two nodes if the corresponding words differ by exactly one letter.

17.6.3 Code Analysis

The code uses two main algorithms:

1. **Breadth-First Search (BFS)**: This finds the shortest distance from the `endWord` to all other words in the graph.

17.6 Example 5: Word Ladder II

2. **Depth-First Search (DFS)**: After BFS determines the shortest distances, DFS builds all possible paths from `beginWord` to `endWord` that adhere to these distances.

17.6.4 Code Walkthrough

Code 17.5: Python Implementation for Word Ladder II

```python
from collections import deque
from typing import List
import string

class Solution:
    def findLadders(self, beginWord: str, endWord: str,
    wordList: List[str]) -> List[List[str]]:
        # Establish distances from each word to endWord
        dist = {endWord: 0}
        q = deque([(endWord, 0)])
        words = set(wordList)

        # Helper function to generate all possible next
        words differing by one letter
        def nextWords(word):
            result = []
            for i in range(len(word)):
                for c in string.ascii_lowercase:
                    if c == word[i]:
                        continue
                    w = word[:i] + c + word[i + 1:]
                    if w in words or w == beginWord:
                        result.append(w)
            return result

        # BFS to build distances from endWord
        while q:
            word, distance = q.popleft()
            if word == beginWord:
                break
            for w in nextWords(word):
                if w not in dist:
                    dist[w] = distance + 1
                    q.append((w, distance + 1))

        solution = []
```

```python
        # DFS to construct paths based on BFS distances
        def dfs(word, res):
            if word == endWord:
                solution.append(res[:])
                return
            for w in nextWords(word):
                if w not in dist:
                    continue
                if dist[w] == dist[word] - 1:  # only
                consider next distance word
                    res.append(w)
                    dfs(w, res)
                    res.pop()

        dfs(beginWord, [beginWord])
        return solution
def main():
    solution = Solution()

    # Test case 1: Expected output with multiple
    shortest paths
    beginWord1 = "hit"
    endWord1 = "cog"
    wordList1 = ["hot", "dot", "dog", "lot",
    "log", "cog"]
    output1 = solution.findLadders(beginWord1, endWord1,
    wordList1)
    print("Test case 1:")
    print(f"Input: beginWord = '{beginWord1}', endWord =
    '{endWord1}', wordList = {wordList1}")
    print("Output:", output1)
    print()

    # Test case 2: No valid transformation path (endWord
    not in wordList)
    beginWord2 = "hit"
    endWord2 = "cog"
    wordList2 = ["hot", "dot", "dog", "lot", "log"]
    output2 = solution.findLadders(beginWord2, endWord2,
    wordList2)
    print("Test case 2:")
    print(f"Input: beginWord = '{beginWord2}', endWord =
    '{endWord2}', wordList = {wordList2}")
```

17.6 Example 5: Word Ladder II

```python
        print("Output:", output2)
        print()

        # Test case 3: Only one transformation needed
        beginWord3 = "hit"
        endWord3 = "hot"
        wordList3 = ["hot"]
        output3 = solution.findLadders(beginWord3, endWord3,
        wordList3)
        print("Test case 3:")
        print(f"Input: beginWord = '{beginWord3}', endWord =
        '{endWord3}', wordList = {wordList3}")
        print("Output:", output3)
        print()

        # Test case 4: Larger wordList with multiple
        shortest paths
        beginWord4 = "a"
        endWord4 = "c"
        wordList4 = ["a", "b", "c"]
        output4 = solution.findLadders(beginWord4, endWord4,
        wordList4)
        print("Test case 4:")
        print(f"Input: beginWord = '{beginWord4}', endWord =
        '{endWord4}', wordList = {wordList4}")
        print("Output:", output4)
        print()

        # Test case 5: Edge case with no transformations
        needed (beginWord equals endWord)
        beginWord5 = "hit"
        endWord5 = "hit"
        wordList5 = ["hit"]
        output5 = solution.findLadders(beginWord5, endWord5,
        wordList5)
        print("Test case 5:")
        print(f"Input: beginWord = '{beginWord5}', endWord =
        '{endWord5}', wordList = {wordList5}")
        print("Output:", output5)
        print()

    if __name__ == "__main__":
        main()
```

17.6.5 Explanation of Test Cases

1. **Test Case 1**: Standard case with multiple shortest transformation paths.
2. **Test Case 2**: Edge case where `endWord` is not in `wordList`, so no transformations are possible.
3. **Test Case 3**: Only one transformation step is required to reach the `endWord`.
4. **Test Case 4**: Smallest example with multiple paths in a minimal word list.
5. **Test Case 5**: `beginWord` is the same as `endWord`, so no transformations are required.

Each test is set up to provide a thorough examination of typical and edge scenarios for the `findLadders` function.

17.6.6 Complexity Analysis

1. **Breadth-First Search (BFS)**:

   (a) **Purpose**: BFS determines the shortest path distances from `endWord` to all other words.

   (b) **Time Complexity**:
   - For each word in the word list, the code generates all possible "one-letter-difference" words. For a word with length L, there are 26×L possible words, where each word is checked for existence in `wordList` (stored as a set, allowing O(1) average-time lookups).
   - Since we process each word in the word list at most once, the BFS takes O(M×26×L)=O(M×L), where M is the number of words in `wordList`.

   (c) **Space Complexity**:
   - The distance dictionary (`dist`) holds distances for each word in the list, requiring O(M) space.
   - The queue q can contain up to M words at a time, leading to an additional O(M) space.

2. **Depth-First Search (DFS)**:

   (a) **Purpose**: DFS is used to construct all possible paths that meet the shortest path criteria.

   (b) **Time Complexity**:
   - In the worst case, all paths from `beginWord` to `endWord` that respect the shortest distance are explored.
   - Let PPP be the number of possible paths. The time complexity here is O(P×L) because each path (of maximum length L) is stored.

17.6 Example 5: Word Ladder II   307

(c) **Space Complexity**:
   - The DFS recursion stack can go as deep as L, giving an O(L) space complexity for the recursion call stack.
   - `solution` stores all paths, so its space complexity is O(P×L)

3. **Overall Complexity**:

   (a) **Time Complexity**: O(M×L+P×L)
      - The O(M×L) term arises from the BFS setup.
      - O(P×L) represents the DFS process to list all valid paths.

   (b) **Space Complexity**: O(M+P×L)
      - O(M) for `dist` and queue.
      - O(P×L) for `solution`.

17.6.7 Edge Cases

1. **No Possible Transformation**: If `endWord` is not in `wordList`, return an empty list immediately.
2. **Begin and End Words are the Same**: If `beginWord == endWord`, return a list with only `beginWord`.
3. **Disconnected Graph**: If `beginWord` or `endWord` are isolated (no possible connections), the algorithm terminates after BFS without finding a path.

17.6.8 Summary

This solution efficiently finds the shortest transformation sequences by using BFS to calculate distances and then DFS to construct valid paths based on these distances. The complexity reflects the cost of finding paths in the graph of words and storing multiple solutions if they exist.

Chapter 18
Union-Find

A set is used to determine if two points belong to the same group. If they are in the same group but not yet merged, the groups are combined. Belonging to the same group implies that two points are connected, either directly or indirectly.

Dynamic connectivity problems involve determining whether two objects are connected within a group where connections may be direct or indirect. Such questions can be abstracted as follows:

- There is a set of objects that make up a disjoint set.
- Union: concatenate two objects.
- Find: Returns whether there is a connected path between two objects.

18.1 Union-Find the Basics

Union-Find determines if two elements belong to the same group (connected component) using a "parent" array, where each element points to its parent in a tree-like structure. When two elements share the same root, they are in the same group.

18.1.1 Algorithm Description

1. **Quick Find (Basic Union-Find)**:
   (a) Each vertex initially has a unique ID.
   (b) When merging two vertices from different groups, all nodes in one group are assigned the ID of the other group.
   (c) This can be slow since it requires updating the IDs of all nodes in the group during each merge.

2. **Quick Union (Improved Union-Find)**:
   (a) Each group is represented as a tree, where nodes point to a parent node.
   (b) Each group has a unique root, and all nodes in a group share the same root.
   (c) To merge groups, only the root of one tree is changed to point to the root of another, rather than updating every node.
3. **Union-Find with Path Compression and Union by Rank** (Optimal Version):
   (a) **Path Compression**: Updates each node's parent directly to the root during a search, flattening the tree for faster future queries.
   (b) **Union by Rank**: Connects the shorter tree under the taller tree's root, maintaining balance and improving efficiency.

18.1.2 Python Code Implementation

Code 18.1: Python Program for the Union-Find Algorithm to Detect Cycles in an Undirected Graph

```python
# Python program for the Union-Find algorithm to detect
cycles in an undirected graph
class UnionFind:
    def __init__(self, n):
        self.parent = list(range(n))
        self.rank = [0] * n  # Rank is used to keep the
        tree flat

    def find(self, x):
        # Path compression optimization
        if self.parent[x] != x:
            self.parent[x] = self.find(self.parent[x])
        return self.parent[x]

    def union(self, x, y):
        # Find roots of the sets x and y belong to
        rootX = self.find(x)
        rootY = self.find(y)

        # Union by rank optimization
        if rootX != rootY:
            if self.rank[rootX] > self.rank[rootY]:
                self.parent[rootY] = rootX
```

18.1 Union-Find the Basics

```python
            elif self.rank[rootX] < self.rank[rootY]:
                self.parent[rootX] = rootY
            else:
                self.parent[rootY] = rootX
                self.rank[rootX] += 1

class Graph:
    def __init__(self, vertices):
        self.V = vertices
        self.edges = []  # List to store graph edges

    def add_edge(self, u, v):
        self.edges.append((u, v))

    def has_cycle(self):
        # Initialize Union-Find
        uf = UnionFind(self.V)

        # Check for cycles
        for u, v in self.edges:
            if uf.find(u) == uf.find(v):
                return True  # Cycle found
            uf.union(u, v)
        return False  # No cycles

# Create a graph and add edges
g = Graph(3)
g.add_edge(0, 1)
g.add_edge(1, 2)
g.add_edge(2, 0)

# Check if the graph contains a cycle
if g.has_cycle():
    print("Graph contains a cycle")
else:
    print("Graph does not contain a cycle")
```

18.1.3 Explanation of Key Parts

- **Union-Find Class**: Manages the parent and rank arrays. The `find` method uses path compression, and the `union` method uses union by rank to keep the trees balanced.

- **Graph Class**: Stores the graph edges and uses the Union-Find class to check if adding each edge forms a cycle.

This implementation efficiently handles large datasets using path compression and union by rank, achieving near-constant time per operation, ideal for large-scale connectivity queries.

18.2 Example 1: Circle Number

18.2.1 Problem

There are N students in a class. Some of them are friends, some of them are not. Their friendship is inherently passive. For example, if A is a direct friend of B, and B is a direct friend of C, then A is an indirect friend of C. And what we define as a circle of friends is a group of students who are directly or indirectly friends.

Given an N*N matrix, M represents the friendship between the students in the class. If M[i][j] = 1, then the ith and jth students are each other's direct friends, otherwise they are not. And you have to output the total number of moments of friends among all students.

Example 1
Input:
  [[1,1,0],[1,1,0],[0,0,1]] output 2
Description: Students 0 and 1 are direct friends, so they are in the circle of friends.
The second student himself is in the circle of friends. So return 2.

18.2.2 Problem Summary

- Given an N×N matrix M, where `M[i][j]` = 1 means that the i-th and j-th students are direct friends, find the number of friend groups.
- We can solve this problem with three methods: Breadth-First Search (BFS), Depth-First Search (DFS), and Union-Find.

18.2.3 Breadth-First Search (BFS) Solution

In this approach, we use BFS to explore each student's friendship group. Once we visit a student, we mark them as "visited" (by setting `M[i][j]` = -1). If we encounter an unvisited friend, we explore their friends recursively.

18.2 Example 1: Circle Number

Code 18.2: BFS to Find the Circle Number

```
from collections import deque
from typing import List

def findCircleNum_bfs(M: List[List[int]]) -> int:
    def bfs(i, j):
        q = deque()
        q.append((i, j))
        M[i][j] = -1  # mark as visited
        while q:
            currx, curry = q.popleft()
            for dirx, diry in ((-1, 0), (1, 0), (0, -1),
            (0, 1)):
                nextx, nexty = currx + dirx, curry + diry
                if nextx < 0 or nextx >= m or nexty < 0
                or nexty >= n or M[nextx][nexty] != 1:
                    continue
                M[nextx][nexty] = -1  # mark as visited
                q.append((nextx, nexty))

    m, n = len(M), len(M[0])
    cnt = 0
    for i in range(m):
        for j in range(n):
            if M[i][j] == 1:
                cnt += 1
                bfs(i, j)
    return cnt
```

18.2.4 Depth-First Search (DFS) Solution

This approach is similar to BFS but uses DFS to explore each student's friend circle. If a student has not been visited, we recursively visit all of their friends, marking each as visited.

Code 18.3: DFS to Find the Circle Number

```python
from typing import List


def findCircleNum_dfs(M: List[List[int]]) -> int:
    def dfs(i, j):
        if M[i][j] == -1:  # visited
            return
        M[i][j] = -1  # mark as visited
        for dirx, diry in ((-1, 0), (1, 0), (0, -1),
        (0, 1)):
            next_i, next_j = i + dirx, j + diry
            if next_i < 0 or next_i >= m or next_j < 0 or
            next_j >= n or M[next_i][next_j] != 1:
                continue
            dfs(next_i, next_j)

    m, n = len(M), len(M[0])
    cnt = 0
    for i in range(m):
        for j in range(n):
            if M[i][j] == 1:
                cnt += 1
                dfs(i, j)
    return cnt
```

18.2.5 *Union-Find Solution*

The Union-Find algorithm is another approach to solve this problem efficiently. Here, each student starts as their own parent. We then union two students if they are directly connected. Each unique root represents a separate friend circle.

18.2 Example 1: Circle Number

Code 18.4: Union-Find to Find the Circle Number

```python
from typing import List


def findCircleNum_unionfind(M: List[List[int]]) -> int:
    def find(x):
        if roots[x] != x:
            roots[x] = find(roots[x])  # Path compression
        return roots[x]

    def union(x, y):
        rootX = find(x)
        rootY = find(y)
        if rootX != rootY:
            roots[rootY] = rootX  # Union the roots
            nonlocal total_cnt
            total_cnt -= 1

    n = len(M)
    roots = [i for i in range(n)]
    total_cnt = n

    for i in range(n):
        for j in range(i + 1, n):  # Avoid duplicate checks
            if M[i][j] == 1:
                union(i, j)

    return total_cnt
```

18.2.6 Test Code

Here's a test function to validate each of the three methods for finding the number of friend circles (BFS, DFS, and Union-Find) given the example input.

Code 18.5: Test Code for the Circle Number

```
from typing import List
from collections import deque

# Define the three friend circle methods
def findCircleNum_bfs(M: List[List[int]]) -> int:
    def bfs(i, j):
        q = deque()
        q.append((i, j))
        M[i][j] = -1  # mark as visited
        while q:
            currx, curry = q.popleft()
            for dirx, diry in ((-1, 0), (1, 0), (0, -1),
            (0, 1)):
                nextx, nexty = currx + dirx, curry + diry
                if nextx < 0 or nextx >= m or nexty < 0
                or nexty >= n or M[nextx][nexty] != 1:
                    continue
                M[nextx][nexty] = -1  # mark as visited
                q.append((nextx, nexty))

    m, n = len(M), len(M[0])
    cnt = 0
    for i in range(m):
        for j in range(n):
            if M[i][j] == 1:
                cnt += 1
                bfs(i, j)
    return cnt

def findCircleNum_dfs(M: List[List[int]]) -> int:
    def dfs(i, j):
        if M[i][j] == -1:  # visited
            return
        M[i][j] = -1  # mark as visited
        for dirx, diry in ((-1, 0), (1, 0), (0, -1),
        (0, 1)):
            next_i, next_j = i + dirx, j + diry
            if next_i < 0 or next_i >= m or next_j < 0 or
            next_j >= n or M[next_i][next_j] != 1:
                continue
            dfs(next_i, next_j)
```

18.2 Example 1: Circle Number

```
        m, n = len(M), len(M[0])
        cnt = 0
        for i in range(m):
            for j in range(n):
                if M[i][j] == 1:
                    cnt += 1
                    dfs(i, j)
        return cnt

    def findCircleNum_unionfind(M: List[List[int]]) -> int:
        def find(x):
            if roots[x] != x:
                roots[x] = find(roots[x])  # Path compression
            return roots[x]

        def union(x, y):
            rootX = find(x)
            rootY = find(y)
            if rootX != rootY:
                roots[rootY] = rootX  # Union the roots
                nonlocal total_cnt
                total_cnt -= 1

        n = len(M)
        roots = [i for i in range(n)]
        total_cnt = n

        for i in range(n):
            for j in range(i + 1, n):   # Avoid
            duplicate checks
                if M[i][j] == 1:
                    union(i, j)

        return total_cnt

# Test function to verify each method
def test_findCircleNum():
    test_matrix = [[1, 1, 0], [1, 1, 0], [0, 0, 1]]
    expected_output = 2
```

```python
    # Test BFS
    result_bfs = findCircleNum_bfs([row[:] for row in
    test_matrix])  # Deep copy for independent tests
    print(f"BFS Result: {result_bfs}, Expected:
    {expected_output}")
    assert result_bfs == expected_output, f"BFS failed:
    expected {expected_output}, got {result_bfs}"

    # Test DFS
    result_dfs = findCircleNum_dfs([row[:] for row in
    test_matrix])  # Deep copy for independent tests
    print(f"DFS Result: {result_dfs}, Expected:
    {expected_output}")
    assert result_dfs == expected_output, f"DFS failed:
    expected {expected_output}, got {result_dfs}"

    # Test Union-Find
    result_unionfind = findCircleNum_unionfind([row[:] for
    row in test_matrix])  # Deep copy for
    independent tests
    print(f"Union-Find Result: {result_unionfind},
    Expected: {expected_output}")
    assert result_unionfind == expected_output, f"Union-
    Find failed: expected {expected_output}, got
    {result_unionfind}"

    print("All tests passed!")

# Run the test function
test_findCircleNum()
```

18.2.7 Explanation

- **Deep Copying** ([row[:] for row in test_matrix]): Each method modifies the input matrix, so we create a deep copy for each test to ensure independence.
- **Expected Output**: The expected output for the provided test case is 2, meaning there are two distinct circles of friends.
- **Assertions**: Each test checks if the result matches the expected output. If any assertion fails, it will output a message showing the discrepancy.

Running this test_findCircleNum() function should verify that all three methods provide the correct output for the given input.

18.2 Example 1: Circle Number

18.2.8 Summary

Each approach provides an effective way to find the number of unique friend circles:

- **BFS and DFS**: Both have a time complexity of $O(N^2)$, as they need to explore each student and their friends.
- **Union-Find**: This is more efficient with path compression and union by rank, resulting in nearly constant time per union-find operation. It is optimal for large friendship matrices.

Chapter 19
Interview Questions

The following is based on some of the author's interview experience, and a few typical interview questions are selected to explain the interview process and requirements.

19.1 Example 1: File System

Problem description: Consider the design of a simple file system metadata structure with two entity types: Files and Directories. Each entity has an integer Entity ID and a Name. File entities also have an additional "size" attribute representing their space consumption in bytes. Like what:

```
=============== Given a file system: ===============
root (id=1)
    dir (id=2)
        file1 (id=4): 100b
        file2 (id=5): 200b
    file3 (id=3): 300b
```

The interviewer should clarify the problem and provide a direct example to ensure the candidate fully understands the question. The purpose is to make the candidate understand the meaning of the topic better, of course, if the candidate can express the meaning of the topic well, there can be a bonus here.

For example, the above topic can be expressed as follows:

```
Filesystem =
{ 1: { type: 'directory', name: "root", children: [2, 3] },
  2: { type: 'directory', name: "dir", children: [4, 5] },
  4: { type: 'file', name: "file1", size: 100 },
  5: { type: 'file', name: "file2", size: 200 },
  3: { type: 'file', name: "file3", size: 300 }
}
```

19.1.1 Problem Summary

The goal is to design a metadata structure for a file system. There are two main entity types in the system:

1. **Files**—Each file has an ID, name, and size.
2. **Directories (Catalogs)**—Each directory has an ID, name, and a list of child entities.

The objective is to calculate the total size of a directory, which includes the sizes of all files in that directory and its subdirectories.

19.1.2 Steps and Solution Outline

1. **Data Structure Representation**:

   (a) The document suggests creating an Entity class with attributes:
   - id: Integer representing the unique identifier of the entity.
   - type: String indicating whether it's a "file" or "directory".
   - name: String representing the name of the entity.
   - size: Integer representing the size (for files only, size is 0 for directories).
   - children: List of child entity IDs (for directories).

2. **Initialization Example**:
    (a) A sample `build_dict` function initializes the data structure with predefined entities:

```
def build_dict(self):
    entities = [
        Entity(id=1, type='directory', name="root",
            size=0, children=[2, 3]),
        Entity(id=2, type='directory', name="dir",
            size=0, children=[4, 5]),
        Entity(id=3, type='file', name="file1", size=100,
            children=[]),
        Entity(id=4, type='file', name="file2", size=200,
            children=[]),
        Entity(id=5, type='file', name="file3", size=300,
            children=[])
    ]
    entity_dict = {entity.id: entity for entity in
    entities}
    return entity_dict
```

3. **Function to Calculate Total Size** (`entity_size`):
    (a) This function computes the total size of an entity by recursively calculating the size of all files within a directory and its subdirectories.
    (b) The function leverages a dictionary for faster lookups of entities by ID.

```
def entity_size(self, entity_id: int) -> int:
    if entity_id not in self.id_to_entity:
        return -1  # ID not found
    entity = self.id_to_entity[entity_id]
    if entity.type == 'directory':
        return self.dfs(entity)
    elif entity.type == 'file':
        return entity.size
    return 0
```

4. **Follow-Up Questions**:
    (a) **Q2**: Caching for optimization when querying multiple entity IDs.
    (b) **Q3**: Discussion on the properties of a valid file system structure (e.g., must be a tree, no loops, no shared files).
    (c) **Q4**: Writing a function to verify the validity of the file system structure.
    (d) **Q5**: Implement a function to retrieve the full path of an entity based on its ID.
    (e) **Q6**: Design a method to add new entities to the file system.
    (f) **Q7**: Writing a function to remove an entity from the file system, including recursive deletion.
    (g) **Q9**: Designing a file system that supports snapshots, allowing for viewing of any previous state of the file system.

19.1.3 Key Takeaways for Interview

- The interview evaluates the candidate's ability to design a data structure that models a hierarchical file system, compute sizes using recursion, and implement optimizations with caching.
- Follow-up questions explore the candidate's understanding of tree data structures, depth-first traversal, and graph properties.
- Some advanced questions assess design skills, particularly around adding and removing entities, maintaining data consistency, and implementing snapshot functionality.

19.1.3.1 Points of Focus in Evaluation

1. **Data Structure Application**: The interview evaluates whether the candidate can create an appropriate data structure to represent the file system and understand the problem.
2. **Depth-First Search (DFS) Algorithm**: The candidate's ability to apply DFS for calculating directory sizes is evaluated.
3. **Advanced Topics**: For candidates with strong backgrounds, further topics include validating the file system, adding/removing entities, and creating snapshots.

19.1.4 Full Code Implementation

Here's the complete code provided in the image:

19.1 Example 1: File System

Code 19.1: Python Code for File System

```python
from collections import deque

class Entity:
    def __init__(self, id, type, name, size, children):
        self.id = id
        self.type = type
        self.name = name
        self.size = size
        self.children = children

class FileSystem:
    def __init__(self):
        self.id_to_entity = self.build_dict()

    def entity_size(self, entity_id: int) -> int:
        # Returns the size of the file or directory
        associated with entity_id
        if entity_id not in self.id_to_entity:
            return -1  # Entity ID not found

        entity = self.id_to_entity[entity_id]

        # If the entity is a directory, calculate its
        total size recursively
        if entity.type == 'directory':
            return self.dfs(entity)

        # If the entity is a file, return its size
        if entity.type == 'file':
            return entity.size

        return 0

    def build_dict(self):
      # Initialize the file system structure
      entities = [
          Entity(id=1, type='directory', name="root",
          size=0, children=[2, 3]),
```

```python
            Entity(id=2, type='directory', name="dir",
            size=0, children=[4, 5]),
            Entity(id=3, type='file', name="file1", size=300,
            children=[]),
            Entity(id=4, type='file', name="file2", size=100,
            children=[]),
            Entity(id=5, type='file', name="file3", size=200,
            children=[])
        ]

        # Create a dictionary to store entities by their ID
        for quick lookup
        entity_dict = {}
        for entity in entities:
            entity_dict[entity.id] = entity

        return entity_dict

    def dfs(self, entity):
        # Perform DFS to calculate the total size of a
        directory
        if entity.type == 'file':
            return entity.size

        if entity.type == 'directory' and len(entity.
        children) == 0:
            return 0

        total_size = 0
        for child_id in entity.children:
            total_size += self.dfs(self.id_to_entity
            [child_id])

        return total_size

def main():
    # Initialize the file system
    fs = FileSystem()

    # Test cases
    test_cases = [
```

19.1 Example 1: File System

```
            (1, 600),    # Root directory, expected size: 600 (sum
            of all files)
            (2, 300),    # Directory "dir", expected size: 300
            (sum of file2 and file3)
            (3, 300),    # File "file3", expected size: 300
            (4, 100),    # File "file1", expected size: 100
            (5, 200),    # File "file2", expected size: 200
            (10, -1)     # Non-existent entity ID, expected
            size: -1
        ]

        # Run tests
        for entity_id, expected_size in test_cases:
            result = fs.entity_size(entity_id)
            print(f"Entity ID: {entity_id}, Expected Size:
            {expected_size}, Calculated Size: {result}")
            assert result == expected_size, f"Test failed for
            Entity ID {entity_id}. Expected {expected_size}, got
            {result}"

        print("All tests passed!")


# Run the main function
if __name__ == "__main__":
    main()
```

19.1.5 Explanation of the Code

1. `Entity` **Class**: This class represents a file or directory, with attributes like `id`, `type`, `name`, `size`, and `children`.
2. `FileSystem` **Class**:
   (a) **Initialization** (`build_dict`): The `build_dict` function initializes the file system with sample entities and stores them in a dictionary for quick lookup.
   (b) `entity_size` **Method**: This method returns the size of a specified entity. If the entity is a directory, it calculates the total size by performing a depth-first search (DFS).
   (c) `dfs` **Method**: This recursive function calculates the total size of a directory, including all files within its subdirectories.

19.1.6 Usage of DFS for Size Calculation

- The dfs function plays a central role, traversing directories recursively to compute the cumulative size of all contained files. If the entity is a file, it returns its size directly. If it's a directory, it recursively calculates the size of its children.

19.2 Example 2: Longest Significant Word Chain

19.2.1 Problem: Longest Significant Word Chain

The problem is to find the longest word chain where you can reduce a word to a single character by consecutively removing letters, ensuring that each intermediate word is also a valid dictionary word. For instance:

1. "I" -> "in" -> "sin" -> "sing" -> "sting" -> "string" -> "staring" -> "starling"
2. "a" -> "at" -> "sat" -> "stat" -> "state" -> "estate" -> "restate" -> "restated" -> "restarted"

Clarification Questions
1. **Input Order**: Check with the interviewer if the words are sorted in any particular order. Here, we assume they are in random order.
2. **Character Set**: Assume all characters are lowercase Latin alphabets (a–z).

19.2.2 Solution

This problem can be represented as a Directed Acyclic Graph (DAG), where each valid transition from one word to another (by adding or removing one character) forms a directed edge. Solving this problem requires finding the longest path within this DAG.

There are two recursive approaches to solve the problem:

1. **Subtraction (Recursive Deletion)**:
    (a) Start with a given word, remove one character at a time, and check if the resulting word is valid.
    (b) Repeat this process recursively for each generated word until you can no longer create valid words.

2. **Addition (Recursive Addition)**:
    (a) Start with a given word and add each character of the alphabet in every possible position.
    (b) Check if the resulting word is valid, then repeat the process recursively for each valid word generated.

19.2 Example 2: Longest Significant Word Chain

Optimization with Caching: To avoid recalculating the chain length for the same word repeatedly, we use caching (memoization). This ensures that previously computed results are reused, reducing the overall time complexity.

19.2.3 Code Implementation

Here's the Python code for both the subtraction and addition approaches, complete with comments.

Code 19.2: Python Code for LongestWordChain

```python
from typing import List, Set, Dict
import string

class LongestWordChain:
    def __init__(self):
        self.cache = {}

    def chain_from_sub(self, word: str, all_words: Set[str], chain_length: int) -> int:
        """
        Recursive function to find the longest chain using
        the subtraction method.
        Removes one character at a time from the word and
        checks if the resulting word is in the
        dictionary.
        Uses memoization to avoid recalculating results
        for the same word.

        :param word: The current word being processed
        :param all_words: Set of valid words (dictionary)
        :param chain_length: Current length of the chain
        :return: Maximum chain length for the given word
        """
        if word in self.cache:
            return self.cache[word] + chain_length - 1
        max_chain_length = 0
        for i in range(len(word)):
            new_word = word[:i] + word[i + 1:]
            if new_word in all_words:
```

```python
                current_chain_length = self.chain_from_
                sub(new_word, all_words, chain_
                length + 1)
                max_chain_length = max(max_chain_length,
                current_chain_length)

        self.cache[word] = max_chain_length
        return max_chain_length

    def longest_subword_chain_sub(self, words:
List[str]) -> int:
        """
        Finds the longest significant word chain using the
        subtraction approach.

        :param words: List of words in the dictionary
        :return: Length of the longest chain
        """
        all_words = set(words)
        max_chain_length = 0
        self.cache = {}

        for word in words:
            current_chain_length = self.chain_from_
            sub(word, all_words, 1)
            max_chain_length = max(max_chain_length,
            current_chain_length)

        return max_chain_length

    def chain_from_add(self, word: str, all_words:
Set[str], chain_length: int) -> int:
        """
        Recursive function to find the longest chain using
        the addition method.
        Adds each character in every position in the word
        and checks if the resulting word is in the
        dictionary.

        :param word: The current word being processed
        :param all_words: Set of valid words (dictionary)
        :param chain_length: Current length of the chain
        :return: Maximum chain length for the given word
        """
```

19.2 Example 2: Longest Significant Word Chain

```
            if word in self.cache:
                return self.cache[word] + chain_length - 1

            max_chain_length = chain_length
            for i in range(len(word) + 1):
                for a in string.ascii_lowercase:
                    new_word = word[:i] + a + word[i:]
                    if new_word in all_words:
                        current_chain_length = self.chain_
                        from_add(new_word, all_words, chain_
                        length + 1)
                        max_chain_length = max(max_chain_
                        length, current_chain_length)

            self.cache[word] = max_chain_length
            return max_chain_length

    def longest_subword_additive(self, words:
    List[str]) -> int:
        """
        Finds the longest significant word chain using the
        addition approach.

        :param words: List of words in the dictionary
        :return: Length of the longest chain
        """
        all_words = set(words)
        max_chain_length = 0
        self.cache = {}

        for word in words:
            current_chain_length = self.chain_from_
            add(word, all_words, 1)
            max_chain_length = max(max_chain_length,
            current_chain_length)

        return max_chain_length
```

19.2.4 Analysis of Time Complexity

1. **Subtraction Approach**:

    (a) Time Complexity: O(N * M), where N is the number of words in the dictionary, and M is the average length of the words.

(b) The recursion depth is bounded by the length of the word, as each recursive call removes a single character.

2. **Addition Approach**:

   (a) Time Complexity: O(M * N * A), where A is the number of letters in the alphabet (26 for lowercase Latin characters).
   (b) This approach can be slower due to the larger number of possibilities created by adding letters.

19.2.5 Test Main Function

Here's a test `main` function to check both methods:

Code 19.3: Test Code for LongestWordChain

```
def main():
    # Sample word list with possible word chains
    words = ["a", "i", "in", "sin", "sing", "sting",
    "string", "staring", "starling", "at", "sat", "stat",
    "state", "estate", "restate", "restated",
    "restarted"]

    # Instantiate the class
    lsw = LongestWordChain()

    # Test subtraction method
    longest_chain_sub = lsw.longest_subword_chain_
    sub(words)
    print("Longest chain length using subtraction
    method:", longest_chain_sub)

    # Test addition method
    longest_chain_add = lsw.longest_subword_additive
    (words)
    print("Longest chain length using addition method:",
    longest_chain_add)

# Run the main function
if __name__ == "__main__":
    main()
```

19.2.6 Conclusion

The problem of finding the longest significant word chain is approached with both recursive subtraction and addition strategies, each with their unique strengths and limitations. By leveraging caching, we optimize the recursion to prevent redundant calculations, improving efficiency.

19.3 Example 3: Combination of Circles

19.3.1 Problem Overview

We are given a list of circles, each defined by their x and y coordinates and radius. Two circles are considered "connected" or "belong to the same group" if they overlap, where overlap is determined by whether the distance between the centers of two circles is less than or equal to the sum of their radii. We need to solve three main problems:

1. **Determine if all circles belong to the same group.**
2. **Count the total number of distinct circle groups.**
3. **Return the k largest circle groups.**

19.3.2 Solution Analysis

This problem can be modeled as a graph traversal problem where:

- **Vertices (Nodes)** represent individual circles.
- **Edges** exist between circles that overlap.

To solve each sub-problem, we can represent the connections between circles using an adjacency list or **adjacency matrix** and then use DFS (Depth-First Search) or BFS (Breadth-First Search) to explore the connected components (groups).

The process can be broken down as follows:

1. **Constructing the Graph**: Use an adjacency list where each circle is a key, and its value is a set of circles that overlap with it. This allows us to easily traverse the graph to determine connected components.
2. **Checking if All Circles are in a Single Group**: Perform DFS/BFS starting from any circle and track all visited circles. If we visit all circles in one traversal, then they belong to the same group.
3. **Counting Total Number of Groups**: Perform DFS/BFS on each unvisited circle to find a new group. Each traversal from an unvisited circle represents a new group.
4. **Finding the** k **Largest Groups**: For each group found, store its size and circles. Then, retrieve the k largest groups using sorting or a min-heap.

19.3.3 Code Implementation

Here is the Python code, broken down into sections with comments for each part.

19.3.3.1 Circle Class

Code 19.4: Python Code for Circle Class

```python
import math
from typing import List, Dict, Set, Tuple
import heapq

class Circle:
    def __init__(self, x: int, y: int, r: int):
        self.x = x
        self.y = y
        self.r = r

    def __hash__(self):
        return hash((self.x, self.y, self.r))

    def __eq__(self, other):
        return isinstance(other, Circle) and self.x == other.x and self.y == other.y and self.r == other.r
```

19.3.3.2 CircleGroup Class

This class handles the functionality of constructing the graph, performing DFS, and solving each problem.

Code 19.5: Python Code for CircleGroup Class

19.3 Example 3: Combination of Circles

```
class CircleGroup:
    def __init__(self):
        self.cache = {}

    def IsOverlapped(self, circle1: Circle, circle2:
    Circle) -> bool:
        """
        Checks if two circles overlap.
        """
        distance = math.sqrt((circle1.x - circle2.x) ** 2
        + (circle1.y - circle2.y) ** 2)
        return distance <= (circle1.r + circle2.r)

    def ConstructAdjacencyDict(self, circles:
    List[Circle]) -> Dict[Circle, Set[Circle]]:
        """
        Constructs an adjacency list where each circle is
        connected to overlapping circles.
        """
        adjacency_dict = {circle: set() for circle in
        circles}

        for i, circle1 in enumerate(circles):
            for j in range(i + 1, len(circles)):
                circle2 = circles[j]
                if self.IsOverlapped(circle1, circle2):
                    adjacency_dict[circle1].add(circle2)
                    adjacency_dict[circle2].add(circle1)

        return adjacency_dict

    def DFS(self, node: Circle, adjacency_dict:
    Dict[Circle, Set[Circle]], current_group:
    Set[Circle]):
        """
        Recursive DFS traversal to mark all circles in
        the same group.
        """
        if node in current_group:
            return
        current_group.add(node)
```

```python
            for neighbor in adjacency_dict[node]:
                self.DFS(neighbor, adjacency_dict,
                current_group)

    def IsSingleGroup(self, circles: List[Circle])
    -> bool:
        """
        Checks if all circles form a single group.
        """
        if not circles:
            return True

        visited = set()
        adjacency_dict = self.ConstructAdjacencyDic
        t(circles)
        self.DFS(circles[0], adjacency_dict, visited)

        return len(visited) == len(circles)

    def CountGroups(self, circles: List[Circle]) -> int:
        """
        Counts the number of distinct groups of circles.
        """
        visited = set()
        adjacency_dict = self.ConstructAdjacencyDic
        t(circles)
        total_groups = 0

        for circle in circles:
            if circle not in visited:
                current_group = set()
                self.DFS(circle, adjacency_dict,
                current_group)
                visited.update(current_group)
                total_groups += 1

        return total_groups

    def GetTopKGroups(self, circles: List[Circle], top_k:
    int) -> List[List[Circle]]:
        """
```

19.3 Example 3: Combination of Circles

```
        Returns the k largest groups of circles.
        """
        visited = set()
        size_and_groups = []
        adjacency_dict = self.ConstructAdjacencyDic
t(circles)

        for circle in circles:
            if circle not in visited:
                current_group = set()
                self.DFS(circle, adjacency_dict,
                current_group)
                size_and_groups.append((len(current_
                group), current_group))
                visited.update(current_group)

        largest_groups = heapq.nlargest(top_k, size_and_
        groups, key=lambda x: x[0])
        return [list(group) for _, group in
        largest_groups]
```

19.3.4 Analysis of Time Complexity

1. **ConstructAdjacencyDict**: This function has a time complexity of O(n^2) because we need to check each pair of circles to see if they overlap.
2. **DFS Traversal**: Each DFS traversal has a time complexity of O(V+E), where V is the number of vertices (circles) and E is the number of edges (overlaps).
3. **IsSingleGroup**: This function also has a time complexity of O(V+E) as it performs a single DFS traversal.
4. **CountGroups**: This function may require up to O(V+E) time for each unvisited circle, but typically remains O(V+E) due to traversing all nodes once.
5. **GetTopKGroups**: This function has an additional OO(klogm) cost for retrieving the top k largest groups.

Overall, the complexity of this solution is dominated by the O(n^2) graph construction time.

19.3.5 Test Function

Below is a `main` function to test each of the functionalities:

Code 19.6: Test Code for CircleGroup Class

```python
def main():
    # Sample circles
    circles = [
        Circle(0, 0, 1),
        Circle(2, 2, 1),
        Circle(4, 4, 1),
        Circle(6, 6, 1),
        Circle(1, 1, 2),
        Circle(5, 5, 2)
    ]

    cg = CircleGroup()


    # Test if all circles are in a single group
    print("Are all circles in a single group?",
    cg.IsSingleGroup(circles))

    # Test counting the total number of groups
    print("Total number of groups:",
    cg.CountGroups(circles))

    # Test finding the top k largest groups
    k = 2
    top_k_groups = cg.GetTopKGroups(circles, k)
    for i, group in enumerate(top_k_groups, start=1):
        print(f"Group {i}: {[f'({c.x},{c.y},{c.r})' for c
        in group]}")

if __name__ == "__main__":
    main()
```

19.3.6 Expected Output

The output of this function will depend on the overlapping circles, but it should provide:

1. Whether all circles form a single group.
2. The total number of groups.
3. The k largest groups by size.

This comprehensive breakdown demonstrates modular coding, analysis of time complexity, and test cases covering various scenarios, ensuring that the solution is adaptable to follow-up questions.

Part III
System Design

Chapter 20
System Design Theory

General system design primarily focuses on object-oriented design or analyzing large-scale data structures. System design interview questions often involve open-ended discussions, where candidates are expected to lead the conversation.

20.1 Design Steps

Here are the steps you can follow to tackle system design interview questions and structure the discussion:

20.1.1 Step 1: Define the Use Case, Constraints, and Assumptions

Start by gathering all the necessary details. Analyze the problem, ask clarifying questions, and discuss assumptions. Consider:

- Who will be using the system, and how?
- What is the system's purpose?
- How many users are expected?
- What are the system's inputs and outputs?
- How much data needs to be processed?
- How many requests per second need to be handled?
- What is the expected read-to-write ratio?

20.1.2 Step 2: Develop a High-Level Design

Create a high-level design by identifying the critical components of the system. Outline the main elements and their interactions to present a clear overview of your approach. This step should highlight the system's foundational building blocks.

20.1.3 Step 3: Focus on Core Components

Dive deeper into the design by discussing the key components in more detail. For instance, if you're asked to design a URL shortening service, you would break it down as follows:

1. Generate and store a hash for the full URL:
   (a) Consider using MD5 or Base62 encoding.
   (b) Address potential hash collisions.
   (c) Decide between SQL or NoSQL databases.
   (d) Discuss the database schema.
2. Translate the hashed URL back to the full URL:
   (a) Look up the full URL in the database.
3. Define APIs and explore object-oriented design.

20.1.4 Step 4: Address Scalability and Extend the Design

Consider how the system will handle scaling and performance. Acknowledge bottlenecks and limitations, and incorporate strategies such as:

1. Load balancing
2. Horizontal scaling
3. Caching
4. Database sharding

These steps will help guide your design process and ensure that you cover all critical aspects in your system design discussion.

20.2 Basic Knowledge Points of System Design

The general big data system structure has the architecture shown in Fig. 20.1, and Fig. 20.1 briefly introduces the basic knowledge points of system design, such as load balancing, caching, and data design.

Figure 20.1 illustrates the architecture of a system designed to handle user requests, likely for a web application or online service. It shows the flow of data from the client to the backend servers and databases, highlighting various components and their roles.

1. **Client**: This represents the user interacting with the system, typically through a web browser or mobile app.
2. **DNS**: The Domain Name System translates the user-friendly domain name (e.g., [invalid URL removed]) into the IP address of the server.
3. **CDN**: A Content Delivery Network caches static content (like images and scripts) closer to the user for faster loading times.
4. **Load Balancer**: This distributes incoming traffic across multiple servers to prevent overload and ensure high availability.
5. **Web Servers**: These handle the incoming requests from users, processing them and generating dynamic content.

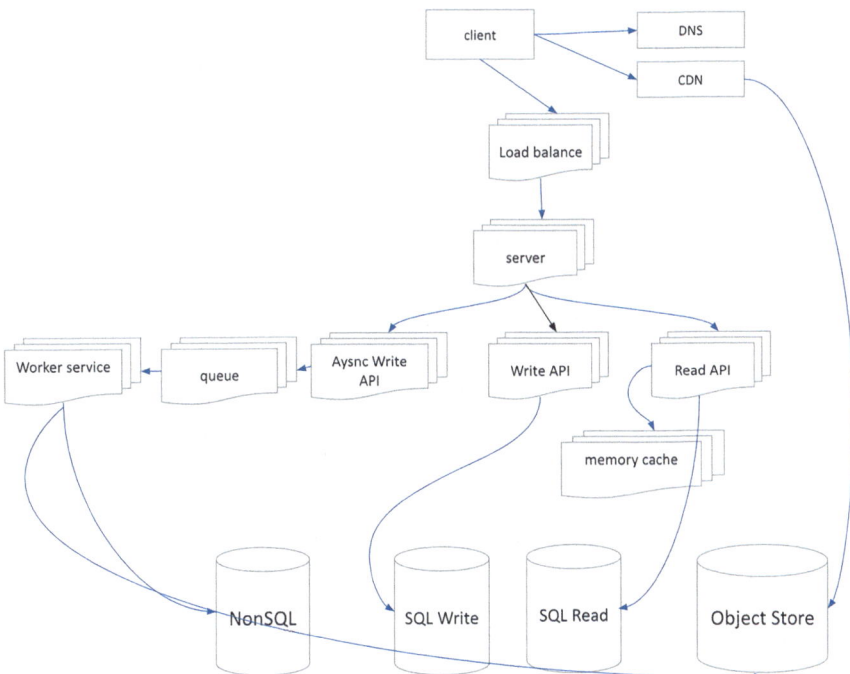

Fig. 20.1 General diagram of big data architecture design

6. **Worker Service (Task Service)**: This component performs background tasks asynchronously, such as processing data or sending emails.
7. **Queue**: A temporary storage for tasks waiting to be processed by the worker service.
8. **Write API**: This interface handles requests to write or update data in the databases.
9. **Read API**: This interface handles requests to read data from the databases.
10. **Memory Cache**: A high-speed cache that stores frequently accessed data in memory for faster retrieval.
11. **NoSQL Database**: This type of database is suitable for storing unstructured or semi-structured data, often used for user profiles, social media feeds, etc.
12. **SQL Write Database**: This database is optimized for writing data, handling frequent updates and insertions.
13. **SQL Read Database**: This database is optimized for reading data, serving read-heavy workloads efficiently.
14. **Object Store**: This storage system is used for storing large files and objects, such as images, videos, and backups.

The arrows indicate the flow of data and requests within the system. For example, a user request might go through the load balancer, then to a web server, which then interacts with the read API to retrieve data from the SQL Read database and the memory cache. The write API is used for updating data in the write database. The worker service handles background tasks and interacts with the queue and various data stores as needed.

20.2.1 Domain Name System

The Domain Name System (DNS) is responsible for converting domain names like http://www.example.com into their corresponding IP addresses. DNS operates hierarchically, with top-level DNS servers overseeing the process. When an IP address is requested (for a domain name), the internet service provider (ISP) or routing infrastructure directs the query to the appropriate DNS server. Lower-level DNS servers store cached mappings, but these caches can become outdated due to propagation delays. Cached DNS results may also be stored in a browser or operating system for a specified duration, determined by the time-to-live (TTL) setting (Fig. 20.2).

- **NS Record (Name Server Record)**: Identifies the DNS server responsible for resolving a specific domain or subdomain.
- **MX Record (Mail Exchange Record)**: Specifies the mail server designated to handle email for a domain.
- **A Record (Address Record)**: Maps a domain name to its corresponding IP address.

20.2 Basic Knowledge Points of System Design

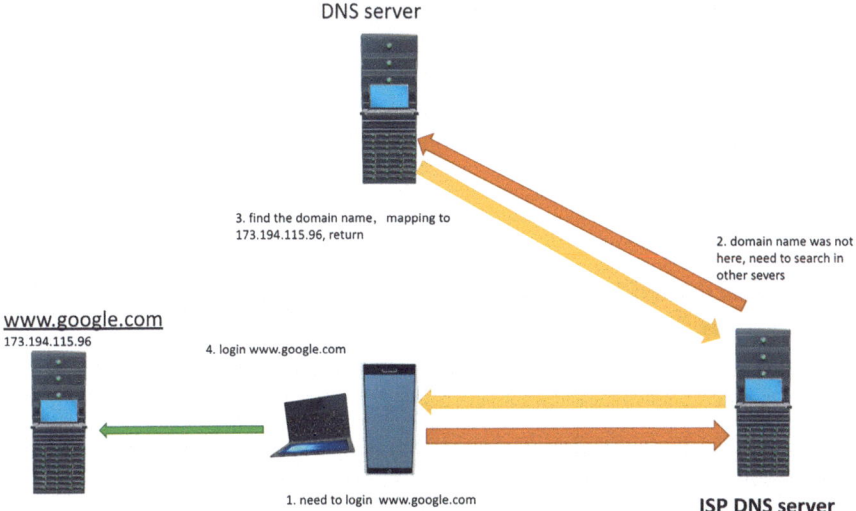

Fig. 20.2 Domain name system

- **CNAME (Canonical Name Record)**: Maps one domain name to another (e.g., example.com to www.example.com) or links to an A record.

Platforms like Cloudflare and Route 53 allow DNS management and offer traffic routing features. Some of these DNS services include:

1. **Weighted Round-Robin Scheduling**:
   (a) Direct traffic away from servers under maintenance.
   (b) Distribute load evenly across clusters of varying sizes.
   (c) Facilitate A/B testing.
2. **Latency-Based Routing**: Routes traffic based on the server with the lowest latency to the user.
3. **Geolocation-Based Routing**: Directs users to servers based on their geographic location.

20.2.2 Load Balancer

A load balancer is responsible for distributing incoming requests to various computing resources, such as application servers and databases. It also routes the response from these resources back to the appropriate client. The primary benefits of using a load balancer are:

1. **Preventing Requests from Reaching Bad Servers**: It ensures that requests are not routed to server that are down or malfunctioning.

2. **Avoiding Resource Overload**: By distributing traffic evenly, the load balancer prevents any single server from becoming overwhelmed, ensuring optimal performance.
3. **Eliminating a Single Point of Failure**: It enhances system reliability and uptime by ensuring that if one server fails, requests are seamlessly routed to other available resources.

20.3 Distributed Caching System Memcached

An overview of distributed caching systems is provided in https://www.memcached.org/. Distributed caching addresses several key challenges:

1. **Horizontal Linear Scaling**: Ensuring that the cache can scale out by distributing the load across multiple servers without performance degradation.
2. **Performance Under High Concurrency**: The cache must maintain optimal performance even under large volumes of simultaneous requests.
3. **Avoiding a Single Point of Failure**: To ensure reliability, distributed caching must use multiple copies of cached data with mechanisms in place for replica consistency.

The core technologies in distributed caching include:

1. **Memory Management**: Efficient allocation, management, and reclamation of memory.
2. **Distributed Management and Algorithms**: Ensuring data is properly distributed across different nodes in the cache system.
3. **Cache Key-Value Management and Routing**: Efficiently managing cache keys and routing requests to the appropriate cache node.

Memcached is a popular high-performance distributed in-memory cache server that helps to improve the speed and scalability of dynamic web applications by caching the results of database queries, thus reducing the number of direct database accesses.

Figure 20.3 illustrates a system architecture that utilizes caching to improve performance and reduce load on the database. Here's a breakdown of the components and how they interact:

- **Browser**: This represents the user interacting with the system, typically through a web browser or mobile app.
- **Application Server**: This is the server responsible for handling user requests, processing data, and generating dynamic content.
- **Memcached**: Memcached is a high-speed, in-memory caching system. It stores frequently accessed data to reduce the need to query the database, resulting in faster response times. Multiple instances of Memcached are shown to distribute the caching load and improve redundancy.

20.3 Distributed Caching System Memcached

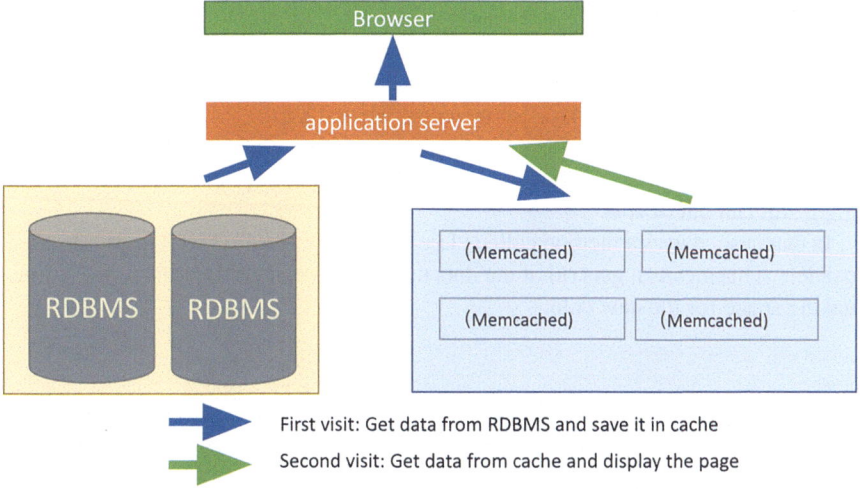

Fig. 20.3 Architectural principles of distributed caches

- **RDBMS**: This refers to a Relational Database Management System, which stores the application's data in a structured format. Two RDBMS instances are depicted, possibly for redundancy or to separate read and write operations.

  How it works:

1. **First Access**: When a user requests data for the first time, the application server fetches it from the RDBMS. This initial access might be slower as it involves retrieving data from disk.
2. **Subsequent Access**: When the same data is requested again, the application server first checks the Memcached cache. If the data is found in the cache (a "cache hit"), it is served directly from memory, resulting in a much faster response. If the data is not found in the cache (a "cache miss"), the application server fetches it from the RDBMS and stores it in the cache for future requests.

   Benefits of this architecture:

- **Improved Performance**: Caching reduces the load on the database and provides faster response times for users.
- **Reduced Database Load**: By serving data from the cache, the system reduces the number of queries to the database, improving its overall performance and scalability.
- **Increased Scalability**: Caching allows the system to handle more user requests without overloading the database.

This architecture is commonly used in web applications and other systems where performance and scalability are critical. By utilizing caching effectively, the system can provide a better user experience and handle increasing traffic demands.

20.3.1 LRU: Principle for Efficient Cache Eviction

Memcached is a system for storing data in memory so it can be accessed quickly. It sometimes needs to make space for new data when it's full.

To do this, Memcached prioritizes reusing space that was previously occupied by data that has expired. However, even after clearing out expired data, Memcached might still run out of space.

In that case, it uses a method called "Least Recently Used" (LRU) to decide what to delete. This means it gets rid of the data that hasn't been used for the longest time, making space for the new data.

20.3.2 Memcached Is Distributed

Although Memcached is referred to as a "distributed" cache server, the distribution of the cache is entirely managed on the client side, not the server side. Here's an illustration of how Memcached implements distributed caching:

Imagine you have three Memcached servers: **node1**, **node2**, and **node3**. The application needs to store several key-value pairs with keys like "tokyo", "kanagawa", "chiba", "saitama", and "gunma".

This diagram illustrates a basic structure for distributing data and requests across multiple nodes in a system. It focuses on how an application interacts with a set of nodes to retrieve data.

Here's a breakdown:

- **Node 1, Node 2, Node 3**: These represent individual servers or machines that hold parts of the overall data.
- **Service List**: This is a list that keeps track of all the available nodes in the system. It acts as a directory to locate where specific data might be stored.
- **Algorithm**: This refers to the logic or method used to determine which node to contact for a specific piece of data. It could be a simple hashing algorithm, a consistent hashing approach, or a more complex method depending on the system's needs.
- **Get("tokyo")**: This represents a request from the application layer to retrieve data associated with the key "tokyo".
- **Application Layer**: This is the layer where user interactions or application logic resides. It sends requests to the system to retrieve or store data (Fig. 20.4).

This structure highlights:

- **Data Distribution**: Data is spread across multiple nodes, potentially for scalability and fault tolerance.
- **Service Discovery**: The service list helps locate nodes responsible for specific data.

20.3 Distributed Caching System Memcached

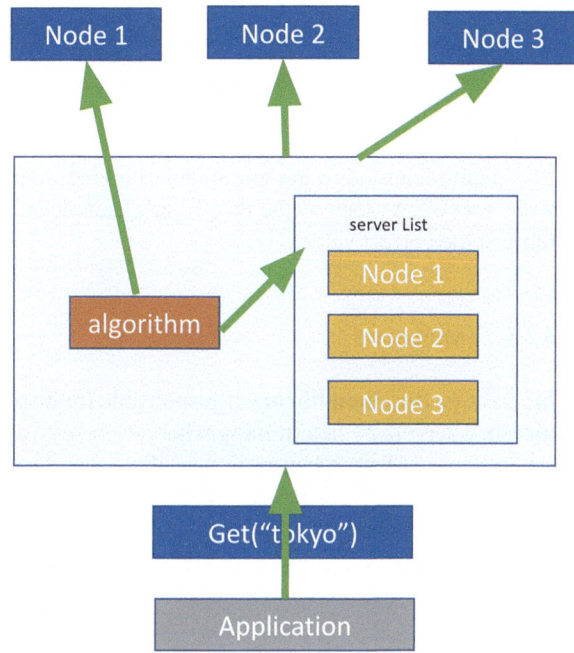

Fig. 20.4 Memcached implements the principle of distributed caching

- **Algorithm for Data Location**: An algorithm determines how data is mapped to nodes.

This is a simplified representation of a distributed system. In reality, there might be more complex interactions, data replication, caching mechanisms, and load balancing to ensure efficiency and reliability.

20.3.2.1 Storing Data

1. When you add the key "tokyo" to Memcached, the **client library** uses an internal algorithm (such as consistent hashing) to determine which of the three Memcached servers should store this data.
2. Based on the key "tokyo", the client selects a server, say **node1**, and sends the command to store the key-value pair ("tokyo", value) on that server.
3. The same process happens for other keys, such as "kanagawa", "chiba", "saitama", and "gunma". Each key is passed to the client library, which uses the same algorithm to select the appropriate server for each one.

20.3.2.2 Retrieving Data

1. When retrieving data for the key "tokyo", the client library uses the same algorithm as it did when storing the data. It passes the key "tokyo" and selects **node1** again (assuming nothing has changed in the server setup).
2. The client then sends a **get** command to **node1**, requesting the value associated with "tokyo". As long as the data hasn't been deleted or expired, the client will retrieve the correct value.

20.3.2.3 Summary

In this process, **the client library** is responsible for distributing data across multiple Memcached servers by determining where each key-value pair is stored. The same algorithm ensures that, when retrieving data, the client queries the correct server where the data was originally stored. This decentralized, client-side distribution is what gives Memcached its "distributed" functionality, even though there is no coordination or communication between the servers themselves.

20.3.3 Hash Consistency

As shown in Fig. 20.5, the hash value of the memcached server (node) is first calculated and configured to a circle of 0~2^{32}. Then use the same method to find out the hash value of the key where the data is stored and map it to the circle. It then starts a clockwise lookup from where the data is mapped, saving the data to the first server it finds. If the server is still not found after 2^{32}, it is saved to the first memcached server.

Add a memcached server from the state in Fig. 20.5. The remainder distributed algorithm affects the hit ratio of the cache due to the large change in the server where the key is saved, but in Consistent Hashing, only the key on the first server counterclockwise where the server is added on the continuum is affected.

As a result, Consistent Hashing inhibits the redistribution of keys to the greatest extent. Moreover, some Consistent Hashing implementations also use the idea of virtual nodes. Using the normal hash function, the distribution of the mapping locations of the servers is very uneven. Therefore, using the idea of virtual nodes, allocate 100~200 points on the continuum for each physical node (server). This suppresses uneven distribution and minimizes cache redistribution as servers go up or down.

Figure 20.5 illustrates a system using consistent hashing to distribute data across a cluster of nodes. Consistent hashing is a special technique used to minimize data movement when nodes are added or removed from the system.

20.3 Distributed Caching System Memcached

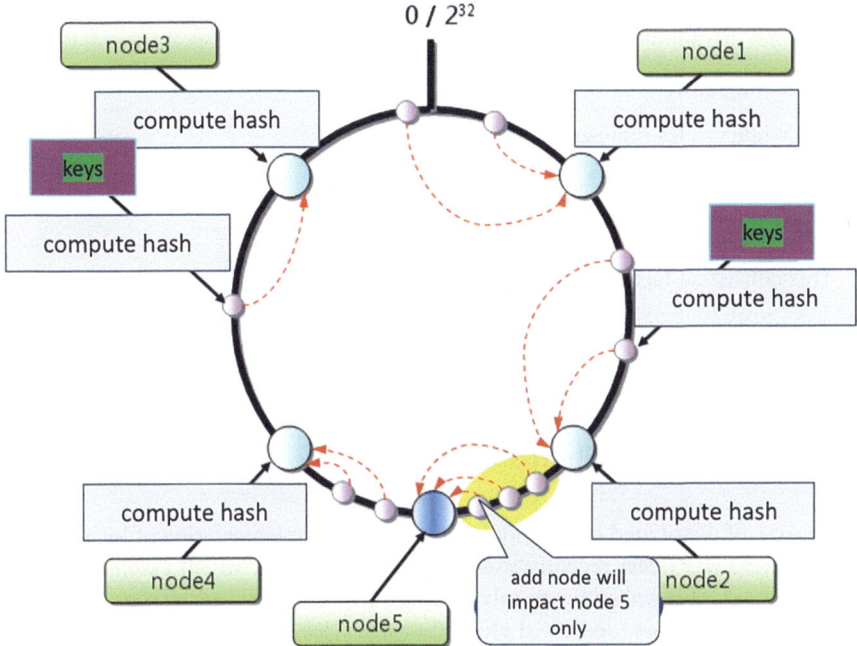

Fig. 20.5 Add a node's hash consistency

Here's how it works:

1. **The Ring**: Imagine all the data keys (like "tokyo" from the previous example) and the nodes placed on a ring. This ring represents the hash space.
2. **Hashing**: Each key and node is assigned a position on the ring using a hash function. This function ensures that keys and nodes are distributed evenly across the ring.
3. **Data Assignment**: A key is assigned to the first node encountered when moving clockwise on the ring from the key's position. For example, in the diagram, the key with the red dotted line would be stored on Node 1.
4. **Adding a Node**: When a new node (Node 5 in the yellow area) is added, it's placed on the ring using the hash function. Only the keys that fall within Node 5's range (highlighted in yellow) need to be moved to the new node. This minimizes data redistribution compared to traditional hashing methods.
5. **Removing a Node**: Similarly, if a node is removed, only the keys that were assigned to that node need to be reassigned to the next node on the ring.

Benefits of Consistent Hashing:

- **Minimizes Data Movement**: When nodes are added or removed, only a small portion of the data needs to be moved.
- **Balances Load**: Ensures that keys are distributed evenly across the nodes, preventing overload.

- **Fault Tolerance**: If a node fails, the other nodes can still handle the load with minimal disruption.

In the diagram:

- The white circles represent data keys.
- The green boxes represent nodes.
- The arrows show how keys are mapped to nodes.
- The yellow area highlights the impact of adding Node 5.

This consistent hashing approach is commonly used in distributed systems like databases, caching systems, and distributed hash tables to ensure scalability, fault tolerance, and efficient data management.

20.4 Design a Distributed Cache

The design of distributed cache should start with the implementation of local cache, such as the LRU (least recently used) caching algorithm, which essentially uses hash table + doubly linked list to solve the problem. The LRU cache runs as a separate process on a host (dedicated cluster) or a service host (co-located), and each cache server will store large chunks of data (shards). Customers should use partitioning algorithms to select shards (e.g., consistent hashes) and the caching client to talk to a caching server that uses the TCP or UDP protocol.

Note the consistent caching, cache consistency, adding or decreasing nodes, and how to update the cache.

20.4.1 The Cache Is Invalid

If data is modified in the database, that data should be invalidated in the cache; otherwise, it can lead to inconsistent application behavior. There are three main types of caching systems:

1. Write-through cache: Only when both the write operation and the cache to the DB are successful, can the write operation be confirmed to be successful, so as to achieve complete data consistency between the cache and storage. In the event of a crash, power failure, or other system outage, nothing is lost. However, in this case, the latency of the write will be higher due to the write operation to two separate systems.
2. Cache Write: Bypass the cache and write directly to the place of the database, which can reduce the wait time (except in one case!). However, because the caching system reads information from the database when a cache miss occurs, it increases the cache misses. This can result in higher read latency in cases

where the application writes and rereads information quickly. Reads must be made from slower back-end storage and experience higher latency.
3. Write back to the cache: Writes are directly performed on the cache layer, and the operation is confirmed as soon as it is completed in the cache. The cache then asynchronously synchronizes that write to the DB. For write-intensive applications, this results in very fast write latency and high write throughput. However, if the caching layer disappears, there is a risk of losing data because the only single copy of the data written is in the cache. This situation can be improved by having multiple replicas to acknowledge writes in the cache.

20.4.2 Cache Eviction Policy

Here are some of the most common cache eviction strategies:

- First-in, first-out (FIFO): The cache evicts the first block of data that is accessed first, regardless of how often or how many times it was previously accessed.
- Last-in, first-out (LIFO): The cache evicts the most recently accessed chunk, regardless of how often or how many times it was previously accessed.
- Least Recently Used (LRU): The least recently used cache is discarded first.
- Recently Used (MRU): The most recently used cache is discarded first compared to LRUs.
- Least Usage (LFU): Calculates how often the required cache is used, discarding the least frequently used chunks first.
- Random Replacement (RR): A candidate is randomly selected and discarded if necessary to make room.

20.4.3 Design a Distributed Key-Value Caching System

Here a distributed key-value caching system is designed, such as Memcached or Redis (the most popular system at the moment). The following questions must be understood:

1. What is the amount of data that needs to be cached?
   This depends on the amount of data being built, which is usually measured in terabytes.
2. What should be the cache eviction policy?
   The focus here is on the LRU cache eviction strategy. If you dig a little deeper, you need to write code about LRUs.
3. What should be the access mode for a given cache or cache invalidation method?
   Let's talk about writeback caching!

4. What is the expected QPS for the system?
   Don't kill the machine! A machine is about to process 1M QPS, and the machine crashes because the query can't answer the query fast enough, and there may be a high risk of high latency!
5. Is latency a very important metric?
   The whole point of caching is low latency!
6. What about consistency and availability?
   Unavailability in the cache system means that there is a cache miss, resulting in high latency due to reading data from a slower machine (disk instead of memory!). Select Availability over Consistency to reduce latency. Accept the eventual consistency as long as you finally see new changes within a reasonable amount of time.
7. What data structures are used to achieve this?
   Map and LinkedList should get the job done! Probably better performance on two-pointer link lists for the remove action.
8. What happens when the machine that processes the debris fails?
   One machine: If there is only one machine per shard, then if that machine fails, all requests for that shard will start hitting the database, so the latency will increase.
   Multiple machines: If you have many machines, you can have multiple machines per shard that maintain exactly the same amount of data. Since there are multiple servers that maintain the same data, the data between the servers may be out of sync. This also means that some keys may be missing on some servers, and some servers may have old values for the same keys.
   Master-slave technology: There is only one active server at a time in a shard, and there is one follower who keeps getting updates. When the primary server fails, the slave server takes over from the primary server. The master and slave servers can maintain a change log with a version number to ensure that they can be captured. If you're satisfied that all servers are ultimately consistent, you can have one primary server take on all the write traffic and many read replicas so that they can also serve the read traffic. Or you can use a peer-to-peer system, such as Apache Casandra, which is a good example of this architecture!

Chapter 21
System Design Practice for Big Data

21.1 Web Crawler Problem

Building a web crawler is more complex than it seems. It's not just about extracting data from websites. To build a truly effective web crawler, especially one that operates at a large scale, you need to think about the bigger picture. This includes:

- **Understanding the challenges**: Websites are complex and dynamic. You must handle JavaScript, prevent website overload, and comply with website rules.
- **Focusing on the goal**: Define the purpose of your crawler and ensure its design aligns with your specific objectives.
- **Prioritizing architecture**: A well-designed architecture is essential for a crawler to be efficient and scalable. This is more important than the specific programming language or tools you use.

Building a successful web crawler requires careful planning and a comprehensive understanding of website behavior.

21.1.1 Architectural Design

To build even a basic web crawler, you need these key parts:

1. **A way to download web pages**: This is like the crawler's hands, fetching pages from the internet.
2. **A way to find links on those pages**: This helps the crawler discover new pages to visit.
3. **A way to avoid visiting the same page twice**: This saves time and resources.
4. **A way to decide which pages to visit first**: Some pages might be more important than others.
5. **A place to store all the information**: This could be a database or a file system.

Building a web crawler that can handle lots of websites at once is much harder. It's like coordinating a team of crawlers, making sure they don't get in each other's way and that they share information effectively. This requires clever ways to manage and store the data, especially when dealing with huge amounts of it.

While downloading and analyzing web pages is important, figuring out how to store and manage all the data efficiently is even more crucial for a large-scale crawler.

Figure 21.1 shows a simplified architecture for a web crawler, highlighting the flow of data and the main components involved. Let's break down each part:

1. **User Program**: This is where the user interacts with the system, likely initiating search requests or defining crawling tasks.
2. **Service Layer**: This layer acts as an intermediary between the user and the core crawling components. It handles user requests, manages resources, and may provide functionalities like authentication and authorization.
3. **Inverted Index Service**: This component is responsible for creating and maintaining an inverted index. This index is a crucial data structure in search engines, mapping words or terms to the documents where they appear. It allows for fast and efficient retrieval of relevant documents based on user queries.

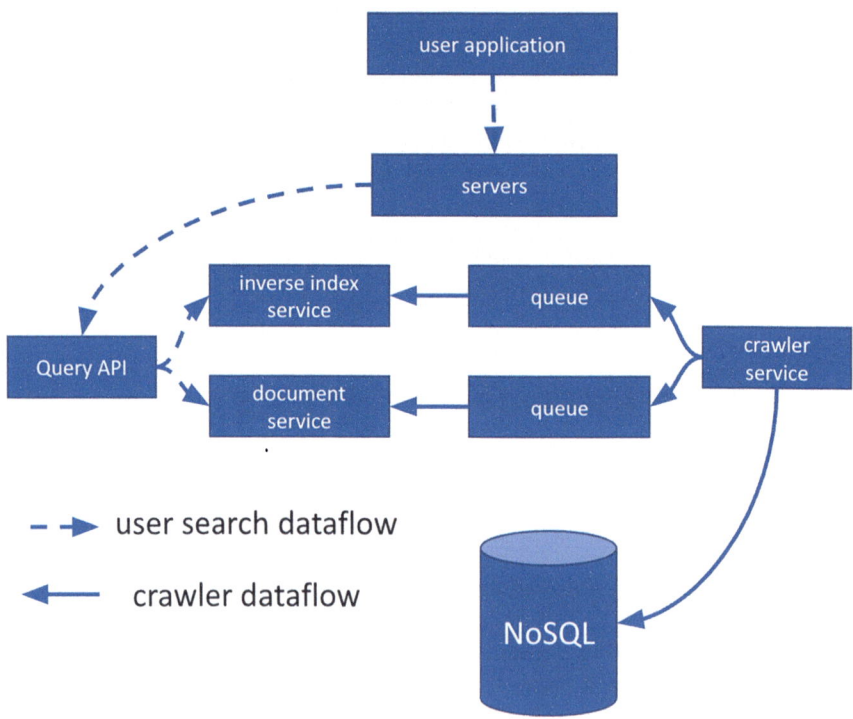

Fig. 21.1 Crawler design

21.1 Web Crawler Problem

4. **Queue**: Queues are used to store and manage URLs that need to be crawled. They act as buffers, ensuring that the crawler works through the URLs in an organized and efficient manner.
5. **Crawler Service**: This is the heart of the system, responsible for fetching web pages from the internet. It follows links, downloads content, and extracts relevant information.
6. **Document Service**: This component handles the processing and storage of crawled documents. It may involve tasks like parsing HTML, extracting text, and storing the data in a suitable format.
7. **NoSQL**: This represents the database used to store the crawled data and the inverted index. NoSQL databases are often preferred for web crawling due to their ability to handle large volumes of unstructured data and their scalability.
8. **User Search Data Flow**: This arrow shows the flow of user search queries through the system, from the user program to the inverted index service, which then retrieves relevant documents.
9. **Crawler Data Flow**: This arrow depicts the flow of data crawled from the web, moving from the crawler service to the document service and finally to the NoSQL database for storage.

In essence, this architecture demonstrates a common pattern in web crawling:

- Users initiate searches or crawling tasks.
- The system fetches web pages, extracts relevant data, and stores it in a database.
- An inverted index is created to enable efficient search.
- Users can then search through the crawled data, with the system quickly retrieving relevant results.

This diagram provides a high-level overview of the system, omitting some details for simplicity. In a real-world scenario, additional components and complexities might be involved.

21.1.2 Crawler Services

Suppose there is an initial links_to_crawl initial listing that is initially ranked based on the overall popularity of the website. If this isn't a torrent that, under reasonable assumptions, can provide crawlers with links to popular websites with external content like Yahoo, DMOZ, etc.

Here, a table crawled_links will be used to store the processed links and their page signatures. links_to_crawl and crawled_links can be stored in a key-value NoSQL database. For the ranking link links_to_crawl among them, Redis can be used with a sort set to maintain the ranking of the page links. At the same time, the trade-offs between use cases and choosing SQL or NoSQL should be discussed.

The pseudocode of the crawler service is as follows:

Code 21.1: Pseudocode for the Crawler Service

> **The Crawler Service** handles each page link in the following loop:
>
> Retrieve the link with the highest priority from the queue
> Detect if crawled_links in a NoSQL database have similar page signaturesIf we have similar pages, lower the priority of page links
> This prevents us from entering the cycle, Continue, or else, scraping the link
> Add the job to the reverse index service queue to generate a reverse index
> Add jobs to the Document Service queue to generate static titles and code snippets
> Generate page signatures
> Remove the link from the links_to_crawl in the NoSQL database
> Insert page links and signatures into crawled_links in your NoSQL database

PagesDataStore is an abstraction in the Crawler service that uses a NoSQL database.

```python
class PagesDataStore(object):

    def __init__(self, db);
    self.db = db

    def add_link_to_crawl(self, url):
    """Add the given link to 'links_to_crawl'."""

    def remove_link_to_crawl(self, url):
    """Remove the given link from 'links_to_crawl'."""

    def reduce_priority_link_to_crawl(self, url)
    """Reduce the priority of a link in 'links_to_crawl' to
    avoid cycles."""

    def extract_max_priority_page(self):
    """Return the highest priority link in 'links_to_
    crawl'."""

    def insert_crawled_link(self, url, signature):
    """Add the given link to 'crawled_links'."""

    def crawled_similar(self, signature):
    """Determine if we've already crawled a page matching the
    given signature"""
```

21.1 Web Crawler Problem

Page is an abstraction in the Crawler service that encapsulates the page, its contents, child URLs, and signatures.

```
class Page(object):

    def __init__(self, url, contents, child_urls, signature):
        self.url = url
        self.contents = contents
        self.child_urls = child_urls
        self.signature = signature
```

Crawler is the main class in the Crawler Service, consisting of Page and PagesDataStore.

```
class Crawler(object):

    def __init__(self, data_store, reverse_index_queue,
    doc_index_queue):
        self.data_store = data_store
        self.reverse_index_queue = reverse_index_queue
        self.doc_index_queue = doc_index_queue

    def create_signature(self, page):
        """Create signature based on url and contents."""

    def crawl_page(self, page):
        for url in page.child_urls:
            self.data_store.add_link_to_crawl(url)
        page.signature = self.create_signature(page)
        self.data_store.remove_link_to_crawl(page.url)
        self.data_store.insert_crawled_link(page.url,
        page.signature)

    def crawl(self):
        while True:
            page = self.data_store.extract_max_priority_
            page()
```

```
if page is None:
    break
if self.data_store.crawled_similar(page.
signature):
    self.data_store.reduce_priority_link_to_
    crawl(page.url)
else:
    self.crawl_page(page)
```

21.1.3 Handle Duplicate Links

It's crucial to prevent a web crawler from getting stuck in an endless loop, which can happen when it keeps revisiting the same pages over and over again. To avoid this, the crawler needs to identify and eliminate duplicate URLs.

For smaller websites, simple techniques like sorting URLs or using data structures that automatically discard duplicates can be used. However, when dealing with massive amounts of data, like billions of links, more advanced techniques like MapReduce are needed to efficiently identify and remove duplicate entries.

Essentially, this is about ensuring the crawler explores new territory and doesn't waste time revisiting pages it has already seen.

```
class RemoveDuplicateUrls(MRJob):

    def mapper(self, _, line):
        yield line, 1

    def reducer(self, key, values):
        total = sum(values)
        if total == 1:
            yield key, total
```

21.1.4 Determine When to Update Crawl Results

Web crawlers must revisit websites periodically to ensure data remains up-to-date, similar to checking emails for new messages.

Here's how crawlers can stay fresh:

- **Keep track of when a page was last visited**: This helps the crawler know when it's time to go back and check for changes.

21.1 Web Crawler Problem   361

- **Revisit pages on a schedule**: By default, a crawler might revisit every page once a week, but some pages might need to be checked more often, like news sites or popular blogs.
- **Analyze how often pages change**: Crawlers can use data analysis to figure out how often a particular website typically updates its content and adjust their revisiting schedule accordingly.
- **Respect website rules**: Some websites have rules about how often they want to be crawled, and good crawlers will follow these rules.

Basically, it's all about finding the right balance between having the latest information and being considerate of website resources.

21.1.5 Designed for Scalability

Figure 21.2 appears to be an expanded and more detailed version of the web crawler architecture we discussed earlier. It includes several new components and shows a more realistic flow of data with multiple instances of certain services. Here's a breakdown of the key elements:

1. **User Program**: Same as before, this is the user interface where interactions with the crawler system originate.
2. **DNS**: This represents the Domain Name System, which translates domain names (like [invalid URL removed]) into IP addresses that computers can understand. This is a crucial step for the crawler to locate and access web servers.
3. **Load Balancer**: This component distributes incoming network traffic across multiple servers to ensure no single server is overwhelmed and to improve overall performance and reliability.
4. **Service Layer**: Now depicted as multiple instances, this layer handles user requests, manages resources, and routes requests to appropriate backend services.
5. **Inverted Index Service**: Multiple instances suggest this service is scaled to handle a larger volume of indexing tasks, improving efficiency and responsiveness.
6. **Queue**: Again, multiple instances are shown, likely to manage different types of URLs or to distribute the workload for better performance.
7. **Crawler Service**: Multiple instances indicate a distributed crawling approach, where several crawlers work in parallel to fetch and process web pages more quickly.
8. **Document Service**: Multiple instances are likely used to handle the increased workload of processing and storing crawled documents from multiple crawlers.
9. **Cache**: This is a new component that stores frequently accessed data in a fast-access location to speed up retrieval times and reduce the load on the database.
10. **Database**: This remains the central storage for all crawled data and the inverted index.

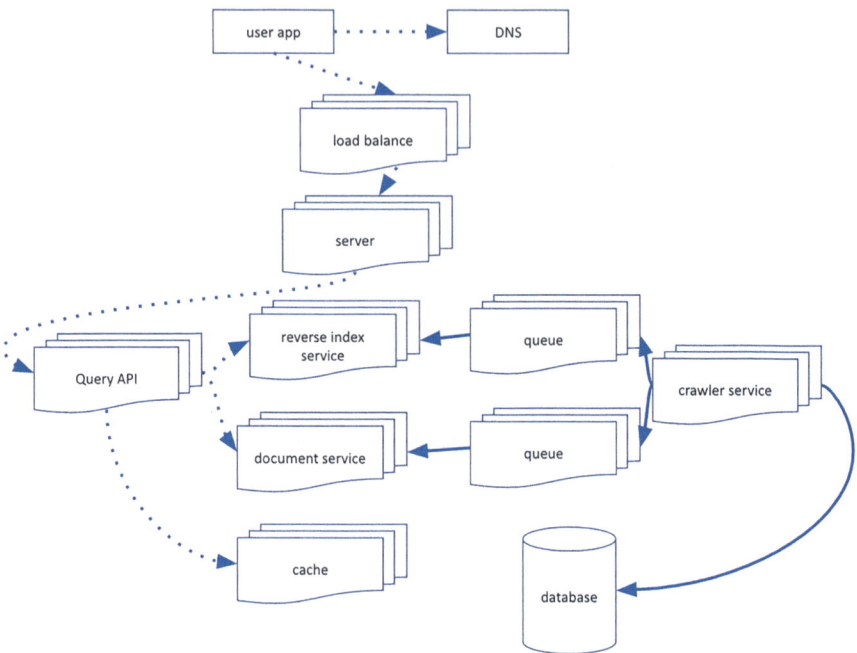

Fig. 21.2 Extended crawler design

This architecture emphasizes scalability and efficiency. By using multiple instances of key services, load balancing, and caching, the system can handle a much larger volume of data and user requests compared to the simpler architecture. This is essential for a web crawler operating at a large scale.

It is important to discuss the bottlenecks that may be encountered in the initial design and how to address each one. For example, what problems can be solved by adding a load balancer to multiple web servers? CDN? Master-slave replicas? What are the alternatives and trade-offs for each scenario?

21.2 Encryption and Decryption of TinyURL

TinyURL is a service that takes long web addresses and makes them shorter and easier to share.

Imagine you have a really long link that you want to send to a friend. Instead of sending the whole thing, you can use TinyURL to create a short, simple link that takes your friend to the same place.

The challenge is to design a system that can:

- **Encode**: Take a long URL and turn it into a short TinyURL.
- **Decode**: Take a TinyURL and turn it back into the original long URL.

21.2 Encryption and Decryption of TinyURL

You have complete freedom in how you design this system. The only requirement is that it can reliably shorten URLs and then expand them back to the original.

21.2.1 Requirements and Objectives of the System

This describes the requirements for building a URL shortening service, similar to TinyURL or Bitly. Here's a simpler breakdown:

What it should do:

- **Shorten**: Take a long web address and create a short, unique "nickname" for it.
- **Redirect**: When someone clicks the short link, send them to the original long address.
- **Customize**: Let users choose their own short "nickname" if they want.
- **Expire**: Have an option for links to expire after a certain time, so they don't last forever.

How it should work:

- **Reliable**: The service should always be available, so links don't break.
- **Fast**: Redirecting to the original link should happen instantly.

Bonus features:

- **Stats**: Keep track of how many times a short link is used.
- **API**: Allow other applications to use the service.

Essentially, this describes a system that's user-friendly, reliable, and efficient for creating and managing shortened web addresses.

21.2.2 Capacity Estimation and Constraints

Traffic:

- **Lots of redirects**: People will click on short links much more often than they create new ones. The example assumes 100 redirects for every new short link created.
- **Estimating usage**: If 500 million new short links are created each month, that means there will be 50 billion redirects in the same period.
- **Queries per second (QPS)**: This is a measure of how many requests the system needs to handle per second. In this case, it's estimated to be 200 new URLs per second and 19,000 redirects per second.

Storage:

- **Storing lots of links**: If the service keeps track of shortened URLs for 5 years, and 500 million are created each month, that adds up to 30 billion URLs to store!
- **Storage space**: Assuming each shortened URL and its associated information takes up 500 bytes, the service would need 15 terabytes of storage.

Bandwidth:

- **Incoming data**: This refers to the data coming into the system when people create new short links. It's estimated to be 100 kilobytes per second.
- **Outgoing data**: This is the data going out when people click on short links and are redirected. It's estimated to be 9 megabytes per second.

Memory:

- **Caching popular links**: To make the service faster, it can store frequently used links in memory (like RAM). This is called caching.
- **Memory needs**: Using the "80-20 rule" (where 20% of the links get 80% of the traffic), the service would need 170 gigabytes of memory to cache the most popular links.

Essentially, this analysis shows that a popular URL shortening service needs to be designed to handle a massive amount of traffic, store a huge number of links, and have enough memory to cache frequently accessed data.

21.2.3 System APIs

We can use SOAP or REST APIs to expose the functionality of our services. Here are the API definitions for creating and deleting URLs:

```
creatURL(api_dev_key, original_url, custom_alias == Noneuser_
name == None, expire_date == None)
```

Parameter:

api_dev_key (string): The API developer key for the registered account. This will be used, among other things, to limit users based on the allocated quota.
original_url (string): The original URL to shorten.
custom_alias (string): An optional custom key for the URL.
user_name (string): An optional username used in encoding.
expire_date (string): An optional expiration date for the shortened URL.
Return: (string)

A shortened URL will be returned for successful insertion; otherwise, an error code will be returned.

```
deleteURL(api_dev_key, url_key)
```

where "url_key" is a string that represents the shortened URL to be retrieved. A successful deletion will return "URL deleted".

How can we detect and prevent abuse? For example, any service can enable abuse by consuming all the keys in the current design. To prevent abuse, we can limit the number of URLs that a user can create or access in a specific period of time through user api_dev_key.

21.2.4 Core Algorithm Design

This describes a simple way to create short URLs, like TinyURL does. Here's the idea:

1. **Assign a number to each link**: Every time a new long URL is given to the system, it gets a number. This number increases by 1 for each new link. So, the first link gets 1, the second gets 2, and so on.
2. **Convert the number to a short code**: This number is then converted into a short code made up of six characters. These characters can be lowercase letters (a–z), uppercase letters (A–Z), or numbers (0–9). This gives a lot of possible combinations! Think of it like a secret code for each link.
3. **Store the code and link together**: The system remembers which short code goes with which long URL. It's like a matching game. This is often done using a "hash table," which is a way to store and quickly find information.
4. **To use a short URL**: When someone clicks a short URL, the system looks up the 6-character code and finds the matching long URL. Then, it sends the person to that original website.

This method is a straightforward way to create short and unique URLs. It's like giving each long web address a short and easy-to-remember nickname.

Code 21.2: How to Shorten URLs

```
class Codec:
    def __init__(self):
        self.count = 0
        self.prefix = "http://tinyurl.com/"
        self.character
        ="0123456789abcdefghijklmnopqrstuvwxyzABCDE
        FGHIJKLMNOPQRSTUVWXYZ"
        self.table={}
    def encode(self, longUrl: str) -> str:
""" Encode the URL to a shortened URL. """
        self.count+=1
        def convertBase62(count):
            strs=""
            for _ in range(6):
                strs=strs+self.character[count%62]
                count = count//62
            return strs
        shortUrl = convertBase62(self.count)
        self.table[shortUrl] = longUrl
        return prefix+shortUrl

    def decode(self, shortUrl: str) -> str:
""" decodes the shortened URL to its original URL. """
        if shortUrl[-6:] in self.table:
            return self.table[shortUrl[-6:]]
```

21.2.5 Database Design

A few observations about the nature of the data we're going to store: (1) We need to store billions of records. (2) Each object we want to store is small (less than 1K). (3) There is no relationship between the records, unless we want to store which user created which URL. (4) Our services are heavy-handed.

For this, we will need two tables in Fig. 21.3, one to store information about the URL mapping and the other to store the user's data.

Since we may be storing billions of rows and **don't need to use relationships between objects—like Dynamo or Cassandra, a NoSQL key-value store is a better choice and** will also be easy to scale. If you choose NoSQL, you can't store the UserID in the URL table (because there is no foreign key in NoSQL), for this we need a third table to store the mapping between the URL and the user.

21.2 Encryption and Decryption of TinyURL

URL	
PK	**Hash: varchar(16)**
	OrignalURL: varchar(512)
	CreationDate: datetime
	ExpirationDate: datatime
	UserID: int

User	
PK	**UserID: int**
	Name: varchar(20)
	Email: varchar(32)
	CreationDate: datetime
	LastLogin: datetime

Fig. 21.3 The database needs to create two tables

21.2.6 Data Partitioning and Replication

Scaling the database to manage billions of URLs requires partitioning data across multiple servers. Here's how we can approach partitioning:

1. **Range-based partitioning**: In this method, URLs are distributed into partitions based on the first letter or a hash key. For instance, URLs starting with "A" are stored in one partition, those starting with "B" in another, and so on. We can even combine less frequently occurring letters into the same partition. This strategy is called range-based partitioning and provides a predictable way to store and retrieve URLs. However, it may lead to server imbalance. For example, if too many URLs start with "E," storing all of them in one partition can cause storage issues.
2. **Hash-based partitioning**: In this approach, we hash the data (e.g., the URL) and determine which database partition the data will be stored in based on the hash. For example, we could use a hash function that maps any key to values between 1 and 256, where each number represents a partition. This method distributes data more evenly but may still result in overload in certain partitions, which can be addressed using consistent hashing.

21.2.7 Cache Design

To improve performance, frequently accessed URLs can be cached. Ready-made solutions like Memcached can store full URLs along with their associated hashes. Before accessing the backend database, the application server can check the cache to see if the desired URL is already stored.

- **Cache size**: Start by caching around 20% of daily traffic and adjust based on usage patterns. For example, with modern servers offering 256 GB of RAM, 170 GB could be used to cache 20% of daily traffic, which may fit on a single server or be distributed across several smaller servers.

- **Cache eviction strategy**: When the cache is full and we need to replace older URLs with newer or more frequently accessed ones, a least recently used (LRU) eviction policy works well. This strategy discards the URLs that have not been accessed recently. We can use data structures like linked hashes to store URLs and their associated hashes while also tracking recent visits.
- **Cache replication**: To distribute the load, cache servers can be replicated. When a cache miss occurs, the server retrieves the data from the backend database, updates the cache, and forwards the new entry to all cache replicas. Each replica will update its cache accordingly, or ignore the update if it already contains the entry.

21.2.8 Load Balancer

Load balancing can be added at three levels:

1. Between the client and application server
2. Between the application server and database server
3. Between the application server and cache server

Initially, a simple round-robin load balancing method can be used to evenly distribute incoming requests across backend servers. This method is easy to implement and doesn't require much overhead. If a server goes down, the load balancer will stop sending traffic to it. However, the round-robin approach doesn't account for the server's actual load. To overcome this, a more advanced load balancing solution could periodically query the backend servers for their load and distribute traffic accordingly.

21.3 Design Autocomplete

21.3.1 What Is Autocomplete?

Autocomplete is a feature that helps you search more efficiently by suggesting possible search terms as you type. It's like a mind-reader for your searches!
Here's how it works:

- **Predicts your query**: When you start typing in a search box, autocomplete analyzes your input and suggests relevant queries.
- **Saves you time and effort**: Instead of typing out the entire search, you can simply select a suggestion.
- **Helps you find what you need**: Autocomplete can guide you towards the right search terms, even if you're not sure exactly what you're looking for.

21.3 Design Autocomplete

It's important to note that autocomplete isn't just about speed. It's also about improving the accuracy and effectiveness of your searches. By suggesting relevant terms, it helps you express your search intent more clearly and find the information you need more easily.

In short, autocomplete is a helpful tool that makes searching easier and more intuitive.

21.3.2 Requirements and Objectives of the System

Feature Requirements: When a user enters something in a query, our service should start with whatever is typed to suggest the top 10 terms. Non-functional requirements: Recommendations should be displayed in real-time, and users should be able to see recommendations within 200 ms.

21.3.3 Basic System Design and Algorithms

This section explains how to build an autocomplete system that can handle a huge number of search terms and provide lightning-fast suggestions.

The Challenge:

Imagine you have a massive dictionary of words and phrases. When someone starts typing in a search box, you need to quickly suggest relevant completions. This requires a clever way to store and access the data.

The Solution:

- **Trie data structure**: This is a specialized way to organize the search terms, like a tree with branches for each letter. It allows for very fast searching and prefix matching.
- **Storing in memory**: To make things even faster, the data is stored in the computer's memory (RAM) instead of on a slower hard drive.

Ranking Suggestions:

- **Frequency tracking**: The system keeps track of how often each search term is used. This helps prioritize the most popular suggestions.
- **Updating frequencies**: As people use the system, the popularity of search terms changes. The system updates these frequencies using a technique called "exponential moving average" (EMA), which gives more weight to recent data.

Adding and Removing Terms:

- **Adding new terms**: When a new search term is added, the system updates the Trie structure and its frequency count.

- **Removing terms**: If a term needs to be removed (e.g., for legal reasons), it's deleted from the Trie, and a filter is added to prevent it from being suggested.

Essentially, this system is designed for:

- **Speed**: Providing autocomplete suggestions with minimal delay.
- **Scale**: Handling a massive number of search terms.
- **Accuracy**: Suggesting the most relevant and popular completions.
- **Dynamic updates**: Keeping the data fresh and reflecting current search trends.

21.3.4 Data Structure: Trie

This section explains how a "Trie" works and how it's used for autocomplete. Think of a Trie like a special dictionary organized for super-fast searching.

How it works:

- **Tree structure**: It's like a family tree, with each branch representing a letter or part of a word.
- **Efficient storage**: Instead of storing every word separately, it groups words with common beginnings. For example, "rest," "restaurant," and "restriction" all share the same "rest" beginning, so they branch off from the same point.
- **Quick lookup**: When you type in a search, the Trie quickly follows the branches that match your letters. This makes finding possible completions very fast.

Search Time:
The text also explains how long a search might take using a Trie:

- **Finding the prefix**: The time it takes to find the part of the Trie that matches what you've typed so far depends on the length of your input (L).
- **Finding the top suggestions**: After finding the matching part, the Trie needs to explore the branches to find the best suggestions (K). In the worst case, it might have to look through the entire Trie (N). However, using a clever technique called a "heap," it can quickly find the top K suggestions.

In simple terms:

A Trie is a clever way to store words that makes autocomplete suggestions very fast. It's like a specialized dictionary designed for quickly finding words with common beginnings. Figure 21.4 shows one application for the Trie.

21.3 Design Autocomplete

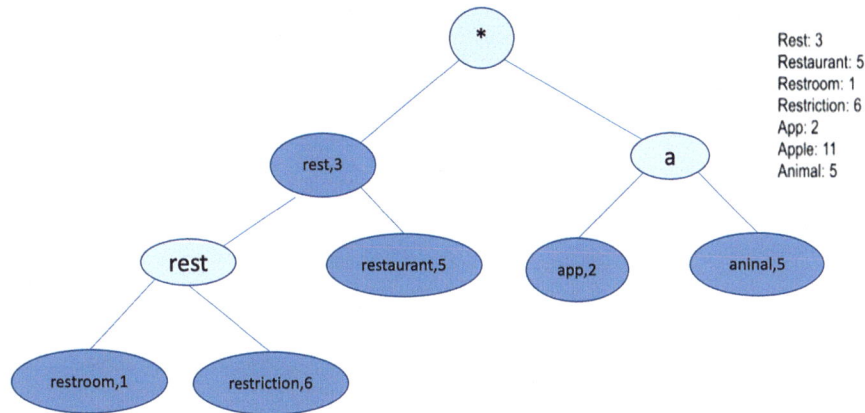

Fig. 21.4 Based on the query words entered by the user

Code 21.3: The Python Program Implements Trie

```
class TrieNode(object):
    def __init__(self):
        self.children = collections.defaultdict(TrieNode)
        self.is_word = False # determines if word is
        completed (end of word)

class Trie(object):
    def __init__(self):
        self.root = TrieNode()

    def insert(self, word):
        current = self.root
        for letter in word:
            current = current.children[letter]
        current.is_word = True

    def search(self, word):
        node = self.root
        return self.dfs(word, node)

    def startsWith(self, prefix):
        node = self.root
        return self.dfs(prefix, node, False)
```

```
def dfs(self, string, node, is_word_given=True):
        # if is_word_given is True: we are looking
        for word
        # if is_word_given is False: we are
        looking for prefix

        # the common part of search and startsWith
    for i, c in enumerate(string):
        if c not in node.children: return False
        node = node.children[c]
    return node.is_word if is_word_given else True
```

Since responsiveness is the most important criterion, let's see if we can do better.

21.3.5 Improvements

21.3.5.1 Storing Sorting Results in a Node

To avoid traversing each subtree to get a prefix, pre-computation can be done and the results can be stored at the node representing the end of the prefix. For example, a sorted list of the top K words that start with that prefix can be saved at that node.

This approach sacrifices storage space for increased performance. A prefix lookup will now take O(L) time, which is significantly faster than before.

Given a prefix, how long would it take to traverse its subtrees? Considering the potential size of the tree due to the amount of data in the index, traversing even a single subtree could be very time-consuming. Since we have strict latency requirements, improving efficiency is crucial. One option is to store the top recommendations directly at each node, which would speed up the search process, but at the cost of requiring more storage.

To meet efficiency demands, we could store the top 10 recommendations at each node to be returned to the user. Instead of storing the entire phrase, we can optimize storage by only storing references to the endpoints. To find the suggested terms, we would need to traverse the tree using the parent references of these endpoints. We also need to keep track of the frequency for each reference to ensure we prioritize the most important recommendations.

How do we build this Trie? We can build the Trie effectively from the bottom up. Each parent node can recursively call its child nodes to calculate the best recommendations and their counts. The parent node will then merge the recommendations from all the children to determine the best ones.

21.3 Design Autocomplete

21.3.5.2 Limiting Word Length

In most cases, users stop typing before reaching 20 characters unless they know exactly what they are searching for, in which case they probably don't need suggestions. Therefore, it's not necessary to build subtrees for longer words or phrases. Instead, we can store frequent long words at their prefix nodes.

21.3.5.3 Caching Layer on Top of the Trie

In practice, 20% of the most frequent requests account for 80% of the traffic. By allocating a small amount of space to handle these requests, the load can be significantly reduced. For example: {'re': ['restriction': 6, 'restaurant': 5], 'a': ['apple': 11, 'animal': 5], 'ap': ['apple': 11, 'app': 2]}

Typically, a Trie is stored in a NoSQL database to ensure durability and scalability, as seen in large systems like Google's TeraTrie. For caching, Redis is a good choice as it supports useful operations for managing cache and sorting. For instance, Redis allows you to update the ranking score of a word without having to fetch, reorder, and reinsert the entire list.

21.3.5.4 Ranking Score Source

Apart from using simple counts for ranking terms, additional factors like freshness, user location, language, demographics, and personal history must also be considered.

To recommend the most frequently searched and up-to-date terms, an aggregator can be used that calculates word scores in real-time. This will ensure that the Trie is continuously updated.

The process works as follows: user searches are sampled and timestamped before being sent to a MapReduce (MR) job. The MR job calculates the frequency ranking scores for the sampled search terms over a specific time period and forwards the results to the aggregator. Low-frequency terms that won't make the top K in the Trie are excluded.

The aggregator will then calculate the new ranking score for each term based on its previous rank and the frequency score (generated by MR + time factor), with more weight given to recent data.

Figure 21.5 depicts a system for processing and aggregating data, likely in the context of generating autocomplete suggestions or similar tasks where data needs to be collected and combined from multiple sources.

1. **MR**: This likely stands for MapReduce, a programming model and associated implementation for processing and generating large datasets with a parallel, distributed algorithm on a cluster. It's commonly used for tasks like indexing web pages or processing log files.

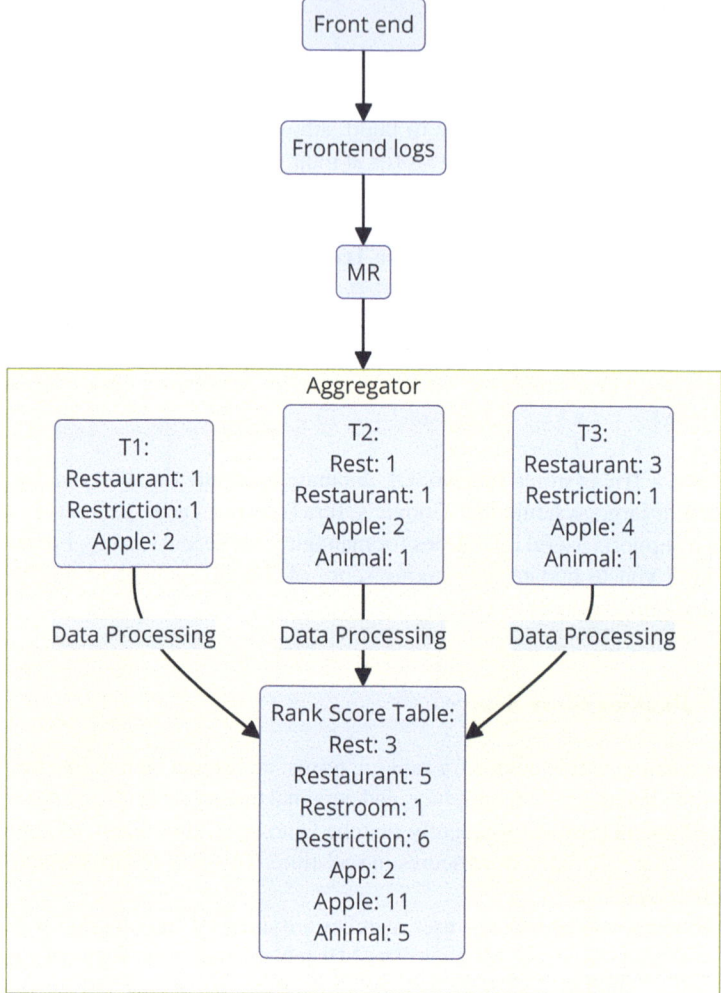

Fig. 21.5 The design of the system for searching for word rankings

2. **Frontend Logs**: This refers to the logs generated by the frontend servers or applications. These logs typically record user interactions, such as search queries, page views, and other activities. In this context, they probably contain information about user search input.
3. **Aggregator**: This component is responsible for collecting and aggregating data from different sources, in this case, the frontend logs. It combines the data into a more manageable and summarized form.
4. **T1, T2, T3**: These likely represent different time intervals or shards of the frontend logs. The aggregator collects data from each of these time intervals.

21.3 Design Autocomplete

5. **Score Ranking Table**: This table stores the aggregated data, likely in the form of search terms and their associated scores or frequencies. This table is used to generate autocomplete suggestions or other ranked results.

In essence, this system demonstrates a common pattern for processing large datasets:

- Data is collected from multiple sources (frontend logs).
- MapReduce is used to efficiently process the data in a distributed manner.
- An aggregator combines the data from different sources or time intervals.
- The aggregated data is stored in a structured format (score ranking table) for further use, such as generating autocomplete suggestions.

This system is designed to handle large volumes of data and provide efficient aggregation and ranking, which are crucial for applications like autocomplete that require real-time responsiveness and accurate suggestions.

21.3.5.5 Updating the Trie

To update the Trie, for each word that has a new score, find its end node and update the score there. Then, proceed upwards from the bottom, updating the list of sorted words at each parent node.

Given that there are about five billion searches per day, this equates to roughly 60,000 queries per second. If we attempt to update the Trie for every single query, this would be highly resource-intensive and would also slow down read requests. To mitigate this, we can update the Trie offline at set intervals.

As new queries come in, we can log them and track their frequency. We don't need to record every single query; instead, we can sample them—for instance, recording every 1000th query. For example, if we don't want to show terms with fewer than 1000 searches, we can safely ignore low-frequency terms. Using a MapReduce (MR) system, we can process the collected data periodically, such as once an hour. These MR jobs will calculate the frequency of all search terms within that period. We can then use the new data to update the Trie by taking a current snapshot and incorporating all the new terms and frequency updates.

We don't want to block read queries during the update process, so here are two potential approaches:

1. **Copy-and-Switch Method**: A copy of the Trie is created on each server and updated offline. Once the update is complete, we can switch to the updated Trie and discard the old one.
2. **Master-Slave Configuration**: A master-slave setup can be implemented for each Trie server. The slave server can be updated while the master server continues to serve traffic. Once the update is finished, the secondary server becomes the new master. The old master server can be updated later and then resume serving traffic.

21.3.5.6 Trie Replication

To handle high traffic and enhance system availability, multiple replicas of the Trie can be deployed. Each replica is updated in sequence. During the update process, the replica will pause serving requests until the update is complete.

21.3.5.7 Snapshots

For additional durability, snapshots of the Trie should be taken at regular intervals. These snapshots can be stored in a service like S3 for safekeeping and recovery purposes.

21.3.5.8 Trie Partitioning

Partitioning the Trie is another method to scale the system to handle increased traffic and a larger footprint. To ensure balanced load distribution, partitions can be created based on the estimated traffic for each prefix. For instance, if the prefixes 'a'-'ea', 'eb'-'hig', and 'hih'-'ke' receive similar amounts of traffic, they can be assigned to shard1, shard2, and shard3, respectively.

Figure 21.6 shows a more complex and detailed architecture for an autocomplete system, likely designed to handle a very high volume of data and user requests. It incorporates several components for data processing, storage, and caching, as well as a distributed approach for scalability.

1. **Frontend Application Service**: This represents the frontend servers or applications that interact with users. They handle user requests, including search queries, and generate frontend logs.
2. **Frontend Logs**: These are the logs generated by the frontend application service, capturing user activity and search queries.
3. **MR**: This likely stands for MapReduce, a distributed data processing framework used to analyze the large volume of frontend logs and extract relevant information, such as search terms and their frequencies.
4. **Aggregator**: This component collects the processed data from MapReduce and aggregates it, combining data from different time intervals (T1, T2, T3) or sources.
5. **Score Ranking Table**: This table stores the aggregated data, likely containing search terms and their associated scores or frequencies. However, unlike the previous diagram, this one suggests a temporary storage, possibly for further processing or transfer.
6. **NoSQL—Trie Datastore**: This is the core database for storing the Trie data structure. It's a NoSQL database, chosen for its ability to handle large volumes of unstructured data and its scalability. The datastore is sharded (shard 1, shard

21.3 Design Autocomplete

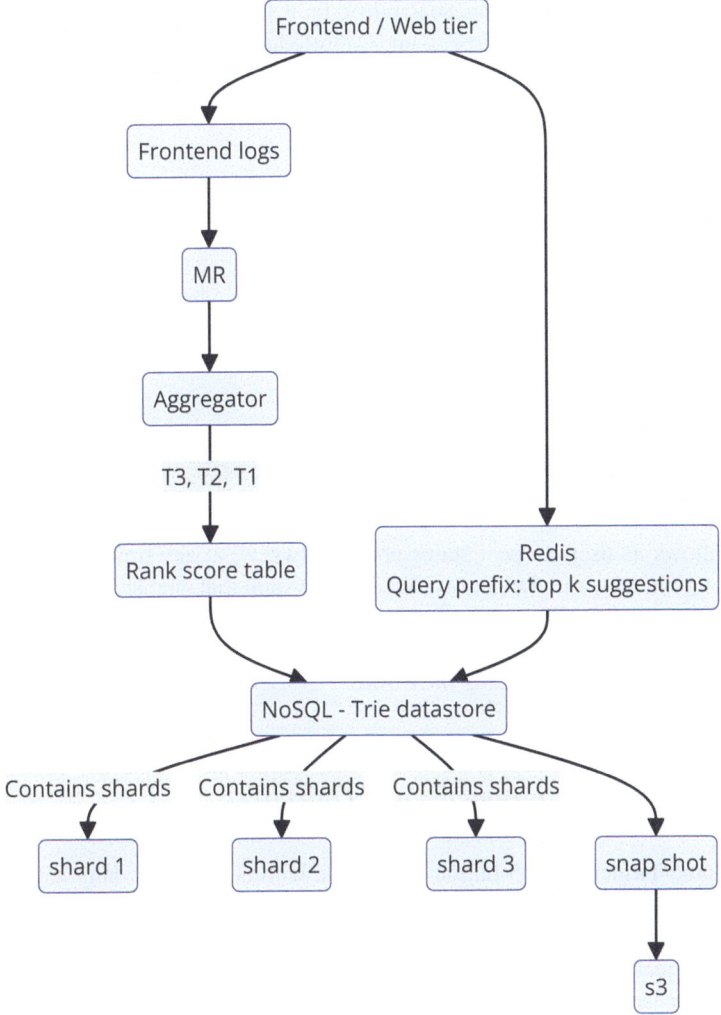

Fig. 21.6 Design of auto-completion system based on Trie partition design

2, shard 3), meaning the data is distributed across multiple servers for better performance and capacity.

7. **Redis**: This is a high-performance in-memory data store used for caching. It stores frequently accessed data, such as the top K suggestions for common prefixes, to provide very fast autocomplete suggestions.
8. **S3**: This likely represents Amazon S3, a cloud-based object storage service. It's used for storing snapshots of the data, possibly for backup, recovery, or offline analysis.
9. **Snapshot**: This indicates the process of taking snapshots of the data in the Trie datastore and storing them in S3.

This architecture emphasizes scalability, fault tolerance, and real-time performance. By using distributed processing (MapReduce), sharding the database, and caching frequently accessed data, the system can handle a massive amount of data and provide quick and accurate autocomplete suggestions even with high user traffic.

21.4 Design Twitter

Twitter is one of the largest social networking services where users can share photos, news, and text-based messages. In this chapter, we will design a service that can store and search for user tweets.

21.4.1 What Is Twitter Search?

Twitter allows its users to post status updates (tweets) at any time. These updates consist of plain text, and the goal is to create a system that enables efficient searching of all user statuses. We aim to design a simplified version of Twitter where users can post tweets, follow or unfollow other users, and view the latest 10 tweets from the people they follow, including their own.

21.4.2 System Requirements and Objectives

Let's assume Twitter has 1.5 billion total users, with 800 million daily active users. Each day, approximately 400 million new tweets are posted. The average size of a tweet is 300 bytes. Additionally, there will be around 500 million searches per day. Each search query will consist of multiple words combined using AND/OR operations, so the system needs to be designed to store and efficiently search through user statuses.

21.4.3 Capacity Estimation and Constraints

With 400 million new tweets per day, and each tweet averaging 300 bytes, the total storage required per day is:

$$400M \text{ tweets} * 300 \text{ bytes} = 112 \text{ GB} / \text{day}.$$

To estimate the storage per second:

$$112 \text{ GB} / 86,400 \text{ s} (\text{in a day}) =\sim 1.3 \text{ MB} / \text{s}.$$

21.4 Design Twitter

21.4.4 System APIs

We may use SOAP or REST APIs to expose the functionality of our services. The following might be the definition of a search API:

```
search(api_dev_key, search_terms, maximum_results_to_return,
sort, page_token)
```

Parameter:

api_dev_key (string): The API developer key for the registered account. This will be used, among other things, to limit users based on the allocated quota.
search_terms (string): A string that contains the search term.
maximum_results_to_return (number): The number of status messages to be returned.
sort(number): Selectable sort modes: Newest First (0-Default), Most Matched (1), Favorite (2).
page_token (string): This token will specify which page should be returned in the result set.
Return Value: (JSON) JSON that contains information about a list of status messages that match the search query. Each result entry can contain the user ID and name, status text, statusID, creation time, number of likes, etc.

21.4.5 Premium Design

At a high level, we need to store all the words in a database, and we also need to build an index to keep track of which words appear in which state. This index will help us quickly find the status of the user's search attempts.

Figure 21.7 illustrates a system designed for high availability and scalability, likely a service that needs to handle a large number of requests and remain operational even if some components fail.

- **User**: This represents the user interacting with the system, likely making requests or accessing services.
- **Load Balancer**: This component distributes incoming user requests across multiple servers to ensure no single server is overwhelmed. This improves performance and reliability.

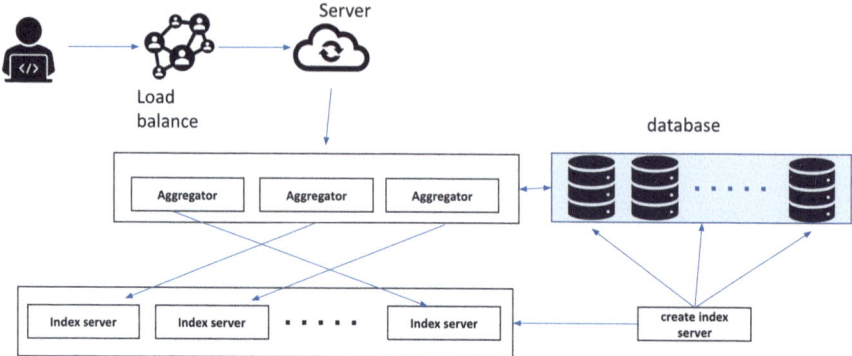

Fig. 21.7 Twitter's high-level design

- **Servers**: These are the workhorses of the system, handling the actual processing of user requests. Multiple servers are shown to provide redundancy and scalability. If one server fails, the others can still handle the load.
- **Index Servers**: These servers likely manage indexes, which are data structures that speed up data retrieval. They could be used for search functionality or to quickly access specific information within the database.
- **Database**: This is where the system's data is stored. Multiple database instances are shown, which could indicate sharding (data is split across multiple databases) or replication (copies of the data are kept on different databases) for increased capacity and fault tolerance.
- **Index Creation Server**: This server is dedicated to creating and updating indexes. Separating this task from the other servers can improve performance and efficiency.

This architecture emphasizes:

- **High Availability**: The use of multiple servers and database instances ensures that the system can continue operating even if some components fail.
- **Scalability**: The system can handle increased traffic by adding more servers or database instances.
- **Performance**: Load balancing and efficient indexing contribute to fast response times.

This type of architecture is common in systems that require high uptime and can handle a large volume of requests, such as web applications, e-commerce platforms, and online services.

21.4.6 Core Algorithm Design

postTweet(userId, tweetId): Creates a new Tweet
getNewsFeed(userId): Retrieves the last 10 tweets. Each Tweet must be made by someone the user follows or by the user himself. Tweets must be sorted chronologically from the most recent start.
follow(followerId, followeeId): Follow a user
unfollow(followerId, followeeId): Unfollow a user

Example
Twitter twitter = new Twitter();
   User 1 sent a new tweet (user id = 1, tweet id = 5).
     twitter.postTweet(1, 5);
   User 1's Acquired Tweets should return a list of Tweets with an ID of 5.
     twitter.getNewsFeed(1);
   User 1 follows User 2.
   twitter.follow(1, 2);
   User 2 sent a new tweet (tweet id = 6).
   twitter.postTweet(2, 6);
   User 1's Acquired Tweets should return a list of two Tweets with IDs of -> [6, 5].
   Tweet ID6 should precede Tweet ID5 as it was sent after 5.
   twitter.getNewsFeed(1);
   User 1 unfollows User 2.
   twitter.unfollow(1, 2);
   User 1's Acquired Tweets should return a list of Tweets with an ID of 5.
   Because user 1 no longer follows user 2.
   twitter.getNewsFeed(1);

This can be done with two hash tables, the first one mapping the relationship between the user's attention to another user, and the second one mapping the relationship between the user's tweets. How to represent the time relationship of a tweet, using a time variable to represent it, the larger the time variable, the more recent the tweet. Of course, the last 10 tweets can be obtained using the priority queue.

Code 21.4: Design Twitter

```
class Twitter(object):

    def __init__(self):
        self.users = defaultdict(set)
        self.followers = defaultdict(set)
        self.reputation = 0

    def postTweet(self, userId, tweetId):
        self.reputation += 1
        self.users[userId].add((tweetId, self.
        reputation))

    def getNewsFeed(self, userId):
        tweets = list(self.users[userId])
        followees = self.followers[userId]

        for user_id in followees:
            tweets += self.users[user_id]

        most_recent_Tweets = sorted(tweets, key = lambda
        posts: posts[1],reverse=True)[:10]

        return [post[0] for post in most_recent_Tweets]

    def follow(self, followerId, followeeId):
        self.followers[followerId].add(followeeId if
        followerId != followeeId else None)

    def unfollow(self, followerId, followeeId):
        self.followers[followerId] -= {followeeId}
```

21.4.7 Improvements

21.4.7.1 Data Storage and Partitioning

Given that we need to store approximately 112 GB of new data every day, an efficient data partitioning strategy is required to distribute this across multiple servers. If we project our storage needs over the next 5 years, we'll need around:

$$112\,\text{GB}^* \, 365\,\text{days}^* \, 5\,\text{years} = 204{,}400\,\text{GB}\,(\sim 200\,\text{TB}).$$

21.4 Design Twitter

To ensure we never use more than 80% of the total capacity, we'll need 240 TB. If we want to keep an additional copy of all the data for fault tolerance, we will require 480 TB of total storage. Assuming each server has a capacity of 4 TB, we will need 120 servers over the next 5 years to accommodate all the data.

We can start with a simple design, using a MySQL database to store the statuses. The data could be stored in a table with two columns: `StatusID` and `StatusText`. A partitioning scheme based on the `StatusID` can be used to distribute the data. We can implement a hash function to map the `StatusID` to the appropriate storage server.

21.4.7.2 Creating a Unique System-Wide StatusID

With 400 million new statuses being created daily, the number of status objects in 5 years would be:

$$400\,\text{million}^* \, 365\,\text{days}^* \, 5\,\text{years} = 730\,\text{billion}.$$

To uniquely identify each status, we'll need a five-byte number for the `StatusID`. We can use a service to generate unique `StatusIDs`, which will be passed through a hash function to determine which server will store the corresponding status object.

21.4.7.3 Indexing

Since users will query status objects using specific words, we need to build an index that maps each word to the status objects that contain it. Let's estimate the size of the index:

- We assume there are approximately 300K common English words and 200K notable nouns, giving us a total of around 500K words.
- The average word length is estimated to be five characters, which means that storing the index in memory will require around 2.5 MB.

If we only index the statuses from the last 2 years, this will involve about 292 billion status objects (out of 730 billion over 5 years). Each `StatusID` will require 5 bytes of memory, so storing these StatusIDs will take around 1460 GB of memory.

To further estimate the total memory needed for the index:

- Each status is associated with about 15 significant words (excluding small words like "the" or "and").
- Each `StatusID` will therefore appear in the index 15 times, resulting in a total of approximately 21 TB of memory.

Given that high-end servers typically have around 144 GB of RAM, we'll need about 152 such servers to store the full index.

21.4.7.4 Sharding the Index

We can shard the index based on two criteria:

1. **Word-based sharding**: Each word is hashed to determine the server responsible for indexing it. The downside of this approach is that some popular words could overload specific servers, leading to performance issues.
2. **Status-based sharding**: The `StatusID` is hashed to determine the storage server, and all the words from the corresponding status are indexed on that server. When querying a specific word, we'll need to query all servers, with each returning a list of `StatusID`s. A centralized server can then aggregate the results.

21.4.7.5 Fault Tolerance

If an index server fails, we can create secondary replicas for each server. In the event of a failure, the secondary server can take over. Both the primary and secondary servers will store identical copies of the index.

In a scenario where both the primary and secondary servers fail, we will need to rebuild the index on a new server. To do this efficiently, we can maintain a reverse index that maps all `StatusID`s to the server where they are indexed. This information can be stored in an Index-Builder server, which keeps a hash table that maps index servers to the `StatusID`s they store. If an index server fails, the Index-Builder server can provide the necessary data to rebuild the index.

21.4.7.6 Caching

To handle popular status objects, a caching layer can be introduced in front of the database. Memcached can be used to store frequently accessed status objects in memory. Before querying the database, the application server can check the cache. The cache eviction strategy should be based on the least recently used (LRU) policy, which ensures that the least accessed data is removed first when the cache is full.

21.4.7.7 Load Balancing

A load balancing layer can be introduced at two points in the system:

1. Between the client and the application server.
2. Between the application server and the backend server.

A simple round-robin load balancing approach can be used to evenly distribute incoming requests across backend servers. If a server fails, the load balancer can automatically remove it from the rotation. However, round-robin balancing does not account for server load. A more sophisticated load balancer could be employed, one that regularly checks the backend server load and adjusts traffic distribution accordingly.

21.4.7.8 Ranking Search Results

To rank search results by various criteria, such as social graph distance, popularity, or relevance, we can assign a ranking score to each status. For example, we could rank statuses based on the number of likes or comments they receive. This ranking score can be stored alongside the index.

Each partition of the index can sort results by popularity before returning them to the aggregator server. The aggregator will then combine and further sort the results based on popularity before sending the top-ranked results back to the user.

21.5 Design Uber/Lyft

The question is open-ended, and taxi-hailing apps can have numerous features. To make the problem more manageable, focus on designing the system around 2–3 core functions, and you can always add more features later. It's important to discuss these features with the interviewer to ensure alignment. Some interviewers may have specific features in mind or may not be concerned about certain aspects.

It's a good idea to ask if they are okay with sticking to a few features first and potentially adding more in the future. Even if this point is not explicitly stated, it's helpful to clarify and make sure you're on the same page.

Here's a good approach to identify the core features:

- What constitutes the minimum viable product (MVP)?
- Would the system feel incomplete without a specific feature?
- For example, the service would be non-functional without the ability to request or hail a taxi.

Here are some basic features you could implement:

- User and driver profiles.
- Users can request a rides and locate nearby drivers, while drivers can accept requests, pick up passengers, and complete drop-offs.

21.5.1 Use Case

The ride-hailing app is state-based, meaning both the driver and the rider move through various states, and the backend system must coordinate these transitions. Below are the various states involved in the process:

Rider:

1. Request a ride
2. Get an estimated time of arrival (ETA)
3. Ride to the destination
4. Complete the ride

Driver:

1. Accept/reject the ride request
2. Pick up the rider
3. Drive to the destination
4. Complete the drop-off

The process begins when a rider selects the "Request a Ride" button. The system searches for available drivers nearby, sending a request to the selected driver. If the driver accepts, the system provides the driver's ETA and shares the rider's location with the driver through periodic updates. At this point, we can assume the driver uses external mapping services like Google Maps to get directions (no need to integrate maps or routes into the system).

Once the driver picks up the rider, the "Pickup" button is selected, and both users see a "Riding" screen. Finally, after reaching the destination and the rider exits, the driver selects the "End Ride" button to finalize the ride.

21.5.2 High-Level Design

Figure 21.8 shows the architecture of a ride-hailing service system.

1. Passengers:
    (a) On the left side, the image shows a passenger with a smartphone who makes a ride request.
    (b) The passenger's request goes through a **Passenger Request Api**, which is balanced by a **Load Balancer** to evenly distribute incoming traffic.
    (c) The request then flows to **App Servers**, which handle the request, and the data is processed using a **Distributed Database** and **Cache.**
2. Drivers:
    (a) On the right side, a driver with a smartphone receives ride requests.
    (b) The driver makes requests using a **Driver Request API**, which is also balanced through a **load balancer**.
    (c) After the ride request is processed, the driver either accepts or rejects the request via a **Driver Accept Request System**.
    (d) A **Matching System** is used to match riders with available drivers.

21.5 Design Uber/Lyft

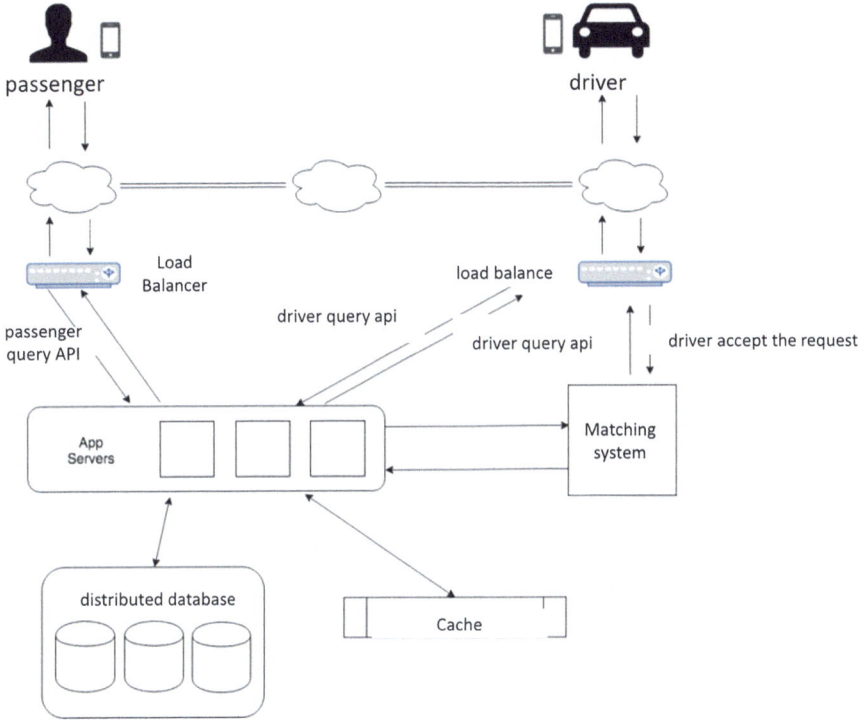

Fig. 21.8 Design the high-level design of the taxi-hailing app

3. Distributed Database and Cache:

   (a) The image includes a **distributed database** and a **cache** that are used to store and quickly retrieve data, such as available drivers and ride requests.

This diagram outlines a typical ride-hailing system flow from when a rider sends a request to when a driver receives and accepts it. The load balancers help distribute the traffic load to the backend servers, and the distributed database and caching systems ensure fast and scalable data management.

21.5.3 What Happens When a User Requests a Ride?

When a rider requests a ride, the application server updates the rider's status to "Requested." The request is then sent to the matching system, which is responsible for finding an available driver.

The matching system keeps a pool of drivers in the "waiting" state. It locates a nearby driver and forwards the request to them. If a driver declines, the system continues sending the request to other nearby drivers until one accepts or all decline.

Once a driver accepts the request, the matching system transmits the driver's details to the app server. The server then updates the driver's status to "PICKING_ UP" and the passenger's status to "WAITING." It also notifies the driver that they are on the way to the rider.

Both the rider and driver receive notifications of status changes, enabling updates to their respective mobile interfaces. For example, when the rider enters the "Waiting" state, the driver's estimated time of arrival (ETA) is calculated and sent as part of the notification to the rider's device.

This process applies to all API requests. Requests are first sent to the app server, which processes them, updating statuses in the in-memory database and making configuration changes in the NoSQL database. It also coordinates requests with the matching system and sends status change notifications to both the passenger and the driver.

21.5.4 How Is the Driver's Location Updated?

For all active drivers (those not in a "NOT_DRIVING" state), their location needs to be regularly updated. This can be handled through the mobile app, which periodically sends the driver's current location to the application server via an HTTP handler.

The app servers store the driver's location in an in-memory database and forward it to the matching system. The matching system tracks each active driver's location to match them with nearby riders. The driver's location is stored in a spatial index enabling efficient querying when locating nearby drivers.

Chapter 22
Multi-threaded Programming

In this chapter, we have reviewed some of the common multi-threaded interview questions and provided the answers.

22.1 Multi-threaded ABC

A thread is an independent execution path within a process. Multiple threads can run concurrently, sharing the same resources of the process while executing different tasks independently. In a process, you can have one or more threads that use the same memory address space and other resources but run separate tasks.

Multi-threading refers to enabling multiple threads to run concurrently. While these threads share resources such as memory, they can execute independently. This allows more efficient CPU usage by running background processes while the main application continues to accept user input, speeding up task execution.

A **process** is a single program or application, while a **thread** is a smaller execution unit within that program. Processes have their own memory space, but threads within a process share the same address space.

Since each thread runs independently, multi-threading increases CPU efficiency by performing multiple tasks simultaneously, like running background operations while the main application is responsive to user input.

A **thread pool** is a collection of threads that are created during the application's startup. These threads are available for executing tasks as needed and are reused after completing their tasks. The main benefit of a thread pool is improving application performance by reusing existing threads rather than creating new ones for each task.

Threads operate in five states: **New**, **Runnable**, **Running**, **Waiting/Blocked**, and **Terminated**.

A **race condition** occurs when multiple threads try to execute the same block of code concurrently, leading to unpredictable outcomes. This issue can be addressed using synchronization methods.

Synchronization ensures that threads run one at a time when necessary, preventing race conditions. By using a **synchronized block**, you can designate specific portions of code to be accessed by only one thread at a time.

Context switching allows the CPU to switch between threads by saving the current thread's state and resuming it later. This is how a single CPU can manage multiple threads or processes.

The **thread scheduler** determines which thread gets CPU time and in what order. **Time slicing** is the method used by the scheduler to allocate CPU time among active threads.

Thread scheduling is determined by the CPU, so different systems may run threads in different orders, which can introduce unpredictability.

A busy spin occurs when a thread idles by executing an empty loop. Unlike methods like `wait()` or `sleep()`, busy spinning retains control of the CPU, preserving the CPU cache.

Thread starvation occurs when low-priority threads are deprived of CPU time due to resource dominance by higher-priority threads.

A thread is considered dead after execution and cannot be restarted.

A **deadlock** occurs when multiple threads are stuck waiting for each other to release resources, leading to a halt in execution. For example, if one thread holds an exclusive lock but requires resources held by other threads, the system can freeze.

An **active lock** is a situation similar to a deadlock, where a thread's state changes but no progress is made (e.g., all threads are stuck in an infinite loop).

Two common Java methods, `wait()` and `sleep()`, are often confused. `wait()` pauses the thread until it's notified by another thread using `notify()` or `notifyAll()`. Meanwhile, `sleep()` pauses the thread for a specified time, allowing other threads to execute before resuming.

Asynchronous programming refers to assigning a single task to one thread, while **parallel programming** distributes a task across multiple threads.

22.2 Example 1: Build H2O

22.2.1 Problem

There are two gases, oxygen and hydrogen. Your goal is to group these threads to form water molecules. Write synchronous code for oxygen and hydrogen molecules to enforce these constraints.

22.2.2 Code Analysis

The key is maintaining a 2:1 ratio of hydrogen to oxygen atoms.

Code 22.1: Python Code for Class H2O

```
from threading import Lock
class H2O:
    def __init__(self):
        self.h=Lock()
        self.o=Lock()
        self.o.acquire()
        self.count=0

    def hydrogen(self, releaseHydrogen: 'Callable[[],
    None]') -> None:
        self.h.acquire()
        self.count+=1
        releaseHydrogen()
        if(self.count==2):
            self.count=0
            self.o.release()
        else:
            self.h.release()

    def oxygen(self, releaseOxygen: 'Callable[[], None]')
    -> None:
        self.o.acquire()
        releaseOxygen()
        self.h.release()
```

1. **Initialization (__init__ method):**

   (a) The class has two `Lock` objects: `self.h` for hydrogen and `self.o` for oxygen.
   (b) `self.o.acquire()` is called, which locks the oxygen lock (`self.o`). This ensures an oxygen thread waits until two hydrogen threads are ready.
   (c) `self.count` is used to keep track of how many hydrogen threads have been processed for a single molecule.

2. **Hydrogen Method** (`hydrogen`):

   (a) Each time a hydrogen thread calls this method, it acquires the hydrogen lock (`self.h.acquire()`), increments `self.count`, and then calls `releaseHydrogen()` to simulate the release of hydrogen.

(b) If `self.count` reaches 2, this means two hydrogen atoms are available, so:
- `self.count` is reset to 0 for the next water molecule.
- The oxygen lock (`self.o`) is released, allowing an oxygen thread to proceed.

(c) If `self.count` is not yet 2, the hydrogen lock (`self.h`) is released, allowing another hydrogen thread to run.

3. **Oxygen Method** (`oxygen`):

   (a) The oxygen thread waits by calling `self.o.acquire()`, which ensures it can only proceed when two hydrogen atoms are ready.
   (b) Once acquired, it calls `releaseOxygen()` to simulate the release of oxygen.
   (c) Finally, it releases the hydrogen lock (`self.h.release()`), allowing a new set of hydrogen threads to proceed.

22.2.3 Test Function

The goal is to simulate the formation of water molecules using multiple threads for hydrogen and oxygen. We can use Python's `threading` library to create these threads.

Here's how a test function might look:

Code 22.2: Test Code for H2O

```
import threading
import time

# Function to simulate releasing hydrogen
def releaseHydrogen():
    print("H", end="")

# Function to simulate releasing oxygen
def releaseOxygen():
    print("O", end="")

# Test function to run multiple threads
def test_h2o():
    h2o = H2O()
```

```
# Number of atoms to test (e.g., for 3 H2O molecules,
we need 6 H and 3 O)
hydrogen_count = 6
oxygen_count = 3

# Creating hydrogen and oxygen threads
hydrogen_threads = [threading.Thread(target=h2o.
hydrogen, args=(releaseHydrogen,)) for _ in
range(hydrogen_count)]
oxygen_threads = [threading.Thread(target=h2o.oxygen,
args=(releaseOxygen,)) for _ in range(oxygen_count)]

# Start all threads
for h_thread in hydrogen_threads:
    h_thread.start()

for o_thread in oxygen_threads:
    o_thread.start()

# Wait for all threads to complete
for h_thread in hydrogen_threads:
    h_thread.join()

for o_thread in oxygen_threads:
    o_thread.join()

print("\nAll H2O molecules formed.")

# Run the test function
test_h2o()
```

22.2.4 *Explanation of the Test*

- **Hydrogen and Oxygen Counts**: We create a specific number of hydrogen and oxygen threads to simulate the formation of water molecules. For each water molecule, we need exactly two hydrogen and one oxygen atom.
- **Thread Creation**: We create lists of hydrogen and oxygen threads, passing `releaseHydrogen` and `releaseOxygen` functions as arguments to print "H" and "O", respectively, when they are released.
- **Starting Threads**: All threads are started in sequence, simulating the random arrival of hydrogen and oxygen atoms.

- **Joining Threads**: The `join()` method is used to wait for all threads to finish execution, ensuring the test does not complete until all water molecules are formed.

22.2.5 Expected Output

The sequence 'HHO' for each water molecule, like this:

```
HHOHHOHHO
All H2O molecules formed.
```

This output pattern confirms that the code enforces the correct ratio of two hydrogen atoms to one oxygen atom for each water molecule.

22.3 Example 2: Print Zero, Even, and Odd Numbers

22.3.1 Problem Overview

The task involves three threads:

1. **Thread A**: Calls `zero()`, which should only output "0".
2. **Thread B**: Calls `even()`, which should only output even numbers.
3. **Thread C**: Calls `odd()`, which should only output odd numbers.

Given an integer n, the expected output sequence should alternate as follows:

- A "0" printed by the `zero()` method.
- Followed by an odd or even number, printed by `odd()` or `even()`, respectively.
- This sequence repeats until all integers up to n have been printed.

For example:

- Input: `n = 2`
- Expected Output: `"0102"`

22.3.2 Code Analysis

The `ZeroEvenOdd` class uses Python's `Lock` objects to coordinate between the threads to ensure they print in the correct sequence.

22.3.2.1 Initialization (`__init__` Method)

```
def __init__(self, n):
    self.n = n
    self.zero_lock = Lock()
    self.even_lock = Lock()
    self.odd_lock = Lock()

    # Lock the odd and even locks initially
    self.odd_lock.acquire()
    self.even_lock.acquire()
```

- `self.n`: The number up to which the sequence will be printed.
- Three `Lock` objects:
    - `self.zero_lock`: Controls access for the `zero()` method.
    - `self.even_lock`: Controls access for the `even()` method.
    - `self.odd_lock`: Controls access for the `odd()` method.
- Initially, `self.odd_lock` and `self.even_lock` are locked, which means the `odd()` and `even()` methods cannot print until the `zero()` method releases them.

22.3.2.2 Zero Method (`zero`)

```
def zero(self, printNumber: 'Callable[[int], None]')
-> None:
    for i in range(1, self.n + 1):
        self.zero_lock.acquire()
        printNumber(0)
        if i % 2 == 1:
            self.odd_lock.release()
        else:
            self.even_lock.release()
```

- The `zero()` method is responsible for printing "0".
- For each iteration, it:
  - Acquires `self.zero_lock`, ensuring that only the `zero()` method can print at this time.
  - Prints "0" by calling `printNumber(0)`.
  - If i is odd, it releases `self.odd_lock`, allowing the `odd()` method to print the next number.
  - If i is even, it releases `self.even_lock`, allowing the `even()` method to print the next number.

22.3.2.3 Even Method (`even`)

```
def even(self, printNumber: 'Callable[[int], None]')
-> None:
    for i in range(2, self.n + 1, 2):
        self.even_lock.acquire()
        printNumber(i)
        self.zero_lock.release()
```

- The `even()` method only prints even numbers.
- For each even number i, it:
  - Waits for `self.even_lock` to be released by `zero()`.
  - Prints the even number by calling `printNumber(i)`.
  - Releases `self.zero_lock` to allow `zero()` to print the next "0".

22.3.2.4 Odd Method (`odd`)

```
def odd(self, printNumber: 'Callable[[int], None]')
-> None:
    for i in range(1, self.n + 1, 2):
        self.odd_lock.acquire()
        printNumber(i)
        self.zero_lock.release()
```

- The `odd()` method only prints odd numbers.
- For each odd number i, it:
  - Waits for `self.odd_lock` to be released by `zero()`.
  - Prints the odd number by calling `printNumber(i)`.
  - Releases `self.zero_lock` to allow `zero()` to print the next "0".

22.3.3 Test Function

To test the `ZeroEvenOdd` class, we can simulate three threads calling `zero()`, `even()`, and `odd()` to verify the output sequence.

```
import threading


# Function to simulate the printNumber function that
prints the number
def printNumber(x):
    print(x, end="")

# Test function for ZeroEvenOdd class
def test_zero_even_odd(n):
    zero_even_odd = ZeroEvenOdd(n)

    # Create threads for zero, even, and odd
    zero_thread = threading.Thread(target=zero_even_odd.
    zero, args=(printNumber,))
    even_thread = threading.Thread(target=zero_even_odd.
    even, args=(printNumber,))
    odd_thread = threading.Thread(target=zero_even_odd.
    odd, args=(printNumber,))

    # Start all threads
    zero_thread.start()
    even_thread.start()
    odd_thread.start()

    # Wait for all threads to finish
    zero_thread.join()
    even_thread.join()
    odd_thread.join()

    print("\nAll numbers printed in sequence.")


# Example usage
test_zero_even_odd(5)   # For n=5, expected output is
"0102030405"
```

22.3.4 Explanation of the Test

1. **Thread Creation**: We create three threads: `zero_thread`, `even_thread`, and `odd_thread`, each corresponding to a different method in `ZeroEvenOdd`.
2. **Starting Threads**: Each thread is started, which will call the respective method (`zero`, `even`, or `odd`), printing "0", even numbers, and odd numbers in the correct sequence.
3. **Joining Threads**: We wait for each thread to finish by using the `join()` method to ensure the output completes before the program exits.

22.3.5 Expected Output

For n = 5, the expected output sequence is:

```
0102030405
All numbers printed in sequence.
```

This pattern confirms that the program correctly alternates between "0" and the appropriate odd or even number, following the expected sequence structure.

Chapter 23
Machine Learning System Design

23.1 Machine Learning Theory

23.1.1 Introduction

This section focuses on some basic concepts, machine learning algorithms, and models in the field of machine learning (ML). Several types of machine learning algorithms are elucidated according to various criteria. These include:

- Identify different types of machine learning problems
- Understand what a machine learning model is
- Understand the general workflow for building and applying machine learning models
- Understand the pros and cons of machine learning algorithms

23.1.2 What Is Machine Learning?

Machine learning often appears to mystify the core concepts of computer science, giving the impression that machines can learn similarly to, or even better, than humans. However, while there is optimism that machines might one day think and learn like humans, today's machine learning systems go beyond merely executing predefined instructions.

The key difference between machine learning algorithms and traditional algorithms (like traffic light control systems) is that machine learning algorithms can adapt based on new data inputs. This adaptation gives the impression that machines are learning. However, beneath the surface, this adaptation follows rigorous rules—every machine learning model operates on detailed instructions coded by humans.

23.1.2.1 What Is a Machine Learning Model?

A **machine learning model** is the output of a machine learning algorithm, which works by uncovering hidden relationships within the data. In essence, this model can be thought of as a mathematical function (F) that takes inputs and provides corresponding outputs. However, unlike predefined fixed functions, machine learning models evolve based on the historical data they are trained on. Consequently, when new data is input, the output changes and the model itself adapts.

For example, in **image recognition**, a model can be trained to identify objects in photos. If the goal is to detect whether a cat is present in a picture, you would provide the algorithm with thousands of labeled images—some with cats, some without. The generated model will then take a digital photograph as input and output a binary value (1 for cat present, 0 for no cat).

23.1.2.2 How Machine Learning Models Map Data

In the case of the image recognition task, the machine learning model performs a mapping from the photo's pixel values (multidimensional data) to binary outcomes. If the image contains three pixels, each with RGB values ranging from 0 to 255, the mapping space between inputs and outputs would be enormous—approximately 33 million possibilities for this simple case.

For real-world images, the complexity multiplies. Images typically have millions of pixels, and each pixel is represented by three color channels (red, green, blue). Therefore, learning this mapping in a real-world scenario is incredibly challenging. The process of discovering the mappings between pixel values and binary outputs is what machine learning attempts to achieve. However, the model often learns an approximation of the true relationship rather than a perfect one.

23.1.2.3 Accuracy of Machine Learning Models

Given the complexity of real-world data, machine learning models rarely achieve perfect accuracy. The outputs they generate are approximations of the underlying data patterns, which is why machine learning models typically have some margin of error. Before the widespread use of deep learning in 2012, the best models could only achieve around 75% accuracy in the **ImageNet visual recognition challenge**. Today, although deep learning models have surpassed human-level performance in some areas with error rates below 5%, no model can claim 100% accuracy across the board.

23.1.3 *Supervised and Unsupervised Learning*

23.1.3.1 Machine Learning Problem Types

When presented with a machine learning problem, the first step is to determine whether it falls under **supervised learning** or **unsupervised learning**. Any machine learning task starts with a dataset composed of samples, where each sample can be represented as an attribute tuple (i.e., a collection of features or variables). Below are the distinctions between the different types of machine learning problems:

23.1.3.2 Supervised Learning

In supervised learning, the goal is to discover a **function** that can generalize well and provide the correct predictions on unseen data. In this type of task, the dataset contains both the input features **X** and the target attribute **y**.

The objective of machine learning here is to train a function **F**, where:

$$F(X) \approx y F(X) \approx y F(X) \approx y$$

The function **F** is trained to predict the target attribute **y** based on the input features **X**. The target attribute serves as a "teacher" or reference, guiding the model to learn correctly. This guidance makes the learning process supervised.

Examples of supervised learning:

- **Classification**: Predict whether an email is spam or not (binary target: spam or not spam).
- **Regression**: Predict the price of a house based on features like square footage and location (continuous target: house price).

23.1.3.3 Unsupervised Learning

In contrast to supervised learning, unsupervised learning deals with data that **does not have predefined target attributes**. Instead, the goal is to identify patterns, structures, or relationships within the data.

Here are some common tasks in unsupervised learning:

- **Clustering**: The goal is to group similar samples together based on shared characteristics. For example, customer profiles can be clustered based on attributes such as purchase history or browsing time. This allows businesses to target specific customer segments with customized marketing strategies.
- **Association**: This task aims to uncover hidden relationships between variables in the data. A common example is analyzing the contents of shopping carts. By

studying which items are frequently bought together (like beer and diapers), a supermarket can strategically place related products nearby to boost sales.

Examples

- **Clustering**: Grouping users on a social media platform based on similar interests or behaviors.
- **Association**: Discovering patterns of product purchases in a shopping basket, such as "people who buy bread are also likely to buy butter."

23.1.3.4 Semi-Supervised Learning

Semi-supervised learning is a hybrid approach, typically used when there is a large dataset available but only a small portion of it is labeled. It leverages both **supervised learning** (for the labeled portion of the data) and **unsupervised learning** (for the unlabeled portion).

A common situation in semi-supervised learning arises when labeling data is time-consuming or expensive. For example, in the **ImageNet project**, researchers at Stanford spent years curating millions of labeled images across thousands of categories. However, while a large portion of images are labeled, there are always some that lack accurate labels (e.g., videos without clear titles or categories).

To handle such datasets effectively, semi-supervised learning combines both techniques:

1. **Supervised Learning**: The model is first trained on the small set of labeled data.
2. **Unsupervised Learning**: Clustering is applied to the large unlabeled dataset. This helps reduce the scope of the model's learning task.
3. **Combination**: Once clustering groups similar samples, supervised learning is applied to individual clusters for further fine-tuning. This leads to a model that performs better than one trained only on labeled data.

Example

- Suppose you want to predict labels for an image dataset, but only 10% of the images are labeled. You can first apply supervised learning to the labeled data to generate a model, and then apply this model to the unlabeled data to predict their labels. Additionally, you might use unsupervised learning techniques like clustering to improve the predictions.

23.1.3.5 Summary

- **Supervised Learning**: The model is trained on labeled data where the input-output pairs are known. It learns to map inputs (X) to outputs (y).
- **Unsupervised Learning**: There are no labels or target attributes. The goal is to find patterns and relationships in the data (e.g., clustering, association).

23.1 Machine Learning Theory

- **Semi-Supervised Learning**: Combines both labeled and unlabeled data. It is often more effective when labeled data is scarce and expensive to obtain.

23.1.4 Classification vs. Regression

Machine learning models can generally be categorized as either **classification** or **regression** models based on the type of output they produce.

- **Classification models**: The output is a **discrete value**. For example, a classification model might output either "yes" or "no" (or any finite set of distinct classes) to indicate whether an image contains a cat or not.
- **Regression models**: The output is a **continuous value**, such as predicting the price of a house, which could be any real number.

23.1.4.1 Classification Model

A **classification model** outputs a discrete value, like whether a certain image contains a cat.

- **Input**: The input image can be represented as a matrix M of size $H \times W$, where H is the height and W is the width in pixels. Each matrix element contains a grayscale value (ranging from 0 to 255) representing the color intensity of each pixel.
- **Output**: The output is a **binary value**: 1 if the image contains a cat, 0 otherwise.

For example, the model receives pixel data from the image, processes it, and then classifies the image either as "contains cat" or "does not contain cat."

23.1.4.2 Regression Models

A **regression model** predicts continuous values, such as the price of a house. In the example of real estate price prediction, the input may include multiple features like the type of house, size, location, and other factors.

- **Input**: A set of features T, where each feature can either be a **numeric** value (like the size of the house) or a **categorical** value (like the type of house).
- **Output**: The model outputs a **continuous value** representing the predicted price, $p \in \mathbb{R}$. For example, $F(T) = p$, where p is the real estate price.

In some cases, these non-numeric (categorical) features might need to be converted into numeric features for the model to process them.

23.1.4.3 Problem Conversion

Some problems may not clearly belong to either classification or regression and they can sometimes be **converted** from one type to the other.

23.1.4.4 Converting Regression to Classification

In the real estate price prediction example, instead of predicting an exact price (a regression problem), the task can be reframed as predicting the **price range** (e.g., low, medium, or high). This would turn it into a classification problem.

23.1.4.5 Converting Classification to Regression

In the case of image recognition (e.g., determining whether a photo contains a cat), the problem can be transformed into a regression task. Instead of predicting binary output (cat or not), the model can output a **probability value** (e.g., 70% chance that the image contains a cat). This allows for a more nuanced evaluation of the model's confidence.

For instance, **logistic regression** is a common algorithm used for classification, but it outputs probabilities (continuous values between 0 and 1), making it a hybrid of regression and classification models.

23.1.4.6 Summary

The boundaries between classification and regression tasks aren't always rigid. You can sometimes improve a model's performance or better fit it to a problem by reframing the problem. For example:

- **Classification tasks** can be framed as **probabilistic regression tasks**.
- **Regression tasks** can be reframed as **classification tasks** by discretizing the output.

In both cases, the goal is to find the most appropriate way to model the underlying patterns in the data.

23.1.5 Underfitting and Overfitting

When building supervised machine learning models (like classification and regression models), two common issues that affect a model's performance are **underfitting** and **overfitting**. Both of these terms relate to how well the model generalizes to **unseen data**—an important aspect of machine learning called **generalization**. A model that generalizes well is one that can make accurate predictions not just on the training data, but also on new, unseen data.

23.1.5.1 Generalization

- **Generalization** refers to how well a model that is trained on a specific dataset can predict outcomes for data that the model has not seen before.
- **Overfitting** and **underfitting** represent two extremes where the model performs poorly on unseen data.

23.1.5.2 Underfitting

- **Definition**: Underfitting happens when a model is too simple to capture the underlying patterns in the data. It fails to perform well even on the training data, leading to poor performance on both training and unseen data.
- **Example**: A linear model (a single line) is too simple to separate different classes of data effectively. The model results in a high number of misclassifications.
- **Cause**:
    - The model is not complex enough to capture the hidden relationships between the features in the dataset.
    - The algorithm used might not be suitable for the given task (e.g., using a linear model for a non-linear problem).
- **How to Solve**:
    - Choose a more complex algorithm that can better capture the underlying patterns of the data.
    - Increase the complexity of the model by adding more parameters or features.

23.1.5.3 Overfitting

- **Definition**: Overfitting occurs when a model is too complex and fits the training data too closely, capturing not only the underlying patterns but also the noise and errors in the data. As a result, while the model performs well on the training set, it performs poorly on new, unseen data.
- **Example**: The model is so finely tuned to the training data that it fits even the noise, leading to poor performance on new data.
- **Cause**:
    - The model is overly complex with too many parameters.
    - It tries to memorize the training data instead of learning the general trends.

- **How to Solve**:
  - **Simplify the model**: Use fewer parameters or reduce the complexity of the model.
  - **Regularization**: Add a regularization term to the algorithm. This technique penalizes the model for becoming overly complex and encourages it to find a balance between fitting the training data and generalizing well to new data.
  - **Cross-validation**: Use techniques like cross-validation to test the model's performance on different subsets of the data during training and avoid overfitting.

23.1.5.4 Summary

- **Underfitting** is caused by models that are too simple to capture patterns in the data. The solution is to increase the model complexity.
- **Overfitting** happens when models are too complex and fit noise in the data, leading to poor generalization. The solution is to simplify the model or use regularization techniques.

The key challenge in machine learning is finding the **right balance** between model complexity and generalization ability to avoid both underfitting and overfitting.

23.1.6 Bias and Variance

Figure 23.1 illustrates the concepts of **bias** and **variance** in machine learning using a dartboard analogy. Here's a breakdown:

- **The Goal**: The center of the dartboard represents the "true" prediction or value a model is trying to achieve. Each dart represents a prediction made by the model.
- **Bias**: Bias refers to the error introduced by approximating a real-world problem, which may be extremely complex, by a much simpler model.
  - **High Bias**: The darts are clustered together but far from the bullseye (targets 1 and 4). This indicates the model is consistently wrong, likely due to oversimplification.
  - **Low Bias**: The darts are closer to the bullseye (targets 2 and 3), suggesting the model is making more accurate predictions on average.
- **Variance**: Variance measures how much the model's predictions change in response to different training data.
  - **Low Variance**: The darts are tightly clustered together (targets 1 and 3), indicating the model's predictions are consistent across different datasets.
  - **High Variance**: The darts are spread out (targets 2 and 4), suggesting the model is highly sensitive to the training data and may not generalize well to new, unseen data.

23.1 Machine Learning Theory

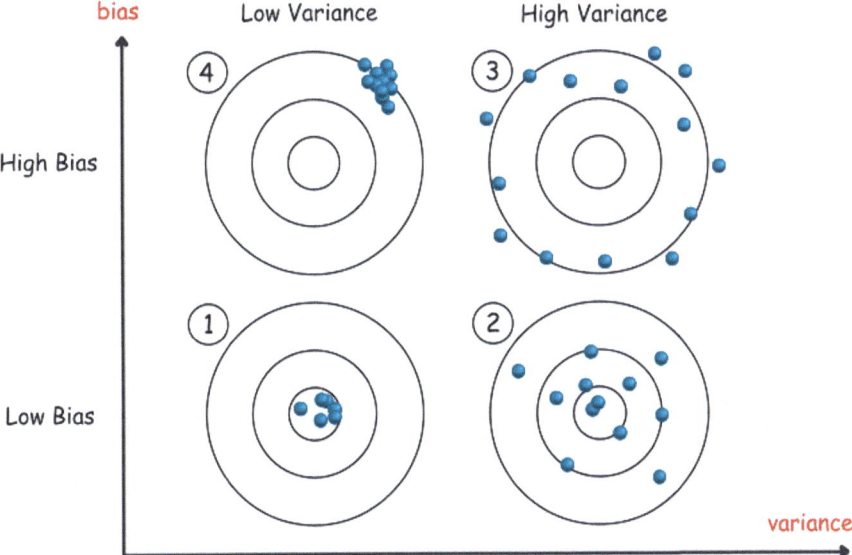

Fig. 23.1 Deviation variance model

The Four Scenarios

1. **High Bias, Low Variance**: The model is consistently wrong but doesn't change much with new data. (Target 1)
2. **Low Bias, High Variance**: The model is accurate on average but its predictions are highly sensitive to the training data. (Target 2)
3. **High Bias, High Variance**: The model is inaccurate and its predictions vary greatly with different data. (Target 3)
4. **Low Bias, Low Variance**: The ideal scenario—the model is accurate and its predictions are consistent. (Target 4)

This visualization helps to understand the trade-off between bias and variance in machine learning. The goal is to find a balance that minimizes both, leading to a model that generalizes well to new data.

Figure 23.2 illustrates the relationship between **model complexity** and **error** in machine learning, highlighting the concepts of **underfitting** and **overfitting**.

- **X-axis**: Represents model complexity, increasing from left to right. This could involve adding more features, using a more complex algorithm, or increasing the depth of a decision tree.
- **Y-axis**: Represents the error of the model. This could be training error or test error.

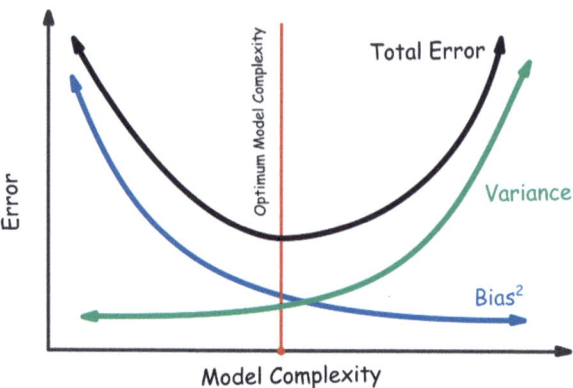

Fig. 23.2 Balance of deviations and variances

The Curves

- **Black Curve (Total Error)**: Shows the overall error of the model. It has a U-shape, indicating that both very simple and very complex models tend to have higher errors.
- **Blue Curve (Bias)**: Represents the error due to bias. It's high for simple models (underfitting) and decreases as complexity increases.
- **Green Curve (Variance)**: Represents the error due to variance. It's low for simple models and increases as complexity increases (overfitting).

Key Concepts

- **Underfitting (High Bias)**: Occurs when the model is too simple to capture the underlying patterns in the data. This results in high bias and poor performance on both training and test data (left side of the graph).
- **Overfitting (High Variance)**: Occurs when the model is too complex and learns the training data too well, including noise and outliers. This leads to high variance and poor generalization to new, unseen data (right side of the graph).
- **Optimal Model**: The point where the total error is minimized (red vertical line). This represents the sweet spot where the model has learned the underlying patterns in the data without overfitting.

In Summary: This graph demonstrates the importance of finding the correct balance between model complexity and error. Increasing complexity can reduce bias but may lead to overfitting. The goal is to find the optimal complexity that minimizes both bias and variance, resulting in a model that generalizes well.

TIP: Bias is the tendency of a learner to repeatedly learn the same incorrect patterns. Variance is the tendency to learn random things that have nothing to do with a real signal. Now, if you've reached this point, then you should be able to understand the statement.

23.2 Machine Learning Theory and Practical Interview Questions

23.2.1 Machine Learning Basic Theory Questions

1. **Explain the difference between supervised, unsupervised, and reinforcement learning.**

   (a) **Solution**:
   - **Supervised Learning**: Models are trained using labeled data where the correct output is known. Examples: classification, regression.
   - **Unsupervised Learning**: Models are trained on data without labeled responses. The goal is to find structure or patterns. Example: clustering, dimensionality reduction.
   - **Reinforcement Learning**: Models learn by receiving feedback from actions taken in an environment, with the goal of maximizing cumulative rewards. Example: game playing, robotics.

2. **What is overfitting in machine learning? How can you prevent it?**

   (a) **Solution**:
   - Overfitting occurs when a model learns not just the underlying pattern but also the noise in the training data, leading to poor generalization on unseen data.
   - **Prevention techniques**:
     - Cross-validation
     - Regularization (L1, L2)
     - Pruning (in decision trees)
     - Early stopping (in deep learning)
     - Dropout (in neural networks)

3. **Describe the bias-variance trade-off in the context of model selection.**

   (a) **Solution**:
   - **Bias**: Error due to overly simplistic models, underfitting data (e.g., linear models for non-linear data).
   - **Variance**: Error due to overly complex models, overfitting data (e.g., a deep decision tree).
   - The goal is to minimize both bias and variance by finding a balance between the two.

4. **What is the purpose of the loss function in machine learning models?**

    (a) **Solution**:

    - The loss function quantifies how well a model's predictions match the actual values. It measures the "cost" or "error" and is used by optimization algorithms to refine the model.
    - **Examples**:
        - Mean Squared Error (MSE) for regression
        - Cross-entropy for classification

5. **Can you explain what a confusion matrix is and what it represents?**

    (a) **Solution**:

    - A confusion matrix is a table used for evaluating the performance of a classification algorithm. It contains:
        - **True Positives (TP)**: Correctly predicted positive cases
        - **True Negatives (TN)**: Correctly predicted negative cases
        - **False Positives (FP)**: Incorrectly predicted as positive
        - **False Negatives (FN)**: Incorrectly predicted as negative
    - **Metrics derived from it**:
        - **Precision** = TP/(TP + FP)
        - **Recall** = TP/(TP + FN)
        - **F1-Score** = 2 * (Precision * Recall)/(Precision + Recall)

6. **What is gradient descent?**

    (a) **Solution**:

    - Gradient descent is an optimization algorithm used to minimize the loss function by iteratively updating model parameters in the opposite direction of the gradient.
    - **Stochastic Gradient Descent (SGD)**: Updates parameters for each training example.
    - **Batch Gradient Descent**: Updates parameters for the entire dataset.

7. **What are some common challenges when working with imbalanced datasets?**

    (a) **Solution**:

    - **Challenges**:
        - The model may become biased towards the majority class.
    - **Solutions**:
        - **Resampling**: Oversampling the minority class or undersampling the majority class.

23.2 Machine Learning Theory and Practical Interview Questions

- **Use of class weights**: Assign higher weights to the minority class.
- **Use advanced techniques** like SMOTE or cost-sensitive learning.

8. **Explain the concept of feature engineering. Why is it important?**

   (a) **Solution**:
   - Feature engineering is the process of creating new input features or transforming existing features to improve the performance of machine learning models.
   - **Importance**: Good features lead to better model performance by providing the model with more relevant information.

9. **What is cross-validation, and why is it used?**

   (a) **Solution**:
   - Cross-validation is a technique to evaluate the performance of a model by splitting the data into multiple subsets (folds) and iterating the training/testing process.
   - **K-fold cross-validation**: Divides the dataset into k subsets, trains on $k - 1$, and tests on the remaining one, repeating this process k times. It reduces overfitting and provides a better estimate of model performance.

10. **Explain what PCA (Principal Component Analysis) is and how it works.**

    (a) **Solution**:
    - PCA is a dimensionality reduction technique that transforms a dataset into a set of uncorrelated variables (principal components) that capture the most variance.
    - It works by finding the eigenvectors of the covariance matrix and projecting the data along these vectors.

23.2.2 Machine Learning Practical Interview Questions

1. **Given a dataset with one million samples, how would you approach building a predictive model?**

   (a) **Solution**:
   - **Data Cleaning**: Handle missing values, outliers, and perform normalization or standardization.
   - **Feature Engineering**: Generate meaningful features and possibly reduce dimensionality.

- **Model Selection**: Choose appropriate algorithms (e.g., linear models for regression, decision trees, or neural networks).
- **Model Tuning**: Use techniques like grid search for hyperparameter tuning.
- **Evaluation**: Use metrics like accuracy, precision, recall, or F1-score for classification; RMSE for regression.

2. **Your model performs poorly on the test set compared to the training set. What might be happening, and how would you address it?**

    (a) **Solution**:
    - The model may be overfitting the training data.
    - **Solutions**:
        - Regularization (L2/L1)
        - Cross-validation
        - Pruning decision trees or reducing neural network complexity

3. **Describe a project where you had to clean the data extensively. What techniques did you use?**

    (a) **Solution**:
    - **Techniques used**:
        - Imputation for missing values
        - Removal of outliers
        - Transformation (log, scaling) of skewed distributions
        - Encoding of categorical variables (one-hot encoding, label encoding)
        - Dealing with inconsistent or duplicate entries

4. **How would you approach hyperparameter tuning for a machine learning model?**

    (a) **Solution**:
    - Use grid search or random search over a range of hyperparameters to find the best set.
    - Alternatively, use Bayesian optimization for more efficient hyperparameter search.

5. **How would you handle class imbalance in a dataset?**

    (a) **Solution**:
    - Resample the data by oversampling the minority class or undersampling the majority class.
    - Adjust class weights in your algorithm to penalize misclassification of the minority class.
    - Use specialized algorithms like SMOTE (Synthetic Minority Oversampling TEchnique).

23.2 Machine Learning Theory and Practical Interview Questions

6. **What would you do if your dataset doesn't fit into memory?**

   (a) **Solution**:
   - Use batch processing or minibatch gradient descent.
   - Employ distributed computing frameworks like Hadoop, Spark, or Dask.
   - Use a database or data streaming service to load data in smaller chunks.

7. **What techniques would you use to reduce the dimensionality of a dataset with many features?**

   (a) **Solution**:
   - **Feature Selection**: Using techniques like Lasso (L1 regularization) or mutual information.
   - **Feature Extraction**: Using PCA or t-SNE (for visualization).
   - **Removing Highly Correlated Features**: This reduces redundancy.

8. **How would you evaluate the performance of a regression model?**

   (a) **Solution**:
   - Common metrics include:
     - **Mean Squared Error (MSE)**
     - **Root Mean Squared Error (RMSE)**
     - **Mean Absolute Error (MAE)**
     - **R-squared score**: Measures the proportion of variance explained by the model.

9. **What is transfer learning, and how would you apply it?**

   (a) **Solution**:
   - Transfer learning involves reusing a pre-trained model (typically a neural network) on a new problem with a smaller dataset.
   - **Application**: You can use pre-trained models like ResNet for image classification and fine-tune the final layers for your specific task.

10. **Have you ever worked with ensemble methods? Can you explain how they work?**

    (a) **Solution**:
    - **Bagging** (Bootstrap Aggregating): Creates multiple models by training on random samples of the data and averaging their predictions (e.g., Random Forests).
    - **Boosting**: Sequentially builds models, with each new model focusing on correcting errors made by previous ones (e.g., XGBoost, AdaBoost).

23.2.3 Deep Learning and Advanced Concepts

1. **What is a neural network, and how does backpropagation work in training it?**

   (a) **Solution**:
   - A neural network is a series of interconnected layers (neurons) where each neuron applies an activation function to the weighted sum of its inputs.
   - **Backpropagation**: It's an algorithm for updating the weights by calculating the gradient of the loss function with respect to each weight using the chain rule.

2. **Explain the difference between CNNs and RNNs.**

   (a) **Solution**:
   - **CNNs** (Convolutional Neural Networks): Primarily used for image-related tasks by applying convolutional filters to detect spatial hierarchies in data.
   - **RNNs** (Recurrent Neural Networks): Used for sequence data (text, speech), where the output depends on the previous inputs.

3. **How would you choose an activation function in a neural network?**

   (a) **Solution**:
   - **ReLU (Rectified Linear Unit)**: Popular for hidden layers due to its efficiency and the ability to reduce the vanishing gradient problem.
   - **Sigmoid or Tanh**: Useful for binary classification tasks, but may suffer from vanishing gradient issues.
   - **Softmax**: Used for the output layer in multi-class classification tasks.

4. **Explain how dropout works in a neural network and why it is used.**

   (a) **Solution**:
   - Dropout randomly "drops" a subset of neurons during training to prevent co-adaptation of features and reduce overfitting.

5. **What are GANs (Generative Adversarial Networks), and how do they work?**

   (a) **Solution**:
   - GANs consist of two neural networks: a generator and a discriminator.
   - The **generator** creates synthetic data, and the **discriminator** tries to distinguish between real and synthetic data.
   - The two networks are trained together in a zero-sum game, where the generator tries to fool the discriminator, and the discriminator tries not to be fooled.

These answers provide a comprehensive understanding of machine learning theory and practical applications, tailored to test a candidate's deep knowledge of machine learning fundamentals, model-building techniques, and advanced concepts like deep learning.

23.3 Machine Learning Scalability

23.3.1 Machine Learning Scalability

Scalability is one of the critical aspects to consider when deploying machine learning (ML) models in industrial applications. As industries generate vast amounts of data and demand real-time or near-real-time insights, machine learning systems must be capable of scaling effectively to handle increasing volumes of data, more complex models, and faster response times. Here are the key factors related to machine learning scalability in industrial contexts:

23.3.1.1 Data Scalability

As industries grow, the amount of data they generate increases exponentially. Machine learning models must be able to process larger datasets efficiently.

- **Challenges**:
  - **Data volume**: High volumes of data can overwhelm traditional ML systems, both in terms of storage and computational capacity.
  - **Data velocity**: In real-time industrial environments (e.g., IoT sensors, streaming data from manufacturing systems), the speed at which data arrives requires models that can process data in real-time or near-real-time.
  - **Data variety**: Data comes in various forms such as structured (e.g., sensor readings), unstructured (e.g., maintenance logs), and semi-structured (e.g., JSON-based telemetry data).
- **Scalability Solutions**:
  - **Distributed Data Processing**: Technologies like Apache Spark, Hadoop, or Dask are used for distributed computing, allowing models to handle large datasets by splitting computations across multiple machines.
  - **Cloud-Based Storage and Processing**: Cloud platforms (AWS, Google Cloud, Azure) offer scalable storage solutions and processing capabilities like serverless computing and GPU/TPU resources, allowing industries to scale as needed.
  - **Incremental Learning**: In some cases, models can be trained incrementally as new data arrives, avoiding the need to retrain from scratch.

23.3.1.2 Model Scalability

As the problem complexity grows (e.g., adding more features, dealing with higher-dimensional data), machine learning models need to scale in terms of both capacity and performance.

- **Challenges**:
    - **Complexity of models**: More complex models, such as deep neural networks (DNNs), require significant computational resources.
    - **Training time**: Training large models on huge datasets can take a long time, which can hinder rapid deployment.
    - **Generalization across different scales**: In industries like manufacturing or finance, models must generalize to both small-scale systems and large-scale operations without losing predictive accuracy.
- **Scalability Solutions**:
    - **Parallelism**: Training algorithms can leverage parallel computing on multi-core CPUs or GPUs, and even across multiple machines in distributed clusters. This reduces training time significantly.
    - **Model Compression**: Techniques such as pruning, quantization, and knowledge distillation can reduce the size of the model without sacrificing accuracy, making it more scalable and faster to deploy on resource-constrained devices.
    - **Transfer Learning**: Instead of training large models from scratch, pre-trained models can be fine-tuned for specific industrial tasks, saving time and resources.

23.3.1.3 Infrastructure Scalability

Scaling machine learning in industrial applications often requires robust and scalable infrastructure to support both data processing and model deployment.

- **Challenges**:
    - **Infrastructure constraints**: Real-time industrial applications (e.g., smart factories, autonomous vehicles) often require low-latency and high-reliability infrastructures.
    - **Edge computing**: In industries like manufacturing, where machines and sensors are deployed in the field, real-time insights need to be generated on-site (edge computing) rather than sending all data to centralized cloud servers.
- **Scalability Solutions**:
    - **Cloud Computing**: Cloud providers offer scalable resources with pay-as-you-go models. Auto-scaling features can automatically adjust computing resources based on workload requirements.
    - **Edge Computing**: Deploying lightweight ML models on edge devices enables faster data processing with minimal latency. This is particularly

important in applications like predictive maintenance or anomaly detection on manufacturing floors.
  - **Hybrid Architectures**: Some systems may use a combination of cloud and edge computing where models are trained on cloud infrastructure and deployed for inference on edge devices.

23.3.1.4 Algorithmic Scalability

Certain algorithms and techniques may not scale well with increased data size or complexity. For industrial applications, choosing scalable machine learning algorithms is essential.

- **Challenges**:
  - **Non-linear scalability**: Some traditional algorithms (e.g., k-NN, decision trees) may struggle with large datasets because their computational complexity grows exponentially with data size.
  - **Real-time constraints**: Algorithms need to provide predictions fast enough for real-time decision-making in industrial systems.
- **Scalability Solutions**:
  - **Online Learning Algorithms**: Instead of batch training, online learning techniques allow the model to update continuously as new data arrives. This approach is essential in streaming data environments.
  - **Approximate Algorithms**: In cases where exact solutions are computationally expensive, approximate algorithms (e.g., approximate nearest neighbors) can provide scalable solutions that still yield accurate results.
  - **Sampling and Dimensionality Reduction**: Techniques like random sampling, Principal Component Analysis (PCA), or t-SNE can be used to reduce the amount of data or the number of features, making it easier for models to scale.

23.3.1.5 Scalable Model Deployment

Once models are trained, deploying them in a scalable manner across industrial applications can be challenging, especially in a production environment where models need to operate 24/7.

- **Challenges**:
  - **Model lifecycle management**: Managing multiple models, from version control to updates, can become complex as the number of applications increases.
  - **Performance and latency requirements**: Industrial applications may require real-time predictions with high reliability.

- **Scalability Solutions**:
  - **Containerization and Orchestration**: Tools like Docker and Kubernetes can be used to package models into containers, making them easy to scale and deploy across different environments.
  - **API-based Model Serving**: Models can be exposed via APIs, allowing them to be scaled across multiple services and accessed in real-time by different applications.
  - **MLOps Frameworks**: MLOps (Machine Learning Operations) tools such as MLflow, Kubeflow, and TFX help automate the deployment, scaling, and monitoring of machine learning models in production environments.

23.3.1.6 Cost Scalability

As industries adopt machine learning at scale, the cost of training and deploying models can become a bottleneck.

- **Challenges**:
  - **Rising cloud costs**: Training large models on the cloud can become expensive, especially as the need for computational resources increases.
  - **Hardware investment**: Specialized hardware (e.g., GPUs, TPUs) for on-premise training and inference may require a significant upfront investment.
- **Scalability Solutions**:
  - **Auto-Scaling**: Cloud providers offer auto-scaling solutions that dynamically adjust the resources based on current demand, reducing unnecessary costs.
  - **Spot Instances**: Cloud services offer spot instances (spare compute capacity at discounted prices) that can be used for non-critical training tasks to save costs.
  - **Optimization for Cost-Efficiency**: Algorithms and models can be optimized to minimize cost while maintaining performance. For example, by choosing less expensive cloud compute instances or reducing the complexity of models to save on GPU hours.

23.3.1.7 Scalable Monitoring and Maintenance

In industrial settings, machine learning models are subject to continuous monitoring and maintenance to ensure optimal performance over time.

- **Challenges**:
  - **Concept drift**: The data distribution in industrial environments may change over time, leading to a phenomenon called concept drift, where the model's performance degrades.

23.3 Machine Learning Scalability

- **Scaling model monitoring**: Monitoring a large number of deployed models for accuracy, performance, and resource utilization can become difficult.
- **Scalability Solutions**:
  - **Automated Model Retraining**: Implement pipelines that automatically retrain the model when performance drops below a certain threshold.
  - **Centralized Monitoring Systems**: Tools like Prometheus and Grafana can provide real-time metrics and monitoring dashboards to observe multiple machine learning models in production.

To achieve scalable machine learning solutions in industrial applications, both the data infrastructure and machine learning systems need to be designed with scalability in mind. The right combination of distributed data processing, scalable algorithms, cloud infrastructure, and regularization techniques can help organizations build robust and scalable machine learning systems that can handle the complex demands of modern industries.

The following are common questions and answers for machine learning scalability.

23.3.2 General ML Scalability Concepts

- **How would you scale a machine learning system for real-time predictions in a production environment with millions of users?**
  - For real-time predictions at scale, you'd want to use a **distributed architecture**. You could employ a **microservices architecture** where each microservice handles a specific ML model or task. **Horizontal scaling** of model inference servers (e.g., using Kubernetes for container orchestration) ensures that more instances can handle higher loads. To reduce latency, deploy models **closer to users** using **edge computing** or **CDNs**. Leverage **load balancing** to distribute requests across multiple servers.
- **What are the key factors to consider when designing a scalable machine learning pipeline?**
  - Some of the key factors include:

    Data volume and velocity: Can the pipeline process large datasets efficiently?
    Model complexity: Can the model be trained and served at scale?
    Compute resources: Ensure efficient use of resources like CPUs and GPUs.
    Fault tolerance and recovery: Can the system handle failures without disrupting the pipeline?

Automation: Consider **CI/CD** pipelines for continuous integration and model deployment.
Monitoring: Ensure proper logging, metrics collection, and model drift detection.

- How does batch processing differ from stream processing in terms of scalability for machine learning workflows?
    - **Batch processing** works well for large, accumulated datasets and is ideal for offline model training. It's typically more resource-efficient for non-real-time applications but can face **latency issues** in use cases needing real-time predictions.
    - **Stream processing** is designed for real-time data ingestion and prediction, which allows models to make predictions on-the-fly (e.g., fraud detection). It's more challenging to scale due to **data velocity** and often requires distributed frameworks like **Apache Kafka**, **Flink**, or **Spark Streaming**.

23.3.3 Data Scalability

- How would you handle and process large datasets (terabytes or petabytes) for model training?
    - For massive datasets, use distributed frameworks like **Apache Hadoop**, **Spark**, or **Dask**. Store data in **distributed storage** systems like **HDFS**, **Amazon S3**, or **Google Cloud Storage**. For preprocessing and feature engineering, use **distributed data processing** to parallelize tasks across clusters. Consider **sharding** or **chunking** large datasets into smaller parts to enable distributed model training.
- How would you address the challenge of handling high-velocity streaming data for real-time machine learning predictions?
    - Implement a **stream processing architecture** using tools like **Kafka**, **Flink**, or **Spark Streaming** to handle data as it arrives. Use **message queues** or **pub/sub systems** to ensure reliable data delivery. For real-time inference, deploy models using **low-latency serving architectures**, and use **model caching** to reduce prediction latency. Scale horizontally using containers (Kubernetes) or serverless platforms (AWS Lambda).
- How would you ensure that data preprocessing and transformations scale effectively as data size increases?
    - Use **distributed data pipelines** like **Apache Beam** or **Spark** for scalable data preprocessing. For feature engineering, consider **map-reduce paradigms** to parallelize the workload. When dealing with very large datasets, implement **data partitioning** or **sampling** strategies to process data efficiently.

23.3.4 Model Training Scalability

- **How would you design a scalable distributed training system for deep learning models across multiple GPUs or machines?**
  - Use distributed training frameworks such as **Horovod**, **TensorFlow Distributed**, or **PyTorch Distributed** to enable **data parallelism** or **model parallelism** across multiple machines or GPUs. For large-scale training, use **parameter servers** or **Ring-AllReduce** algorithms to synchronize gradients between machines. Opt for **GPUs/TPUs** in the cloud to optimize training speed, and use cloud infrastructure like **AWS Sagemaker**, **Google AI Platform**, or **Azure Machine Learning** for dynamic scaling.
- **How would you approach model training for a large-scale dataset that cannot fit into memory?**
  - Use **minibatch training** where only a subset of the data is loaded into memory at a time. For very large datasets, use **distributed data pipelines** (e.g., Apache Spark) to preprocess the data. Implement **out-of-core learning** algorithms like those found in **scikit-learn** or use frameworks like **Dask** that support chunked data processing.
- **Explain the challenges of hyperparameter tuning at scale and how you would address them.**
  - Hyperparameter tuning at scale is resource-intensive, especially for deep learning models. Use distributed hyperparameter tuning frameworks like **Ray Tune** or **Google Vizier** to parallelize trials across multiple machines. Techniques like **random search**, **Bayesian optimization**, or **genetic algorithms** can help explore the hyperparameter space efficiently. **Automated machine learning (AutoML)** platforms can further streamline the tuning process by using these methods efficiently.

23.3.5 Model Deployment and Serving at Scale

- **How would you design a system to deploy and serve machine learning models for real-time predictions with low latency and high throughput?**
  - Use a **microservices architecture** to serve models with **containerized deployments** using **Kubernetes** or **Docker Swarm**. Employ **gRPC** or **REST** APIs to communicate between services. Utilize **horizontal scaling** and **load balancers** to handle high traffic, and **caching mechanisms** like **Redis** to reduce latency for frequently requested predictions. For low-latency serving, consider **model quantization** or **distillation** to make the model lightweight.

- How would you ensure scalability when deploying multiple versions of machine learning models in a production environment?
  - Implement **model versioning** using tools like **MLflow** or **Kubeflow**. Use a **canary deployment** strategy to test new models on a small percentage of traffic before fully rolling them out. In complex systems, deploy models behind a **model registry** and a **model orchestration** layer that can manage model selection dynamically (e.g., **Seldon** or **Triton Inference Server**). **A/B testing** and **multi-armed bandit approaches** can help in selecting the best model versions.

23.3.6 Infrastructure and Resource Management

- How would you design a scalable cloud-based infrastructure to support machine learning workflows for training, testing, and deploying models?
  - Use a **cloud-native architecture** with services like **AWS Sagemaker**, **Google AI Platform**, or **Azure ML** for end-to-end workflows. Use **auto-scaling** clusters like **Kubernetes** to dynamically allocate compute resources. For distributed data processing, utilize **Spark on EMR** (AWS) or **Dataproc** (GCP). For model training, use **cloud-based GPUs** and **TPUs** that can scale on demand. Ensure **CI/CD pipelines** are in place for automated deployment and testing.
- How would you manage distributed resources efficiently (e.g., across multiple VMs, GPUs) when training a large machine learning model?
  - Efficient resource management in distributed training involves using **schedulers** (e.g., **SLURM**, **Ray**), which allocate resources dynamically. Use **auto-scaling** to provision more compute resources when needed and to shut down idle instances to save costs. **Gradient checkpointing** can be used to minimize memory usage by offloading computations. For large models, use **model parallelism** to distribute parts of the model across GPUs/VMs.

23.3.7 Model Monitoring and Maintenance at Scale

- How would you design a monitoring system to ensure that machine learning models deployed at scale are performing as expected?
  - Use **monitoring tools** like **Prometheus** or **Datadog** for collecting metrics on model performance (e.g., latency, throughput, error rates). Implement **model performance logging** to monitor metrics like accuracy, precision, and recall. Use **drift detection algorithms** to monitor changes in data distribution and alert for model retraining. **Model explainability tools** (e.g., **SHAP**, **LIME**) can help detect issues in decision-making.

23.4 Machine Learning System Design

- **How would you set up a system to handle automatic model retraining when performance starts to degrade?**
  - Set up **triggers** for model retraining based on performance metrics and drift detection. Use **automated pipelines** with tools like **Kubeflow Pipelines** or **MLflow** to automatically retrain models when necessary. Set up a feedback loop where new data is continuously fed back into the system and triggers retraining jobs when significant drifts or performance degradations are detected.

23.4 Machine Learning System Design

23.4.1 Machine Learning System Design

Machine learning (ML) is the study of computer algorithms that are automatically improved based on experience. ML is designed to solve numerous complex problems and has made great strides in speech understanding, search ranking, credit card fraud detection, and more.

Figure 23.3 shows a central concept labeled machine learning with eight related application surrounding it. Each concept is illustrated with a small picture and label. These concepts, translated to English, are:

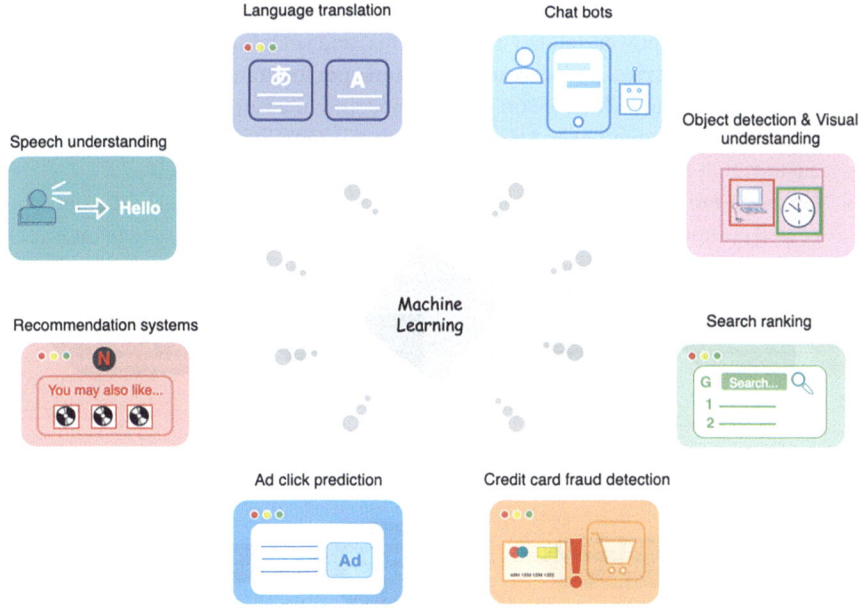

Fig. 23.3 Application areas for machine learning

- Translation, showing the translation between Japanese "あ" and English "A".
- Chat depicted by a chat window on a mobile phone.
- Language understanding, with an arrow pointing from speech to the word "Hello."
- Object detection and visual understanding, showing a computer detecting a clock in an image.
- Recommendation system, illustrated with "You may also like…" and a list of music records.
- Search ranking (Search ranking), with a search engine results page.
- Advertising click prediction, showing an ad with the label "Ad".
- Credit card fraud detection, with a credit card and a warning sign.

Companies in a variety of industries, from healthcare and agriculture to manufacturing and retail, are leveraging these technologies to succeed. As a machine learning engineer, this is exciting and lucrative.

Figure 23.4 illustrates a sequential process, likely related to building and deploying a machine learning model. Each block represents a stage in the process, with the connecting lines and arrow indicating the flow. Here's a breakdown of the steps:

1. **Deepen the understanding of the problem**: This initial stage, marked by a head with a coin, emphasizes the importance of thoroughly understanding the business problem or objective before applying machine learning. It suggests that a clear definition of the problem and desired outcome is crucial.
2. **Understand system requirements**: This step, shown with a computer and server rack, highlights the need to consider the technical constraints and requirements of the system where the model will be deployed. This includes factors like processing power, latency requirements, and scalability.
3. **Determine metrics for measuring system performance**: Represented by a checklist, this stage focuses on defining specific, measurable, achievable, relevant, and time-bound (SMART) metrics to evaluate the model's success. This ensures that the model's performance aligns with the initial goals.
4. **Envision end-to-end system architecture**: This step, visualized with interconnected computer components, involves designing the complete system architec-

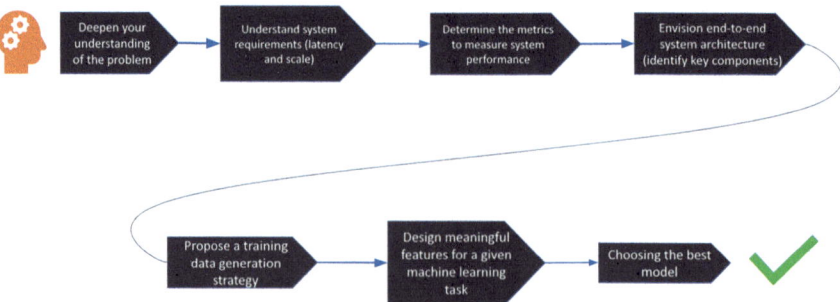

Fig. 23.4 The process of interviewing machine learning

23.4 Machine Learning System Design

ture, including data acquisition, preprocessing, model training, deployment, and monitoring. It emphasizes a holistic view of the system.

5. **Envision end-to-end system architecture**: This seems to be a duplicate of the previous step, possibly an error in the diagram.
6. **Propose a training data generation strategy**: Illustrated with a data flow diagram, this stage emphasizes the importance of a robust strategy for acquiring, cleaning, and preparing the data used to train the machine learning model.
7. **Design meaningful features for a given machine learning task**: This step, shown with a magnifying glass over data, highlights the critical role of feature engineering in selecting, transforming, and creating relevant features that improve the model's accuracy and efficiency.
8. **Choose the best model**: Represented by a flowchart with different model options, this stage involves selecting the most suitable machine learning model based on the problem, data characteristics, and performance requirements.
9. **Choose the best model**: Again, this appears to be a duplicate step, likely an error in the diagram.
10. **Train a competent model**: This step, shown with a progress bar, focuses on the actual training process, where the selected model learns from the prepared data and optimizes its parameters to achieve the desired performance.
11. **Design meaningful features for a given machine learning task**: This is another repetition of a previous step, indicating a potential error in the diagram.
12. **Deploy the model**: This final stage, marked with a green checkmark, represents the deployment of the trained model into a production environment where it can be used to make predictions or decisions on new data.

Overall, the picture depicts a comprehensive workflow for developing and deploying machine learning models, emphasizing the importance of careful planning, data preparation, model selection, and evaluation throughout the process. The repetitions in the diagram suggest potential errors that need to be addressed for clarity.

23.4.2 Machine Learning Workflows

Figure 23.5 shows the work flows for machine learning:

1. Data-Centric Approach
   (a) Data is the fuel for machine learning models. The entire process revolves around the dataset, which defines how the machine learning model will be constructed.
   (b) Without accurate and relevant data, it is impossible to build effective models. Therefore, data preparation is critical.

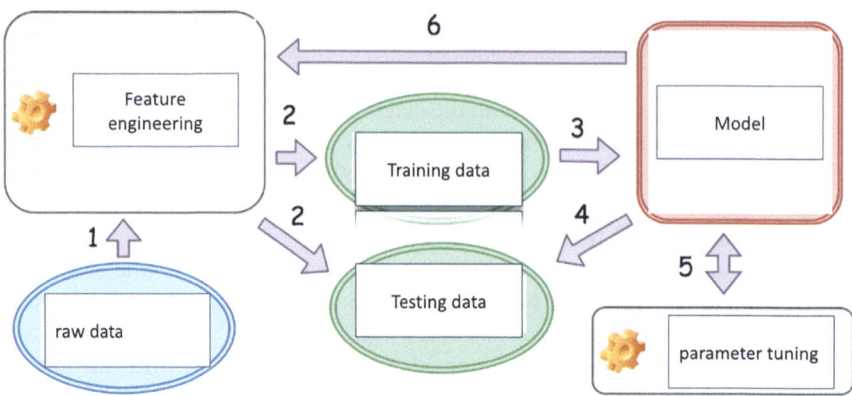

Fig. 23.5 Workflows for machine learning

2. Identify the Problem Type

    (a) **Supervised Learning**: If the dataset includes a **target attribute** (i.e., the desired output), it is a **labeled dataset**. In supervised learning, the goal is to predict the target attribute. For example, if the task is to determine whether a photo contains a cat, the target attribute might be [Yes | No].
    (b) **Unsupervised Learning**: If no target attribute exists, the task falls under unsupervised learning, where the model must discover patterns without pre-defined labels.

3. Model Type: Classification or Regression

    (a) **Classification**: The output is **discrete** (e.g., predicting whether an image contains a cat).
    (b) **Regression**: The output is **continuous** (e.g., predicting the price of real estate).

4. Feature Engineering

    (a) Once the model type is determined, feature engineering is performed to transform raw data into a format suitable for the machine learning algorithm.
    (b) **Handling missing data**: Real-world datasets often have missing values. These can be addressed through various techniques, such as filling missing entries with the average of other data points.
    (c) **Encoding categorical variables**: Some algorithms require numeric inputs, so categorical data (e.g., country, gender) must be converted into numbers using methods like one-hot encoding.

5. Split the Dataset

    (a) The dataset is split into two parts:
    - **Training Set**: This part of the dataset is used to train the model.
    - **Test Set**: This part of the dataset is reserved for testing the model's generalization on unseen data.

23.4 Machine Learning System Design

6. Training Process
   (a) During training, the algorithm is fed the training dataset, and the model learns patterns in the data.
   (b) Once trained, the model is then evaluated using the test set in the **testing process** to check how well it performs on new data.
7. Hyperparameter Tuning
   (a) It's rare to be satisfied with the first trained model. The next step involves adjusting **hyperparameters**—the external parameters that define the model's behavior.
   (b) **Hyperparameters** control aspects such as model complexity, learning rate, or in the case of a decision tree, the maximum tree height. These adjustments affect the underlying parameters learned by the model during training.
   (c) For example, in a decision tree model, the tree's maximum height defines how deep the tree can grow, affecting the number of branches and leaves.
8. Iterate and Improve
   (a) Machine learning is an iterative process. After initial training and testing, one often revisits previous steps to refine the model, enhance performance, and ensure better generalization.

In conclusion, building a machine learning model involves data preparation, problem identification, model selection, training, and iterative tuning of hyperparameters to optimize the model's performance.

23.4.3 ML Interview Concepts and Techniques Overview

23.4.3.1 Performance and Capacity

When building machine learning systems, our aim is to improve key metrics like user engagement while staying within the limits of our system's capacity and performance. This means we need to meet certain service level agreements (SLAs), such as responding to 99% of requests within 500 ms. We also need to consider how much traffic our system can handle (e.g., 1000 queries per second).

To achieve this, we focus on two main aspects:

- **Training**: Determining the right amount of data and computing power needed to create effective prediction models.
- **Evaluation**: Ensuring our models and system can meet the required performance standards and handle the expected load.

For systems like search ranking, recommendations, and ad prediction, a "funnel" approach works well. This means starting with a simple, fast model to handle a large volume of initial requests (e.g., a search for "Computer Science" yielding

100 million results). Then, as the number of items to process decreases, we can use more complex and accurate models, like deep neural networks, for the final decision. This approach allows us to balance speed, accuracy, and system resources effectively.

23.4.3.2 Train Your Data Collection Strategy

Machine learning models learn directly from the data they are given. This means the quality and amount of data used for training is incredibly important. Poor-quality data leads to poor results, even with the best algorithms.

Here are some ways to collect training data:

- **From users**: Collect data as users interact with your system.
- **Manual labeling**: Use crowdsourced platforms, public datasets (like BDD100K), or hire professionals to label data.
- **Creative techniques**: For example, use data from user interactions to personalize your product, or generate synthetic data with a GAN (generative adversarial network) for visual tasks like object detection.

Other important factors to consider:

- **Data segmentation**: Splitting data into different sets for training, testing, and validation.
- **Data volume**: Ensuring you have enough data to train your model effectively.
- **Data filtering**: Cleaning and preprocessing data to remove errors and biases.

Filtering is crucial because it directly affects what your model learns. The goal is to create a model that is as unbiased and accurate as possible.

23.4.3.3 Online Experiments

To build successful machine learning systems, we need to rigorously test how they perform in different situations. This testing process can even spark new ideas for improving the model itself. "Success" for a machine learning system can be measured in various ways, depending on its goals.

A/B testing is a valuable technique for online experiments. It helps us understand the impact of new features or changes by comparing the original system (the control) against a modified version (the variant). This comparison involves formulating two hypotheses: the null hypothesis (assuming no significant difference) and the alternative hypothesis (suggesting a real difference).

Beyond A/B testing, we can also assess the long-term effects of our system through techniques like backtesting (evaluating the model on past data) and long-running A/B tests, which provide insights into sustained performance over time.

23.4.3.4 Embed

Embedding is a way to represent things like words, documents, images, and even people as lists of numbers (vectors) in a way that captures their meaning. This allows computers to understand relationships between these things.

Think of it like translating words into a secret code that computers can understand. This code preserves the meaning of the words, so words with similar meanings have similar codes.

Here are two common ways to create these "codes" for words:

- **CBOW (Continuous Bag of Words)**: This method looks at the words surrounding a target word to predict the target word itself. Imagine trying to guess a missing word in a sentence based on the words around it.
- **Skip-gram**: This method does the opposite; it uses the current word to predict the surrounding words. It's like trying to guess what words might come before and after a given word.

Both of these methods help computers learn the relationships between words and their meanings, allowing them to do things like translate languages, understand sentiment in text, and answer your questions accurately.

23.4.3.5 Other ML Interview Concepts and Techniques

This is a brief overview of key concepts and techniques used in machine learning interviews and system design. To become truly proficient, you should explore these areas further:

1. **Transfer learning**: This involves adapting a pre-trained model for a new, but related, task. It's like leveraging your knowledge of Spanish to learn Italian more quickly.
2. **Model debugging and testing**: This is crucial for identifying and fixing errors in your models to ensure they perform as expected.
3. **Training data filtering**: This focuses on cleaning and preprocessing data to remove noise and biases, which can significantly impact model accuracy.
4. **Model building and iterative improvement**: This involves a cyclical process of building, evaluating, and refining your models to achieve optimal performance.

By delving deeper into these topics, you'll gain a more comprehensive understanding of machine learning and be better equipped to tackle real-world challenges.

23.5 Example 1: Design Google Lens

When drafting interview questions for a role related to **Google Lens**, you should focus on several key areas, including **computer vision**, **machine learning**, **image processing**, and **system design**. The questions should assess the candidate's technical knowledge, problem-solving ability, experience with large-scale systems, and familiarity with product design and optimization. Here's a set of sample interview questions that could be tailored to various roles related to Google Lens:

1. **Understanding the Product**:

    (a) Can you explain what Google Lens is and how it works at a high level?

    (b) What are the key use cases for Google Lens, and how do they influence design decisions?

2. **Challenges and Opportunities**:

    (a) What are some challenges Google Lens faces in terms of image recognition and real-time processing on mobile devices?

    (b) How might you improve the user experience for a feature like text extraction in Google Lens?

23.5.1 Technical Questions (Computer Vision and Machine Learning)

3. **Image Classification and Object Detection**:

    (a) How would you design an object detection system for Google Lens that can identify objects in real-time using a smartphone camera?

    (b) What techniques would you use to handle edge cases, like blurry or low-resolution images?

4. **Image Segmentation**:

    (a) Describe the process of **image segmentation** and how it could be applied in Google Lens for better object recognition and interaction (e.g., identifying and selecting a specific object from an image).

5. **Optical Character Recognition (OCR)**:

    (a) Explain how Optical Character Recognition (OCR) works. What steps would you take to improve OCR accuracy for different languages and fonts in Google Lens?

    (b) How would you handle cases where the text is on a curved or uneven surface?

6. **Multi-Modal Learning**:

    (a) How would you integrate both text and image data into a model used for Google Lens to improve search results?

    (b) How do you handle cases where visual and textual data are misaligned?

23.5 Example 1: Design Google Lens   431

7. **Transfer Learning**:

    (a) Google Lens often needs to identify objects in domains with limited amount of labeled data. How would you use **transfer learning** to adapt pre-trained models to a new domain with minimal data?

23.5.2 System Design and Scalability

8. **Large-Scale Image Processing Pipeline**:

    (a) How would you design a scalable image processing pipeline that allows Google Lens to process millions of images in real-time?
    (b) What considerations would you have for latency and throughput in a cloud-based architecture for Google Lens?

9. **Mobile Optimization**:

    (a) Google Lens needs to process images in real-time on mobile devices with limited computational power. How would you optimize a machine learning model for efficient inference on mobile devices?
    (b) What techniques could you use to reduce latency in image recognition while maintaining accuracy?

10. **Edge AI**:

    (a) How would you balance edge computing (processing on-device) versus cloud-based processing for Google Lens, and what trade-offs would you need to consider?
    (b) How would you design a fallback mechanism for when Google Lens loses internet connectivity but still needs to process images locally?

11. **Model Deployment and A/B Testing**:

    (a) Explain how you would handle **continuous deployment** and **A/B testing** for new features in Google Lens to ensure minimal disruption to users and model performance.
    (b) How would you measure the performance and success of new features in production (both from a technical and user perspective)?

23.5.3 Algorithm Optimization and Debugging

12. **Algorithm Accuracy and Bias**:

    (a) How would you approach identifying and mitigating bias in the Google Lens object recognition system, especially when recognizing culturally diverse objects?

(b) What steps would you take to optimize the model's accuracy without increasing computational complexity?

13. **Handling Noisy Data**:

    (a) In real-world scenarios, images captured by users may be noisy, blurry, or poorly lit. How would you design an image enhancement algorithm for improving the performance of Google Lens under such conditions?

    (b) What preprocessing steps would you apply to clean the input image before feeding it into the model?

14. **Handling User Feedback**:

    (a) How would you incorporate user feedback (like whether Google Lens correctly identified an object) into the training loop to improve the model's performance over time?

    (b) How would you design a system to adaptively learn from user corrections while ensuring data privacy?

23.5.4 Advanced Topics

15. **Augmented Reality (AR)**:

    (a) Google Lens sometimes provides real-time AR overlays on physical objects. How would you integrate AR into the Google Lens experience, and what are the technical challenges of aligning virtual objects with real-world items?

    (b) How would you ensure that the AR annotations appear accurately on fast-moving objects in real-time?

16. **Generative AI**:

    (a) How could **Generative AI** (such as GANs) be applied to improve the capabilities of Google Lens, for example, in filling in missing parts of an image or generating enhancements?

    (b) Describe a scenario where generative models could enhance the object recognition pipeline for better contextual understanding.

23.5.5 Data Management and Privacy

17. **Handling Private Data**:

    (a) Google Lens processes a lot of personal and sensitive data (e.g., identifying text from documents). How would you ensure data privacy and compliance with regulations (e.g., GDPR) in the design of Google Lens?

23.5 Example 1: Design Google Lens

    (b) What techniques would you implement to anonymize or encrypt data while ensuring that models can still be trained and improved?

18. **Data Labeling and Quality Control**:

    (a) Google Lens relies heavily on large amounts of labeled data for training. How would you design an efficient and scalable data labeling pipeline for different types of image data (e.g., object detection, OCR)?

    (b) How do you ensure the quality of labeled data and manage edge cases where the data might be ambiguous or mislabeled?

23.5.6 Metrics and Evaluation

19. **Evaluation Metrics**:

    (a) What metrics would you use to evaluate the performance of Google Lens's image recognition models?

    (b) How would you design an evaluation pipeline to assess both accuracy and user satisfaction with the system? What would you consider when dealing with ambiguous or subjective results?

20. **Error Analysis**:

    (a) Suppose Google Lens consistently fails to recognize a certain type of object (e.g., certain brands or rare objects). How would you diagnose the issue and improve the model's ability to recognize that object class?

    (b) What tools or processes would you implement for monitoring model performance over time and detecting issues before they affect the end user?

23.5.7 Cross-functional and Product Questions

21. **Collaboration with Product and UX Teams**:

    (a) How would you collaborate with UX designers and product managers to ensure that technical decisions align with the user experience goals for Google Lens?

    (b) How would you prioritize which features to develop or improve in Google Lens, given limited resources and competing demands?

22. **Explaining AI to Non-technical Stakeholders**:

    (a) How would you explain how Google Lens's image recognition technology works to a non-technical audience (such as product managers or end users)?

    (b) What strategies would you use to communicate model performance, limitations, and risks effectively to non-technical stakeholders?

23.5.8 Final Thought Questions

23. **Future Directions**:

    (a) How do you see the role of **AI and machine learning** evolving in Google Lens over the next 5 years?

    (b) What new features would you add to Google Lens to improve its functionality and user experience?

24. **Ethical Considerations**:

    (a) What ethical challenges do you see in deploying a product like Google Lens, and how would you address these in the design and deployment process?

    (b) How would you ensure that Google Lens respects cultural and ethical differences when providing object recognition services globally?

23.5.9 Summary

These questions span technical, product, and system design aspects related to Google Lens, covering topics such as **computer vision**, **OCR**, **real-time processing**, **scalability**, **data privacy**, and **product integration**. Depending on the role being interviewed for, you can adjust the focus towards more technical design, machine learning model optimization, or cross-functional collaboration.

When drafting interview questions for a role related to **Google Lens**, you should focus on several key areas, including **computer vision**, **machine learning**, **image processing**, and **system design**. The questions should assess the candidate's technical knowledge, problem-solving ability, experience with large-scale systems, and familiarity with product design and optimization. Here's a set of sample interview questions that could be tailored to various roles related to Google Lens:

23.5.10 General Questions About Google Lens

1. **Understanding the Product**:

    (a) Can you explain what Google Lens is and how it works at a high level?

    (b) What are the key use cases for Google Lens, and how do they influence design decisions?

2. **Challenges and Opportunities**:

    (a) What are some challenges Google Lens faces in terms of image recognition and real-time processing on mobile devices?

23.5 Example 1: Design Google Lens   435

(b) How would you improve the user experience for a feature like text extraction in Google Lens?

23.5.11 Technical Questions (Computer Vision and Machine Learning)

3. **Image Classification and Object Detection**:
   (a) How would you design an object detection system for Google Lens that can identify objects in real-time using a smartphone camera?
   (b) What techniques would you use to handle edge cases, like blurry or low-resolution images?

4. **Image Segmentation**:
   (a) Describe the process of **image segmentation** and how it could be applied in Google Lens for better object recognition and interaction (e.g., identifying and selecting a specific object from an image).

5. **Optical Character Recognition (OCR)**:
   (a) Explain how Optical Character Recognition (OCR) works. What steps would you take to improve OCR accuracy for different languages and fonts in Google Lens?
   (b) How would you handle cases where the text is on a curved or uneven surface?

6. **Multi-Modal Learning**:
   (a) How would you integrate both text and image data into a model used for Google Lens to improve search results?
   (b) How do you handle cases where visual and textual data are misaligned?

7. **Transfer Learning**:
   (a) Google Lens often needs to identify objects in domains with limited labeled data. How would you use **transfer learning** to adapt pre-trained models to a new domain with minimal data?

23.5.12 System Design and Scalability

8. **Large-Scale Image Processing Pipeline**:
   (a) How would you design a scalable image processing pipeline that allows Google Lens to process millions of images in real-time?

(b) What considerations would you have for latency and throughput in a cloud-based architecture for Google Lens?

9. **Mobile Optimization**:

    (a) Google Lens needs to process images in real-time on mobile devices with limited computational power. How would you optimize a machine learning model for efficient inference on mobile devices?

    (b) What techniques could you use to reduce latency in image recognition while maintaining accuracy?

10. **Edge AI**:

    (a) How would you balance edge computing (processing on-device) versus cloud-based processing for Google Lens, and what trade-offs would you need to consider?

    (b) How would you design a fallback mechanism for when Google Lens loses internet connectivity but still needs to process images locally?

11. **Model Deployment and A/B Testing**:

    (a) Explain how you would handle **continuous deployment** and **A/B testing** for new features in Google Lens to ensure minimal disruption to users and model performance.

    (b) How would you measure the performance and success of new features in production (both from a technical and user perspective)?

23.5.13 Algorithm Optimization and Debugging

12. **Algorithm Accuracy and Bias**:

    (a) How would you approach identifying and mitigating bias in the Google Lens object recognition system, especially when recognizing culturally diverse objects?

    (b) What steps would you take to optimize the model's accuracy without increasing computational complexity?

13. **Handling Noisy Data**:

    (a) In real-world scenarios, images captured by users may be noisy, blurry, or poorly lit. How would you design an image enhancement algorithm for improving the performance of Google Lens under such conditions?

    (b) What preprocessing steps would you apply to clean the input image before feeding it into the model?

14. **Handling User Feedback**:
    (a) How would you incorporate user feedback (like whether Google Lens correctly identified an object) into the training loop to improve the model's performance over time?
    (b) How would you design a system to adaptively learn from user corrections while ensuring data privacy?

23.5.14 Advanced Topics

15. **Augmented Reality (AR)**:
    (a) Google Lens sometimes provides real-time AR overlays on physical objects. How would you integrate AR into the Google Lens experience, and what are the technical challenges of aligning virtual objects with real-world items?
    (b) How would you ensure that the AR annotations appear accurately on fast-moving objects in real-time?

16. **Generative AI**:
    (a) How could **Generative AI** (such as GANs) be applied to improve the capabilities of Google Lens, for example, in filling in missing parts of an image or generating enhancements?
    (b) Describe a scenario where generative models could enhance the object recognition pipeline for better contextual understanding.

23.5.15 Data Management and Privacy

17. **Handling Private Data**:
    (a) Google Lens processes a lot of personal and sensitive data (e.g., identifying text from documents). How would you ensure data privacy and compliance with regulations (e.g., GDPR) in the design of Google Lens?
    (b) What techniques would you implement to anonymize or encrypt data while ensuring that models can still be trained and improved?

18. **Data Labeling and Quality Control**:
    (a) Google Lens relies heavily on large amounts of labeled data for training. How would you design an efficient and scalable data labeling pipeline for different types of image data (e.g., object detection, OCR)?
    (b) How do you ensure the quality of labeled data and manage edge cases where the data might be ambiguous or mislabeled?

23.5.16 Metrics and Evaluation

19. **Evaluation Metrics**:

    (a) What metrics would you use to evaluate the performance of Google Lens's image recognition models?

    (b) How would you design an evaluation pipeline to assess both accuracy and user satisfaction with the system? What would you consider when dealing with ambiguous or subjective results?

20. **Error Analysis**:

    (a) Suppose Google Lens consistently fails to recognize a certain type of object (e.g., certain brands or rare objects). How would you diagnose the issue and improve the model's ability to recognize that object class?

    (b) What tools or processes would you implement for monitoring model performance over time and detecting issues before they affect the end user?

23.5.17 Cross-functional and Product Questions

21. **Collaboration with Product and UX Teams**:

    (a) How would you collaborate with UX designers and product managers to ensure that technical decisions align with the user experience goals for Google Lens?

    (b) How would you prioritize which features to develop or improve in Google Lens, given limited resources and competing demands?

22. **Explaining AI to Non-Technical Stakeholders**:

    (a) How would you explain how Google Lens's image recognition technology works to a non-technical audience (such as product managers or end users)?

    (b) What strategies would you use to communicate model performance, limitations, and risks effectively to non-technical stakeholders?

23.5.18 Final Thought Questions

23. **Future Directions**:

    (a) How do you see the role of **AI and machine learning** evolving in Google Lens over the next 5 years?

    (b) What new features would you add to Google Lens to improve its functionality and user experience?

24. **Ethical Considerations**:
    (a) What ethical challenges do you see in deploying a product like Google Lens, and how would you address these in the design and deployment process?
    (b) How would you ensure that Google Lens respects cultural and ethical differences when providing object recognition services globally?

23.5.19 Summary

These questions span technical, product, and system design aspects related to Google Lens, covering topics such as **computer vision**, **OCR**, **real-time processing**, **scalability**, **data privacy**, and **product integration**. Depending on the role being interviewed for, you can adjust the focus towards more technical design, machine learning model optimization, or cross-functional collaboration.

23.6 Example 2: Search Rankings

23.6.1 Problem Statement

An interviewer asks you to design a search relevance system for a search engine, specifically focusing on how to display relevant results on the search engine results pages (SERP). To clarify the problem, we can break it down into three key aspects: scope, scale, and personalization. The following sections will reference the approach described in https://www.educative.io/courses/grokking-the-machine-learning-interview/problem-statement-xlXBOEW7gkJ.

23.6.1.1 Scope of the Problem

The interviewer's question is broad and to avoid any ambiguity, it's important to ask clarifying questions. Thinking out loud as you work through possible solutions will help narrow the problem space. A good initial question for the interviewer would be: "Are we focusing on a general-purpose search engine like Google or Bing, or a specialized one like Amazon Product Search?"

Once you've defined the context, you can start refining the scope of the problem. In this example, let's assume you're working with a general-purpose search engine like Google or Bing to return relevant results. However, the techniques discussed can be applied to a wide range of search engines.

The final problem statement can be described as follows: "Design a generic search engine that delivers relevant results for queries such as 'Richard Nixon', 'programming languages', and so on." This would require building a machine learning system that ranks search results based on their relevance to the user's query, addressing the challenge of search ranking.

23.6.1.2 Scale

Once you've established that you're working on a general-purpose search engine, understanding the scale of the system is crucial. There are two important questions to consider:

1. *How many websites will this search engine need to index?*
2. *How many requests per second (QPS) do you expect the system to handle?*

Let's assume you're working with billions of documents and that the search engine will need to process around 10,000 queries per second (QPS). Understanding this scale will guide the design of your system. For example, later in the process, you might implement a funnel-based approach, where the complexity of the model increases as the set of documents is narrowed down in such a large-scale search system.

Another key consideration is whether the user is signed in or not. This will influence how much personalization can be applied to improve the relevance of the search results. In this case, assume that the user is signed in and their profile, including historical search data, is available. This will enable you to leverage personalization features to provide more tailored and relevant search results.

23.6.2 Evaluation Metrics

Let's examine some metrics that can help you define what a "successful" search solution looks like. Selecting the right metric for your machine learning model is crucial. Machine learning models learn purely from data, without any human intuition embedded into them. Therefore, if you choose the wrong metric, the model may optimize for an entirely incorrect objective.

There are two primary types of metrics used to evaluate the success of a search query: (1) online metrics and (2) offline metrics.

Online metrics are calculated based on real-time user interactions within the system. In contrast, **offline metrics** evaluate the quality of search results using offline data, without requiring direct user feedback.

23.6.2.1 Online Metrics

In an online environment, you can gauge the success of a search session by observing the user's actions. At the query level, success can be defined by user engagement, such as clicking on a search result. A straightforward metric to track this is the **click-through rate (CTR)**.

23.6 Example 2: Search Rankings

CTR is calculated by dividing the number of clicks by the number of impressions. For example, when a search engine displays a results page and the user views it, that counts as an impression. If the user clicks on a result, it is considered a success.

However, CTR has some limitations. For example, even unsuccessful clicks can contribute to a positive search outcome. This could include scenarios like a user clicking on a result but quickly returning to the search results, indicating dissatisfaction. To address this, you could filter the data to include only "successful clicks," such as those where the user stays on the page for a longer period.

Another factor to account for is **zero-click searches**, where the search engine results page (SERP) answers the query directly, eliminating the need for further clicks.

While these examples focus on single-query search sessions, search sessions can also span multiple queries. For instance, a user might start by searching for "Italian food," fail to find the desired results, and then refine the query to "Italian restaurant." In some cases, users may need to explore multiple results before finding what they're looking for.

Ideally, you want users to find the most relevant results with the fewest number of queries and with as many relevant results as possible on the results page. Therefore, **time to success** is another important metric to measure and track the performance of a search engine.

23.6.2.2 Offline Metrics

Offline methods for evaluating search success typically involve using human evaluators. These evaluators are tasked with objectively scoring the relevance of search results based on specific guidelines. Their ratings are then aggregated across a sample of queries to create a baseline for evaluation.

23.6.3 Architectural Components

Let's take a look at the architectural components of a search ranking system and their role in answering searcher queries.

23.6.3.1 Architecture

Let's take a look at the architectural components that are essential when creating a search engine.

Figure 23.6 shows a flowchart of an information retrieval system, likely a search engine. It outlines the process from receiving a user's query to delivering search results. Here's a breakdown of the steps:

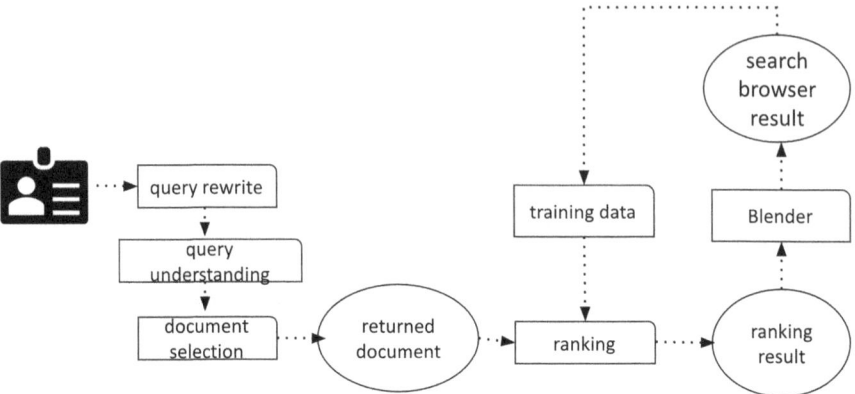

Fig. 23.6 Architectural components of a search engine

1. **User Input**: The process begins with a user (represented by an ID icon) submitting a query. This could be a question or a set of keywords.
2. **Query Understanding**: The system analyzes the query to understand the user's intent and information needs. This might involve natural language processing techniques to identify key concepts and relationships within the query.
3. **Document Selection**: Based on the understood query, the system selects relevant documents from its index or database. This step involves matching the query terms with the content of the documents.
4. **Retrieved Documents**: The selected documents are then gathered for further processing. This could be a large set of potentially relevant documents.
5. **Ranking**: The retrieved documents are ranked based on their relevance to the query and other factors like authority and popularity. This step ensures that the most relevant documents are presented first.
6. **Training Data Generation**: The system generates training data from user interactions, such as clicks and feedback on search results. This data is used to improve the system's performance over time.
7. **Blender (Mixing/Combining)**: This step likely involves combining different ranking signals and algorithms to produce the final ranking of documents. This could include factors like user preferences, context, and freshness of the content.
8. **Ranking Results**: The final ranked list of documents is presented to the user as search results. This is the output of the system that the user sees.

Let's take a brief look at the role of each component in answering searcher queries.

23.6.3.2 Query Rewrite

Search queries are often imprecise and fail to fully capture the searcher's actual intent. To address this, we use query rewriting to improve recall, meaning we retrieve a broader range of relevant results. Query rewriting involves several components, as outlined below:

1. **Spell Check Process**
   Spell-checking is an essential part of the modern search experience. It automatically corrects common spelling mistakes in queries (e.g., changing "ITLIAN RESTAURAT" to "Italian Restaurant").
2. **Query Expansion**
   Query expansion enhances search result retrieval by adding relevant terms to the user's original query. This helps reduce the gap between the searcher's input and the available documents. For instance, after fixing any typos, we might expand a query like "Italian restaurant" by adding related terms like "food" or "recipe" to capture a wider array of potential results (such as web pages).

23.6.3.3 Query Comprehension

This phase involves figuring out the main intent behind the query, for example, the query "gas station" is most likely to have local intent (interest in nearby places), while the query "earthquake" may have news intent. Later, this intent will help select and rank the best query documents. In our current scope, you don't need more details about this.

23.6.3.4 Document Selection

The web contains billions of documents, so the first step in document retrieval is identifying a large set of documents relevant to the user's search query. For instance, popular searches like "sports" might correspond to millions of web pages. Document selection is the process of narrowing down this vast collection to a smaller subset of the most relevant results.

This stage prioritizes recall, utilizing simpler techniques to filter through the billions of web pages and gather documents that could be relevant to the query. At this point, the exact ranking of the selected documents is not a priority. The ranking component, which follows document selection, is responsible for determining the exact relevance (precision) of each document and organizing them appropriately for the search engine results page (SERP).

By providing the ranking component with documents that have already undergone an initial round of filtering, the system reduces the workload. This enables the use of more advanced machine learning models (focused on high precision) within the ranking stage, without negatively impacting system performance or capacity.

23.6.3.5 Ranking

Ranking systems heavily rely on machine learning to determine the optimal order of documents (commonly referred to as learning to rank). If the number of documents retrieved during the document selection stage is substantial (e.g., over 10,000), and the system faces high traffic (e.g., more than 10,000 queries per second), it's often necessary to implement multi-stage ranking with models of varying complexity and sizes.

These multiple ranking stages allow the use of simpler, faster models in the early stages and reserve more complex models for the final stages, where precision in ranking is critical. This approach helps manage computational costs, especially in large-scale search systems.

For instance, a potential configuration might involve retrieving 100,000 documents, which are then passed through two ranking stages. In the first stage, you could apply a lightweight linear machine learning model that operates quickly (in nanoseconds). In the second stage, you could employ a more computationally demanding model, such as a deep learning model, to precisely rank the top 500 documents filtered by the first stage. When selecting an algorithm for this process, it's essential to consider the model's execution time, as balancing cost and performance is a crucial factor in large-scale machine learning systems.

23.6.3.6 Blender

Blender delivers relevant results across various search domains, including images, videos, news, local listings, and blog posts. For example, a search for "Italian Restaurant" might present a combination of websites, local results, and images. The main goal of blending is to enhance the searcher's experience by providing more engaging and relevant results.

An additional key factor is ensuring result diversity—it's important not to display all results from the same source or website. Ultimately, Blender processes the searcher's query and generates a comprehensive search engine results page (SERP).

23.6.3.7 Training Data Generation

This component shows the circular way in which machine learning is used to compose a search engine ranking system. It takes online user engagement data from the SERPs displayed in response to the query and generates positive and negative training examples. The resulting training data is then fed into a machine learning model that is trained to rank search engine results.

23.6.3.8 Hierarchical Model Approach

Above, we briefly discussed the multi-tier funnel, which goes from a large number of documents selected for the query to the most relevant ones. This configuration for large search systems is described in detail Fig. 23.7.

23.6 Example 2: Search Rankings

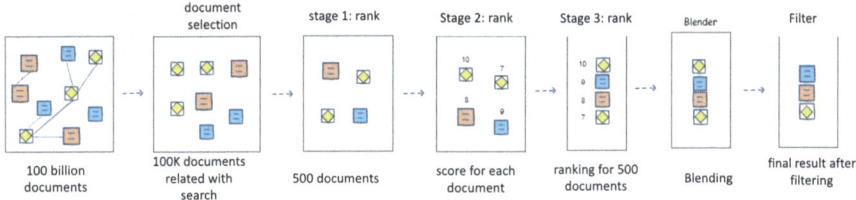

Fig. 23.7 Hierarchical model approach

These steps translate into a hierarchical model approach that allows you to choose the appropriate ML algorithm at each stage, also from a scalability perspective.

The example configuration above assumes that you first select 100,000 documents from the index for a searcher's query, and then use a two-stage sorting, the first stage is reduced from 100,000 to 500,000 documents, and the second stage is then ranking those 500 documents. The mixer can then mix results from different search domains, and the filter will further filter out irrelevant or offensive results, resulting in good user engagement. This is just an example configuration, and it's important to note that you should choose based on your capacity needs as well as your experiments to see the impact on relevance based on the documentation scored on each tier.

23.6.4 Training Data Generation

Let's take a look at ways to generate training data for search ranking problems.

23.6.4.1 A Point-by-Point Approach to Training Data Generation

This describes two different ways to train machine learning models for ranking tasks, like showing the most relevant search results.

1. Peer-to-Peer Approach:
Imagine each document as a competitor in a race. This method trains the model to predict a "relevance score" for each document individually, like assigning each runner a speed. Then, it simply sorts the documents by their scores, with the highest score at the top, just like ranking runners by their speed to determine the winner. This approach focuses on comparing documents directly against each other.
2. Point-by-Point Approach:
Instead of focusing on individual scores, this method simplifies the problem by grouping documents into categories. Think of it like sorting emails into "important" and "not important" instead of trying to rank them by exact importance

level. This approach uses classification algorithms to assign each document to a category, making it simpler to train and sometimes more efficient. For example, a model might classify documents as either "relevant" or "irrelevant" to the search query, creating a basic ranking system.

Essentially, these are two different strategies for teaching a computer to rank items. The first focuses on individual comparisons, while the second simplifies the task by grouping items into categories.

23.6.4.2 Positive and Negative Training Examples

Basically, they're trying to predict which websites you'll find useful based on your search query.
Think of it like this:
You search for "Paris Tourism" and see three websites:

- Paris.com
- Eiffeltower.com
- Lourvemusuem.com

You skip the first one, but click on "Eiffeltower.com"and spend 2 min browsing before signing up for something. Then, you go back to the search results and click on "Lourvemusuem.com," but only stay for 20 s.

The search engine learns from this! It sees that you were really interested in "Eiffeltower.com" (positive example) but not so much in "Paris.com" (negative example). "Lourvemusuem.com"might be somewhere in between.

This information is used as "training data" to improve the search engine's ability to show you relevant results in the future. The more people use the search engine, the more it learns and the better it gets at predicting what you'll find useful.

23.6.4.3 Warning: Fewer Negative Examples

This explains how search engines gather massive amounts of data to train their ranking algorithms, even when faced with a common issue: people often only click on the first few results.

Here's the breakdown:

- **The Problem**: If users only click the top result, the search engine doesn't get enough information about what's *not* relevant. It's like only knowing what "good" food is, but not having any examples of "bad" food.
- **The Solution**: To overcome this, search engines use "random negative examples." They assume that results buried deep down in the search results (like page 50) are probably not relevant. This helps them learn what to avoid showing you.
- **Data Explosion**: Imagine millions of searches happening daily. Each search generates data about what people click on (positive examples) and what they

ignore (including those random negative examples). This quickly adds up to millions of data points every day!
- **Capturing Weekly Patterns**: People use search engines differently throughout the week. Weekends might see more searches for entertainment, while weekdays might have more work-related searches. To account for this, search engines collect data for a whole week to capture these variations.
- **Massive Dataset**: With millions of searches daily, and data collected over an entire week, the search engine ends up with a gigantic dataset (around 70 million examples in this case) to train its algorithms. This massive dataset helps them fine-tune their ability to show you the most relevant results.

23.6.5 Ranking

The aim is to develop a model that displays the most relevant results for a searcher's query. Since users primarily focus on the first few results on the Search Engine Results Page (SERP), it is crucial to prioritize relevance in the initial results.

23.6.5.1 Learning To Rank (LTR)

LTR refers to a collection of techniques that utilize supervised machine learning (ML) to solve ranking problems.

23.6.5.2 Phased Approach

As explained in the Schema Components section, the number of documents that match a single query can be enormous. Therefore, large search engines adopt a multi-tiered funnel approach. The top tier of the funnel processes a large number of documents using a simpler, faster algorithm. In the next phase, a more complex machine learning model ranks a smaller subset of documents.

For instance, the first phase may receive 100,000 related documents from the document selection component. After initial ranking, this number is reduced to 500, ensuring that the most relevant documents proceed to the second stage (also known as document recall). In the second stage, documents are re-ranked to ensure they are in the correct order, focusing on the precision of the ranking.

The model's first phase emphasizes recall by retrieving the top five to ten relevant documents from the initial 500 results, while the second phase focuses on precision by ranking these results accurately.

Phase 1: At this stage, we aim to reduce the large collection of documents to a smaller subset, while ensuring that highly relevant documents aren't missed. This can be achieved using a pointwise approach, approximating relevance or irrelevance through binary classification. Logistic Regression: Linear algorithms, such as logistic regression or small MART (Multiple Additive Regression Tree) models, are ideal for scoring large volumes of documents. Here, the ability to quickly score each document is crucial for efficiently managing a large document library. Phase 2: The primary goal of the second phase is to refine the ranking order. This is achieved by switching from a pointwise target (e.g., click or session success) to a pairwise target. Pairwise optimization for learning to rank involves ordering document pairs correctly rather than minimizing classification errors.

23.6.5.3 Pairwise Learning Algorithms

LambdaMART: LambdaMART is a variation of MART, but focuses on improving pairwise rankings. Tree-based algorithms are known for generalizing well with moderate training data. If your training data comprises millions of examples, LambdaMART is one of the best options for the second phase of pairwise ranking. This approach is also ideal for optimizing offline NDCG (data from human evaluations).

LambdaRank: LambdaRank is a neural network-based method that employs a pairwise loss function to rank documents. However, neural network-based models are typically slower and require more extensive training data. Hence, the availability of a large dataset is essential before opting for this approach. Pairwise methods for online training data generation can produce ranking examples for a vast number of search engines, allowing for the creation of a substantial number of document pairs.

23.6.5.4 LambdaRank Learning Process

For a given query, let's say we need to rank two documents. The model assigns scores to each document based on their feature vectors, and these scores are used to predict which document should rank higher. The optimization function works to minimize incorrect rankings.

Both LambdaMART and LambdaRank are extensively covered in the paper "From RankNet to LambdaRank to LambdaMART: An Overview". https://www.educative.io/courses/grokking-the-machine-learning-interview/problem-statement-xlXBOEW7gkJ. To compare the performance of different models, the NDCG score of the ranking results can be calculated.

23.6.6 Filter the Results

Even after finding relevant search results and ranking them, search engines still need to filter out results that are unsuitable for everyone to see. This includes things like:

- **Offensive content**: Anything that's sexually explicit, violent, or promotes hate speech.
- **Misinformation**: False or misleading information, like fake news or conspiracy theories.
- **Content inappropriate for children**: Material that is sexually suggestive, violent, or promotes harmful behavior.
- **Discriminatory content**: Anything that attacks or demeans a particular group of people.

To do this, search engines use special machine learning models. These models need three things:

- **Training data**: Examples of "bad" content so they can learn what to filter out. This data can come from human reviewers who identify problematic content or from user reports of inappropriate results.
- **Features**: Specific characteristics of websites and pages that can help identify unsuitable content. These might include the words used on the page, the website's history of being reported, or the types of images used.
- **Trained classifiers**: Algorithms that can analyze the features and predict whether a result is unsuitable.

Think of it like training a spam filter. You give it examples of spam emails, teach it to recognize common features of spam (like suspicious subject lines or lots of exclamation points), and it learns to filter out unwanted messages. Search engines do something similar to keep their results safe and appropriate for everyone.

23.7 Example 3: Short Video Recommendation System

When designing a recommendation system for short videos on YouTube (like YouTube Shorts), the goal is to provide personalized, relevant, and engaging video content to users based on their preferences, behavior, and platform-wide trends. The system must scale to handle millions of users, video uploads, and interactions per second.

Here's an approach to designing the system:

23.7.1 High-Level Architecture

The system can be broken down into several components:

- **User Service**: Manages user information such as user profiles, history, likes, dislikes, subscriptions, and watch history.
- **Video Service**: Manages the metadata and storage of the videos (such as duration, category, and tags). Also manages the upload process, video processing (encoding), and storage on a CDN (Content Delivery Network).

- **Recommendation Engine**: Generates personalized recommendations based on user interactions, video metadata, content engagement metrics, and trends.
- **Data Storage and Caching**: Manages structured (e.g., user profiles, video metadata) and unstructured (e.g., video files, video embeddings) data. Caches frequently accessed content and video recommendations.
- **Feedback Loop**: Gathers user interaction feedback (likes, dislikes, shares, comments, etc.) to retrain models and update the recommendation system.

23.7.2 System Components

23.7.2.1 User Profile Management

- **Purpose**: Stores and manages user behavior, preferences, and demographic information.
- **Data Stored**: Watch history, likes, dislikes, search history, subscriptions, geographic location, etc.
- Tech Stack:
  - **Data Storage**: SQL database (MySQL, PostgreSQL) for structured data like user profiles, preferences, and watch history.
  - **NoSQL Databases** (e.g., Cassandra or MongoDB) to manage large-scale data and unstructured information such as user interactions.
  - **In-Memory Cache** (e.g., Redis or Memcached) for quick access to user profiles and frequently accessed data.

23.7.2.2 Video Metadata Service

- **Purpose**: Manages metadata for all uploaded videos and handles video encoding.
- **Metadata Stored**: Video duration, category, tags, uploader, upload time, views, likes, etc.
- Tech Stack:
  - **SQL/NoSQL Database** for storing structured data related to video metadata.
  - **Blob Storage/CDN** for storing actual video content (e.g., Amazon S3 or Google Cloud Storage).

23.7.2.3 Recommendation Engine

- **Purpose**: Provides personalized video recommendations based on user preferences, video metadata, and engagement metrics.

23.7 Example 3: Short Video Recommendation System   451

- Components:
    - **Content-Based Filtering**: Recommends videos similar to previously watched videos by analyzing video metadata, tags, and embeddings (using NLP or visual features).
    - **Collaborative Filtering**: Recommends videos based on the behavior of similar users (i.e., users who watched similar content).
    - **Deep Learning-Based Embedding Models**: Converts videos into vector embeddings based on video content (frames, captions, etc.) using techniques like convolutional neural networks (CNN) or BERT embeddings for captions.
    - **Trending/Popular Content Algorithm**: Surfaces videos that are currently trending globally or locally using metrics such as views, engagement, and recency.
    - **Real-Time Behavior Tracking**: Tracks real-time user behavior (such as video watch duration, skips, etc.) and adjusts recommendations dynamically.
- Tech Stack:
    - **Machine Learning models**: TensorFlow, PyTorch for training and deploying recommendation models.
    - **Message Queues** (Kafka, RabbitMQ) to collect and process real-time engagement data.
    - **Data Pipelines**: Apache Spark, Flink for real-time and batch processing of logs, watch history, and metadata.

23.7.2.4 Data Storage and Caching

- **Purpose**: Handles storage for metadata, user behavior logs, and recommendation results.
- Tech Stack:
    - **Distributed file systems** (HDFS or GCS) for storing logs and metadata.
    - **NoSQL databases** like Cassandra for user logs and engagement metrics.
    - **Redis/Memcached** to cache frequently accessed recommendations and video metadata.

23.7.2.5 Feedback Loop

- **Purpose**: Continuously improves recommendation models by using user interactions (such as likes, dislikes, time spent, shares, etc.).
- How it works:
    - Collect user interactions with videos in real-time.
    - Use these signals to update user preference profiles.
    - Feed this data into machine learning models to retrain them.

- Tech Stack:
  - **Real-time event streaming**: Use Kafka or AWS Kinesis to collect real-time user interactions.
  - **Data pipelines**: Use Apache Flink or Spark to process interaction data.
  - **Model retraining**: Models are retrained at regular intervals using user feedback.

23.7.3 Video Processing and Delivery

23.7.3.1 Video Upload and Encoding

- Users upload videos, which are processed and encoded into different resolutions and formats for efficient streaming.
- Tech Stack:
  - **Encoding Service**: FFmpeg or cloud-based transcoding solutions (AWS MediaConvert, GCP Transcoder) to process videos.
  - **CDN (Content Delivery Network)**: Videos are cached and served from a CDN (e.g., Cloudflare, Akamai) for low-latency delivery to users worldwide.

23.7.3.2 Video Serving

- After processing, videos are hosted on the CDN and served based on the user's geographic location and network bandwidth.

23.7.4 Algorithmic Flow for Recommendation

The recommendation algorithm involves the following steps:

1. User Engagement Data:

   (a) Start with the user's watch history, interactions (likes, comments), and preferences.

2. Content Retrieval:

   (a) Fetch a large candidate set of videos (e.g., 10,000) based on user preferences, trending content, and collaborative filtering.

3. Initial Ranking:

   (a) Use lightweight models (e.g., logistic regression) to rank the top 500 videos based on metadata like category, tags, and recent views.

4. Refined Ranking:
   (a) Apply complex models (e.g., deep learning-based models) to the top 500 videos, analyzing video embeddings, user embeddings, and engagement patterns.
   (b) Rank the top 10–20 videos to display to the user.
5. Real-time Feedback:
   (a) Update recommendations dynamically as the user watches more videos, likes, or skips content. Feedback loops improve recommendation accuracy for future sessions.

23.7.5 Deep Learning-Based Recommendation Algorithms

Deep learning-based recommendation systems are highly effective at generating personalized accurate recommendations by learning complex patterns in user behavior, content, and context. These models go beyond traditional recommendation systems (like collaborative filtering and content-based filtering) by utilizing neural networks that can automatically learn representations from raw data, such as user-item interactions, text, and images. Below, we explore various deep learning architectures and techniques used for building recommendation algorithms.

Recommendation systems provide personalized suggestions for users. The most common approaches are:

- **Collaborative Filtering (CF)**: Predicts user preferences based on the preferences of similar users or items. Matrix factorization (e.g., SVD, ALS) is a common technique.
- **Content-Based Filtering (CBF)**: Recommends items based on the content/features of the items (e.g., item metadata like genres, keywords) and compares them to user preferences.
- **Hybrid Systems**: Combine collaborative and content-based methods.

In deep learning, we combine these ideas with deep neural networks to model more complex relationships.

23.7.5.1 Neural Collaborative Filtering (NCF)

Neural Collaborative Filtering (NCF) extends matrix factorization by replacing the dot product operation with deep neural networks.

- **How It Works**:
  - The input consists of user-item pairs (typically in a sparse matrix format).
  - The model learns embeddings for users and items.

- Instead of computing the dot product of user and item embeddings (as in matrix factorization), it concatenates these embeddings and feeds them into a feedforward neural network.
  - The neural network learns non-linear interaction patterns between users and items.
- **Advantages**:
  - Can model complex, non-linear relationships between users and items.
  - Flexible and adaptable to different data sources.

Loss Function: Can use Mean Squared Error (MSE) for rating prediction or cross-entropy loss for click prediction.

23.7.5.2 Autoencoders for Collaborative Filtering

Autoencoders are neural networks used for unsupervised learning, typically for dimensionality reduction or representation learning. In recommendation systems, **Autoencoders** can be used to learn low-dimensional embeddings of user preferences.

- **How It Works**:
  - The input is the user-item interaction matrix (ratings, clicks, etc.).
  - The autoencoder tries to reconstruct the input matrix from a compressed hidden representation (embedding).
  - The hidden layer acts as a latent representation of the user's preferences, which can then be used to generate recommendations.
- **Advantages**:
  - Handles sparse data well by learning compressed representations.
  - Suitable for cold-start problems where user-item interactions are limited.

23.7.5.3 Deep Learning with Content Features (DL-CBF)

In **content-based filtering**, deep learning can be used to learn powerful representations from the item's content features, such as text, images, or audio. This is particularly useful for recommending items such as articles, movies, or products with detailed attributes.

- **How It Works**:
  - Uses **Convolutional Neural Networks (CNNs)** or **Recurrent Neural Networks (RNNs)** to process text or images.
  - Embeddings generated from content (e.g., video frames, article text) are concatenated with user embeddings to predict interactions.

- **Text-Based Recommendation**:
  - Use pre-trained embeddings (e.g., **BERT**, **Word2Vec**) to extract features from text.
  - Fine-tune the embeddings based on user-item interaction data to predict user preferences.
- **Image-Based Recommendation**:
  - Use **CNNs** to extract features from images (e.g., product images in an e-commerce store).
  - The extracted image features can be combined with user preferences to improve the quality of recommendations.

23.7.5.4 Recurrent Neural Networks (RNNs) for Sequential Recommendations

RNNs are suitable for capturing **sequential patterns** in user behavior. They can model time-dependent user interactions and make recommendations based on the history of user activities.

- **How It Works**:
  - The model processes user interaction sequences (e.g., watched videos, purchased products) over time.
  - RNNs (or their variants like **LSTMs** or **GRUs**) can learn the temporal dependencies between items in the interaction sequence.
  - The final hidden state of the RNN represents the user's current preference, which can be used to recommend the next item in the sequence.
- **Advantages**:
  - Captures sequential dependencies in user behavior.
  - Suitable for recommendation systems where time plays a critical role (e.g., playlists, news articles, shopping sequences).

23.7.5.5 Attention Mechanisms in Recommendations

Attention mechanisms can enhance the performance of recommendation systems by focusing on the most relevant aspects of user-item interactions.

- **How It Works**:
  - **Self-Attention**: Each item in a user's interaction history is assigned a weight, representing how important that interaction is to the recommendation.
  - The attention mechanism learns to give higher weights to more relevant items and lower weights to less relevant items.

- **Transformer-Based Models**:
  - Models like **Transformers** (e.g., used in BERT) can be adapted to recommendation systems, especially for modeling sequences of user interactions.
- **Advantages**:
  - Improves accuracy by focusing on the most relevant parts of the user's interaction history.
  - Scalable and efficient for processing large sequences of interactions.

23.7.5.6 Hybrid Deep Learning Models

Many real-world recommendation systems use **hybrid models** that combine multiple deep learning techniques.

23.7.5.7 Wide and Deep Model

- **Wide** component handles memory-based models (e.g., linear models or collaborative filtering) to capture general patterns.
- **Deep** component uses neural networks to capture complex feature interactions.

This approach allows the model to capture both memorized user-item interactions (via the wide component) and more generalizable patterns (via the deep component).

23.7.5.8 DeepFM (Deep Factorization Machines)

- **Factorization Machines (FM)** model pairwise feature interactions and are effective in sparse data scenarios.
- The **DeepFM** model combines a **factorization machine** with a **deep neural network** to capture both low-order and high-order feature interactions.

23.7.5.9 Challenges in Deep Learning for Recommendations

Although deep learning-based recommendation systems can yield state-of-the-art performance, they also pose challenges:

1. **Cold-Start Problem**:
   (a) New users/items don't have enough interaction data to generate accurate recommendations.
   (b) Solution: Use content-based features (e.g., video tags, product descriptions) or embeddings learned from similar users/items.
2. **Scalability**:
   (a) Real-world recommendation systems need to scale to millions or even billions of users and items.

23.7 Example 3: Short Video Recommendation System

(b) Solution: Use distributed training frameworks (e.g., TensorFlow, PyTorch) and deploy models on powerful infrastructure (e.g., GPUs, TPUs).

3. **Interpretability**:
   (a) Deep learning models can be black-box, making it difficult to understand why a recommendation was made.
   (b) Solution: Use attention mechanisms or interpretable layers to provide insight into the recommendation process.

23.7.5.10 Evaluation Metrics

To evaluate the performance of deep learning-based recommendation systems, common metrics include:

- **Precision@K/Recall@K**: Measures how many of the top K recommended items are relevant.
- **Mean Average Precision (MAP)**: Evaluates the ranking of items in terms of their relevance.
- **Normalized Discounted Cumulative Gain (NDCG)**: Measures the quality of recommendations by considering the position of relevant items in the list.
- **Click-Through Rate (CTR)**: Measures how often users click on recommended items.

23.7.5.11 Conclusion

Deep learning-based recommendation algorithms have revolutionized the field of recommendations by leveraging neural networks to learn complex, non-linear interactions between users, items, and features. They outperform traditional methods in terms of scalability, accuracy, and personalization, but also present new challenges such as cold-start, scalability, and interpretability. To build an effective recommendation system, hybrid approaches and careful tuning of deep learning models are often required to balance precision, scalability, and performance.

23.7.6 Scalability Considerations

1. Data Storage:
   (a) The system needs to handle petabytes of data (user data, videos, interactions). Distributed databases like Cassandra or HBase can help scale storage horizontally.
2. Caching:
   (a) Frequently accessed recommendations and videos should be cached using Redis to reduce database and recommendation engine load.

3. Load Balancing:
   (a) Use load balancers (e.g., Nginx, AWS ELB) to distribute traffic evenly across backend services.
4. Horizontal Scaling:
   (a) Each service (video processing, recommendation engine, metadata storage) should scale horizontally to handle increasing user requests and data.

23.7.7 Metrics for Measuring Success

1. **Click-through rate (CTR)**: Measures how often users click on recommended videos.
2. **Watch time**: Measures how long users watch videos, indicating the relevance and engagement of recommendations.
3. **Video completion rate**: Tracks how often users watch videos until the end.
4. **Bounce rate**: Measures how often users leave without interacting with recommendations.

23.7.8 Challenges and Solutions

1. Cold-Start Problem:
   (a) For new users with no watch history, recommend trending videos, category-based videos, or popular videos in the user's geographic location.
2. Real-Time Updates:
   (a) Use real-time data pipelines to process user interactions quickly and update recommendations without lag.
3. Scalability:
   (a) Employ distributed databases, sharding, and horizontal scaling to ensure the system can handle millions of users simultaneously.

23.7.9 Conclusion

The YouTube Short Video Recommendation System needs to combine machine learning algorithms (collaborative filtering, content-based filtering, and deep learning models) with scalable infrastructure (distributed databases, CDNs, data pipelines) to deliver highly personalized video recommendations to millions of users in real-time. The architecture should prioritize scalability, personalization, and low-latency video delivery to provide a seamless user experience.

Chapter 24
Large Language Model System Design

24.1 Example 1: Building a Text-to-Image Generative AI System

Scenario: You are tasked with designing a text-to-image generation system similar to DALL·E or MidJourney. The system's goal is to generate high-quality images from textual descriptions provided by users.

Requirements

- **Text-to-Image Generation**: Given a user's input (e.g., "A dog playing in a park under a sunset"), the system should generate a realistic image matching the description.
- **High-Quality Output**: The generated images should be high-resolution and photorealistic.
- **Scalability**: The system should handle thousands of users generating images simultaneously.
- **Real-Time Processing**: The system should provide users with image outputs within a few seconds.
- **User Interaction**: The system should allow users to make refinements to their image outputs (e.g., "Make the dog larger" or "Change the sunset to a cloudy sky").
- **Multi-modal Input**: The system should potentially allow additional inputs like sketches or image references.

24.1.1 Model Architecture

- What type of generative model would you use to generate images from text (e.g., GANs, diffusion models, transformers)? Explain your choice and the trade-offs.

- How would you design the system to handle complex prompts with detailed descriptions (e.g., multi-object scenarios)?

Solution

For a text-to-image system, you can use a Generative Adversarial Network (GAN) or a Diffusion model.

- **GANs**: GANs have been widely used for generating images. The generator network creates images based on input text, and the discriminator evaluates the quality of the generated images. However, GANs often struggle with stability during training and producing fine-grained details.
- **Diffusion models**: Diffusion models such as **DALL·E 2** and **Stable Diffusion** have recently demonstrated state-of-the-art performance in text-to-image generation. Diffusion models use a process that gradually adds noise to an image and then learns to reverse the process to generate an image from noise.
- **Transformers**: Combining transformers with diffusion models allows better handling of long, complex textual descriptions, as transformers can model relationships between words in a prompt more effectively.

Trade-offs: GANs may be faster but less stable and detailed. Diffusion models are computationally expensive but more effective at producing high-quality, detailed images.

24.1.2 Data Pipeline and Preprocessing

- How would you collect and preprocess the data (e.g., text-image pairs) for training such a model?
- How would you ensure the text data captures nuances and detailed descriptions that can be used to guide image generation?

Solution

- A large dataset of text-image pairs would be required. Publicly available datasets like **COCO**, **LAION**, or **OpenImages** could be a starting point.
- Preprocessing for text: Use **tokenizers** like **BERT** or **GPT** to preprocess the text descriptions, turning them into embeddings or token sequences that the model can understand.
- Preprocessing for images: Resize, normalize, and possibly augment images to make them suitable for model training.
- **Attention Mechanisms**: To handle nuances and detailed descriptions, use attention mechanisms that allow the model to focus on important parts of the input text while generating corresponding parts of the image.

24.1.3 Model Training and Fine-Tuning

- How would you handle the training process, given the massive computational resources required for training a generative model?
- How would you fine-tune the model to generate high-quality, domain-specific images (e.g., artistic images, cartoons, or photorealistic landscapes)?
- What strategies would you use to handle bias in the training data, especially when it comes to generating sensitive or diverse content?

Solution

- **Training**: Distributed training with **data parallelism** or **model parallelism** using frameworks such as **PyTorch** or **TensorFlow**. Leverage **cloud GPUs** or **TPUs** from platforms like **AWS**, **GCP**, or **Azure**.
- **Fine-tuning**: Pretrain the model on large general datasets, then fine-tune it on domain-specific datasets (e.g., photorealistic images, artistic images).
- **Handling bias**: Use **diverse data augmentation** techniques, or apply post-processing filters to ensure fairness. Train with **adversarial debiasing** techniques to avoid biased image generation.

24.1.4 Inference and Real-Time Generation

- Generating high-quality images from scratch is computationally expensive. How would you design the system to generate images in real-time or near-real-time for end users?
- What infrastructure would you use to ensure fast and scalable inference (e.g., GPU clusters, cloud services, caching mechanisms)?

Solution

- **Speed optimization**: You can use **quantization** or **pruning** techniques to reduce the model's size and improve inference speed.
- **Infrastructure**: Deploy models on **GPU clusters** or use **on-demand cloud services** like AWS EC2 with GPU instances. Consider using **serverless architecture** for dynamic scalability. Pre-cache common or frequently used prompts to reduce latency.
- **Latency handling**: Partition the generation task so that some tasks (e.g., image refinement) run asynchronously while generating a rough image quickly for user feedback.

24.1.5 Scalability and Performance

- How would you scale the system to handle thousands of concurrent requests while maintaining low latency?
- What kind of architecture would you propose for load balancing, ensuring the system remains responsive even under heavy load?

Solution

- **Scalability**: Utilize **horizontal scaling** by distributing the model inference across multiple GPU nodes or serverless endpoints (e.g., **AWS Lambda** with GPU, **GCP Vertex AI**).
- **Caching**: Implement **distributed** caching for common or repeat requests (e.g., Redis or Memcached) to reduce redundant processing.
- **Load balancing**: Use **load balancers** like **AWS ELB** or **GCP Load Balancing** to evenly distribute traffic across servers.

24.1.6 Refinement and Iterative Generation

- Users may want to refine their generated images based on new instructions (e.g., "make the dog larger"). How would you design a feedback loop that allows users to refine images without regenerating them from scratch?
- How would you integrate multi-modal inputs like sketches or image references to guide the model in generating or refining images?

Solution

- You can implement a feedback loop where the user interacts with **latent vectors** that represent the generated image. For instance, **StyleGAN** allows the user to modify certain features without regenerating the entire image.
- For multi-modal inputs, such as sketches or image references, use a model like **CLIP** (Contrastive Language-Image Pre-training), which can align text and images. The user can refine the image by inputting both a text prompt and an image reference, and the model will adjust the image accordingly.

24.1.7 Evaluation and Quality Metrics

- How would you assess the performance of the text-to-image generation system? What metrics would you use (e.g., FID score, user satisfaction, image diversity)?
- How would you address subjective user feedback, considering that users may have varying perceptions of image quality?

24.1 Example 1: Building a Text-to-Image Generative AI System

Solution

- **Metrics**: Use **Frechet Inception Distance (FID)** to measure the quality of the generated images by comparing them to real images. **Inception Score (IS)** and **CLIP Score** can also be used to measure how well the generated images align with the text prompts.
- **A/B testing**: Run **A/B tests** to gather user feedback on generated images, and use the results to iterate on model improvements.
- **Subjective feedback**: Incorporate a **rating system** or **thumbs up/down** mechanism to allow users to provide feedback, helping the system learn preferences.

24.1.8 Handling Unseen Prompts and Out-of-Domain Requests

- How would the system deal with unusual or unseen prompts that the model hasn't been trained on?
- What fallback mechanisms would you implement to ensure the system generates something meaningful in such cases?

Solution

- **Zero-shot learning**: Use a **CLIP model** to understand and map unseen prompts to relevant image concepts.
- **Fallback mechanism**: If the model encounters an unseen or incomprehensible prompt, return a **default image** or a message like, "This request is outside the model's knowledge. Would you like to try something else?"
- You can also leverage **transfer learning** to adapt pre-trained models to new domains without training from scratch.

24.1.9 Ethics and Safety

- How would you ensure the system doesn't generate inappropriate or harmful content?
- What measures would you implement to filter and moderate generated images, ensuring alignment with platform guidelines?

Solution

- **Content moderation**: Use **adversarial filtering** or fine-tuning techniques to prevent the generation of harmful or inappropriate images.
- **Safety filters**: Implement **post-processing filters** that can blur or block out offensive content.
- **Compliance**: Ensure compliance with regulations such as **GDPR** by anonymizing and securing user data. Provide users with options to opt out of data collection or generation.

24.1.10 Bonus Questions

- How would you handle storage and retrieval of previously generated images if users want to regenerate or tweak them later?
- How would you handle versioning of the model as it evolves over time to ensure backward compatibility for user-generated content?

Solution

- Storage and Retrieval:
  - Solution: Store generated images in a **distributed file system** (e.g., **S3, Google Cloud Storage**) with unique IDs. Store latent vectors along with images, so users can retrieve and tweak previously generated images without starting from scratch.
- Versioning of the Model:
  - Solution: Use **ML model versioning tools** (e.g., **MLflow** or **DVC**) to manage and track changes to the models. For user-facing versions, ensure that generated content is tagged with the model version used, ensuring backward compatibility when retrieving older outputs.

These solutions provide a comprehensive guide to addressing the challenges and design decisions involved in creating a generative AI system for text-to-image tasks.

24.2 Example 2: Design the ChatGPT Model

Developing a model like ChatGPT involves multiple steps, including choosing the architecture, gathering data, training the model, fine-tuning it, and deploying it. Here's an overview of the process, broken down into key steps:

24.2.1 Choosing the Right Model Architecture

The architecture underlying ChatGPT is a **Transformer-based** model, specifically **GPT (Generative Pre-trained Transformer)**. The steps involved are:

- **Start with Transformer Architecture**: GPT models are based on the Transformer architecture, which was introduced in the paper "**Attention is All You Need**". This architecture is well-suited for processing sequential data and is highly efficient for language modeling tasks.
- Select a Model Type:
  - GPT (Generative Pre-trained Transformer): The core architecture. It is a decoder-only architecture that generates text based on a given input prompt.

- Alternative Architectures: Other architectures to consider are BERT (for bidirectional text comprehension tasks) or T5 (a unified text-to-text framework), but for a chatbot, GPT-style models are preferred due to their strong generative capabilities.

24.2.2 Gathering Data for Pre-training and Fine-Tuning

Training a model like ChatGPT requires vast amounts of text data, and you will need both pre-training and fine-tuning datasets.

- Pre-training Data:
  - Use publicly available text datasets such as Common Crawl, BooksCorpus, Wikipedia, Reddit conversations, and OpenWebText.
  - For pre-training, you aim to teach the model the structure of language, grammar, facts, reasoning, and some world knowledge.
- Fine-tuning Data:
  - You'll need dialogue-specific data to fine-tune the model for conversational abilities. You can use datasets like Persona-Chat, DSTC (Dialogue State Tracking Challenges), or create custom datasets using platforms like Amazon Mechanical Turk for human annotations.
  - Fine-tuning should also involve ethical guidelines and content filtering so the model behaves responsibly.
  - Reinforcement Learning from Human Feedback (RLHF): This step is used in models like ChatGPT to ensure the model can align with user expectations. It involves collecting human feedback on responses and adjusting the model's output accordingly.

24.2.3 Training the Model

Training a model like GPT from scratch is extremely resource-intensive and requires access to significant computational power, typically TPUs or GPUs.

- Model Size:
  - Small models (e.g., GPT-2 small): Easier to train with moderate resources, often using millions of parameters.
  - Large models (e.g., GPT-3): Requires huge computational power and can take weeks to train using supercomputing resources like clusters of TPUs or GPUs.

- Frameworks:
  - Use PyTorch or TensorFlow for training the model. Hugging Face's Transformers library provides implementations of GPT, GPT-2, GPT-3-like models which are very useful for fine-tuning or extending existing models.
  - Distributed Training: You'll likely need to implement data-parallel or model-parallel training to distribute the model across multiple GPUs/TPUs.
- Pre-training Objectives:
  - Train the model to predict the next word in a sequence using causal language modeling (i.e., the model only looks at preceding tokens and predicts the next one).
  - You will need to define a tokenizer that breaks input text into subwords and a vocabulary to feed to the model.

24.2.4 Fine-Tuning for Specific Use Cases

Once pre-trained, the model needs fine-tuning for specific use cases like conversations.

- Supervised Fine-Tuning: Use conversation datasets to train the model to follow prompts and instructions, provide informative answers, and maintain conversational context.
- Reinforcement Learning Fine-Tuning: Use RLHF (Reinforcement Learning from Human Feedback) where human evaluators rate the model's responses, and the model learns to improve its performance.
- Safety and Bias Mitigation: Fine-tuning should involve steps to minimize harmful outputs, mitigate bias, and ensure that the chatbot behaves according to ethical standards. You can fine-tune on datasets that contain appropriate behavior.

24.2.5 Model Evaluation and Testing

Before deployment, you need to thoroughly evaluate the model:

- Evaluation Metrics:
  - Perplexity: Measures how well the model predicts the next word in the sequence (lower perplexity is better).
  - Human Evaluations: Let human evaluators interact with the model and provide ratings on various aspects like fluency, accuracy, safety, and relevance.
- Testing for Bias and Toxicity:
  - Ensure the model does not generate harmful or biased content by testing it on sensitive or controversial topics.

24.2.6 Deploying the Model

Once trained and evaluated, the next step is deploying the model for real-world use:

- Hosting: You will need a platform capable of serving large-scale models. Options include Google Cloud AI Platform, AWS Sagemaker, Azure AI, or Hugging Face Inference API.
- Optimizing for Inference:
    - Quantization: Convert model weights from float32 to int8 to reduce memory usage and speed up inference.
    - Pruning: Remove unimportant connections from the model to make it more lightweight and efficient.
    - Model Distillation: Train a smaller model (student) to mimic a larger model (teacher) to serve faster responses.
- Scalability: Use load balancers and horizontal scaling to handle high traffic during peak times. You can also serve different versions of the model based on user needs, with lighter models for faster interactions and heavier models for high-quality responses.

24.2.7 Real-Time Updates and Feedback Loop

Post-deployment, constantly update and improve the model:

- User Feedback: Use user feedback to improve the chatbot's performance through fine-tuning.
- Active Learning: Implement active learning where uncertain outputs are flagged and later manually labeled for further fine-tuning.
- Continuous Learning: Retrain the model periodically with new data and user interactions to keep it updated with current trends.

24.2.8 Tools and Resources

1. Frameworks and Libraries:
    (a) **PyTorch** or **TensorFlow** for training.
    (b) **Hugging Face's Transformers** for easy access to pre-trained models and fine-tuning.
2. Cloud Platforms:
    (a) Google Cloud AI, AWS SageMaker, Azure Machine Learning for training and deployment.

3. Training and Inference Hardware:

    (a) Use **NVIDIA GPUs** or **Google TPUs** for large-scale training and deployment.
    (b) On-device inference using TensorRT or ONNX for optimization.

4. Data Sources:

    (a) Use publicly available datasets like **Common Crawl**, **Reddit**, **Wikipedia**, and **BooksCorpus** for pre-training.
    (b) Create synthetic or crowd-labeled dialogue data for fine-tuning.

24.2.9 Summary of Steps to Build a ChatGPT-Like Model

1. Choose the Architecture: Transformer-based model (GPT).
2. Data Collection: Use large-scale datasets for pre-training, unsupervised or weakly supervised data for fine-tuning.
3. Model Training: Train on GPUs/TPUs with techniques like distributed training, and consider starting with a pre-trained model.
4. Fine-Tuning: Focus on specific conversational abilities using dialogue datasets and reinforcement learning from human feedback.
5. Evaluation: Test for accuracy, fluency, safety, and bias with quantitative metrics and human evaluators.
6. Deployment: Optimize for fast inference and scalability. Use cloud services or model distillation for lightweight serving.
7. Continuous Improvement: Use feedback and active learning for ongoing updates.

Building a ChatGPT-like model is resource-intensive but feasible with access to cloud platforms, modern deep learning frameworks, and significant computational power.

The manufacturer's authorised representative in the EU is Springer Nature Customer Service Centre GmbH, Europaplatz 3, 69115 Heidelberg, Germany. If you have any concerns regarding our products, please contact ProductSafety@springernature.com

Printed and bound by CPI Group (UK) Ltd, Croydon, CR0 4YY

26/03/2026

02078953-0011